Londoner **Sean Egan** has contributed to a range of ~~Billboard~~, *Billboard*, *Book Collector*, *Classic Rock*, *Record Collector*, *Tennis World*, *Total Film*, *Uncut* and RollingStone.com. He has written or edited nineteen books, including works on The Beatles, Jimi Hendrix, The Rolling Stones, *Coronation Street*, Manchester United and Tarzan. His critically acclaimed novel *Sick of Being Me* was published in 2003, while *Don't Mess with the Best*, his 2008 collection of short stories, carried cover endorsements from Booker Prize winners Stanley Middleton and David Storey.

THE MAMMOTH BOOK OF

The Rolling Stones

Sean Egan

ROBINSON

RUNNING PRESS
PHILADELPHIA · LONDON

Constable & Robinson Ltd
55–56 Russell Square
London WC1B 4HP
www.constablerobinson.com

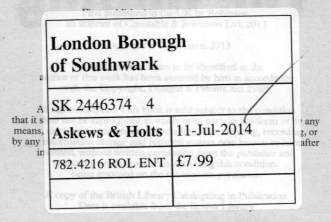

UK ISBN: 978-1-78033-646-6 (paperback)
UK ISBN: 978-1-78033-647-3 (ebook)

1 3 5 7 9 10 8 6 4 2

First published in the United States in 2013 by Running Press Book Publishers,
A Member of the Perseus Books Group

All rights reserved under the Pan-American and International Copyright Conventions

Books published by Running Press are available at special discounts for bulk
purchases in the United States by corporations, institutions, and other organizations.
For more information, please contact the Special Markets Department at the
Perseus Books Group, 2300 Chestnut Street, Suite 200, Philadelphia, PA 19103,
or call (800) 810-4145, ext. 5000, or e-mail special.markets@perseusbooks.com.

US ISBN: 978-0-7624-4814-2
US Library of Congress Control Number: 2012942537

9 8 7 6 5 4 3 2 1
Digit on the right indicates the number of this printing

Running Press Book Publishers
2300 Chestnut Street
Philadelphia, PA 19103-4371

Visit us on the web!
www.runningpress.com

Printed and bound in the UK

CONTENTS

Contents

INTRODUCTION

"It's hard to remember just what that period was like," Mick Jagger said of the sixties in 1987, "but I can assure you it was extremely different from now. Things you take for granted now they wouldn't then: social values, the way people mix, racial segregation, sexual segregation and orientation, the opportunities people would or wouldn't have, class and money."

What Jagger was uncharacteristically too modest to say was that so many of those injustices were rectified partly because of the group of which he has now been the lead singer for half a century. The Rolling Stones were unlike any rock or pop ensemble before them in their refusal to wear a suit uniform, their unruly mops of hair and their shrugged dismissal in both interviews and recordings of social conformity and tradition. Whereas The Beatles, at first anyway, were smiling and solicitous, the Stones' casualness and surliness seemed to represent a new social order: an antidote to a censorious, authoritarian and grey society, whether it be class-bound Britain, white-picket-fence America or communist-yoke Russia. As the years passed, the young increasingly emulated and took their cue from the Stones' outlaw attitude. So seriously did the Establishment take their enemies-of-society mien that in 1967 Jagger and Stones guitarist Keith Richards were given harshly discriminatory prison sentences for drugs offences, while fellow guitarist Brian Jones was hounded by the police via repeated raids in suspicious circumstances. Nothing the

Establishment did, however, would stop the Stones' influence seeping into the DNA of the generation about to assume power.

Meanwhile, the band effortlessly made classic records, moving with awe-inspiring speed from being the best rhythm-and-blues covers merchants on the scene to creating their own sound via the Jagger/Richards songwriting axis that swiftly rivalled Lennon/McCartney. They defiantly littered the buttoned-up sixties with brilliant 45 rpm anthems of disaffec-tion and sensuality like "(I Can't Get No) Satisfaction" and "Let's Spend the Night Together", while turning out classic albums like *Aftermath*, *Beggars Banquet* and *Let It Bleed*. Come the seventies, the disintegration of The Beatles and their own appointment of virtuoso guitarist Mick Taylor saw the Stones acquire a new swaggering, if "wasted", confidence. They became the undisputed template for a rock band via their manes of rebelliously long hair, their gargantuan and decadent tours, and masterpiece LPs like *Sticky Fingers* and *Exile on Main St.*

Although marriage, family and sated artistic hunger plus the emergence of younger, more relevant acts inevitably meant a dilution of their impact and powers, the Stones were still able to knock out the odd superb record like 1978's *Some Girls*, while their enduringly profitable tours proved what nobody had suspected back when they started: that a rock band could remain active and sustain appeal across generations.

The Mammoth Book of The Rolling Stones presents a bumper collection of writing, old and new, on the group correctly described at various times as both "The greatest rock 'n' roll band in the world" and "A way of life".

Sean Egan

CYRIL DAVIES AND THE STONES IN JANUARY 1963

John Pidgeon

First published on www.rocksbackpages.com, April 2009

The first time I hear Cyril Davies blow his harmonica is January 1963 at Leo's Jazz Club in Windsor. As I approach, shoulders hunched against the cold, I watch billows of cigarette smoke, lit pink and yellow by the lights inside, spill from an open door, before the thin, chill evening air is split by an inhuman scream, a siren wail that rises a tone, then subsides. The sound nails me momentarily to the pavement, then propels me to the entrance of an unprepossessing British Legion Hall, which by day is a hang-out for pensioners who have served time, as most have, in the armed forces. At a folding table by the door I fumble distractedly in my pocket for the four shilling (20p) entry fee, entirely absorbed by the source of this extraordinary sound: a balding, badly dressed man, who looks middle-aged to my teenage eyes.

I struggle to relate the sound I hear to what I can see. Davies's hands are cupped in front of his mouth, a cable trailing from his fingers, but his instrument is invisible, apart from a glinting sliver revealed whenever he parts his hands, a movement matched by a modulation in the sound.

Unseen it might be, but what I'm listening to is as powerful and evocative an instrumental voice as Little Richard's piano, Buddy Holly's guitar or Ray Charles flat-top Wurlitzer soloing the opening bars of "What'd I Say?". Davies can make this thing he had hidden in his hands cry, shout, and howl so my hair stands on end. And there is no room for doubt, these sounds can only be coming from him, because the other instruments on stage are drums, bass, guitar and piano, and I know the sounds they make. So does my companion – a jazz fan, hence our visit to Leo's Jazz Club – who is soon hissing from the side of his mouth that what the R & B All-Stars are playing is little different from rock 'n' roll, an opinion to which I am able to nod urgent agreement, without letting on that this is not the least of the reasons that I love it. I don't want to piss him off. He's the one with the driving licence and his mother's car.

As the set progresses, a beanpole singer with a blond fringe and a teasing smile takes his turn at the microphone, but his singing is too smooth, too jazzy for my taste. Meanwhile, a black female vocal trio attempt an approximation of the Raelettes, Ray Charles' backing singers, whose visceral harmonies I know from my live *Ray Charles at Newport* album. Indeed Davies and the Velvettes recreate Charles' "(Night Time Is) The Right Time", though without the sex-fuelled fire of Marjorie Hendricks, and, anyway, all I have ears – and open-mouthed wonder – for are Cyril Davies and his harmonica.

The wail of Cyril Davies's harmonica tears straight to the centre of my heart, and the next day, a Saturday, I catch a bus into town and find a Hohner Marine Band harmonica in the music shop. On the way home I slip it from its snug blue box to study its simple features: twelve holes to be sucked or blown, each of them numbered – pointlessly, it seems to me, since the numbers are lost from sight even before the instrument is pressed to one's lips. On the face of it, there is even less here to master than on a recorder, and yet the repertoire of sounds conjured from it by Davies is infinitely more expansive. This comparison triggers a suspicion that learning to play like him isn't going to be easy.

In my bedroom I cup the harmonica the way I saw Davies do last night. I try some experimental sucks and blows, enough to teach me that the blow is only a tuneful means of emptying my lungs before switching to the suck that creates the more evocative notes. Remarkably, the modulated suck that "bends" the notes a semi-tone comes to me quickly, and by lunchtime I am able to ape Davies' wail at different points on the scale, but I have no records from which I can learn melodic sequences and none that I heard him play have stayed in my head. I know I have to see Davies and his R & B All-Stars again.

Fortunately, in spite of his aversion to amplified "beat music", my Leo's companion has taken a pointless shine to one of the Velvettes who, he has convinced himself, was giving him the come-on. I don't openly question why he imagines a statuesque African professional singer should have been eyeing up a grammar school sixth-former, barely out of short-back-and-sides, but gratefully accept his invitation to revisit the club the following Friday.

Although Cyril Davies thrills me as before, [Long John] Baldry's unctuous vocalising is even less to my taste, while the Velvettes' strident harmonies grate on my ears. During the week I have listened to *Ray Charles at Newport*, cementing my opinion that these three are no match for the Raelettes. As the All-Stars step off stage for the interval break, Davies waiting for no one as he hustles to the bar, my companion, blaming the smoky atmosphere, but perhaps also seizing the chance to play hard-to-get, insists that we should stretch our legs and clear our lungs.

Minutes from the British Legion Hall, in a narrow street that sides the Star & Garter Hotel, I stop, astonished, at the sound of more upbeat blues and another harmonica. I search for the sound with my eyes and see dancers silhouetted in the open windows of an upstairs room attached to the back of what is plainly more pub than hotel. On either side of the doorway that leads upstairs, black posters with white lettering announce The Ricky Tick Club and The Rolling Stones Every Friday 5/-. Judging by those cooling off outside, the Ricky Tick crowd is younger and hipper, and the girls prettier, than at Leo's. There are studenty types and some snappy dressers. While I move involuntarily, and, I hope, inconspicuously, to a spirited version of Benny Spellman's "Fortune Teller", the rhythm driven by maracas, my eyes lock with the wide-eyed gaze of a girl wearing black ski pants, whose dark hair is cropped as short as Jean Seberg's in *À Bout De Souffle*, but, as if struck by a thought, she looks away, grinds her cigarette under her heel, and disappears inside.

Hands, as always, in my pockets, I weigh the two half-crowns my mother has given me as petrol money for my driver, who has halted a few yards further on and is giving me the hurry-up sign with a finger on his watch face. I shout, "I'll see you at the car at ten thirty," and duck into the doorway.

Once I've seen The Rolling Stones at the Ricky Tick, there is no going back to Leo's. The Stones are what I've been looking for without expecting to find: a young white English group playing black American music. And they really have mastered the idiom. They won't become famous because they wear their hair like girls or urinate on a garage forecourt or get busted for drugs, but because they are white boys who play black music better than anybody has before.

The group's residency at the Ricky Tick lasts six months, from January to July 1963, but more than forty years later I can revisit those Friday nights at will: I can see the upstairs room with the bar against one wall, a small, barely raised stage in the opposite corner, and, incongruously, fishing nets hung from the ceiling; I can hear the crowd singing along with the Stones' closing "Bye Bye Johnny", answering Mick's circling wave of a hand; I can feel the floor move under my feet as I dance with my Jean Seberg lookalike, the bouncing boards and rafters loosing plaster from the ceiling below on to the roof of the Stones' parked van, inside which Ian Stewart is trying to grab some sleep before driving the band back to their West London flat.

Norman Jopling cannot claim to be the first journalist to write about The Rolling Stones: that accolade belongs to local reporter, Barry May, who penned a piece on them in the issue of the Richmond and Twickenham Times dated 13 April 1963. However, Jopling's feature on the group in the edition of New Record Mirror for the week ending 11 May 1963 was vastly more important, and not just because it was the band's first coverage in the music press and the first in a national publication.

Jopling recalls: "New Record Mirror's senior journalist Peter Jones was pally with Giorgio Gomelsky who was pestering him to see a group at his club in Richmond. Peter saw them, then told me I should see them and write the article because I was the self-appointed authority on rhythm & blues. But I hated British R & B and refused. ('They're British – they can't be any good!') Eventually he wore me down and I went, and took a photographer. It was an epiphany."

"The Rolling Stones: Genuine R & B!" (the dropped "g" in "Rolling" throughout the article was not reflected in the heading) occupied a half-page of the then almost A3-sized paper along with a photograph wherein the boys struck surprisingly angelic poses. Jopling misspells Ian Stewart's surname and renders Bo Diddley's "Mona" as "Moaner" but that pales into insignificance beside his perspicacity in declaring that the ensemble will "soon be the leading R & B performers in the country". The article reveals that, contrary to the myth that it was foisted on the Stones by their soon-to-be manager, debut single "Come On" was part of the band's repertoire. Amusingly, the band are quoted as scorning the idea of original numbers.

That soon-to-be manager – who guided them to superstardom – came into the group's orbit as a direct consequence of the feature. Jopling continues: "The article didn't appear for a couple of weeks – we didn't rush into print because they didn't have a record to plug. In fact, it was the first time Record Mirror had ever published an article on a group without a record. Peter then told Andrew Oldham that I was writing a rave piece on the group, and advised him to check them out. And that was that. I was nineteen and so was Andrew – but he was very smart!" Have Mick and the boys ever thanked Jopling for his part in their superstardom? Jopling: "Ha-Ha!"

THE ROLLING STONES – GENUINE R & B!

Norman Jopling

First published in *New Record Mirror*, May 1963

As the trad scene gradually subsides, promoters of all kinds of teen-beat entertainments heave a long sigh of relief that they have found something to take its place. It's Rhythm and Blues, of course – the number of R & B clubs that have suddenly sprung up is nothing short of fantastic.

One of the best known – and one of the most successful to date – is at the Station Hotel, Kew Road, in Richmond, just on the outskirts of London. There, on Sunday evenings, the hip kids throw themselves about to the new "jungle music" like they never did in the more stinted days of trad.

And the combo they writhe and twist to is called the Rollin' Stones. Maybe you've never heard of them – if you live very far away from London the odds are you haven't.

But by gad you will! The Rollin' Stones are probably destined to be the biggest group in the R & B scene if it continues to flourish. And by the looks of the Station Hotel, Richmond, flourish is merely an understatement considering that three months ago only fifty people turned up to see the group. Now club promoter bearded Giorgio Gomelsky has to close the doors at an early hour – over four hundred R & B fans crowd the hall.

And the fans who do come quickly lose all their inhibitions and proceed to contort themselves to the truly exciting music of the boys – who put heart and soul into their performances.

The fact is that, unlike all the other R & B groups worthy of the name, the Rollin' Stones have a definite visual appeal. They aren't the Jazzmen who were doing trad. eighteen months back and who have converted their act to keep up with the times.

They are genuine R & B fanatics themselves, and they sing and play in a way that one would have expected, more from a coloured US R & B team than a bunch of wild, exciting white boys who have the fans screaming – and listening – to them.

Lineup of the group is Mick Jagger, lead vocal and harmonica and student at the London School of Economics. The fierce backing is supplied by Brian Jones, guitar and harmonica, and also spokesman and leader of the group. He's an architect, while Keith Richards, guitar, is an art student. The other three members of the group are Bill Wyman, bass guitar, Ian Stuart, piano and maracas, and drummer Charles Watts.

Record-wise, everything is in the air, but a disc will be forthcoming. It will probably be the group's own adaptation of the Chuck Berry number, "Come On" (featured on Chuck's new Pye LP). The number goes down extremely well in the club's session on Sundays – other Chuck Berry numbers that are in the group's repertoire are "Down The Road Apiece" and "Bye, Bye, Johnny" – which is one of the highlights of the act.

Even though the boys haven't dead-certain plans for a disc, they do have dead-certain plans for a film. For club promoter Giorgio is best known as a film producer, and he has made several imaginative films dealing with the music scene. But for the Rollin' Stones film, there are some truly great shots of the team in action, singing and performing "Pretty Thing", the Bo Diddley number. The film itself lasts for twenty minutes, and will be distributed with a main feature film.

The group are actually mad about Bo Diddley, although pianist Ian is the odd man out. Diddley numbers they perform are "Crawdad", "Nursery Rhyme", "Road Runner", "Moaner" and, of course, "Bo Diddley".

They can also get the sound that Bo gets too – no mean achievement. The group themselves are all red-hot when it comes to US beat discs. They know their R & B numbers inside out and have a repertoire of about eighty songs, most of them are the numbers which every R & B fan in the country knows and near enough loves.

The boys are confident that, if they make a disc, it should do well. They are also confident about their own playing, although on Sundays at the end of the session at Richmond they are dead-beat. That's because on Sunday afternoons they also play the R & B session at the Ken Colyer Club.

But despite the fact that their R & B has a superficial resemblance to rock 'n' roll, fans of the hit parade music would not find any familiar material performed by the Rollin' Stones. And the boys do not use original material – only the American stuff. "After all," they say, "can you imagine a British composed R & B number – it just wouldn't make it."

One group that thinks a lot of the Rollin' Stones are The Beatles. When they came down to London the other week, they were knocked out by the group's singing. They stayed all the evening at the Station Hotel, listening to the group pound away. And now they spread the word around so much in Liverpool that bookings for the group have been flooding in – including several at the famed Cavern.

All this can't be bad for the R & B group who have achieved the American sound better than any other group over here. And the group that in all likelihood will soon be the leading R & B performers in the country . . .

"COME ON"

Sean Egan

Along with The Beatles and Bob Dylan, The Rolling Stones are the most important artists of twentieth-century popular music, which in the era of their prime – a time when pop stars took on the status of figureheads for a querulous generation – necessarily meant they were also politically important. Achieving such plateaux is, of course, always unthinkable at the outset of a career and the professional origins of the Stones are as unprepossessing as they come.

The nucleus of the band that ultimately became a component of the Holy Trinity of rock was Mick Jagger, Keith Richards and Brian Jones. Jagger and Richards hail from Dartford. Located in the county of Kent, it is one of those London suburbs that seem quaintly sleepy to people from the capital only a short train journey away. Born at the same hospital in 1943 – Jagger on 26 July, Richards on 18 December – they originally lived one street apart and attended a mutual primary school before their paths were diverted by the "eleven-plus": Jagger's success in said examination gained him entrance to a grammar school. They reconnected when they were in further education, their mutual love of blues, especially rhythm and blues, cementing a bond of friendship. Richards joined Jagger's band, Little Boy Blue and the Blue Boys, of which Mick was lead vocalist and sometimes guitarist. Perhaps it was the acknowledged revitalization of the band that Richards' arrival brought, but it was from there only a short matter of time before Jagger was beginning to see his hobby group as a possible future profession and his studies of secondary importance, a highly illogical conclusion that may have been intertwined with a subliminal rejection of the bourgeois values of his parents.

Jagger and Richards met Brian Jones (born on 28 February 1942) in April 1962 at Alexis Korner's weekly R & B club in the Ealing Club, West London, of whose existence they were amazed to discover via music weekly, *Melody Maker*. The posh, Cheltenham-raised Jones was a more unlikely devotee of the music of the oppressed black American than even these two products of the English welfare state. Yet his clipped tones and preternatural politeness went hand-in-hand with more bohemian attributes, among them an extraordinary golden-haired beauty, the fact that he was already the father of two illegitimate children, a somewhat tormented psyche mani-fested in displays of insecurity and violence, and musical activities and ambitions totally at odds with the dentistry ambi-tions harboured for him by his extremely strait-laced parents. The first time Jagger and Richards saw him, he was styling himself "Elmo Lewis" and playing slide guitar.

Jagger, Richards and especially Jones would have been horrified to learn back in '62 that they would one day become widely known and perceived as "The greatest rock 'n' roll band in the world." In the early days, the group made pains to point out to such sections of the media that were interested in them that they were an R & B outfit. Jones even had a habit of writing letters to the music press about what constituted rhythm and blues. One such missive was to *Jazz News* in October 1962: "Surely we must accept that R & B is the American city Negro's 'pop' music – nothing more, nothing less. Rhythm & Blues can hardly be considered a form of jazz. It is not based on improvisation as is the latter. The impact is, and can only be, emotional." Such keen intelligence and abso-lute devotion to the form are what originally made Jones the undisputed leader of the band.

Such debates were no doubt entered into in the Edith Grove flat in Chelsea, in which Jagger, Richards and – off and on – Jones lived in squalor from the latter half of 1962 onwards in their pursuit of their musical dreams. Jagger had started on his journey to being the most famous frontman in the world by securing gigs with Blues Incorporated, singing three songs on Saturdays at the Ealing Club and three at the Marquee Jazz Club in Soho on Thursdays. Blues Incorporated's appearance

on BBC radio's *Jazz Club* on 12 July 1962 provided the stage
entrée to The Rolling Stones. The budget of the programme
didn't extend to including Jagger in the line-up, so he and the
rest of the band were free to play the Marquee in the absence
of Blues Incorporated. "Mick Jagger and The Rolling Stones",
as they were billed, played support to Long John Baldry. The
rest of the line-up was made up by long-time musical associate
of Richards and Dartford native Dick Taylor on bass, Ian
"Stu" Stewart, a pianist possessed of a harrumphing blues
purism that made him lift his fingers in protest at minor keys,
and future Kinks member Mick Avory, one of several stand-in
drummers that the group would employ. There were also
stand-in bassists after September '62 when Taylor left to
pursue his art course (he ended up in The Pretty Things). Bill
Wyman (born William Perks on 24 October 1936) became the
permanent bassist in December 1962. Fellow Londoner Charlie Watts (born 2 June 1941) agreed to become the permanent
drummer in January 1963.

The "Mick Jagger" prefix was quickly dropped – as was
occasionally the "g" in "Rolling" – but the band persisted with
their new name despite the fact that Stewart thought it was the
stuff of corny Irish show bands and despite the fact that its
origin was completely ad hoc. Brian Jones came up with "The
Rolling Stones" on the spur of the moment when on the phone
to *Jazz News*, who naturally wanted to know the name of the
group whose first gig they would be listing. Depending on
whom you believe, the guitarist's inspiration was the title of
"Rolling Stone Blues" by Muddy Waters (source: Richards) or
a line in the same artist's "Mannish Boy" (source: Jagger's
friend, Dave Godin). Either way, it was a great name. It appropriately came from the blues tradition but it somehow seemed
to allude to rock. It would also come to endear itself to journalists because it lent itself to all manner of puns and allusions
along the lines of "Gather No Moss", "Still Rolling", "Rolling
On", "Stone Me" . . . Moreover, it naturally lent itself to the
colloquial "the Stones", an act of abbreviation that conferred
coolness on the abbreviator.

Like the vast majority of R & B groups, the Stones did not
write their own material – unless you counted jams predicated

on generic blues changes. However, there was something a little different about them. Even then, people noted the onstage extroversion of Jagger, although at the time it was restricted to no more than shaking his head around. Additionally, the band spurned the conventional idea of lead and rhythm guitars, with Richards and Jones both concentrating on a non-virtuoso approach but one whose interchangeable nature created a powerful sonic mesh. Meanwhile, although Watts and Wyman were the archetypal Quiet Ones personality-wise and were not musically showy, they were an outstanding rhythm section and each was capable of flashes of virtuoso brilliance. Then there was an easy-on-the-eye quality not common for bluesmen. In addition to their collective youthful vigour, Jagger and Jones shimmered with beauty, and one that was by no means quintessentially male. Moreover, there was a fascinating duality to Jagger's beauty: his large lips sometimes made it as easy to believe he was ugly. Meanwhile, Richards – his swaggering peacock days a few years ahead of him – exuded an acnescarred menace that had its own compulsion.

Band archivist Wyman is usually a reliable source of information but he has given three different dates at three different venues in three different books for the debut of the first classic Stones line-up: 14 January 1963 at the Flamingo (*Stone Alone*); 12 January 1963 at the Ealing Jazz Club (*Rolling with the Stones*); and 11 January 1963 at the Ricky Tick Club (*Blues Odyssey*). In any case, it could be argued that the classic lineup had still not been arrived at because Stewart – whose name and face is unknown even to many who have everything the Stones ever released – was still a member.

Andrew Loog Oldham was a nineteen-year-old publicist (he'd previously worked for The Beatles) who usurped Giorgio Gomelsky as the band's manager in late April 1963. Although Oldham brought on board older impresario Eric Easton for his money and contacts, his partner wasn't interested enough in modern music to have had any part in Oldham's decision that, although Stewart's resemblance to Desperate Dan might have been acceptable in blues circles, it was impractical for the pop milieu. Oldham was also sceptical of the ability of teenagers' brains to assimilate six members. When in May 1963 the Stones acquiesced to the shunting aside of Stewart to the role of road manager and occasional session and stage keyboardist (with a sixth share in mechanical royalties up to 1969), it was symbolic: this was the act not of a band content to preach to the converted in R & B clubs but one who craved the sort of mass audience that their blues heroes, such as Muddy Waters and Howlin' Wolf, had never known. Despite Jones' insistence on purist delineation of genre, The Rolling Stones proved to have their eyes on the main chance.

Oldham signed the group to Decca. That the label was one of those that had turned down The Beatles wasn't that big a deal in itself – so had every other British record label except Parlophone. However, Decca's rejection was the one that had entered popular legend because it was allegedly accompanied by the dismissive comment from the man responsible, Dick Rowe, that "guitar groups are on the way out". Rowe furiously denied he had ever said such a thing and some attribute the story to spite on the part of Beatles manager Brian Epstein. True or not, the quote was widely circulating and making Rowe a figure of ridicule. Oldham pounced, securing his charges a record deal with Decca on the back of Rowe's embarrassment. "You just had to go to the person who turned down The Beatles," Oldham later said. "It was logical. Dick Rowe should be remembered not as the man who turned down The Beatles but the man who signed The Rolling Stones." It should be pointed out that Oldham was probably pushing at an open door with Rowe for another reason: The Beatles' George Harrison had already sung the Stones' praises to him. The deal Oldham secured with Decca was highly advantageous: following some advice from legendary producer Phil Spector, Oldham only agreed to lease the band's masters to the label. A less bright idea from Oldham was to make Richards pretend his surname was Richard, a confused exploitation of the fame of middle-of-the-road UK chart idol Cliff Richard. It wasn't until the late seventies that Richards formally reverted to his birth name. Many older journalists to this day refer to him as Richard.

By the time they recorded their debut single, The Rolling Stones were comparative studio veterans. In October 1962,

Jagger, Richards, Jones, Stewart and stand-in drummer Tony Chapman (no bassist) entered the Curly Clayton Sound Studio and committed to tape Bo Diddley's "You Can't Judge a Book by the Cover", Muddy Waters' "Soon Forgotten" and Jimmy Reed's "Close Together". The results garnered them a rejection from EMI. In March 1963, Glyn Johns – later a superstar producer but then a lowly engineer and friend of the band – supervised a session for them at London's IBC studios, where they recorded Bo Diddley's "Diddley Daddy" and "Road Runner", Jimmy Reed's "Honey What's Wrong" and "Bright Lights, Big City" and Muddy Waters' "I Wanna Be Loved". Years later, Brian Jones said that these recordings captured the true essence of the band in a way that their hits did not but Glyn Johns' boss found no takers when he hawked them around record companies. Roger Savage was the engineer when the group entered Olympic Studios, London, in May 1963 to record what would become their entrée to the wider world, although how this squares with Johns' claim that he recorded a version of "Come On" is not clear. A session at Decca Studios, London, six days after the Olympic one resulted in a re-recording that was not used.

The standalone single no longer plays an important part in the music industry, at least in the physical form that it once did, so history books and critical evaluations now tend to focus on albums. Yet, for their first seven years as a recording outfit, the records that made the Stones' name and reputation were not to be found on what were then called LPs. Not one of the Stones' fifteen UK sixties' singles appeared on an album. The situation was, of course, different in the States where it was inconceivable to try to sell an album that didn't have a hit on board, but prior to December 1967, their American albums were mongrels compared to the purebred British products, thrown together randomly by London Records and aurally thinned out by artificial stereo.

As with every other group of the time, the singles were what originally defined the band, with albums merely a very pleasant bonus for those who could afford them (which was by no means all of their fans in the beginning). They initially charted a gradient of lightning-fast aesthetic development as they journeyed from covers band to compositional self-sufficiency. Before too long their singles were sociopolitical manifestoes as their subject matter – and the band's presentation of their music – proceeded incrementally to tweak the noses of the Establishment and their notions of what was proper behaviour. The singles were also, without exception, brilliant, juggling with apparent effortlessness the requirements to both grab the ear of the casual listener and to fulfil an artistic and increasingly attitudinal milestone with each new release.

They started fairly modestly, though, with "Come On" on 7 June 1963 (UK release date, as are all herein except where indicated) backed by "I Want to Be Loved". Although the Stones – Keith in particular – loved Chuck Berry and although Berry, despite his rock 'n' roll anthems, was always a rhythm-and-blues artist, the band have claimed that the song was not their choice. Richards said, "At the time it was done just to get a record out. We never wanted to hear it. The idea was Andrew's." Jagger went as far as to sneer, "It was shit." The band have even said that they expressed their contempt for the song by not playing it at gigs, itself a daring act when it was the only thing of theirs that was known by the vast bulk of the public. Yet the legend that the song was forced on them by their philistine manager is open to question. Norman Jopling recalls: "Brian told me that 'Come On' could be the choice for a single. That was before Andrew got involved. I remember being surprised when it actually was their first single because I always thought it was a bad choice and that Andrew would make them pick something more typical of their sound. I guess he went with what the group wanted."

One member of The Rolling Stones who has publicly expressed something other than derision for "Come On" is Ronnie Wood, who has commented, "I think it's brilliant." He wouldn't be a member of the band until a dozen years after the single's release, yet it is Wood who is right. Berry's original – one of his more obscure songs – has an even-tempered, even whimsical tone that completely belies the lyric's catalogue of irritants: that feeling of being infuriatingly out of sync with the world when in a bad mood, one in this case caused by being dumped. Only Berry's use of the word "jerk" – deemed too risqué by the Stones or their managers and replaced by "guy" – conveys frustration. The Stones crank up the intensity on their faster arrangement, which Jagger – aside from one melancholically delivered verse – veritably spits out. Everything is perfectly judged in a wonderful performance, from the bobbing bass intro to the clipped, perpetual rhythm guitar to the bear-with-a-sore-arse vocal delivery to the falsetto echoing of Mick's enunciation of the title phrase to the epic echo given to Brian's locomotive-whistle mouth harp to the way that Charlie guides things home by starting to work the hi-hat in the final verse. Willie Dixon's stop-start twelve-bar blues "I Want to Be Loved" makes for a powerful B-side, especially Jones' fluttering harmonica.

The commercial sheen of "Come On" in combination with the surreptitious nudging of sales in the sprinkling of shops that – pre-barcode scanners – returned figures was sufficient to ensure that the Stones' opening salvo reached a healthy position. There were four competing charts at the time, which were aggregated into a single chart once the BBC's TV chart programme, *Top of the Pops*, began in 1964. *The Guinness Book of British Hit Singles* is now the industry's standard reference book and relies for chart stats for the early sixties on the hit parade published in *Record Retailer*, where "Come On" made no. 21.

"I WANNA BE YOUR MAN"

Sean Egan

Quite why the Stones retrospectively acquired a contempt for their first record and its naked commercialism is a mystery. Another mystery is why they have not exhibited anything like as much disdain for the follow-up single even though recording a Lennon and McCartney number was a far more cynical measure than covering "Come On". Of course, the Stones would not have stooped so low as to record something like "Bad to Me", "Hello Little Girl" or "Love of the Loved", saccharine John and Paul songs that were UK hits for Billy J. Kramer and the Dakotas, The Fourmost and Cilla Black that year. Nonetheless, riding on The Beatles' hallowed coat-tails for a virtually guaranteed hit was another act that begged the question of where the blues purism had gone so quickly.

Perhaps the band – Jagger and Richards, in particular – have always been more inclined to be easy on themselves in this respect because the entire process of being gifted "I Wanna Be Your Man" is intertwined with the successful assumption of their own identity, wrapped up in which was their appreciation of the fact that songwriting was an attainable goal. The legend is well-known that Oldham, in a chance meeting, told The Beatles' songwriting axis that the group were having trouble deciding on a follow-up to "Come On", a recording of the Leiber/Stoller song "Poison Ivy" and another of Allen Toussaint's "Fortune Teller" having been deemed unsuitable for release. (Stones versions of both tracks would appear on the Various Artists album *Saturday Club* at the end of January 1964.) The Beatles-versus-Stones rivalry propounded by the press never actually existed – not only had George Harrison arguably got them a record deal but the two groups would in time coordinate their releases so as not to detract from each other's sales. It was perfectly natural for the Fab Four's song-writing team to knock off a second verse for an incomplete song in the Stones' presence – a process by whose brevity the latter were astounded. Although it would be a while before Mick and Keith were writing anything by which they weren't a little embarrassed, this demystification of composition was crucial to a personal growth that would ultimately see them become among the most important songwriters of the decade, behind only Lennon and McCartney and Bob Dylan. How, then, could they see this record in anything other than a positive light?

On *With The Beatles*, released in the fourth week of November 1963, "I Wanna Be Your Man" was a scrap tossed to Ringo to sing and, while mildly enjoyable, sounded like it. In the Stones' hands three weeks earlier, it was a whirlwind of guitar, high-leaping bass, yowling vocal, distorted guitar solo and breakneck tempo. This all lends a small degree of gravitas to what is essentially a nursery rhyme. The "Nanker, Phelge" to be found in the parentheses underneath the title of the B-side, "Stoned", was the pseudonym used for the group-composed songs – often, like this, blues instrumentals – with which the band would fill out albums and singles in the early days. Oldham also got a cut of this publishing arrangement. The Nanker part was the Stones' word for a band party trick involving pushing up one's nose while pulling down the skin below one's eyes; James Phelge was a former flatmate of Keith, Mick and Brian at their Edith Grove hovel. "Stoned" is pretty good musically (with Ian Stewart shining on piano) and atmospherically (cavernously echoey). In the title's daring allusion to drugs (to the bulk of the populace, the word still meant "drunk"; hipper folk were aware the meaning was transmuting into something else) can be detected one of the first public stirrings of the spirit that would make the Stones the foremost rebels of their generation. Another example was the fact that following their promotion of "Come On" at Oldham's behest in matching houndstooth jackets, they had insisted on dressing in their own way, becoming the first major chart group to spurn ties and a uniform look. Ridiculously unremarkable today, such an act was virtually revolutionary in an age when lack of adherence to social convention could mark one out as degenerate.

THE ROLLING STONES EP/"NOT FADE AWAY"

Sean Egan

If the importance of singles has rather been forgotten by rock historians, it is as nothing compared with the way that Extended Play releases have been treated.

EPs had their own chart in Britain up to 1967 and sometimes their lead track received as much airplay and hence fame as hit singles. The format was not common in the States, so Stones EP cuts tended to be shoved on to US-only albums instead, with the EP origination often only vaguely apprehended by American rock critics who are in large part responsible for chronicling the medium. While the Stones never captured the popular imagination in the manner of the title track of the Fab Four's *Twist and Shout* with any of their EP cuts, they released three highly regarded EPs in their homeland consisting of material originally unavailable elsewhere in the UK and which equates to a whole album's worth of material. As the EP became a defunct platform, several of their EP tracks acquired a rarity status. Even the Americans, who rarely missed a trick when it came to hunting down every obscurity while slapping together another pseudo-album, failed to notice some of them. Usefully, in 2011, ABKCO mopped up all The Rolling Stones' UK EP tracks on the prosaically titled *60's UK EP Collection*.

The first Stones EP was an eponymous affair released on 10 January 1964 and was reputedly a testing of the water by Decca as to whether the kids adored the band enough to make the jump from spending their pocket money on a Stones single to saving up their pocket money for an album. Its topping of the EP chart suggests that indeed they were – as, of course, does the fact that the group are still with us.

Keith Richards peculiarly retained a teenage-like devotion

to Chuck Berry decades after his own compositional abilities
had transcended Chuck's narrow melodic skills. Although
Berry was not renowned for a great variety of tunes, he was
celebrated for his sparkling lyrics. Unfortunately, that gift was
not on display in "Bye Bye Johnny", a peculiar sequel to
"Johnny B. Goode" seen through the eyes of Johnny's mum
and nothing like as inspired as its parent song. The Stones
covered it competently for the opening track of their first EP.
Their version of "Money" is decent enough, if a little
ramshackle, but The Beatles had recently made irrelevant
every other interpretation of this Berry Gordy and Janie Bradford song, a US hit for both Barrett Strong and The Kingsmen,
with the berserk version that closed *With The Beatles*. Interestingly, "You Better Move On" was listed first on the EP's cover
as though Decca considered this Arthur Alexander ballad the
track most likely to propel it into the chart's upper echelons.
The Stones winningly perform a number that straddles pop
sentimentality and blues grit. The record closes with a recording of "Poison Ivy" different to the one discarded for the
band's second single. Previously a transatlantic hit for The
Coasters, it so happened that it made the UK charts again in
the hands of The Paramounts in the month of this EP's appearance. The Stones inject some muscle in their take on the song,
which doesn't prohibit some prettily cascading guitar lines.

At this juncture, the nascent Jagger/Richards songwriting
team operated in parallel to the Stones: with few exceptions,
Mick and Keith considered their compositions too soft for
their own group. Nonetheless, they were no doubt pleased at a
couple of milestones for their partnership that occurred in
January 1964. Firstly, they placed songs with outside sources.
"Will You Be My Lover Tonight" b/w "It Should Be You" was
a January 1964 Decca single by George Bean, produced by
Andrew Loog Oldham and with backing almost certainly
provided by the Stones. The B-side is very mainstream, inoffensive but perfectly enjoyable pop. Despite its risqué title, the
A-side is cut from the same Moon-in-June cloth, although
with its French horn, strings and cavernous production it is
given a slight grandeur in keeping with Oldham's hankering
(soon to become very pronounced) to be a British Phil "Wall

of Sound" Spector. This extremely obscure record seems to just predate "That Girl Belongs to Yesterday" but, crucially, the latter became the first hit written by Jagger/Richards when US singer Gene Pitney took it to no. 7 in Britain and no. 49 in his home country. Pitney said that he customized the song somewhat and it certainly fits into his established melodramatic, semi-operatic template.

Although "That Girl Belongs to Yesterday" was not considered good enough for a Stones record despite the way it demonstrated the commercial potential in Mick and Keith's craft, this does not mean that they were becoming purist regarding their singles. "I Wanna Be Your Man" had made no. 12 upon its November 1963 release. "Not Fade Away" was its follow-up in February 1964. The band can claim with their dying breaths that their raw arrangement elevated it into something more than a cynical lunge for the big time, but a cover of a Crickets song had nothing to do with the blues and everything to do with Mammon.

Although it was an original song, The Crickets' record was an interesting purloining of Bo Diddley's trademark shave-and-a-haircut-two-bits rhythm. The very definition of staccato – apart from a typical, blurred Buddy Holly solo – it relied on silence for its power as much as it did The Picks' cooing vocal underscoring of the riff and Holly's plaintive singing. The Stones' version spurns any gaps, filling the soundscape with scrubbed acoustic guitar, handclaps, wailing harp, maracas (played by a visiting Phil Spector), a relentless rhythm section and a guileless Mick vocal. As the original is a fine recording, it's quite an achievement that the Stones' very different version is just as interesting. Nonetheless, Oldham's famous claim that "I considered it to be like the first song Mick and Keith wrote" was pushing it. Within a year, the Stones themselves would surely consider this record to be juvenilia.

Phelge/Spector was the publishing credit for the B-side, "Little by Little", although the anecdotal evidence suggests that the song was a collaboration between Jagger and Phil Spector. Gene Pitney was also in the crowded Regent Sound studio and he and Ian Stewart sat at the same piano for what is a rather nifty and authentic blues boasting attractively downhome guitar work, bright harmonica (from Mick this time) and quite lengthy instrumental passages. There were umpteen R & B bands in Britain at the time and the fact that they all drew from the same pool of material made it difficult to adjudge any as being much better than any other, but it was recordings like this that showed whom among them had the potential to transcend their influences.

This article by sixties "gear bird" journalist Maureen Cleave reeks of manipulation by Andrew Loog Oldham – and of the journalist playing along with the manager's attempts to portray the Stones as the people the kids should idolize because their parents hated them. Nonetheless, it does give a flavour of just how shockingly unconventional the world found The Rolling Stones in 1964.

THIS HORRIBLE LOT – NOT QUITE WHAT THEY SEEM

Maureen Cleave

First published in the *Evening Standard*, March 1964

"But would you like your daughter to marry one?" is what you ask yourself about the Rolling Stones. They've done terrible things to the musical scene – set it back, I would say, by about eight years.

Just when we'd got our pop singers looking neat and tidy and, above all, *cheerful*, along come the Rolling Stones, looking almost like what we used to call beatniks. (I use this démodé word deliberately. I hope you can remember what beatniks looked like.)

The Stones, which is what they are called by intimates, have wrecked the Image of the Pop Singer of the Sixties.

"We're a horrible looking bunch," they say of themselves, and there is not a murmur of dissent. Girls stop to stare and giggle in the street, men shout things that are unrestrainedly rude, the Hilton Hotel shows them the door and so do many provincial pubs.

They do take a bit of getting used to. And certainly no prospective mother-in-law is going to accept them in their present condition.

Their ages range from 19 to 22. There is Keith Richard who has a pert face, pert manners and was eating an apple; there is Charlie Watts who is keen on clothes and considered by his manager to have the bone structure of Steve McQueen and therefore a great future in films; there is Brian Jones who has floppy yellow hair and is the one best-liked by me; there is Bill Wyman who bears a marked resemblance to both Charles I and Charles II, an essentially Stuart face; and then there is Mick Jagger who is indescribable.

On television they look curiously appealing with their great heads shaking vaguely, Mick Jagger jerking like a jack-in-the-box but his feet rooted to the spot.

They possess no uniforms: "We couldn't adapt ourselves to a uniform," they say. They will walk on to the stage in the outfits depicted above, tie or no tie as the case may be. They sell a lot of records. Their "Not Fade Away" is in at No. 3. Their manager, a young man with red hair called Andrew Loog Oldham, is passionately devoted to their scruffy image.

"Aggressive," he said with satisfaction. "They don't wash too much and they aren't all that keen on clothes. And they don't play nice-mannered music: it's raw and masculine. I get letters from the kids begging me not to let them appear at the Palladium or go to America and get all tidied up."

Often he is asked if they are as stupid as they look. "People," said Mr Oldham nonchalantly, "keep asking me if they're morons."

Indeed the Stones are not what they seem. You discover that one was a graphic designer, another did engineering, another went to the London School of Economics.

Brian Jones now lives in a village in Berkshire but shortly moves to Belgravia where, he says, he will live next door to Lady Dartmouth.

He hires a different make of car each week so as to get to know them all.

Charlie Watts has invested a lot of his money in the Rock of Gibraltar which the others think is pretty stupid.

They originally created a stir in a club in the Station Hotel, Richmond. The place held 140 people and on a good night there would be 500 dancing in the street. Sometimes you would find the Salvation Army at one end of the street and the Stones at the other.

"The kids used to hang off the ceiling," said Brian, "taking their shirts off and that. They liked the way we raved. In places like Cardiff they kiss us, getting the sweat off our faces on to their faces."

As the Stones would say, the kids "reckon" them like mad. They claim to have a disruptive influence on other pop singers, many of whom long to throw away their blue mohair suits and rebel.

And of course their effect on the poor young man in conventional employment is to make him extremely discontented. He is forever confiding in the Stones how he longs to wear his hair down his back only his bosses and teachers won't let him. "From that quarter," Mick Jagger said, "there seems to be some sort of opposition."

Two weeks ago, they scored a victory over the grown-ups in the north. They appeared on *Scene at 6.30*.

"Get those horrible people off the screen," cried the adults, switching over to *Top of the Pops*. There, gaping at them smugly from *Top of the Pops*, were the Stones.

"We're quite clean really," Brian Jones says, just for your information. "What we want to do is bring a lot of pleasure to people. Thereby earning a bomb!"

THE ROLLING STONES

Sean Egan

UK release: 17 April 1964

Produced by: Andrew Loog Oldham and Eric Easton for Impact Sound

Charts: UK no. 1

Tracklisting:
Route 66
I Just Want to Make Love to You
Honest I Do
Mona (I Need You Baby)
Now I've Got a Witness (Like Uncle Phil and Uncle Gene)
Little by Little
I'm a King Bee
Carol
Tell Me (You're Coming Back)
Can I Get a Witness
You Can Make It If You Try
Walking the Dog

In a sense, the "real" Stones starts here.

The first EP may not have been marked by quite as much cynicism as the opening trio of singles, but on their eponymous debut long-player, The Rolling Stones were at last free to purvey on vinyl the kind of material that had made their name around the clubs in London.

Keith Richards has always claimed both that much of this album comprises dubs and that it was a work-in-progress – recorded at tiny Regent Sound Studios in London's Denmark

Street – that was authorized for release by a precipitous Andrew Oldham (credited as on all the Stones work up until 1967 as producer, though always dependent on good engineers, in this case Bill Farley). That other bands' rough mixes should sound half as good. This is easily the best album to come out of the British R & B scene and although the fact that there are only three originals rules it out of contention as a grand artistic statement, it is still one of the Stones' finest long-playing efforts to this very day.

Opener "Route 66", was written by Arthur Troup back in the 1940s, although it had latterly been revived by Chuck Berry both as a straight cover and as a rewrite in the form of "Sweet Little Sixteen". This litany of the sights along the highway that ran almost from coast to coast in the States in some senses epitomized why young men of the Stones' generation wanted to be in rock 'n' roll or R & B groups. A fairly matter-of-fact song for most Americans, in Britain, where highways hadn't come into existence until a half-decade previously (and were dubbed motorways when they did) and in which air travel for the average Briton was unattainable, its litany of place names would have been less glamorous than mystical. Jagger's performance is endearing rather than impressive but behind him the band cook impressively, especially Jones on angular rhythm guitar. "I Just Want to Make Love to You" is one of the many Willie Dixon songs made famous by Muddy Waters. The number is mildly daring in a culture where discussion of sex was still taboo in the media, something emphasized by the way that a pause is inserted before the lascivious enunciation of the word "love", which itself is accompanied by a bang of instrumentation. As with the opener, the handclaps are a tacky touch but it's an excellent band performance. When the tempo is urgently raised in the bridge, the metaphor about the rhythms of the sexual act become crystal clear. "Honest I Do" is a pop-blues number from the pen of Jimmy Reed. The Stones version is sensual. It's also very well produced: when Mick conjures some lonesome harmonica, it sounds like he's on a mountain ledge, while cymbal splashes are mixed dramatically high. Bo Diddley's "Mona (I Need You Baby)" possesses an unexpectedly surreal ambience, with the beat slurred, the guitars floating and shimmering, and the vocal placed in the middle distance, collectively making for the quality of a dream. The track enriches the album as much for its refreshing change of tone as its artistic excellence. "Now I've Got a Witness (Like Uncle Phil and Uncle Gene)" is a "Nanker, Phelge" song, the first half of whose title alludes to a cut on side two of the album. The parenthetical section of the title is a nod to Spector and Pitney, who were present in the studio when it was laid down. It's the type of blues instrumental where generic becomes plagiaristic, with Ian Stewart's organ indeed picking out the riff of "Can I Get a Witness", but it has its own fine original attributes, particularly Brian's mouth harp. "Little by Little" further swells the Stones' publishing coffers by gaining a second airing here to close side one of the original vinyl configuration.

In the grand tradition of blues innuendo, the lyric of Slim Harpo's "I'm a King Bee" suggestively declares "I'm a king bee buzzin' around your haaave." Guitar lines are appropriately stinging and some purring bass from Wyman resembles buzzing. After the relatively exotic fare of much of what has preceded it, "Carol" – an identikit Chuck Berry rocker – can't help but sound a little ordinary, and there are more of those gauche handclaps. Nonetheless, it's an enjoyable, thumping rendition. "Tell Me (You're Coming Back)" marks the milestone of the first Rolling Stones-released recording featuring the publishing credit of Mick Jagger and Keith Richards. The songwriting axis that was soon to be one of the world's greatest kicks things off respectably enough but in no way remarkably. The track impresses for the way its tumbling acoustic guitar figures, booming drum fills, chinka-chinka electric guitar and wailing harmonies adhere with utter professionalism to the conventions of a melodramatic balladry that would be the very antithesis of the Stones' stock-in-trade.

"Can I Get a Witness" – a US hit for Marvin Gaye – marked the occasion of the first time the Stones issued a cover of a song from Motown, the hit factory whose product was actually of far more interest to young African-Americans than the Stones' beloved blues, considered by them to be old man's music. It's not one of the better creations of the magnificent

Holland/Dozier/Holland songwriting team, being rather plodding in structure and over-plaintive in nature. The gospel-like "You Can Make It If You Try" was a Ted Jarrett song recorded by Gene Allison. Jagger sounds too callow to be dispensing life advice but the proceedings are well intentioned enough to engender indulgence in the listener and the band provide pleasing swells and rolls. "Walking the Dog" brings things to a fine close. A surreal Rufus Thomas song with bizarre imagery, it features slinky guitar and some gruff backing singing from Brian Jones, the only time the latter's voice would ever be prominently heard on a Stones record.

The album's major flaw is the lead singer. Mick Jagger might have been steeped in the blues but at this point in time he doesn't quite sound the real downhome deal. Not yet having developed his famously louche vocal style, he tends to resemble an angelic kid trying on for size the music of a far more case-hardened breed. However, where he is merely endearing, his colleagues are more convincing. Instrumentation being a far easier means by which to effect a façade, Keith, Brian, Bill and Charlie make us believe with their tight, punchy and raw playing across thirty-two minutes that they are something other than fresh-faced, well-fed honkies.

The album's American equivalent was released six weeks later. Its rechristening as *England's Newest Hit Makers* – a title that instantly dated the product insofar as the next group of Anglo hit-makers were theoretically just around the corner – was the type of crass move that would be the bane of British groups' lives for several more years, as would the type of tampering with tracklistings evident here. On the latter score, this album got off lightly, with "Not Fade Away" (which opened proceedings) displacing "Mona (I Need You Baby)". The American version did pretty well, reaching no. 11. Contrary to popular memory, the Stones did not attain their status as cultural and commercial bookends to The Beatles across the Atlantic until 1965, with compatriots such as the Dave Clark Five being considerably more successful than they were in the States before then. However, that bookend status arrived pretty quickly in their home country. *The Rolling Stones* knocked *With The Beatles* off the top of the charts in May '64.

Sean Egan

As the latter album had itself displaced The Beatles' first album *Please Please Me*, this made the Stones the first act other than the Fabs to occupy the LP top spot since May 1963. The feat created a virtuous circle, generating inevitable newsprint centred on whether the Stones were the "new" Beatles, and so on.

Although the excellence of the product played its part in those sales figures, so did their co-manager's spark. A contemporary of his young charges he might have been, but Andrew Oldham's considerable experience as a PR man showed in the way the album was packaged. Even The Beatles – who had stunned everybody with their stylish, moody sleeve for *With The Beatles* – had not dared to market their product without their name on the front cover, and this even though they were literally the four most recognizable people on the planet. *The Rolling Stones* featured a half-length, dimly lit, unsmiling group photograph and no lettering except Decca's logo. "The Rolling Stones are more than just a group – they are a way of life," Oldham declared on the back. Whether his sleevenotes were marked by canniness or are prescient only in hindsight is debatable. The boastful banalities that followed ("For the Stones have their fingers on the pulse of the basic premise of 'pop' music success – that its public buys sound, and the sound is what they give you with this their first album . . .") suggest that this opening sentence had no wellspring other than a hypester's desire to increase interest. Quite remarkably, though, that line became true as the Stones proceeded to epitomize the desire for change felt by a generation.

"IT'S ALL OVER NOW"

Sean Egan

The Stones single "It's All Over Now" was released in Britain on 26 June 1964 and a month later in the States. Written by Bobby and Shirley Womack, its initial recording was by The Valentinos. American DJ Murray the K didn't allow his self-proclaimed status as the "Fifth Beatle" to prevent him from alerting their theoretical rivals to the song's qualities. When the Stones acted upon his recommendation, Bobby Womack was furious to find a competing record blowing asunder the chances of his group's original version becoming a hit. That is, until such time as massive royalty cheques started coming through his door.

The single was the first recorded fruits of the Stones' sessions in the second week of June at the legendary Chess Studios in Chicago, which had been responsible for so many of their favourite records. Unlike The Beatles, who rarely ventured outside of their recording comfort zone at EMI's studios in Abbey Road, north London, the Stones were happy to knock out tracks while on the move. By doing so, they were able to avail themselves of recording technology that staid old British studios had yet to deign with their attention.

Oldham's previously mentioned contention that "Not Fade Away" was the first Stones composition would actually be more appropriate to "It's All Over Now". Although it was a cover job, you'd swear it wasn't. As with "Come On", the Stones completely rearranged the number and in the process, as they did with that earlier song, injected the appropriate spite in a creation whose jaunty musical timbre did not previously match its seething lyric. In so doing, they invented their sound. The staccato riff, the anthemic feel, the reedy harmony vocals from Keith and the air of recrimination-bordering-on-misogyny all make it sound uncannily like the sort of Jagger/Richards Stones song with which we would become happily familiar. That quasi-misogyny, incidentally, wasn't sinister in '64 but more an act of rebellion, a spurning of the solicitousness of the romantic pop song that was so rarely a part of people's everyday relationship experiences as to seem phoney.

The lyric is the vengeful exultation of a badly treated man that, with the tables turned, it is now his former lover's turn to cry. In 1964, "Because I used to love her, but it's all over now" – the repeated line that constitutes the chorus – was novel (and exhilarating) in its brutal matter-of-factness. It's also colloquial in a song packed with everyday expressions, albeit ones mainly from black American neighbourhoods. Colloquialism is, of course, often ungrammatical and phrases like "She done me wrong" and – daringly, at least stateside, where people would have understood it – "half-assed game" were the types of things creating consternation in the great and the good who were lamenting the increasing informality of culture; in the UK this informality somehow seemed wrapped up in the increasing proliferation of Americanisms. Chiming twelve-string rhythm guitar offsets the clangourous main riff and, thanks to the expertise of Chess's engineer Ron Malo, both are treated with a reverb that provides a larger-than-life scale, especially in the introduction. Although it has a grim subject, there is something joyful about the track.

An earlier UK recording, "Good Times, Bad Times", occupied the flipside. It is differentiated from a thousand and one generic blues songs only by its acoustic instrumentation. However, that it was a Jagger/Richards song was lucrative indeed, for B-sides generated the same amount of writer/publisher mechanical royalties as hit sides and "It's All Over Now" achieved the vital milestone of becoming the group's first UK no. 1. That achievement would have to wait in the States, where it only climbed as high as no. 26. The same month, the Stones had notched up their first top 40 US hit in a rather curious manner. "Tell Me" had been lifted off the first album and its soppy-ish strains had climbed to 24, 27 and 26 in the *Billboard*, *Cash Box* and *Record World* charts respectively. (*Billboard* positions will be cited from hereon for reasons similar to those for preferring the *Record Retailer* charts for the UK.) Lost in the mists of time is the fact that this hit kicked off a brief period when what would become the archetypal dirty rock 'n' roll band were known as balladeers, with three of their first four top 40 US hits being downtempo. Or as Keith later put it, "it was the fuckin' soul ballads that happened for us in America". (At least the Yanks buying their first Stones product in "Tell Me" got a blast of the band's true nature in the form of the B-side, "I Just Want to Make Love to You".)

The day after the release of "It's All Over Now", the BBC TV show *Juke Box Jury* accorded the group the same privilege granted The Beatles in December 1963 by inviting them to make up the show's normally varied panel. In their assessments of the discs whose merits they were asked to judge, the Stones, as was their wont, were candid, which may not sound such a big deal but public forthrightness in the achingly polite/dishonest culture of pre-psychedelic Britain was considered by many almost insurrectionary. Those parts of the public who didn't like the length of their hair, their unmatching clothes or their disobliging miens were already psyched up to find their high ratio of "misses" and their dismissal of the exalted Elvis Presley's new record "There's Gold in the Mountain" as "dated" to be an outrage. The Stones were probably no more disrespectful or impolite in their assessment of the records than had been the Fabs, but The Beatles' overall cheeriness could, in the viewer's mind, transform any dismissive comment into endearing schoolboy cheekiness. Column inches were generated by the "furore", just as had happened a few weeks previously when – in an incident manufactured by the canny Oldham – Stones members snarled their displeasure in the press at being refused admission to the restaurant in their hotel because they were not wearing ties. That a generation was becoming impatient with quasi-militaristic pettiness was why so many teenagers were increasingly taking so much pleasure in their parents' fury at the Stones. Plays, films, books and even political speeches also articulated the questioning outlook of a society that, freed from the draft and austerity, now had sufficient time and freedom to be able to question the authoritarian models of government that dictated their behaviour, their dress and their living arrangements. However, in terms of a critical combination of a visual and aural shorthand and aesthetic pleasure, nothing could quite match the force of pop, and the Stones were at the forefront of it.

FIVE BY FIVE EP / "TIME IS ON MY SIDE"

Sean Egan

14 August 1964 saw the release of the Stones' second UK EP, the drolly titled *Five by Five*.

The five members recorded its five tracks at Chess in the same sessions as gave rise to "It's All Over Now". Opener "If You Need Me" (Wilson Pickett/Robert Bateman) is an organ-dominated, slow-burning soul number with a spoken-word interlude. If that description puts the reader in mind of a soon-to-be-released Stones song called "Time Is on My Side", they would be right. As with that song, Jagger emotes impressively to simpatico backing. In "Empty Heart" (Nanker, Phelge), the falsetto swoops behind Mick's lead vocal are among the things that mark the carving of a distinct identity among the usual throwing of blues/soul shapes. "2120 South Michigan Avenue" – the title the postal address of the Chess studio – is another Nanker, Phelge blues instrumental, but again shows a band learning to rise above the generic. Stewart's organ dominates and Brian's mouth harp is sparkling. Wyman has claimed that, not for the last time, a bass riff of his kicked off the composition.

Side two opens with "Confessin' the Blues", a twelve-bar dating from the forties written by Walter Brown and Jay McShann, but which the Stones probably knew from more recent recordings by Little Walter or Chuck Berry. That it sounds a little staid compared with the Stones' self-generated material on this record may be a yardstick of their progress. In the Stones' hands, "Around and Around" sounds something more than another grid-written Chuck Berry celebration of youth and rock, courtesy mainly of Brian's bullet-headed rhythm guitar. Mick's vocal is a little lacking in passion but the track has an impressive swing, with the guitar work approaching flamenco-style in places.

The EP was a small step rather than a great stride forwards for the band but was naturally enthusiastically received by their fans, who sent it to no. 1 in its chart. Over in the States, it was of course ignored except for the purposes of plundering for LP tracks. America instead got a new single, that is, a genuinely new recording as opposed to something lifted off an LP (a practice if not unknown then largely frowned on in the British market). The Regent Sound-recorded version of "Time Is on My Side", released on 26 September 1964, remained unique to America for twenty-five years, displaced by a new recording (ironically recorded at Chess) made for the British market and which was subsequently included – apparently erroneously – on American hit compilations.

Written by Norman Meade (a.k.a. Jerry Ragovoy), the song had its lyric fleshed out by Jimmy Norman, although the latter's credit has disappeared in one of those murky sagas of publishing attribution common to the era. This soul ballad's narrator is sanguine about the restlessness of his lover in the conviction that she will come running back to him after satisfying her wanderlust. Such thinking is rather unusual in a medium in which romantic relationships are usually predicated on exclusive and immediate terms. It makes for an altogether refreshing and generous-hearted experience, one that Mick assists with a quavering execution of lines like "I got the real love – the kind that you *need.*"

The B-side was the high-quality "Congratulations", a rebuke to a heartless Lothario with plenty of acoustic guitar cascades. That the composers were Jagger and Richards was a real fillip this time out, for the record was the first Stones fare to climb into the US top 10, making no. 6. This was possibly because, and not just in spite, of the furore the Stones created by their appearance on *The Ed Sullivan Show* on 25 October, the day after the release of their second American album, *12 x 5.* The group performed "Around and Around" and came back to close the show with "Time Is on My Side". The appearances of The Beatles on the same programme eight months before had charmed America, but disgust was closer to the feelings of at least those sections of the States aged over thirty at the sight of this band with by now astoundingly abundant hair (collar-length), mismatched clothes and a pigeon-toed, stick-thin lead singer dressed in a sweatshirt. Sullivan was not impressed by the audience disrespectfully screaming all the way through an exchange with Jagger. Afterwards, he fulminated, "I promise you they'll never be back on our show." The crusty Sullivan had made such threats before and kept to his word but the threats of even the host of the most popular variety show on American TV were so much bluster in the face of the Stones' snowballing popularity, which ironically he may have intensified: "Time Is on My Side" was hovering around the 50 mark in the charts when he signalled to the country's youth that these people were on their side in the generation war.

12 x 5 – a hodgepodge of previously released singles and EP tracks plus three new recordings – made the US no. 3 spot.

"LITTLE RED ROOSTER"

Sean Egan

Although their accommodation of philistinism via US mongrel albums was clearly something that they had convinced themselves didn't really count (it was only America), the Stones' next UK single was the very opposite of such shamelessness in its insistence on artistic integrity over commercialism. With their first no. 1 under their belts, the band dispensed with the policy of being incrementally more populist with their singles by committing what seemed commercial suicide.

Their fifth 45 was a downbeat twelve-bar blues. Sam Cooke had actually brushed the US top ten in late '63 with what he titled "Little Red Rooster", but that hardly augured chart success for the Stones, who used only his title as they dispensed with his soul rearrangement and took the song back to its roots when it was known as "The Red Rooster". It had originally been recorded by Stones favourite Howlin' Wolf. Like many of the Wolf's songs, it was written by Willie Dixon, although as was standard with blues it was to some degree an adaptation and aggregation of motifs from previous records.

The band seem to have apprehended that merely slapping a lacklustre, generic blues workout on an A-side wouldn't cut it, teen idols or no. The stately pace, the pattering percussion, the mordant vocal and the juxtaposition of acoustic guitar and electric slide all make for something richer and warmer than any blues they had ever attempted before. In many ways, this is Brian Jones' record. Always the biggest blues purist in the band, he is the member who would have been most enthusiastic about its release. Additionally, it is his playing that makes the record via both the cawing bottleneck that is its most prominent feature and his closing harmonica (mimed by Mick for television appearances). B-side "Off the Hook" is a boring mid-tempo song about a couple engaging in telephonic tit for tat. Despite its artistic shortcomings, it was another valuable addition to the growing Jagger/Richards publishing catalogue.

It was arguably the strangest or at least most exotic disc in the history of the British singles charts thus far, but "Little Red Rooster" made no. 1. Jagger's 1969 comment, "I still dig 'Little Red Rooster', but it didn't sell", suggests that actual units shifted were not that impressive compared with those of their previous 45s. This may be due to its lack of danceability (an important requirement then) or it may have been due to the fact that the band didn't appear on *Top of the Pops* in a dispute over bookings that had been arranged by their recently dispensed-with co-manager Eric Easton. Either way, it mattered little. However illusory that no. 1 position may have been, it was psychologically important in enabling the band to claim vindication.

That the song's lyric is a litany of the innuendoes common to the blues was a matter of little importance: they passed over the heads of the vast majority of the purchasers as well as unhip radio programmers.

THE ROLLING STONES NO. 2

Sean Egan

UK release: 15 January 1965

Produced by: Andrew Loog Oldham and Eric Easton for Impact Sound

Charts: UK no. 1

Tracklisting:
Everybody Needs Somebody to Love
Down Home Girl
You Can't Catch Me
Time Is on My Side
What a Shame
Grown Up Wrong
Down the Road Apiece
Under the Boardwalk
I Can't Be Satisfied
Pain in My Heart
Off the Hook
Susie-Q

Easy as it is to mock the American pseudo-Stones albums, it has to be conceded that that second American LP was a far better listening experience than the real deal, released in Britain three months later.

Excuses for the artistic failure of *The Rolling Stones No. 2* are pretty much non-existent. With the band members still not composing much, they were in the same position as they had been on their first LP, relying upon American R & B records for their material, in which resided a vast repertoire of good to classic songs. Yet faced with this limitless aural bounty, they came up with an uneven record. Although there are high points, too often they plump for songs that are either individually weak or else tedious in conjunction. There is also some noticeably uninspired playing.

"Everybody Needs Somebody to Love" almost acts as a summary of what is wrong with the album. A recent Solomon Burke record, which the artist had written with Bert Berns and Jerry Wexler, it has a patience-wearing, vainglorious, spoken-word intro, jerky feel and comical guitar solo, and makes for a most peculiar opener. Although it gets exciting in a bridge that builds to a crescendo, it is overall a meandering number undeserving of its long-for-the-era five minutes' duration. (An alternate take included on the US album *The Rolling Stones, Now!* is little better but at least detains the listener for two minutes less.)

"Down Home Girl" – an Alvin Robinson record written by Jerry Leiber and Arthur Butler – stakes a claim for fashionability with its nod to the fact that rhythm and blues was transmogrifying into soul. The Stones turn in a slinky performance decorated with impressively liquid guitar lines. "You Can't Catch Me" is a Chuck Berry-penned celebration of an outlaw of the road. Musically, it chugs along agreeably but there's no disguising the monotony of the verses. The version of "Time Is on My Side" here differs from the take that appeared on the US single and *12 x 5* in that it has a guitar rather than organ intro, a more mellifluous intonation of the title line, less echo on Mick's voice and a clean, not faded, ending. It achieves the remarkable feat of making the first released version sound flawed (specifically by being watery and overstylized). It is exquisite from its opening lilting guitar figure onwards, with Mick contributing a nigh-perfect vocal, all the more impressive for the fact that its humility is something with which we have never really associated him.

"What a Shame" had already been heard in the US. In December 1964 London Records had refused to countenance releasing "Little Red Rooster" and made the Jagger/Richards soul ballad "Heart of Stone" the follow-up to "Time Is on My Side". "What a Shame" – also penned by Mick and Keith

– was its flipside. "Heart of Stone" reached no. 19. A tradition
in the States, created by airplay's influence on chart positions,
was for B-sides to sometimes make an appearance on the Hit
Parade, and "What a Shame" was the first Stones track to
manage that feat, albeit only in its "Bubbling Under" nether
regions (124). The Stones rarely adhered to the pattern of
many artists in throwing substandard tracks on their flipsides,
but "What a Shame" is archetypal B-side fare with its awkward
percussion, hesitant guitar plucking and repetitive melody.
"Grown Up Wrong", another Mick and Keith effort, is even
clunkier, with heavy-handed drumming doing no favours to
an irritatingly unresolved tune.

   "Down the Road Apiece" opened side two. Don Raye's
forties song was probably familiar to the band through Chuck
Berry's recording. Its flowing, jazzy melody provides a
perfectly sound bedrock for a good performance but the
Stones' playing never rises above perfunctory. The Drifters'
hit "Under the Boardwalk" (written by Arthur Resnick and
Kenny Young) may be an almost shockingly mainstream song
for this group to cover but it comes as a blessed relief in the
midst of this mediocrity, its depiction of alfresco lovemaking
given a blissfully languid and atmospheric arrangement.
Mick's singing is the most conventionally pleasant it has yet
been. Amazingly, the track's polished production was achieved
in the humble environs of Regent Sound.

   Muddy Waters' "I Can't Be Satisfied" is theoretically more
familiar territory for the Stones, but although superficially
similar to "Little Red Rooster" in its twelve-bar structure and
oodles of Jones slide, it sounds arch, something not helped by
the echo slapped on Jagger's voice. "Pain in My Heart", an
Allen Toussaint song that had been recently revived by Otis
Redding, has a richer feel than almost anything else here, prin-
cipally by dint of its dense rhythm section and dramatic
instrumentation. Following the first British outing for "Off the
Hook" (completing a triumvirate of original songs that hardly
suggested Mick and Keith were destined for great things),
Dale Hawkins' "Susie-Q" – written by the artist with Stan
Lewis and Eleanor Broadwater – is a strong closer, a snaky
song of devotion with some attractively distorted guitar.

However, the handclap loop left playing after the instrumentation has been faded is symptomatic of a lethargic approach to the whole album.

The bad smell hanging over this enterprise was completed by the sleeve. Schoolboy daring motivated its scatological title while Oldham's sleevenotes were similarly distasteful and juvenile in their advice to fans who desired the LP: "If you don't have the bread, see that blind man, knock him on the head, steal his wallet . . ." For once, the guardians of morality were in the right when they objected and the note was hastily amended. About the only thing classy about the whole enterprise was the cover photo, which took the debut LP's daring minimalism even further. Once again, there was no typography, while the group picture – taken by snapper-of-the-moment David Bailey – seemed designed to warn off, not entice, the potential purchaser: the half-shadowed Stones stare out menacingly, with a pock-marked Keith particularly unsettling.

Like "Little Red Rooster", *The Rolling Stones No. 2* proved the Stones' status could send a record to the top of its relevant chart regardless of obvious commerciality and, in this case, quality.

"THE LAST TIME"

Sean Egan

February '65 saw the release of another US Stones LP with a title that emphasized how supposedly of-the-moment the contents were and thus instantly dated them: *The Rolling Stones, Now!* It made no. 5. Its Jagger/Richards-written track "Surprise, Surprise" would not see the light of day in the band's home country until 1971. Seeing as it is an I-was-gonna-dump-*you*-anyway plodder, Britons weren't missing much.

Back in Blighty, it was time for another Stones milestone, one even more important than their first chart-topper or the assertion of "Little Red Rooster" that purism could be balanced with success. Mick and Keith had cut their writing chops on material that had been unsuitable for a Stones A-side by dint of its being too generically bluesy or not bluesy enough. With "The Last Time", they considered themselves finally to have an original song of sufficient integrity on their hands to be worthy of single status. Well, original to a point. Keith Richards later described "The Last Time" as a song that "goes back into the mists of time". The most recent permutation was called "This May Be the Last Time" by The Staple Singers, which had been issued as a single in 1955 but which the Stones most likely heard on the 1962 album *Swing Low*. "It had a strong Staple Singers influence," Richards admitted. "And I didn't actually realize until after we'd written it . . ."

That Roebuck "Pops" Staples – leader of the gospel group in question – had copped the publishing on his group's recording was fair enough, as the issue of who was the original composer was probably dead before the notion of copyright was born. Similarly, no legal action could result from Jagger and Richards sticking their names in the parentheses beneath the title on their own record label, although their colleagues may have felt a grievance about not being cut in on that deal considering that it was a collective performance that had made the result almost unrecognizable from its antecedent. The Stones discarded the Staples' funereal pace and bare arrangement, ramping up the tempo and placing a circular Brian Jones guitar lick centre-stage. Rather than a tribute to God, the lyric was now the rumination of a man contemplating ditching his lover. The record is a love-it-or-hate-it proposition – that riff is as much repetitive as it is hypnotic, and the lack of a bridge adds an impression of one-dimensionality – but on its UK release on 26 February 1965 the group once again sailed to no. 1. The disc did impressively well upon its 13 March US release, too, making it to no. 9. With the Jagger/Richards songwriting team now validated, there would not be another official, studio, non-original Stones A-side for more than twenty years in the UK or the US.

On both sides of the Atlantic, the B-side was "Play with Fire", which made no. 96 on the *Billboard* Hot 100. Mick and Keith are the only Stones on the track. With the other band members asleep, two producers, friends of the band, filled the gaps: Phil Spector handled guitar and bass, and Jack Nitzsche keyboards and tam-tams. However, the Nanker, Phelge publishing credit seems to be explained by Wyman's contention that several different versions were recorded and that the wrong master was given to Decca. The track was quite a startling slab of class warfare and malice for the period. Its power has been somewhat diluted – the threat in the narrator's admonition to his poor-little-rich-girlfriend that playing with him is playing with fire is empty in a society where the law takes domestic violence profoundly more seriously than it did back then. However, the track continues to impress for its indigenous flavour. The Stones spent most of their time pretending to be black Americans but here Mick sings in something approaching his own accent as he juxtaposes the rough area of Stepney with the upmarket locale of Knightsbridge against a frilly and quintessentially English backdrop dominated by acoustic guitar and harpsichord.

"(I CAN'T GET NO) SATISFACTION"

Sean Egan

Bill Wyman once revealed in a BBC radio interview that in 1965 all five Stones had an equal vote in what should be released as a single. In a ballot in the middle of that year, which also involved Ian Stewart and Dave Hassinger – the engineer who had become a trusted ear since they had moved their stateside recordings to RCA studios in late 1964 – Keith Richards and Mick Jagger came out against issuing "(I Can't Get No) Satisfaction" as an A-side. Not only were they outvoted by all the others, but the mix that was commercially released was considered by Richards to be unfinished. Both the composition about which the songwriters were expressing their lack of confidence, and the recording of it that one of them deemed substandard, are still – despite all the intervening years in which great records have been released – easily among the greatest in the history of popular music. While this fact remains clear, what is receding from the popular memory is the society that gave vent to the broadside of frustration that is "Satisfaction". Also forgotten is the measure of just how confrontational and vulgar the record was in the context of that society.

"Music as Social Statement" is an overused notion, particularly when applied to belligerent punk tracks that make no impact beyond the already converted. When it blasted from radios, Dansettes and television screens in the summer of '65, the snarling ambience of "Satisfaction" reached everyone from innocent children to rebellious teenagers to uninterested mothers to conservative businessmen to reactionary senior citizens. A record whose snarling music and seditionary lyric were in no sense mainstream became so by dint of the widest imaginable exposure granted it by the existing popularity of the group purveying it. A virtuous circle then resulted as its familiarity and the affection in which it was held helped change the definition of mainstream.

The album for which the Stones were prepping at the time would turn out to have a soul flavour, so it makes sense that Keith has subsequently revealed that the lick he heard in his head for this creation was played with horns. Remnants of that soul vision remain on the finished record in the shape of Charlie's stomping, Stax-like drum beat and Mick's Otis Redding-esque chant of "No, no, no!" However, Richards' fleeting infatuation with the new toy that was the fuzzbox turned the track into something else completely. It was possibly the opening entry in the ferocious, distortion-loving genre retroactively christened "freakbeat". The resultant buzzsaw guitar riff sounded thrillingly as if it were cutting its way through speaker grilles.

The track is a perfect synchronization of sound and spirit. Bolted to that angry riff is a Jagger lyric that possesses all of soul's passion but is channelled in a direction no soul singer had ever imagined. While offering no specific social comment or political analysis, the song was instantly recognizable as summing up the contempt that sixties youngsters held for the values of their elders that hemmed in their lives. The sexual allusion in the title/chorus line – the result of Keith (not Mick) mishearing "If I don't get no satisfaction from the judge" in Chuck Berry's "Thirty Days (To Come Back Home)" – was a cocked snook at intercourse-leery media, as was a reference to the problems posed to that activity by menstruation in the section in which the narrator reveals that his girl has told him to come back next week because she's on a losing streak. Elsewhere, Jagger hollers his resentment of babbling voices on his car radio telling him stuff about which he is clearly supposed to be excited but by which he is bored and of television commercials that insist (successfully, judging by the narrator's revealed attitudes) that he is defined by his consumption modes. The way Mick softly sighs the choruses gives them an unreal ambience perfectly counterpointed by the quarrelsome verses.

Compared with subsequent rock outrage like The Sex Pistols effing and blinding on teatime TV or the swaggering bad-boy antics of a multitude of subsequent bands from Led Zeppelin to Oasis, all of this may sound inchoate where it doesn't just seem like kindergarten stuff. However, the latter acts were operating in a much liberalized landscape that was to a large extent the product of the pioneering of the Stones. "Satisfaction" was an exhilarating breath of fresh air to those fed up to the back teeth with the banal window-dressing in which the world was then presented.

Twelve-bar blues of a modernistic and wry flavour graced the US and UK B-sides of "Satisfaction", respectively "The Under Assistant West Coast Promotion Man" and "The Spider and the Fly". The former Nanker, Phelge creation was inspired by London Records' George Sherlock, with whom the band had become acquainted on their first American tour. The quintessential American-ness of his title (the grandiosity of its length undercut by its own sub-clauses) was grist to the mill for musicians from a race ever ready to mock (or, in their native parlance, "take the piss out of") pomposity. "The Spider and the Fly" is more adventurous both musically and lyrically, a syncopated tune bearing a tale of a lonely travelling musician reduced to the borderline desperate act of engaging in congress with a woman of the advanced age of thirty. There is some excellent harmonica work that is the handiwork of Jagger.

Although "Satisfaction" was released in America on 6 June 1965, British sensibilities didn't get to be shaken up by it for two and a half months, a quite astounding fact from today's globally harmonized perspective. When it was granted a UK release on 20 August, it had long become the band's first US no. 1. British acts that had topped the American chart was a category still containing fewer than a dozen. The Stones had been beaten to the feat by The Beatles, of course. Less predictable was that the likes of Manfred Mann, Freddie and the Dreamers, Wayne Fontana and the Mindbenders and Herman's Hermits had also pipped them to the post. Looking at that fact from this end of the timeline, it seems absurd that such lightweight-to-risible bands should have scaled the summit stateside before such artistic giants as the Stones. On the other hand, that value inversion was made up for in spades.

"Satisfaction" sat at the summit for a month. Moreover, its effect on the Stones' career both in the States and elsewhere was incalculable. The Stones had issued great discs before, but this was a special record, an anthem, a signature, a cultural milestone, an artistic high-water mark and everything else that makes a song one that it would be unthinkable not to play live at every concert.

It was also, of course, self-composed. It is simply astounding that just eighteen months after placing their first song with another artist – which itself wasn't long after having first written together – Jagger and Richards had come up with something so immortal.

It's interesting to note that another of the acts who beat the Stones to number one in the States were The Animals. The Newcastle group were similar in so many ways: a quintet absolutely steeped in the blues and adroit at rejigging their favourite records sufficiently to distinguish themselves from multitudinous other acts drawing from the same well of material. In fact, it's easy to imagine many observers on the pop scene to have considered The Animals to be the band with the greater potential: their lead singer Eric Burdon had a magnificent and authentic blues voice that made Jagger sound like an imposter, while, good musicians though the Stones were, none were in the same league as The Animals' virtuoso keyboardist Alan Price. That all changed with "Satisfaction". The record's jaw-dropping brilliance and its colossal commercial success – and the huge effect this must have had on Mick and Keith's confidence in their own abilities – put the Stones into a rocket ship and left The Animals puttering along in their Commer FC van.

Needless to say, when "Satisfaction" was issued in Britain, it stormed to no. 1. Although their already elevated status in their home country meant it didn't quite have the same bridgehead impact it did across the Atlantic, it did have the significant effect of fully legitimizing a debate that endured throughout the sixties: Beatles or Stones?

Stating a preference was almost always a matter of adopting a stance or – wittingly or unwittingly – revealing a mindset. Beatles fans adored the warmth and humanity that radiated from the Fab Four's music and personalities; Stones fans who loved the uncooperative aura and spiritual bite of their records viewed that mop-topped sunniness as a form of compromise, a kowtowing to Establishment mores. Yet rock critic Greil Marcus made the interesting point, "it was The Beatles who opened up the turf the Stones took as their own – there was no possibility of a left until The Beatles created the centre". In any case, the reality was that most people revered both groups and even for those who insisted on nailing their colours to the mast of one of them, it was simply bliss to be able to take for granted that for once little, backward, impoverished, grey, one-bath-a-week, class-ridden, slightly comical Britain had one over on the Yanks.

There was another dimension to the debate. Namely, it became so taken for granted that the Stones and The Beatles occupied more or less equally an artistic plateau several levels above any other contender that when people were asked their favourite group, they would give their reply of "The Yard-birds", "The Animals", "Small Faces" or what-have-you on the full understanding that they meant "apart from The Beatles and the Stones". Everybody liked *them*.

The national pride engendered by the two best and most popular musical ensembles on the planet being British was truly profound, especially considering the figureheads-of-progressivism status increasingly enjoyed by them. The most important pop groups were British. It naturally followed therefore that some of the most important and influential people in the world were British.

OUT OF OUR HEADS

Sean Egan

UK release: 24 September 1965

Produced by: Andrew Loog Oldham

Charts: UK no. 2

Tracklisting:
She Said Yeah
Mercy, Mercy
Hitch Hike
That's How Strong My Love Is
Good Times
Gotta Get Away
Talkin' 'Bout You
Cry to Me
Oh, Baby (We Got a Good Thing Going)
Heart of Stone
The Under Assistant West Coast Promotion Man
I'm Free

As for the reason for the postponement of "Satisfaction" in the country that took such patriotic pride in The Rolling Stones . . .

In its trappings of triviality, the *Got Live If You Want It!* EP (or *got LIVE if you want it!* as rendered by the sleeve) was the polar opposite to "Satisfaction". In 1965, an in-concert pop record meant a band trying vainly to make themselves heard against a wall of screaming teenagers. Compounding the dubious worth of such an enterprise is the possibility that it is, to a greater or lesser extent, bogus. The sound clarity of some tracks doesn't suggest recordings made, as claimed, at the Edmonton Regal, Liverpool Empire and Manchester Palace. Additionally, while one can admire the chutzpah involved in hiving off the fans screaming "We Want The Stones" into a separate track of that name and claiming the publishing rights for Nanker, Phelge, what possible artistic worth can a thirty-six-second snatch of "Everybody Needs Somebody to Love" be claimed to possess? Nonetheless, there's no denying the raw power and toe-tapping pleasure of renditions of "Pain in My Heart" and "Route 66", however devised. Side two of the EP was given over to songs not previously released by the group. Hank Snow's uptempo wanderlust anthem "I'm Moving On" and Bo Diddley's "I'm Alright" are given punkily energetic readings. The UK fans who sent this record (whose title punningly alluded to Slim Harpo's "I've Got Love If You Want It!") to no. 1 in the EP chart upon its release on 11 June 1965 had no idea how their teenybopper minds were about to be blown with their idols' next single.

By the time of that next single, the Stones' rebel credentials had been ratcheted up by the prosecution and conviction on 22 July 1965 of Jagger, Jones and Wyman on charges of insulting behaviour. The case related to an incident on 18 March 1965 when they were refused permission to use a garage's lavatory facilities apparently because of their unconventional appearances (the attendant described Wyman in court as a "shaggy-haired monster"). Their profane and liquid response ("We'll piss anywhere, man," was one of the comments uttered as trousers were unzipped) might today seem merely an act bathed in self-aggrandizement. However, it possessed a far more layered significance in 1965: the behaviour of the forecourt attendant was symptomatic of the everyday pettiness of minor figures of British authority and was intertwined in a vague feeling of powerlessness felt by the majority.

The second half of 1965 saw a transatlantic synchronization of a Rolling Stones album title for the first time. However, the US and UK versions of *Out of Our Heads* boasted significantly differing tracklistings. The American album was released on 30 July and was the usual arbitrary collection of new and previously issued cuts, including, fatuously, "I'm

Alright" from the *Got Live If You Want It!* EP. "One More Try", a sprightly Jagger/Richards blues that exhorts the listener to keep his chin up, would not be made available in Britain until 1971. The inclusion on the American album of "The Last Time" and "Satisfaction" makes it unsurprising that it spent three weeks atop the US albums chart.

The UK album released nearly two months later is, although a rather short affair lasting less than half an hour, far more substantial than that lacklustre second domestic LP. Moreover, although it isn't quite as enjoyable an aural experience as the debut, it improves on it in the sense of containing both more and better original songs. While retaining one foot in their established sound, *Out of Our Heads* was something of a surprise in the way it saw the band exploring another, contrasting, form of American black music: there is as much smooth soul as gritty blues.

"She Said Yeah" was a Larry Williams number written by Sonny Christy (an early alias of Sonny Bono) and Roddy Jackson. The rough-hewn complexion provided by its abrasive guitar riff and excited vocal provides a misleading idea of what will follow on the platter. However, it's good stuff and one wishes it didn't run to a mere minute and a half. Don Covay's "Mercy, Mercy" (written by the artist and Ronnie Miller) sees a narrator pleading for sensitivity from an increasingly uninterested lover. The Stones' excellent version mixes a smooth-rolling arrangement and creamy backing vocals with rough-edged guitar work. The version of Marvin Gaye's US hit "Hitch Hike", written by Gaye, Clarence Paul and Mickey Stevenson, is a sharp and snappy reading. The Stones move from Motown to Stax in the space of two tracks as they proffer a rendition of the Roosevelt Jamison composition made famous by Otis Redding, "That's How Strong My Love Is". Jagger emotes impressively against a backdrop that sounds grand despite featuring no horn charts. Intentionally or not, Redding returned the compliment by including a version of "Satisfaction" on *Otis Blue*, released a couple of months after *Out of Our Heads* in the US, which Keith liked because it transposed his riff to the horns he had always envisaged playing it. The lack of similarity of Jagger's and Redding's voices is a given and one would think the same applied to Sam Cooke. However, Jagger unexpectedly sounds uncannily like Cooke on a cover of the latter's "Good Times", a typically suave creation from the man who purportedly invented soul. The backing vocals are surprisingly velvety and, as with several tracks here, the tidiness of the instrumentation is underlined by an unfussy, clean ending. The original vinyl side one closed with "Gotta Get Away", a kiss-off to a faithless partner. Its fine ebbing-and-flowing melody is capped by a tongue-twisting, semi-yodelling of the title phrase. In no way does this Jagger/Richards creation feel like it's drawn from inferior stock to the standards by which it's surrounded.

Stones albums at this point had an obligatory Chuck Berry number. This album's tribute to Keith's hero is "Talkin' 'Bout You", which opens side two. Not only do the band change the title from its original "I'm Talking About You", they also slow down the pace of Berry's hardly uptempo tribute to a ladylove, making for a peculiarly languid, if enjoyably so, interpretation. Solomon Burke's "Cry to Me" (written by Bert Russell) is another song in that then-new tradition wherein a love song is made to feel like a sermon from the mount ("Doncha feel like crying?"). As such it would probably have sounded silly coming from Mick's mouth on the first album. That he was now a man, not a boy, is evident in the fact that he acquits himself as well as his colleagues in an assured performance.

"Oh, Baby (We Got a Good Thing Going)" is a delightfully brisk and smartly played rendition of blueswoman Barbara Lynn's good-hearted love anthem. "Heart of Stone" – the Jagger/Richards song that had been a minor hit in the US at the beginning of the year – gets its first UK airing. Its love-as-melodrama approach means it fits in happily here. "The Under Assistant West Coast Promotion Man" is also belatedly introduced to UK fans. Its bluesy strains remind us just how little of this type of music the album contains.

The album closer, "I'm Free", sees the Jagger/Richards team exult in that incredible sense of liberation experienced by boys and girls entering adulthood when they suddenly realize they are autonomous men and women pretty much beholden to nobody, a sensation that, of course, was ratcheted up for this particular pair by the exhilaration of their being increasingly wealthy idols. Rather than opt for a bellicose arrangement for this declaration of independence, the band float it on gentle and radiant instrumentation, which includes organ from Jones. This was the first example of the penchant he would increasingly display for broadening the Stones' musical horizons through his multi-instrumentalism. The result is appropriately beatific and a sweetly mellow end to a high-quality record.

For the first time, a British Stones album featured the group's name on the cover, but there was still something revolutionary about the artwork: the monochrome shot by Gered Mankowitz confined the group to a small portion of the sleeve, depicting them gazing at the purchaser down a triangular tunnel formed by a building site's hoardings.

"GET OFF OF MY CLOUD"/ "19TH NERVOUS BREAKDOWN"

Sean Egan

"I remember after 'Satisfaction', which was a time of great triumph, a worldwide hit, Mick and I were sitting back in some motel room, in San Diego . . . We gave this big sigh of relief and it was exactly at that moment that there was a knock at the door and the phone started ringing and people wanted the next hit."

So said Keith Richards of the aftermath of the life-changing success of "Satisfaction". Elsewhere he said, "It's really difficult now to realize how important it was to have a hit single. If the last one didn't do as well as the one before, that meant you were out, you were sliding out . . . So each one had to be better and *do* better, it didn't just have to be better."

The first quote can be taken with a pinch of salt: the guitarist seems to have a tendency to compress protracted sequences of events into pithy and poetic recollections (he seems to be the source of the myth that Oldham locked him and Jagger in a room until they came up with their first song). However, the point made in the second quote that a 45 rpm manifesto was required from sixties· pop groups at dauntingly regular intervals is indisputable.

Following up "Satisfaction", of course, was somewhat less daunting than impossible. In the event, Richards and his writing partner offered "Get Off of My Cloud". "[T]hey're crap. It's nothing," said Jagger later of the lyric he contributed to the song. "I never dug it as a record," shrugged melody writer Richards in 1971. Richards had changed his mind by 2003, by which time he was saying he loved it. The world had cottoned on to how great was the record long before he did: it topped the charts on both sides of the Atlantic and became an anthem of the autumn of '65.

In several ways, the record is "Satisfaction Part Two", featur-ing a stomping soul beat, a vocal melody line that is more chant than tune, a belligerent chorus and a lyric featuring an appar-ently arbitrary litany of contemporary irritants. The narrator is volubly peeved by pushy marketing men informing him he has won a prize, zealous traffic wardens and neighbours complain-ing about the noise of his household (the title phrase deriving from its location on the ninety-ninth floor of his block). As not all of these things can be put at the feet of those in power and none of them are exactly gross injustices, this may seem banal-grievance-bordering-on-child's-whine but, as with the gripes in "Satisfaction", the era made the act of complaint progressively political in itself. The chorus – a call-and-response, fist-pumping affair – is actually better than that of "Satisfaction". However, the same can't be said for the riff. This is not a matter of shame – few have devised a riff as good as "Satisfaction" and nobody has come up with a better one – but the trebly, liquidy affair here doesn't grab the lapels in the way a great riff should, not least because it's buried way back in the mix.

Nonetheless, this is a truly powerful record, one that saw the Stones leapfrog The Beatles in one respect. On *Rubber Soul*, released that December, the Fabs' lyrics were still mainly romance-based and therefore broadly unremarkable. At this point in history, at least, the Stones stood shoulder to shoulder at pop's pinnacle with Bob Dylan – whose epic blast of venom, "Like a Rolling Stone", had been sandwiched by the releases of "Satisfaction" and "Get Off of My Cloud".

The B-side in the States – where "Get Off of My Cloud" was released on 25 September 1965 – was "I'm Free". Britain – in which the single was issued on 22 October – was treated to a new Jagger/Richards song on the flipside, one that showed that Mick and Keith could turn their hand to Beatles-like courtly romance should they so wish. "The Singer Not the Song" was both a common phrase and the title of a 1961 Dirk Bogarde film based on a book by Audrey Erskine Lindop. Wherever they heard it, the Stones create a ballad around it that celebrates one particular lover over intimacy in general. The lyric is draped with chiming electric and picked acoustic guitars to create a disarmingly guileless piece of work.

"Get Off of My Cloud" was the last Stones product released
in Britain in '65. On 4 December, the hungrier (by dint of
being wealthier) American market got another album with
ridiculously arbitrary contents (each side closing with a cut
from the live EP) and a fatuous title – *December's Children
(And Everybody's)*. It made no. 4 in the US. Two of its tracks
would not see the light of day in Britain until the seventies.
"Look What You've Done" is a good version of an above-
average Muddy Waters twelve-bar blues. Whereas that is a
blast from the Stones' rapidly disappearing covers-dominated
blues past, "Blue Turns to Grey" was representative of their
new era of self-reliant pop and rock. It's also a sign of how
effortlessly prolific the Jagger/Richards songwriting team were
becoming. They were now reaching the stage where they could
discard worthy material. Although the Stones have never
played it live and probably barely remember it, UK chart
legend Cliff Richard had a top 20 hit with the song in early
1966. It's a ballad but in no way sappy; perceptive about the
self-deceit common to the aftermath of a love affair, it contains
both a pleasingly melancholic title phrase and a sweet little
flourish of a guitar refrain.

The Stones did their home country the lately rare honour of
letting them hear their next single first, releasing it on 4 February 1966, eight days before its US release. "Dunno about you
blokes, but I feel about ready for my 19th nervous breakdown,"
Jagger is supposed to have remarked on a tour of the States.
"We seized on it at once as [a] likely song title," said Mick of
this alliterative and memorable phrase. As this explanation
from Jagger is a contemporaneous one, it's difficult to know
how to evaluate it: their interviews in the sixties were jam-
packed with fibs, half-truths and self-mythologizing, especially
where telling the truth would have been too controversial even
for a band who courted strong reaction. It would have been
taboo to mention (and perhaps also indicative of a sense of
societal discretion that has been regrettably lost) that, like
many Jagger songs of the period, "19th Nervous Breakdown"
is almost certainly rooted in the singer's relationship with
Chrissie Shrimpton. He and the sister of model Jean Shrimpton
had been stepping out since 1963, although many wondered

why they stuck together, such was their propensity for public arguments and even physical fights. Shrimpton was considered a mentally fragile figure and, indeed, would attempt suicide at the culmination of their relationship, an event that took place at the close of the very year of the release of "19th Nervous Breakdown". That the relationship was destructive and its termination good for both parties is probably confirmed by the fact that Jagger's exploration of her challenged psyche was not exactly sympathetic.

The song depicts a neurotic young survivor of a wealthy but negligent upbringing. She is soured towards the world by a previous, bad relationship, and the resultant anomie infects even those who try to help her, including her current partner, the narrator. This is all conveyed in a conversational, matter-of-fact style (first line: "You're the kind of person you meet at certain dismal, dull affairs") that is impressive in a medium where stylized and gimmicky phraseology is the norm. Adding to the air of adventure is the unusually long playing time of just shy of four minutes. Mick's vocal, though clear enough, is somewhat low in the mix, a common enough grievance for Stones records at this time as to have been discussed in the letters columns of the music press. Despite the mildly murky ambience, the record is more melodic than most self-written Stones singles thus far, even actually boasting a bridge. The crowning glory is little moments to which the listener looks forward: an intro where the two guitars, bass and drums announce their presence in turn, a blaring horn-like guitar part prior to each chorus and Wyman's burbling bass runs at the close. For those hip enough, there was also the delicious frisson attending the knowledge that the "trip" referred to at one point was a stationary journey.

American B-side was the mid-tempo "Sad Day" (Jagger/ Richards), in which the narrator realizes that a relationship he thought was going fine is over. The rising inflections at the end of the lines make the melody seem slightly forced but it's an enjoyable affair. How appropriate it is that the British B-side was "As Tears Go By", a song associated with Marianne Faithfull, the woman who was soon to replace Shrimpton in Jagger's affections. Jagger, Richards and Oldham had written this glum rumination on loneliness and the passage of time in 1964, and had seen Faithfull acquire a top 10 UK hit with it (no. 22 in the States). Jagger has admitted that the band were too embarrassed to put out their own version at first. When they did, they slowed down the tempo and added plucked acoustic guitar passages and chamber strings for an effect rather reminiscent of The Beatles' "Yesterday".

The latter had been issued as a US-only single the previous year. "As Tears Go By" provided a US no. 6 for the Stones when it was issued on 18 December 1965 (a fortnight after it had appeared on *December's Children*) with "Gotta Get Away" as the B-side. (A translated version – "Con le Mie Lacrime" – was a hit for them in Italy.) Although this was lucrative and helped emphasize the Stones' lesser-known melodic credentials, it also created an impression, which ballooned over the years, best summed up by John Lennon in his caustic 1971 interview with *Rolling Stone* magazine publisher Jann S. Wenner: "I would like to just list what we did and what the Stones did two months after on every fuckin' album." Just months before, the Stones had been streets ahead of The Beatles in terms of mature and cutting-edge lyrics, but it was as a consequence of releases like "As Tears Go By" that the Stones from around this point onwards would always seem followers to The Beatles' leaders.

"19th Nervous Breakdown" was the first UK Stones single not to climb to the top spot since "Not Fade Away". In the States, it also stalled at no. 2, kept off the top spot in a three-week battle of generations and ideals by Sgt Barry Sadler's celebration of patriotic and military values, "Ballad of the Green Beret".

AFTERMATH

Sean Egan

UK release: 15 April 1966

Produced by: Andrew Loog Oldham

Charts: UK no. 1

Tracklisting:
Mother's Little Helper
Stupid Girl
Lady Jane
Under My Thumb
Doncha Bother Me
Goin' Home
Flight 505
High and Dry
Out of Time
It's Not Easy
I Am Waiting
Take It or Leave It
Think
What to Do

By 2 April 1966, The Rolling Stones had racked up sufficient chart entries in the States to justify a greatest-hits album, the mysteriously titled *Big Hits (High Tide and Green Grass)*. The album also inadvertently served to mark the passing of a Stones era, for two weeks later came the UK release of *Aftermath*, the first Stones album to be entirely made up of original material. From this point onwards, covers would only feature in the Stones output, if at all, sparingly.

That the fourteen tracks on *Aftermath* were exclusively
Jagger/Richards compositions was mathematically impressive:
of the thirty-six cuts on their three previous UK albums, just ten
had been written by them or collectively with their bandmates.
That achievement becomes even more impressive when the fact
is taken into account that the LP was written on the fly. In October–December 1965, Gered Mankowitz was the Stones'
embedded photographer on their fourth American tour. "They
were under pressure to write because they were booked into the
studio," he recalled. "I had one long evening somewhere in the
middle of the tour with Mick just hanging out with him and I
remember him saying words to the effect of, 'We've got twelve
songs to write and it's really hard because of the schedule',
which meant that they would fly out straight after the show and
get into the next place at two, three in the morning." Of course,
none of that alone is what makes the album so impressive. Any
halfway competent bunch of musicians can throw together
enough generic, derivative or mediocre material to fill an LP. In
addition to George Bean, Gene Pitney and Marianne Faithfull,
Jagger/Richards songs had already been released by Adrienne
Poster, The Mighty Avengers, Bobby Jameson, West Five, Lulu,
Dick and Dee Dee, Jimmy Tarbuck, Vashti, Thee and The Herd.
None of those compositions were included here. Mick and
Keith waited until they had enough material that was brilliant
and/or pioneering. Moreover, at over fifty-three minutes, *Aftermath* is an unusually long album (the last Beatles album had
been a mere thirty-five minutes). Only Bob Dylan was making
albums so lengthy at this point.

Although Jagger and Richards were coming into their pomp,
the fact should not be ignored that the same can be said of Brian
Jones. This idea might come as a surprise to Mick and Keith, who
were having to put up with increasingly erratic behaviour from a
man whose damaged psyche and deep-rooted paranoia were
made worse by the effects of his prodigious drug use and his
resentment at the fact that he could no longer be regarded as the
leader of the band when the songwriting axis was now his meal
ticket. Yet even as he was indicating that he did not care about the
group's records by his absences from sessions and his dilettante
behaviour when he did attend, Jones was enriching and

broadening the group's sound. *Aftermath* featured contributions
from him on such wholly non-blues instruments as sitar, dulcimer, koto, harpsichord and marimbas. Charlie Watts has damned
Jones' multi-instrumentalism as merely another manifestation of
a short attention span but the fact that Jones could master any
given instrument – percussion, string or wind – sufficiently to
wrest pleasing sounds from it before moving on to another is not
only remarkable but its results are indisputable: the sweetening he
applied to several *Aftermath* tracks – and to multiple Stones
recordings from this point forward – made very good cuts great.
(It also gave ammunition to Stones fans inclined to engage in
those "Who's the best?" debates: the Fabs had to hire outside
musicians to effect such layering.)

"Mother's Little Helper" provides a forceful entrée. The
opening salvo mixes modern slang with the sort of insolence
that was increasingly ticking people off about the Stones
("What a drag it is getting old!"). Then Jagger launches into an
attack on the housewife pep-pill culture and implicitly (explicitly being out of the question when no pop star dared talk
publicly about drug use) the older generation's hypocrisy in
being in favour of harsh sanctions for recreational use of the
sort of drugs favoured by the Stones' generation. Jones
provides some sweeping sitar. The cockneyisms that Mick
throws in were then rarely heard in pop, nor was the straight-
talking contempt with which this track is suffused. Although
cogently and melodically argued by a bunch of young peacocks,
"Mother's Little Helper" is simply and unmistakably a "Fuck
You" to the prevailing order (or at least their wives).

"Stupid Girl" is presumably another song rooted in Jagger's
dysfunctional relationship with Chrissie Shrimpton. It's utterly
infectious in its marching mean-spiritedness. On "Lady Jane",
dulcimer from Jones, harpsichord from Jack Nitzsche and
courtly phraseology in Jagger's lyric ("I pledge my troth")
disguise the song's chilling mercenariness. The narrator
declares himself a humble servant to the titular woman and
then unblushingly informs in turn Anne and Marie, to whom
he has also been suitor, that his decision is based on Jane's
station. The glittering intelligence of this remarkable track
must have bewildered those who viewed the band as bestial,

although, that said, the track that succeeds it, "Under My Thumb", isn't exactly marked by civilization's finest qualities. The narrator boasts that his "squirming dog" keeps her eyes to herself while he can still look at someone else, although he does claim that this is a matter of the tables having been reversed. The insistent staccato rhythm, Jones' evocative marimba riff and the vibrato-assisted lead guitar work make it impossible to spurn the track, however discomforting.

The album's first semblance of blues comes on the clopping, slide-decorated "Doncha Bother Me", a demand by a hip figure not to be the victim of a follower's copycat tendencies ("your clothes and your hair – I wore it last year"). The unusual lyric, swishing bridge and Jagger's artful singing demonstrate that the band are now masters of the form of which they could once only write pastiches. Side-closer "Goin' Home" is in one sense cut from far more traditional blues cloth, but this touching lament of a road-weary rocker pining for the comforts of the hearth becomes revolutionary simply by dint of its taking an inordinately long time to conclude. "While we were playing it, we awaited a signal to stop but no one signalled," recollected Wyman. Everybody improvised after the "proper" song was exhausted and the resultant cut was nearly eleven-and-a-quarter minutes. "It was the first long rock-and-roll cut," Richards later observed. Technically, he was right – Bob Dylan's "Desolation Row" from the previous year exceeded it by around five seconds but was essentially a folk number – but being first doesn't necessarily confer quality. As can be seen elsewhere on this album, when an artist tests the boundaries, he sometimes discovers in the process that the uncharted territory beyond is fertile. As can be seen on this track, on other occasions he finds barren ground that demonstrates why those boundaries exist. Because these are fine musicians, there are flashes of good playing in the extemporization section – particularly some thrumming bass lines from Wyman – but overall it turns a song that would have been fine at three minutes long into a something flabby and tedious and, moreover, the album's only weak cut.

"Goin' Home" also presaged a new ruthlessness about its composers: by all rights, a predominantly improvised generic blues should have engendered a collective band publishing credit, but – with one bizarre exception – there would never be another Nanker, Phelge song. Wyman, future members Mick Taylor and Ronnie Wood and future sidemen Billy Preston and Ian McLagan would harbour and publicly air grievances about the fact that songs to which they felt they contributed – and in some cases were even the main composer – were attributed by dint of their power in the band to Mick and Keith. Brotherly love was never a Stones forte.

The remainder of *Aftermath* is underrated. While the first side boasts several tracks about which a lot has been written, the only cut much discussed on side two is "Out of Time", which became a UK no. 1 in the hands of Chris Farlowe in mid-1966. One complaint commonly made is that the material is "un-Stonesy" but, in fact – this soon into their songwriting self-reliance – an archetypal original Stones sound had yet to be established. The songs on the second side are certainly not as groundbreaking or grandstanding as those on side one but nonetheless they constitute a thoroughly enjoyable collection of material whose very quietude and quirky or poppy nature provide an extra dimension to both the LP and the group.

A peculiarly faraway-sounding piano passage, which includes a snatch of the "Satisfaction" riff, introduces "Flight 505", a song about a man who catches a flight on a whim and finds to his – what can only be described as – bemusement that it will be the last for him and everyone on the plane. A brittle pop arrangement is decorated by some more vibrato-treated guitar. "High and Dry" is the Stones' inaugural sojourn into what was then called country and western (although it could be posited as occupying the intersection between that genre and country blues). As with all their explorations of this territory, the Stones do rather sound like they're taking the piss, but that doesn't detract from a crisply played, wryly observed song about a man lamenting the fact that he has been dumped because his partner had latched on to his mercenary motives. Such is the hypnotic nature of the tune that, though far from being the album's best song, it's the one whose melody you're most likely to find turning in your head.

Although nothing like as long as "Goin' Home", "Out of Time" feels epic, not just because of its unusually protracted 5:37 playing time but for the depths of its malice as the narrator exults in and minutely dissects his fickle ex's downfall. The mid-tempo arrangement is decorated by marimbas (Jones), piano (Nitzsche), organ (Stewart) and bopping backing vocals. Being an artist on Oldham's Immediate Records, Farlowe clearly had something akin to a "bagsy" arrangement with Jagger/Richards songs, but this was the only one to provide him with a big hit: the prior "Think" and the subsequent "Ride On, Baby" only made nos 37 and 31 respectively.

"It's Not Easy" is the other side of the coin to the sentiment of "Out of Time", as well as a counterblast to the accusations of this being a woman-hating album: in another brisk pop arrange-ment, the narrator notes how dreary life is after a break-up and concedes that "to take his girl for granted" is "a big failing in a man". The delicate "I Am Waiting" is vaguely Far Eastern in both its melody and its air of mystery, being an opaque anthem of anticipation. ("Waiting for someone to come out of some-where" is as close as it comes to definition.) "Take It or Leave It" is a gorgeous little creation, propelled by acoustic guitar and featuring multiple key switches and some sweet "oh la la ta ta la la la" trilling as the narrator dissects honestly and maturely a relationship where the woman sometimes goes mysteriously absent but is not painted as a villainess for doing so ("But you can be so kind"). The Searchers released the song on single just before *Aftermath*'s appearance and secured a UK no. 31 with it. "Think" rather feels like walking in on a couple's argument, its recriminations only half-comprehensible. Richards plays the fragmentary and wispy (if clever) lyric against a melody that is almost anthemic. The closing "What to Do" is a brief but intriguing song of inertia.

The front cover once again did not feature the band's name. Guy Webster's pink-tinted band photograph is merely graced by the title (actually rendered as "After-Math"). The album remained at no. 1 on the UK albums chart for two straight months. Curiously, considering their status both musically and sociologically and their host of chart-topping singles, the Stones would have another no. 1 album in their homeland in this decade only by the skin of their teeth – *Let It Bleed* making the top spot on 20 December 1969.

"PAINT IT BLACK"/"HAVE YOU SEEN YOUR MOTHER, BABY, STANDING IN THE SHADOW?"

Sean Egan

Despite having released, in *Aftermath*, an album that was far more adventurous than The Beatles' (admittedly splendid) previous long-playing effort *Rubber Soul*, come 7 May 1966 (13 May in the UK) the Stones were once again dogged by that accusation of deferentially following in the Fab Four's footsteps. The reason was the sitar and the Indian/mystical ambience of their latest single, "Paint It Black". (The comma inserted after the title's second word on the original label was a record company error.)

On "Norwegian Wood", one of the minority of tracks on *Rubber Soul* (December 1965) characterized by innovation rather than exquisite craftsmanship, George Harrison had become the first Western pop musician to utilize the exotic strains of the sitar. By dint of The Beatles' being the most successful musicians on the planet, "raga-rock" was briefly all the rage. That acts as talented as The Byrds, The Hollies, The Mamas & The Papas, Eric Burdon & The Animals and The Pretty Things used either sitar or an effect meant to convey sitar on their records in the Fabs' wake makes the ridicule that in some quarters attended the Stones' deployment of it rather unfair, although that itself may be a function of the fact that – Dylan aside – they were the only contenders for the status of artists as important as The Beatles. It's additionally unfair in the sense that the Stones arguably made better use of the instrument than anybody, including The Beatles.

Inevitably, it was Brian Jones who decided to tackle the sitar. His opening coiling figure on "Paint It Black" is unrepresentative of what will follow as he proceeds to strum, not pluck, the strings. Such was Jones' demonstrated vast respect for foreign sounds and musical cultures, it would be difficult to postulate this unusual approach as an example of a Westerner misusing the instrument out of ignorance, so perhaps it's wisest to put it down to innovation, especially as there are passages later on in the record where Jones does indeed show that he is willing and able to play it more conventionally. In any case, the propulsive effect is exciting, lending the air of mystery that is one of the sitar's attributes while dispensing with the suffocating, greasy qualities that is one of its drawbacks.

The sitar propels along a recording that is shrouded in shadow. This is possibly the first Stones track on which Watts' drumming is special rather than highly competent. His Arabian-esque two-beat would be exotic already without being treated with echo. Jagger's lyric about a man who has lost his woman – quite possibly in a fatal sense – is surreal, littered with non-rock phraseology ("until my darkness goes", "foresee", "my love"), and its non-Western aura is deepened by oddly placed conjunctions. The Eastern stuff is really piled on in the final forty-five seconds, which feature no vocal at all but rapidly strummed acoustic guitar, weirdly thrumming bass and Mick humming like an extra in a market scene in *The Thief of Baghdad*.

The record was a transatlantic no. 1. America got "Stupid Girl" (previously unreleased in that country) as the B-side. Britain was treated to the sublime "Long Long While". Although not a cast-iron classic like the A-side, it's a tightly played, piano-dominated soul ballad shot through with disarming vulnerability and self-criticism.

Aftermath got its belated US release on 2 July, losing three tracks in the process. One of the tracks omitted was "Mother's Little Helper", which was released as a single stateside in June. It reached no. 8, with its B-side, "Lady Jane", charting at no. 24. 23 September 1966 (the following day in the States) saw the release of the "proper" new Stones single. The bizarre, elongated title of "Have You Seen Your Mother, Baby, Standing in the Shadow?" was as nothing compared with the promotional film directed by Peter Whitehead (who helmed the little-seen Stones documentary *Charlie Is My Darling* the same year). It saw the band dressed as women, two of them militaristically so, an image also to be seen on the single's picture bag. An added provocative touch was that Wyman – one of the uniformed Stones – was in a wheelchair. There is something vaguely disturbing about the tableau, which prefigured the grotesque visual stylings of punk by a decade and must have confirmed for some the sentiment previously expressed by the *Chicago Daily News* journalist who declared of the band in general in November 1965, "This is the end of the line. Beyond the Stones, one simply cannot go and still maintain civilization."

Although Richards has always claimed that "Have You Seen Your Mother" was not given a proper mix, no blame for this is attached to Glyn Johns, who engineered it at IBC Studios in London. Rather, it was released in a rush to fulfil the release date. One wonders, though, whether what Keith would consider a proper mix would have improved the chances of the Stones' lowest-charting single since "I Wanna Be Your Man" in their home country (it made no. 5) and a record that climbed no higher than no. 9 stateside. Following a science-fiction-soundtrack-like opening, we are treated to an extravaganza containing surreal lyrics, growling bass, a brass section, massed backing vocals and a finger-popping interlude. It all sounds very ambitious and worthy but the sound is murky, the brass reedy and the whole never gels. The Dylanesque lyric is daring ("Have you had another baby?") but that dated quality is its only attribute, while the instrumentation lacks coherency. It would have made for an interesting, intriguing album track but was a bizarre (if brave) choice for a single.

Flip "Who's Driving Your Plane?" is a piano-heavy 12-bar with a lyric consisting of another put-down of a neurotic female cleverly and modishly drawn by Jagger, who also sings well.

"LET'S SPEND THE NIGHT TOGETHER"

Sean Egan

The Stones went as far as making "Have You Seen Your Mother" the opening cut of the UK version of *Big Hits (High Tide and Green Grass)*, released on 4 November 1966. Interestingly, the compilation – which had a tracklisting slightly different from the US release – closed with the song that marked the last time the Stones had taken such a chance with a single, "Little Red Rooster". The album made no. 4.

Over in the States, 10 December 1966 saw a step back from daring singles to crass commercialism with the release of *Got Live If You Want It!* That the Stones did not sanction the release of this in-concert album (which differed from the 1965 UK EP but, like that disc, also had its title eccentrically rendered as *got LIVE if you want it!*) indicated their feelings about its worth. It purported to be an affair recorded at the prestigious Royal Albert Hall in London but in fact the City Hall, Newcastle, and Colston Hall, Bristol, were the sorts of modest venues from which the tracks emanated. Certain of the contents were barely live (Wyman: "Some tracks featured overdubs from Mick, Keith and Stu") and "I'm Alright" was clearly the instrumentation from the British *Got Live* EP track with a new vocal. Other tracks were not remotely live: "Fortune Teller" is the studio recording that had appeared on the *Saturday Club* album, while the Otis Redding song "I've Been Loving You Too Long" is an RCA track dating from mid-1965, both with screaming layered on.

That such a worthless artefact as the *Got Live If You Want It!* album climbed as high as no. 6 in the US chart was clearly a manifestation of the Stones' cachet. Their next record demonstrated why they possessed that prestige. In its combination of two songs of contrasting moods but consistent magnificence,

"Let's Spend the Night Together" b/w "Ruby Tuesday" surely ranks alongside "Hey Jude"/"Revolution" by The Beatles and "Sunny Afternoon"/"I'm Not Like Everybody Else" by The Kinks as one of the greatest singles of all time. The A-side was started in America before the engineering baton was passed from Hassinger to Glyn Johns at Olympic Studios in Barnes, London, the location of many Stones recordings over the rest of the sixties, including "Ruby Tuesday".

While the pure aesthetic merits of the record are still readily appreciable nearly half a century after its release, the incendiary nature of the A-side is barely comprehensible to modern sensibilities. To get an idea of how much in 1967 discussion of or reference to sex was taboo in the mainstream media, it should be noted that even ten years beyond that point, sitcoms on both sides of the Atlantic conveyed the impression that they were being incredibly naughty by alluding to "it". Pop in '67 being the preserve of children and teens – post-Elvis popular music did not largely have an adult demographic until its fans had grown up with it – the idea of mentioning sex within its environs was something considered completely inappropriate, including no doubt by those people tasked with wiping down the seats in venues that had just hosted concerts by the likes of The Rolling Stones. Pop songs discussed kissing, holding hands and romantic heartbreak but the scenarios were sexless ones. Occasionally, there would be allusions to couples living in sin ("She said that living with me was bringing her down" in The Beatles' "Ticket to Ride" or "making love" in The Drifters' "Under the Boardwalk") but they could be overlooked because the lack of direct, explicit explanation made it possible to still posit them as not involving "it" – even if in the same manner as people affecting not to notice that someone has broken wind. For a record to appear in the charts with the bald, unapologetic title "Let's Spend the Night Together" was simply shocking.

Jagger was rapidly acquiring the status of Public Enemy No. 1 (at least within popular culture), yet was actually a fairly polite and diplomatic media presence (studied obnoxiousness and profanity were stacked behind sexual frankness in the "Taboos to Be Broken" queue). Accordingly, he said in interviews adjacent to the single's release on 13 January 1967 (the following day in the States) that the song didn't necessarily refer to a boy and a girl sleeping together. There again, the "What – me?" pseudo-guilelessness of statements like "If people have warped, twisted, dirty minds, I suppose it could have sexual overtones" probably only intensified the state of apoplexy to which the record reduced the socially conservative.

This horny anthem is dressed up in strangely conventional clothes: there is un-Stonesy ba-da-da chanting of the main melody line and the song is propelled by a relatively dulcet piano motif, played by Jack Nitzsche and Richards. However, it has a driving beat, one punctuated at regular intervals by blurred tattoos from Watts. Although "We could have fun just grooving around" and "I'll satisfy your every need" are the closest the narrator comes to a direct reference to matters carnal, the title refrain is more than enough to convey the message, as is the general air of dry-mouthed desperation.

"Ruby Tuesday" is exquisite. Another track with Nitzsche piano decoration, it is a wistful farewell to a mysterious, free-spirited female whose ethereal lyric is summed up by the first line, "She would never say where she came from." The "Jagger/Richards" publishing credit is possibly the first example of its being a business convenience rather than an indication of contribution. The haunting words are not the work of Jagger ("Neither of which I wrote," he has said about the melody and lyric). Instead, the track is a real breakthrough for Richards, the man largely restricted to melody hitherto. The Stones' intimate friend, bodyguard and drug dealer Tony Sanchez seemed to think that the credit should have read "Jones/Richards". Certainly, Brian's pretty, fluttering recorder is a massively important part of the heart-tugging soundscape and it is he in combination with Nitzsche who provides the best part of the record: they bring the proceedings to a close in a coda where piano and recorder coil deliciously around each other. Although it's a delicate ballad, the Stones manage the trick of injecting muscle into it: the choruses are uptempo, with emphasis on rolling drums.

When promoting the record, the Stones sported a new image of floppy hats, satin shirts, candy stripes and trailing scarves. This dandy look would evolve over the course of '67 into the even more outlandish flower-power fashions of the Summer of Love.

The frankness of "Night" caused significant problems in puritanical America, with *The Ed Sullivan Show* insisting Jagger replace "the night" with "some time" and some radio stations ludicrously bleeping out the offending phrase. Inevitably, many US DJs gravitated to the less problematic B-side. "Ruby Tuesday" reached no. 1 stateside, with "Night" only making an appearance at no. 55. In Britain, the controversy around the single was actually significantly less pronounced than that created by a television furore analogous to the I'll-never-book-them-again Ed Sullivan fuss of 1964. As the single stalled at no. 3, it can be stated that this furore failed to yield the chart dividends of the prior scandal. After performing the song on *Sunday Night at the London Palladium* – a variety show whose format and place in the nation's affections was the equivalent of Sullivan's show across the Atlantic, with the difference that the titular venue was the "star" – the Stones refused to participate in the traditional schmaltzy programme finale whereby all the guests would mount a revolving podium and smile and wave at the crowd and cameras. Oldham later said Jagger was behind this defiance and that his motive was embarrassment at the fact that UK newspapers had picked up on him having backed down on *The Ed Sullivan Show* a week previously. Oldham contended that with no attempt by the Palladium to censor either "Night" or their other song that evening, the new and bluntly drug-oriented "Connection", Jagger, "in another huff and puff, blindly looks around for another house to blow down". The resultant tumult was considerable, with newspaper coverage tending towards a who-the-hell-do-they-think-they-are? tone.

"Let's Spend the Night Together" was a sociological milestone. Never before had what was then called the hit parade played host to such matter-of-fact candour. Although it didn't single-handedly open the doors to the permissive culture, it played a massive part in facilitating it. In a contemporary culture where every single public comment can and tiresomely often is smirkingly interpreted as an innuendo by TV and radio show hosts, one could legitimately question whether society is ultimately better off for this, but the impetus for the song was valid in its mocking of the almost agonized refusal to acknowledge the act central to – and indeed responsible for – people's lives.

BETWEEN THE BUTTONS

Sean Egan

UK release: 20 January 1967

Produced by: Andrew Loog Oldham

Charts: UK no. 3

Tracklisting:
Yesterday's Papers
My Obsession
Back Street Girl
Connection
She Smiled Sweetly
Cool, Calm & Collected
All Sold Out
Please Go Home
Who's Been Sleeping Here?
Complicated
Miss Amanda Jones
Something Happened to Me Yesterday

A week after "Let's Spend the Night Together" came the UK release of the band's new album, *Between the Buttons*. America got a tweaked version on 11 February that, naturally, included both sides of their latest hit. That stateside tweak made the album feel more substantial. The British configuration, although it impresses by the deepening of the band's melodic skills and its overall charming and sweet atmosphere, remains a collection of unfamiliar and often understated-to-the-point-of-underwhelming material. That Jones makes very modest, in some cases no, contributions to several tracks is a sign of the

fact that, though he shines when he does contribute, his dilet-
tantism was in danger of making him a part-timer.

The vaguely obscene-sounding title comes from a misun-
derstanding by Watts, who drew the back-cover cartoon, of
Oldham's explanation of the title, a term meaning undecided.
The cover picture by Gered Mankowitz of a bleary Stones in
a public park after an all-night recording session is utterly
beautiful. On the original vinyl pressings, the band's name and
album title could only be seen in tiny lettering on two of the
buttons of Charlie's coat.

The LP starts strongly with "Yesterday's Papers". Jones
contributes haunting marimbas while Richards provides a
floor-shaking vibrato guitar figure. This, Nitzsche's harpsichord and doo-doo-doo cooing harmonies provide a
misleadingly gentle ambience for a thoroughly callous dismissal
of a former lover whose usefulness to the narrator is equated
to a twenty-four-hour-old *Times* or *Daily Sketch*. Considering
how nimble is the melody, it's impressive that Jagger has cited
this as his first-ever solo composition. The track makes immediately noticeable the band's new richer sound, although
whether that lushness is due more to Olympic, Glyn Johns or
the maturation of the Stones is unclear.

"My Obsession", though, demonstrates many of the faults
of *Between the Buttons*. Its circular, directionless arrangement
mirrors the inchoateness of the lyric. The narrator bewilder-
ingly states, "My obsessions are your possessions", and notes
that he didn't realize that the object of his lust was so young
but then goes on to say that he could almost be her son.
Capping the thoroughly unimpressive and muddled proceedings is a finish that consists of Watts banging uncertainly on a
drum skin. "Back Street Girl" is far more impressive. A sugar
daddy makes it plain to his (we infer) younger and (we are
told) unsophisticated mistress that he is happy with her
compartmentalized place in his married life, yet the lyric at no
time feels like it is endorsing the cold point of view conveyed:
this is clearly critique via impersonation and a subject in keeping with the class warfare of the sixties. Jones shines on both
organ and accordion in an arrangement with a French café
ambience.

"Connection" is now a well-known term for a supplier of illegal drugs but in 1967 only the hip (a category that did not proliferate in the media) understood it. This album's brief, two-minute song of that title predated Richards' first use of cocaine, let alone heroin, but grass, pep pills and, lately, LSD were in the picture. Keith (whose composition this mainly is, according to Jagger) makes things a little easier for the uninitiated with lines like "My bags they get a very close inspection." This is all wafted on a breezy pop melody. The daring subject matter probably makes the song feel more substantial than it is.

"She Smiled Sweetly" – one of Jones' no-shows – is a celestial and highly contemplative track with a sweet melody and markedly gospel-ish organ. "Cool, Calm & Collected" is another uncertain, unresolved cut, this one with a jackass undertow. Jagger affects an upper-class English accent in his celebration of a ladylove. The lyric is nuanced – rather than idealized, the woman is posited as masking insecurities with a cheerful public face – but one doesn't know what to make of the way vaudeville piano and kazoo are bizarrely juxtaposed with sitar. The breathless ragtime finale at least impresses.

Side two opens with "All Sold Out", a sinewy but still poppy denunciation of someone not a million miles from the subject of "19th Nervous Breakdown". The arrangement relies upon aural disconnection: swells of backing vocals, rumbles of piano, flecks of guitar and warbles of recorder wash in and out almost at random. A Bo Diddley beat is treated with space-age sound effects on "Please Go Home". The surrealism is aided by Jones on Theremin and Mellotron in a track that's passable but hardly justifies running over three minutes. "Who's Been Sleeping Here?" is positively Dylanesque with its rolling melody, slashes of harmonica, mysterious ambience and references to the likes of "the butler, the baker, the laughing cavalier". It's an impressive pastiche in parts but its purpose is puzzling.

"Complicated" is another nuanced – indeed, complicated – discussion of an adored female. Once again the swirling nature of the track and more of the peculiar, non-rock drumming patterns common on this album create something that's nothing more than uncertain. The blaring, distorted guitars on

"Miss Amanda Jones" are the album's first glimpse of rock power, although it remains within its pop parameters. Lady Jane Ormsby-Gore, with whom Jagger had a fling, is rumoured to be the subject of "Lady Jane" but it seems far more likely that she is the focus of this good-natured number about a debutante embracing bohemia.

The lengthy (nearly five minutes) closer, "Something Happened to Me Yesterday", starts to wend its bizarre path with a sarcastic brass fanfare. Like "Connection", it goes as far as it safely can in addressing a drug experience, although, that said, lines like "It's really rather drippy but something oh so trippy" are not exactly opaque for the halfway with-it and had it not been for the irredeemable squareness of the Establishment would have been astonishing hostages to fortune in a legal scenario in which the Stones would soon find themselves embroiled. Trombone, trumpet and tuba – all handled by the versatile Jones – make for a cartoonish soundscape, added to by whistling and Richards (in his vocal debut) alternating lead vocals with Jagger. The latter provides a *Dixon of Dock Green* spoken-word sign-off to a track that – like the album overall – is utterly unlike anything in the Stones' canon.

Brian Jones said in a May 1964 interview, "We've become kind of figureheads for all the kids who would like to rebel against authority. We are expressing something they cannot say or do." That the guitarist was holding forth about his band's sociological significance when the Stones had been a chart act for less than a year was not presumption: the stories currently running in the press about a headmaster in Coventry who had suspended eleven pupils with Stones haircuts and told them not to return until they were of acceptable length (which he had explicitly defined as Beatle-like) demonstrated that for those in power The Rolling Stones had quickly become a yardstick for the degeneracy of the generation that would – God forbid – one day succeed them.

Although he probably didn't intend to carve out such a role – the linguistic and social ease bequeathed by his very elevated upbringing was more likely responsible – Brian Jones became the band member who provided the verbal dimension to a sociopolitical manifesto that the Stones otherwise communicated by deed or music. This interview from the NME in the wake of the scandal caused by their refusal to mount the podium at the London Palladium is a perfect example of his penchant for cogently outlining what the Stones – and by extension their peers – saw as wrong with the world.

THE ROLLING STONES: OUR FANS HAVE MOVED ON WITH US

Keith Altham

First published in the *New Musical Express*, February 1967

Let us consider that unique phenomenon – the Rolling Stones' public image!

When the Stones began rolling approximately three years ago they founded their personal approach upon a direct appeal to young people's impatience with authority and the basic premise that no one likes to be told what to do – especially a teenager. The Stones became "the defiant ones" – representatives of the eternal struggle between youth and the aged; champions of the "it's my life and I'll do what I like with it" school.

The parents spotted the declaration of war upon their authority and rejected the Stones – the Stones promptly rejected the parents.

Today there exists a huge social barrier between the older generation and the Stones – a barrier which some critics argue must be broken if the group are to "appeal to a wider market" and make the transition like the Beatles into films.

Since their early days the group has progressed immeasurably both musically and lyrically – take a good listen to "Ruby Tuesday" – and Jagger, with the exception of that recent abortive presentation on the Palladium TV, is without equal on stage as an agitator and interpreter of musical excitement.

Any improvement in the group as entertainers has been largely overshadowed by the regular bursts of shock publicity and personal life exposés in a National Press apparently as dedicated to a policy of "with the Rolling Stones only bad news is good news" as the group themselves are to their uncompromising attitudes and opinions.

I took up the subject with Brian Jones in a bar off Kensington High Street last Monday, where he supped a pint of Guinness and flicked fag ash into his untouched oxtail soup at irregular intervals.

"Why should we have to compromise with our image?" posed Brian. "You don't simply give up all you have ever believed in because you've reached a certain age.

"Our generation is growing up with us and they believe in the same things we do – when our fans get older I hope they won't require a show like the Palladium.

"The recent pictures of me taken in Nazi uniform were a put-down. Really, I mean with all that long hair in a Nazi uniform, couldn't people see that it was a satirical thing? How can anyone be offended when I'm on their side? I'm not a Nazi sympathiser.

"I noticed that the week after the pictures of me taken in that uniform appeared there were photographs of Peter

O'Toole in the same newspaper wearing a German uniform for a film he is making. But no one put him down for wearing that!

"The photographs taken of my flat in a terrible mess recently was another misrepresentation. An Italian film company was filming in the room and we pushed everything into one corner to make room for the camera crew. We were not even aware of the photographs that were being taken were for publication in a paper here.

"You've seen my flat – I don't live in that kind of mess normally. I've complained to the Press Council about the whole episode."

At this point enter Mr Keith Richard in his maroon leather jacket, University of Hawaii T-shirt and orange neckerchief, full of apologies for being late as he had forgotten it was his chauffeur's day off. How does he see the possibility of coming to terms with the older generation as the Beatles appear to have done?

"You can't suddenly become accepted overnight by cutting your hair, putting on a suit and saying 'Look, aren't I nice?' – it's not us – it's not honest, and why should we?" asked Keith.

"We haven't got the same PR set up as the Beatles," added Brian. "Anyway, I think you must realise that certain of the Beatles share a great many of our ideas and opinions."

We moved on to just who exactly are the Stones' fans now. Brian obliged by describing one who had "passed on".

"'Margaret Stokes' was a Stones fan three years ago but she 'copped' out," he said. "Now she's probably married with a kid and another on the way. She and her husband go to the same pubs as her parents and they are both bored with life. If she goes to see a pop group at all she'll go and see Dave Dozy and Speakeasy!

"Sometimes we get the old characters like the one we met in a country club over the weekend. He came up to us and said he was a fan and that he'd been in the business 40 years and prophesied that we'd be all right 'as long as you keep yer 'armonies'.

"Our real followers have moved on with us – some of those we like most are the hippies in New York, but nearly all of them think like us and are questioning some of the basic immoralities which are tolerated in present day society – the war in Vietnam, persecution of homosexuals, illegality of abortion, drug taking. All these things are immoral. We are making our own statement – others are making more intellectual ones.

"Our friends are questioning the wisdom of an almost blind acceptance of religion compared with total disregard for reports related to things like unidentified flying objects which seems more real to me. Conversely I don't underestimate the power or influence of those, unlike me, who do believe in God.

"We believe there can be no evolution without revolution. I realise there are other inequalities – the ratio between affluence and reward for work done is all wrong. I know I earn too much but I'm still young and there's something spiteful inside me which makes me want to hold on to what I've got.

"I believe we are moving towards a new age in ideas and events. Astrologically we are at the end of the age called the Pisces age – at the beginning of which people like Christ were born.

"We are soon to begin the age of Aquarius, in which events as important as those at the beginning of Pisces are likely to occur. There is a young revolution in thought and manner about to take place."

Returning the conversation to any kind of level related to pop music proved difficult and a chance remark of mine as to Gene Pitney's marriage brought the retort, from Brian, "You've been trying to reduce the conversation to that level all afternoon!"

However we did manage to ascertain what they thought of Max Bygraves' action on the Palladium last week when he produced a can of aerosol and sprayed the stage on mentioning the Rolling Stones by name.

"Brilliant," said Keith sarcastically, "I mean all that and 'Tulips From Amsterdam' too!"

"Did he do it without wearing a wig?" retorted Brian. "I mean that's a bit avant garde for Max Bygraves – putting down the Stones without wearing a wig!"

We stepped over Max Bygraves and conversationally circumnavigated the death of President Kennedy – something else that Mr Jones has very definite opinions about and cares about almost obsessively. A neat swerve in discussion bought us to what if anything or anyone is following the Rolling Stones.

"I'd like to see the Move," said Brian. "They are really an extension of our idea of smashing conventions. Those kind of smash ups they have – destroying TV sets, cars, etc., are all a part of dissatisfaction with convention.

"Pete Townshend's tendency to smash guitars is a physical reproduction of what is going on in his mind – I wish he'd write a book!"

A somewhat disturbing interview was rounded off by Brian insisting that the Muzak version of Ravel's *Bolero* was turned up over our heads – "it builds to a great climax" – and we finally left the restaurant – Mr Jones in his Rolls – Mr Richard in his girl friend's dirty red sports car, and me by cab.

Nothing it seems is going to change the Rolling Stones – except perhaps old age!

"WE LOVE YOU"

Sean Egan

15 July 1967 saw the release of another American pseudo-album. The title *Flowers* could be posited as a desperate attempt to artificially involve the Stones in a Summer of Love in which adverse circumstances had caused them to forfeit real participation. It rounded up the two tracks displaced from *Between the Buttons* when that album was released in America but was otherwise arbitrary in its selection of contents; "Let's Spend the Night Together" and "Ruby Tuesday" were included again – a measure of the way the American label did not give a damn about either fleecing the fans or artistic integrity, something further underscored by "Out Of Time" being remixed and shortened by two minutes. As a final twist of ruthless greed, three tracks were included which even Stones completists could not already possess in the shape of *Out of Our Heads* out-take "My Girl" and *Aftermath* out-takes "Ride On, Baby" and "Sittin' on a Fence". "My Girl", the Temptations hit also covered memorably by Otis Redding, would have made perfect sense on *Out of Our Heads*. Here, it is anachronistic. However, few mortals can resist the blissful, summery Smokey Robinson/Ronald White composition and the Stones render it more than competently. Even the strings presumably added by Oldham are sweet on the ear.

The other two "new" songs are Jagger/Richards creations. Jones' frilly harpsichord refrain in "Ride On, Baby" is incongruous in another thoroughly modern dissection of a damaged female ("I could pick your face out in an FBI file"). The lyric is actually clever enough to temporarily make us put aside our misgivings that this is over-familiar territory for the Stones and that it is even more callous than "19th Nervous Breakdown" (the narrator is telling the object of his scorn to get out and ride on, baby). "Sittin' on a Fence" is arguably the apotheosis of the Stones' rejection of the bourgeois convention of matrimony as the only permissible manifestation of sexual love. The narrator's sneering at friends who "just get married 'cause there's nothing else to do" may seem banal now, but in a society where the majority of teenage schoolgirls had no loftier aspiration than to be engaged and where sex was shrouded in taboo and littered with obstacles, it was genuinely relevant. Even if we have to view the sentiments of the lyric as a period piece, unblemished by the passage of time is the gorgeous, suitably languorous instrumentation, the chief component of which is extraordinarily elongated, lilting acoustic guitar lines. This wonderful track would have enhanced even a great album like *Aftermath*. Only a band of the Stones' stature could discard it.

Flowers would be the final American travesty album as the Stones insisted (just as The Beatles did that year) in art over commerce from hereon. A coordination of LPs ensued, although the band could never quite persuade (even had they been inclined to) American labels to refrain from the very un-British propensity to flog an album to death by releasing singles from it, and multiples of singles as the years wore on.

On 27 June 1967, Mick Jagger was found guilty of drug possession following his arrest at a party at Keith Richards' Sussex house, Redlands, the previous February. He was remanded in custody while the trial of Richards, busted at the same time for allowing his home to be used for the consumption of illegal drugs, continued. Two days later, the guitarist was also found guilty. Richards was handed down a sentence of a year, with Jagger getting three months. (Their art dealer friend Robert Fraser received six months for possession of heroin.) With Brian Jones facing trial for possession of cocaine and hashish following his arrest on 10 May – the very day Jagger and Richards were formally charged – it would seem that the Establishment was out to destroy The Rolling Stones.

Mick and Keith were granted bail pending an appeal. At this point, *The Times* weighed in on the Stones' side in a famous editorial titled "Who Breaks a Butterfly on a Wheel" ("It should be the particular quality of British justice to ensure that Mr Jagger is treated exactly the same as anyone else, no better and no worse. There must remain a suspicion in this case that Mr Jagger received a more severe sentence than would have been thought proper for any purely anonymous young man"). Possibly as a result of this unexpected disapproval from the Establishment's newspaper of record, the pair's appeals were heard unusually quickly (on 31 July) and, also possibly as a result, the appeal courts quashed Richards' conviction and reduced Jagger's punishment to twelve months' probation.

"We Love You" b/w "Dandelion" was the first original Stones output since the tumultuous legal events that had threatened the very existence of the band. Written and recorded after Jagger and Richards' release but before the confirmation of their appeal hearing, it was therefore a creation informed by uncertainty. In any other year, a record commenting on their treatment by the judicial system would have been marked by biting condemnation, either the veiled kind in which pop stars felt able to deal only prior to 1967 or the more full-on broadsides that became socially acceptable after that year. However, "love" being for the first and only time in history the prevailing sociopolitical philosophy, they clearly felt compelled to temper their righteous anger with forgiveness. The strange thing is that although the Stones chant the title phrase to the people who "hound[ed]" them and who put them in "uniforms" – doing so on the grounds that "love is all around" – the record doesn't possess anything like the beatific atmosphere of Scott McKenzie's "San Francisco (Be Sure to Wear Flowers in Your Hair)", The Beatles' "All You Need Is Love", Eric Burdon & The Animals' "San Franciscan Nights" or any of the other concurrent flower-power anthems. Even with the peculiar use of the "we" pronoun in place of "us" that made it sound olde-worlde but was also in the inclusive spirit of the year, the record sounds . . . well, snotty. "We Love You" provided an example of the fact that though the Stones were clearly on the good-guy axis in life – if we define the good-guy axis as those in favour of liberal reform – there was always something a little edgy about them (or at least Jagger, Richards and Jones). Three years later, the promotional film for The Beatles' single "Something" provided another such contrast. By then The Beatles

had shrugged off any inclination to project an inoffensive
image so it was sincerity that informed the love-suffused
montage of them frolicking with their respective partners to
the strains of George Harrison's sumptuous ballad. Had The
Rolling Stones made such a video, they would simply have
been laughed at.

Not that the unconvincing assumption of the peacenik
mantle prevents "We Love You" from being a truly magnificent record. It opens with footsteps and the closing of heavy
doors, sound-effect allusions to their travails that will recur
herein. In the second Stones single in a row dominated by
piano, Nicky Hopkins' dark, rippling motif underscored by
Wyman's menacing bass turns out not to be the prelude to
R & B, rock, pop or any other form associated with the Stones
but an extravaganza whose unprecedented margins are drawn
by Brian Jones' quite extraordinary Mellotron, which is set to
Arabian brass. Throughout, Hopkins' splendid riff snakes
hither and thither, and massed chanting repeatedly rushes into
the listener's face. In a fine performance from Watts, the drumming is also in the Far Eastern spirit. This cinematic soundscape
gets ever more phantasmagorical until brought to a close past
the four-minute mark by something resembling an orchestral
car crash.

Although aesthetically inferior, "Dandelion" is a far more
successful attempt by Jagger and Richards at passing themselves off as giving a shit about peace and love. Their insistence
that the childhood game of decision-making via the puff-
forced dispersion of the titular flower's head is one in which
adults can also exult is accompanied by the type of pseudo-
naïve melody popular at the time and is as aurally fancy as a
paisley shirt courtesy of harpsichord, organ, saxophone
(Jones) and massed backing vocals (which include contributions from Lennon and McCartney). Watts once again shines
with busy and unconventional patterns. The song repays the
favour of "We Love You" in reprising a snatch of the song on
the other side.

The triumph of "We Love You" was purely artistic. Such
had been the public outcry and the sense of loyalty stimulated
in their fans by the Stones' treatment by the judiciary that it

was assumed by many that "We Love You" would shoot to the top of the charts on both sides of the Atlantic. Perhaps that would have happened if Jagger or Richards had ben still incarcerated or their freedom in jeopardy upon its 18 August 1967 release (2 September in the US). In the eventuality, it did even worse than "Have You Seen Your Mother, Baby . . .", making only no. 8. Stateside, DJs preferred "Dandelion", but even that made it only as far as no. 14, with "We Love You" topping out at no. 50. The song has never been performed live by the band, is rarely played on radio and is unknown to many people who feel they know a lot about the band.

Much of the artistic triumph of "We Love You" was due – quite incredibly – to Jones. Although a record more different from "Little Red Rooster" is hard to imagine, "We Love You" must surely equal that one as Brian's finest hour. That this man could wrench from himself such artistic inspiration is astounding – he was going through hassles with the authorities just as bad (if not as widely discussed, at least these days) as those of Jagger and Richards and which would persist after his colleagues' reprieve, and he was also trying to deal with the trauma of losing his girlfriend Anita Pallenberg to Richards. Although the Mellotron – a precursor of the synthesizer and the sampler – was fashionable, it was not on the surface a device that enabled virtuosity. Jones, however, found a way to deploy it in a somewhat more than prosaic manner. As George Chkiantz, who assisted Glyn Johns in the engineering, has marvelled, "The instrument was a dreadful device. It's like a tape recorder with fifty or sixty tapes and a pitch wheel that goes down when you press each key, which slowed down the whole caboodle. For him to play this thing meant he had to be anticipating the beat by variable amounts." No wonder Chkiantz adjudged Jones' evocative, fluid playing on this track "a fucking miracle".

The single was accompanied by a revolutionary promotional film directed by Peter Whitehead. The "We Love You" promo interlaced footage of the Stones pretending to record the track (in which Jones is clearly stoned) with courtroom drama sequences based on the trial of Oscar Wilde, featuring Jagger as defendant, Richards as judge and Marianne Faithfull as Lord

Alfred Douglas, with a supporting role for the fur rug famous from the reportage of the Redlands bust as the only thing standing between Faithfull (or Miss X as she was called) and indecency. A smirking Jagger emerges from the rug's folds. There are better contenders for first pop "video" – The Beatles' promos for "Penny Lane" and "Strawberry Fields Forever" of the previous February the most prominent – but not many. Additionally, no mainstream pop group had ever tweaked the nose of the Establishment in this way. For no reason related to legal impediments, the BBC banned it and it was foreign territories that got its benefit. Such was the way of the world at the time.

THEIR SATANIC MAJESTIES REQUEST

Sean Egan

UK release: 8 December 1967; US release: 9 December 1967

Produced by: The Rolling Stones

Charts: UK no. 3; US no. 2

Tracklisting:
Sing This All Together
Citadel
In Another Land
2000 Man
Sing This All Together (See What Happens)
She's a Rainbow
The Lantern
Gomper
2000 Light Years from Home
On With the Show

Having already released an album at the beginning of the year and not having, unlike The Beatles and Dylan, previously established a pattern of two albums per annum in their homeland, the Stones could easily have sat out the rest of 1967. One wonders whether an anxiety about needing to issue a response to *Sgt. Pepper's Lonely Hearts Club Band,* The Beatles' titanic masterpiece of June, was the impetus for their second album of '67. The fact that an album as magnificent but less acclaimed appeared the same month as *Pepper* might have ramped up that anxiety: that The Jimi Hendrix Experience's *Are You Experienced* was by veritable new boys potentially made the Stones look passé. Alternatively (or additionally), perhaps the

Stones felt that the music they had been making throughout
the year would not have currency for much longer. Promoting
"We Love You", Jagger had alluded to the short shelf-life he
felt flower power to possess when he said of the single, "I'm
not involved in this love-and-flowers scene but it is something
to bring people together for the summer . . . In the winter we'll
probably latch on to snow!"

Their Satanic Majesties Request is possessed of the same
gushing and unconvincing benevolence as "We Love You" but
extended to over forty minutes. Quite simply, the Stones look
silly in Michael Cooper's cover photograph: though the array
of colour involved in their sitting dressed in medieval-cum-
Arthurian-legend costume is dazzling, they resemble sullen
schoolboys forced to participate in the school play, something
not helped by the badly constructed, childlike, painted backdrop. It also looks like an imitation of *Sgt. Pepper*'s similarly
ornate and similarly fold-out (then still unusual) cover, once
again giving rise to that old monkey-see-monkey-do jibe about
their relationship to The Beatles. (The cover looked more
impressive first time out when it was rendered in 3D but that
expensive effect was shortly dropped, as was the gatefold
sleeve, consigning the maze-that-went-nowhere inside to
history.)

A more persuasive adoption of the season's fashions was
the exotic instrumentation: although it might be said to be
pulling the Stones away from their main R & B-based strength,
courtesy of Jones this group had been utilizing instruments
rarely heard on rock and pop records well before most. Brian
– when interested or compos mentis, both states increasingly
uncommon – goes to town here, heard on exotic instruments
like flute, trumpet and Mellotron.

The title of *Their Satanic Majesties Request* derives from the
legend to be found on British passports ("Her Britannic
Majesty's Secretary of State requests and requires", etc.). The
proposed original version – *Her Satanic Majesty Requests* –
would have created a Sex Pistols-size scandal a decade before
"God Save the Queen" stormed the charts, as well as no doubt
occasioning even more hassle from the authorities. The
compromise version at least gave journalists a handy form of

shorthand for the band – "Their Satanic Majesties" – in the period in which they possessed a demonic and/or haughty aura (roughly 1968–76).

The band themselves have spoken of the virtual miracle of their coming up with any output in the circumstances in which they found themselves that year. This turmoil was not restricted to matters legal. During the recording, the band dispensed with their manager/producer when Oldham's absence from the country – dictated by fear that he would also be busted – was interpreted as a lack of loyalty. Their management was now solely in the hands of Allen Klein, the pit-bull New Yorker brought in as co-manager on Oldham's suggestion in July 1965. The band are credited with the album's production, although engineer Glyn Johns' sure hand can also be audibly discerned. Considering the turmoil and the adoption of unconvincing trappings, it's even more of a miracle just how good much of the contents of the album are.

The participatory spirit of "Sing This All Together", the opener of what the Stones term the "Front Side", cleaves to the We-Are-One ethos of the season. With its brass fanfares and massed singing, it's mildly intoxicating but it sags in the middle courtesy of another fleetingly fashionable philosophy – "musical rules are made to be broken, maaan" – that results in directionless noodling on indeterminate instruments. "Citadel" is where the Stones' journey into psychedelia works best. This crunching hard rock crossed with sword-and-sorcery imagery is punctuated by the most unearthly Morse code beeping to brilliant effect.

Although The Beatles had thrown George and even Ringo a publishing bone, aside from the rapidly disappearing Nanker, Phelge compositions Jagger and Richards had hogged the songwriting credits on Stones product. Only the chaos of '67 could have allowed any other member an official credit. In the days before mobile phones, Glyn Johns was unable to reach Bill Wyman when he was in transit to a *Satanic* session that had – in an example of the album's protracted, bitty genesis – been cancelled. As a consolation for his wasted trip, Johns asked Wyman if he had any songs he wanted to demo. Watts and Nicky Hopkins assisted in getting his creation on to tape, with The Small Faces' Steve Marriott fetched from the studio next door to add vocal gravitas. Jagger, Richards and Jones were played the rough mix of what was originally titled "Acid in the Grass" the next day. Having enthused about it after this blind test, they could hardly leave it off the album when told the identity of the composer and singer. "In Another Land", as it was eventually called, is indeed a marvellous track, thoroughly in keeping with the dreamlike ambience of the era and this particular album. Even the tremolo effect that Wyman insisted be applied to his voice out of insecurity about its strength contributes to that surrealism. In the serene verses the narrator blissfully navigates a land of castles and floating feathers hand in hand with his lover but in the uptempo chorus reality comes crashing down on his despondent form when he realizes ("Is this some kind of joke!") that he has been dreaming. The acutely clever lyric is perfectly complemented by an excellent melody in a cut that demonstrates what a criminal waste was Wyman's exclusion from Stones songwriting in all other circumstances.

Jagger and Richards spitefully added Wyman's surreptitiously taped snoring to the end, something of which the bassist was unaware until he played the finished album. However, the track was at least given the honour of being the lead-off single for the album in America – albeit in a peculiar way, being credited to Wyman alone, despite the fact that the rest of the Stones beefed it up with overdubs and Jagger can clearly be heard on backing vocals. (The album's "The Lantern" was the flipside.) The bizarre decision not to credit it to the Stones inevitably meant lack of interest from DJs and it climbed only as high as no. 87.

Futurism was somehow thought to be a component of the philosophy variously called flower power, peace-and-love and psychedelia insofar as one of its tenets was remaking the world in a better fashion. It was inevitable therefore that *Satanic Majesties* would feature a couple of science-fiction-oriented tracks. In 1967, the year 2000 was often utilized as a piece of shorthand for a future that we imagined would be full of robots, jetpacks and streets in the sky. "2000 Man" posits a man more in that imagined future than the present, to the bewilderment of his family. While lines like "I am having an affair with a random computer" are now as amusingly dated as that robot-dotted landscape that never came to pass, musically the track is delightful. We are taken on a quite dizzying ride wherein a lilting acoustic segment melds into an uptempo section, which itself segues into an even more uptempo part before a return to the gentle verses. Weirdly mixed drumming is in the "far out" spirit.

After three high-quality tracks, the side staggers to a messy close with possibly the worst thing ever to appear on a Stones record. With "Sing This All Together (See What Happens)", we are force-fed another bite of a hardly appetizing cherry. The ordeal continues for eight and a half minutes. Exotic percussion is banged and tapped, voices emit screeches and squawks, instruments play odd, disconnected phrases and the only example of singing is a repeat of parts of the lyric of the first instance of the song. This track has dragged the whole reputation of the record down. The inclusion of the snatch of dialogue, "Where's that joint?", incidentally, seems insane in light of recent circumstances.

Though no singles were plucked from *Satanic Majesties* in the UK, it yielded a second single in the States in the form of the track that opened the "Back Side" (boom-boom), "She's a Rainbow", which reached no. 25. Nicky Hopkins' piano is as important to "She's a Rainbow" as it was to "We Love You". Here it is treated to sound almost glockenspiel-like and meanders its mellifluous path through a tribute to a fair damsel that has a saucy undertow ("She comes in colours everywhere"). A sweeping strings-and-brass arrangement from a pre-Led Zeppelin John Paul Jones and a French-tinged "ooh-la-la" vocal backing complete a kaleidoscopic picture. With "The Lantern", futuristic sound effects – industrial warbles, washes and blinkings – decorate a lyric that harks back to a rustic, mythical past. The musical accompaniment is a pageant of riches. "Gomper" evades meaning as much as its title but is pleasingly impressionistic and poetic ("To and fro she's gently gliding") and steeped in times gone by, if only in the imagination of the likes of sword-and-sorcery writer Robert E. Howard. Tablas help create the impression of the languorous events taking place in exotic climes. However, around the two-minute mark, what has so far been a pretty little creation morphs into a formless din that continues for a further three minutes.

During his incarceration in prison, Jagger began writing a song. It eventually became "2000 Light Years from Home", in which his emotional devastation and isolated terror was filtered through a science-fiction perspective. (It would be the B-side of "She's a Rainbow" in the US.) Lamenting the absence of the people he has left on earth, he appropriates the imagery of SF quite impressively ("We're setting off with soft explosion"). Although the track has less momentum than one might like, it has a real atmosphere (or should that be lack of atmosphere?), with Jones on Mellotron expertly evoking the icy cold of the cosmos.

"On With the Show" closes the album with Jagger doing his posh voice as master of ceremonies in a strip joint (the adoption of this role being uncomfortably reminiscent of the compere of *Sgt. Pepper*). The track has a driving beat and, as with many places on the LP, Keith's guitar is treated to sound surreally razor sharp, but the point of the whole enterprise is puzzling and though it never descends into the chaos of the extemporized sections elsewhere, parts of it are unfocused, impressionistic washes of sound.

Like *Between the Buttons*, *Satanic Majesties* is dissimilar to anything else in the Stones' corpus. Unlike with the previous album, though, those who are prepared to assert that *Satanic Majesties* is a neglected, substantial work are not found in any abundance. The grounds for this dismissal seem to be the perception that the Stones were engaging in a contrived and imitative project that ended up making them look hapless and undignified. However, take away the unfortunate sleeve, the back end of "Gomper" and the entirety of "Sing This All Together (See What Happens)" and throw in "We Love You" and you have – whisper it lightly – a brilliant LP.

It is now receding into history that there was once a Mick Jagger whose speech was peppered with words like "uptight", "groove", "gas", "scene", "freaky" and "man", but then the sixties are equally quaintly distant. This interview with him by Barry Miles (then commonly known just by his surname) in the underground bible International Times *(commonly known as* IT*) captures Jagger buzzing with the revolutionary zeitgeist, conducted as it was a few days after he and Miles attended an anti-Vietnam War demonstration outside the American Embassy in Grosvenor Square.*

The interview often sounds like the babblings of two people sharing a joint, but in point of fact the ideas in the air in the sixties – ones not previously addressed in the modern age – caused many discourses to be indistinguishable from the wide-eyed notions of the stoned. The effect is intensified by the fact that Miles – in the unorthodox spirit of the age – does a minimal amount of editing.

Jagger is sometimes naïve for a man of his intellect: knowing what we know now about Altamont and why it happened, his comment about gigs, "If they had no police there, there wouldn't be any trouble," is rather chilling. In one sense, though, his quasi-utopianism has been vindicated: one passage of the interview is suffused with Jagger's residual resentment at the authoritarian religiosity that permeated his education, an experience common to British people of his generation but today a thing of history.

MICK JAGGER *INTERNATIONAL TIMES* INTERVIEW

Barry Miles

First published in *International Times* as "JAGGER (MILES)", May 1968

MJ: "London's great because people are around but I can't do anything because all the time there are people coming round. And I can't say 'Fuck off' to them. I can to some of them in the nicest possible way. I can say, 'Well, really I can't make it. I'm too busy. I mean, I must do something,' but you can rarely get into anything for longer than an hour, because at the end of an hour something interrupts you, and it doesn't matter what it is, if you're there you're available.

"What's the point of going upstairs and locking myself in the room? Whereas if you're in the country, the only people that see you are the people that really want to come. London's great but I only want to be here weekends, or the equivalent of a weekend, like Monday and Tuesday."

M: "Are your surroundings important to you?"

MJ: "London doesn't make me uptight enough to get into those uptight scenes which are very good for creation, 'cause it's much easier to express my very uptight mood than it is my very relaxed and happy mood. I find it difficult to express my relaxed mood and when I express it my way, I just look at it and I just tear it up."

M: "This is writing, not the music?"

MJ: "Just the writing . . . it does relate to the music but as I'm involved in it . . . it's more obvious in the words than it is in the music, though they both fit together . . . yeah . . . they're all great to write when you're in New York, you know. You can knock off four a day in a hotel room in New York [laughs]. It just makes you so uptight, people knocking on the door all the time. It's insanity, and yet . . . London doesn't give me that feeling. It's still very rushing about, but it's pretty relaxed as cities go, it really is."

M: "Is the quieter happy music the thing you're trying to get at?"

MJ: "No. I'm not trying to get *at* anything! I'm really not trying to get *at* anything at all. I would like to be able to find it. To be able to express everything equally as well . . . to be able to express every varying mood. I know what I'm good at and I know what I really can't do and I would like to be able to express every mood as well as the ones I can."

M: "As a response to an environment?"

MJ: "Yes, to environment, to people ... people influence me more than what you call environment, which is totality ... but ... It's always the *same people*! And you have to put them down. I don't like saying that, because it sounds so obvious, because the sounds aren't them really. They're only used ... just as ... just used as examples, and you have to keep going back to them again, back into these people, specially women, go get into them, to different kinds of them, they're all such a groove! But when there are no songs, it nearly always means I'm very contented and I can't be bothered to write about it! I'm too busy to be worried about writing about it. It doesn't worry me, I don't want it, I don't want to write about it. Don't want to work, don't want to do anything, just want to ... just carry on. But then someone phones up and says ... 'Mmmm, got to make a record.' But it's good that they're there, because otherwise we might not ever do anything ... which might be great if we never did ... sometimes when you don't do anything, you can really get into this groove, you know, 'Why did I ever bother?' but then suddenly you get thrown back into it and you think, 'Wow, really such a gas to do things!' I just found that my ego and everything was just being totally submerged. But I think in the wrong way."

M: "Submerged rather than rid of?"

MJ: "Yeah."

M: "How much are you into that scene?"

MJ: "I've cut myself off from that now, I really have. I'm just trying to forget it ... just living, not just working, just being very spiritual, being very religious or being very ... enthused with one ... into my own head ... just getting into all that. I've just thrown it out. Because my body keeps telling me all the time, to forget it, my soul just tells me ... it keeps telling me what's right and what isn't right for me to do at the present time and I just follow it."

M: "Doesn't this bring you into confrontation with authorities?"

MJ: "What have they got to do with it?"

M: "They usually stop any expression of freedom."

MJ: "Yes . . . but they can only stop things when they know they're going on. They can't do anything. They are you, really. I mean, they're part of it, they're *that* part of it, they're very essential for *it*. People that branch out are essential to it because in the end they often show the whole thing the way to go. Or it may show the others that that isn't the way for them to go. They're part of the whole thing. It wouldn't exist without the other."

M: "It wouldn't exist as an alternative?"

MJ: "No."

M: "I'm interested in the idea of an alternative society growing out of what's happened in the last few years. Not a specific hippie thing or even drugs thing, but just a general re-evaluation of things that a lot of people are getting into, which is beginning to threaten a lot of barriers that old-style society has put up. I think it will mean the ending of one society and the starting of another, rather than a natural flow of just changing the old society into the new one."

MJ: "I think that about most cyclic changes. There's no doubt that there's a cyclic change, a *vast* cyclic change, on top of a lot of smaller ones. I can imagine America becoming just ablaze, just being ruined . . . but this country's so weird, you know, it always does things slightly differently, always more moderately, and always very boringly, most of it, the changes are so suppressed. The people suppress them. For instance, everyone knew about the white backlash in England, everyone forgot about it, but everyone knew. It's weird to see it, but you tend to forget, there definitely is this fantastic split and it even cuts across class, which shows how strong it is, because there's very few things in England that do transcend class. All extremes meet at the other end, but that's the point in this one, it isn't one of those."

M: "Do you ever try and analyze what the cause of the backlash might be?"

MJ: "I think it's quite simple – it's simple on every level. I think it's amusing, though, because it's them, their grandfathers and great-grandfathers of the dockers, all these freaks, these people . . . it's their great-grandfathers that broke up a civilization, a tribal grouping which had been going on for perhaps 30 million years, people didn't think it was 30 million years, maybe it isn't maybe it's 6 million maybe it's 30. But they *broke it up* and it's breaking *them* up! Those people can break up societies not as old. I mean, our society is a white European race, an island kingdom. As a race, not very old, but it's very proud and it's quite old, and it's not been changed around too much and it's been preserved and it's . . . and you know . . . get five million black people in and it . . . it really changes things. Because they just are different and they do act differently and they don't live the same, not even if they were born here they don't. I mean, why should they? They don't, they just don't, and it breaks up the society and not only does it break up the society within its other side, it breaks the whites into like, getting on with black people and not getting on with black people. It makes all that scene, Liberals and Conservatives."

M: "It's shown a lot of people that the left wing wasn't left wing for humanitarian reasons but for self-interest reasons. Everyone was relying on the dockers as the great communists who fought against the fascists."

MJ: "Of course they're not, you know. Of course they're not! They're just totally self-interested, they can't see further than their noses. *And who can blame them?* Why can't they see further than their noses? Part of the reason, they were very strictly brought up."

M: "They were taught to 'hold back' all the time."

MJ: "That scene is very weird, you know, I used to have friends who were dockers' sons. That is something completely freaky, I don't even know what it's about, it's something that's before Victorian schooling, because they don't take any notice of schools and they're not like me, or my friends who you could say are the product not only of their family but of their school. These people aren't. They're not products of some working class school or bad education. It's a family thing, it's something from before compulsory schooling."

M: "A tribal grouping?"

MJ: "Yes, and very aware of its own identity and everything, there's still those very freaky bits like that. Everyone must have been like that at one time. Every group and every craft group, families, and that's a survival thing."

M: "Horrific thought."

MJ: "It's freaky, isn't it? 'Cause they've all got their own self-interest which is why they form unions but the unions have become so big now that they don't mean anything, really. I don't know, they probably do though. I don't know anything about it. All those small unions are like that. And if you're born into it, quite often I think that the family and the craft thing is much stronger than the school thing and you stay in it and you have these values in it. And your whole life revolves around, you know, not sort of, not just to get more money and that but . . . there's a whole lot of other things involved. It's fantastically backward and they won't change or open up."

M: "They feel threatened by anything new."

MJ: "They don't even think why, they're ever so conservative. I mean they *really are*, you know."

M: "They don't know why they shout at people in the streets."

MJ: "Oh no, they have no idea. But anthropologically it's a very simple thing: people react, and the way they cringe and the way they get frightened . . . you can *see* frightened people. It all depends how many of them there are. Like, reverse their positions: like, if you do go into a place which is full of fifty black people and they're all doing something, you don't half feel strange. You know, until you break down the communication barrier between you, until you get into their scene, until you're one of them, you know, till you're accepted as one of them as far as it goes, as far as you can be, as far as you want to be."

M: "The communications barrier is the armoring they've built around themselves . . . but that occurs in everybody."

MJ: "Yes, well that's supposedly the thing which keeps you on the side of some kind of sanity. Your logic system is the thing which keeps your mind together because when you start destroying it, if you're not ready for it to be destroyed you don't know what follows. All your life is built up on a logic system. When you're a kid and people tell you this, that and the other. You've got it inherently anyway. You just build it up and the whole thing's, like, so that nothing goes wrong in the circuit, so that each follows on."

M: "Do you think you have it inherently?"

MJ: "Oh yes!"

M: "You don't think that it's part of society and your reactions to it? Because you can bring children up in a different way and have no character armoring."

MJ: "Oh yes he'll have a totally different logic system but he'll still have one. He's got to. I mean there's probably so many variations on it as there are brain cells but still you've got to have it. I don't know where that got us . . . I got lost! I think there's many reasons underneath, that aren't understood by Western society, or by Eastern society. I think some people know why, as a global thing, man behaves in these ways and there are so many different ways out of it, so many explanations, because you don't know. You can start with whatever premise you want, you can start with, 'Well, I think man is really naturally very honest, truthful and loves beauty, and that somehow it gets completely screwed up because when he gets born, the people already there tell him it's not cool.' Is that Christian? No! The Christian thing is that man is inherently evil! [laughs] Now that's where you've got your education scene coming in, your religion, your Western world and all that because when you're really young 'You're a naughty little boy, aren't you?' And when you go to school you're evil and there's some weird scene in the garden of Eden, and 'You're so awful that God gave his only son and suffered for you because you're so rotten.' Thank you, well wow! You know? Am I really that bad? So you think . . . I'm pretty evil and you *know* you're not, you really do! You know you're really not. I mean, it's absolute rubbish, I don't know where they got the idea from. I'm really not a theologian, maybe George Harrison should be here to talk with me, but it just seems that that isn't right, that can't possibly be right. But it's not right, you know, the other thing's not right either. 10,000 years ago the whole thing might have been totally different, but it's a state of evolution of man. But he can change that so it is hereditary. I think that's possible. So what is it that my Sunday newspapers tell me this week, that man suffered a brain explosion in the Cleosticene era and never got over it, and it was all too much, and what was the reason? That man is a schizophrenic. It's pretty incredible, but it's true in a certain way, because he's got it. Koestler said it and a lot of people must have read it. It was a very funny thing to put on the front of a paper, it seemed to me, because it was right down with it."

M: "Koestler in a book written in 1943 said that we were on the edge of a rebirth, the age of economic man was at an end, and a new society with new ethical values would take over. He was predicting it then and it hasn't happened yet, but maybe it's beginning."

MJ: "Of course it's happening! I mean *it's happening*! But I think it's always been happening, always more than it's ever been happening, whenever you were, you know. When did your grandfather turn round and say, 'It was happening more than it is now!' It's always happening more than it ever *has* been happening. It's always accelerating itself, but it all depends which cycle of change you're on. I mean there are so many cycles. Look at history, look at Europe in the last three thousand years. You can see cycles: two hundred years, three hundred years, you can see changes. You can go to two thousand years and see changes: Christianity, for instance, if you wanted to and there's lots of them. You could see the others . . . well, I can see the others because when you learn about them there's so little known that they divide them up rather arbitrarily, I always feel, into like ten or fifteen thousand year cycles. Then there's millions. Which change are we going through? [laughs] Do you think that we're going through a big one? I think we're going through one, it's the death of economic man. The death of the Western Christian economic unit. It's the change of that unit."

M: "Into what?"

MJ: "Into what? And what might be the mutation, I mean the biggest changes are caused by mutations, some of the biggest mutations can be caused by radioactivity."

M: "Is that an area which concerns you at all? I mean, what's going to happen in the year 3000?"

MJ: "Yeah, I'll be there! I think I have great difficulty in putting all my thoughts together to make one unit. I freak off into what I term history, or . . . and then I find it very difficult to relate it to my whole life or spirituality. Or, d'you know what I mean, so I just get turned on by just bits and pieces, I just get enthusiastic about them and I retain them and then sometimes I just fit them all together and they go completely mad and wrong. But I just have a great time and I don't take it too seriously. I mean, I don't feel a call of . . . I don't feel a spiritual call."

M: "You've been reading quite a lot about Buddhism."

MJ: "Yeah, I've been swept along the river."

M: "The river of fashion?"

MJ: "Well fashion's like fad, like interest, fashion's for shoes. Yes, it's fashion but it's a realization of a need for some sort of spirituality which is living. You know what I mean? Which doesn't look like a corpse, which is existing, strongly, say, but even so it's not as strong as it used to be. Perhaps I'm confusing the issue. Every master would know."

M: "Can the world's religions be revitalized?"

MJ: "Do the world's masters know . . . they must know . . . religion doesn't mean anything. Religion and religion. Religion nothing. Religion's outdated because the world is no longer separated, d'you know what I mean?"

M: "Spirituality from physical matter? Like the alchemical blending of science and spirituality?"

MJ: "It's merging with higher physics."

M: "Aren't they finding more and more smaller particles in the DNA chain?"

MJ: "I don't know, it's very difficult to understand. They're finding out just the same story in a different way . . . The Buddhist form, I think, is easier. The Buddhist approach is easier to compare with higher physics, than the Christian approach to the same thing. The symbolism, I think. I think that's a realization."

M: "How do you feel when students riot when you're on stage? Do you pick up on any energy?"

MJ: "Yes! Wow! Tingle with it! The energy's great! I mean, they give you *so* much energy, just don't know what to do with it man! And it lasts, too, every performer has felt that. It's just the way you are, the way the energy is, the way you react, I don't really know why . . . I know I try and do it, but then I never went on stage with the idea of keeping everything cool. I never wanted it to be peaceful. Even if I did before I went on the stage, soon as I got on there and felt what they felt, I've wanted to make . . . I mean, they were totally in control, as much as I was. I mean, I was in control, but they were also."

M: "So it becomes a dialogue."

MJ: "Yeah. And if you've got nobody in between, that's when it becomes funny. Because it can turn on you, see, if you haven't got any policemen it's weird, because then they don't know what to do. I mean, I'm not talking about girls and that sort of scene, I'm talking about what you're talking about, like these students. 'Cause then they don't know what to do but then there's very rarely no police. That's a mistake the authorities make, they never ought to have any police there at all. If they had no police there, there wouldn't be any trouble. Not because the police make trouble, because they are more brutal or . . . or you know, all the reasons which are true, you know they are, etc. But that's not really the reason that there's trouble, it's just 'cause they're there. It's the only symbol there. It's the only outlet you can get, especially in the Western world, you can't really touch anything can you? What can you touch? You can only touch the police."

M: "Do you think that's a short-circuiting?"

MJ: "Yeah, totally, and they know it, and that's why it doesn't make any difference."

M: "Some people think that, by attacking symbols of authority, you're attacking authority itself."

MJ: "Not at all, not at all, you won't do anything."

M: "If you really want an alternative that's not who you should be demonstrating with, with all those fuzz, if we really want to be anything we have to go straight to all kinds of different places, and MUST try and bypass the police. And if we want to demonstrate we have to meet them on their own ground. If they want to use horses, we'll have 10,000 people on horses."

MJ: "And that's what I thought when I was there. I didn't march with Vanessa Redgrave, didn't feel like it."

M: "I felt very frustrated by that demonstration."

MJ: "But that's what it should have been!"

M: "An expression of frustration?"

MJ: "But that's just fun, you see! Because that's your own inherent violence. That's our way out. 'Cause we love it! And it's our excuse, see? We can't be guerillas. We're so violent, we're violently frustrated. We haven't got enough violence, we've no opportunity. We don't want to be in the army, it doesn't do anything anyway, I mean, so what? There's nothing. It's a whole drag, the army's all over, the army! There's no guerillas, there's no . . . well, there's Welsh nationalists. You can go and join them, but what a joke! I mean there's nothing in this country . . . and there's all this violence. If you want to talk about it, it's here, it's there, you know. It's not a question of having to meet people, it's fun. You can push, you can push everyone into a situation."

M: "I wonder . . ."

MJ: "You can! You can see the last war, that was a situation, you could get nearly all the youth of this country, with very few exceptions, into a situation where they will defend their country. Maybe they were not defending their country, maybe they thought they were defending their families. And they were. Maybe they were defending their . . . whatever they were, they were defending something. And not only that, they were defending lots of other people's, like America's. They had this weird sort of illusion. But you can always get people into a situation where they can do it. It's rubbish to say that you can't, because it's so obvious!"

M: "I agree that you can get people into that situation, but whether or not that's constructive . . ."

MJ: "It isn't constructive, but you know you have to. It does impress the establishment, I'm sure. The establishment is not used to it in this country. It's used to seeing it in Germany and Japan, but it's not used in this country to seeing such violence."

M: "It wouldn't take them long, though."

MJ: "Oh, they'll soon get used to it, I guess. But you can tell by the reaction from the press, and the television. It puts them pretty uptight! I think it's a short circuit – there's far better ways of doing it, I mean. What are you aiming for? To have a proper revolution. To have a change. There is no alternative society. There is none. There are lots but they're not alternatives, they're not really! You can have a left-wing revolution. I mean, there's all those but they're just the same. It's the same thing. It's all the same. I can't see it as an alternative society; the only thing I can see, looking at it a lot, is that you're in a fantastic change period, though. Everyone keeps saying so and probably we are, And, like, you're just the first charge-off, so that, you know, it just happens."

M: "The first charge-off is usually put down by a war. Like Paris between the wars; and before the First World War there were the pre-Raphaelites."

MJ: "Oh yes, you can be sure. And that will be the biggest change. That's the mutation of the race."

M: "I think that's the kickback. Can't you envisage another society?"

MJ: "Another society . . . yeah!"

M: "A society where a person can do anything he likes with his own mind and body providing he doesn't mess with other people's mind and bodies."

MJ: "That will come within this society."

M: "I don't think so."

MJ: "I don't really think so, but that's a *this* society thing!"

M: "A prerequisite to that is an inherent social responsibility towards other people. That's unlikely to happen in this society."

MJ: "No you won't get the change, unless it's a thousand year change. You won't make the society."

M: "Not through education?"

MJ: "No."

M: "Reorganization?"

MJ: "No."

M: "How very depressing."

MJ: "I don't think so."

M: "I do."

MJ: "No, it isn't a depressing thought. If you keep hammering at it you won't get anywhere except depressed. The only other way is for each person to understand himself. You know there's ways of doing it aren't there?"

M: "Yes, well this is where the change would be. First those that understood themselves would be the alternative society and as it grew it would be the society itself. This is happening in America now, on a very big scale, but the combined students and hippies and everything amount to millions of people, really, who are all re-evaluating society."

MJ: "Yes, well, they haven't got an alternative, and: they've still got all the things of the other society, in other words their society. The other society's veneer. The other society's veneer of society and behavior patterns and education is so thin, theirs is even thinner! They're both valuations of . . . their valuations of values are destructible. They're the thinnest film on water, you can't float a boat on it, I mean, but they're just veneers, they're looking at each other and they're the same fucking thing! And they'll degenerate to the same thing, they'll degenerate to putting helmets on and fighting each other and when they come out they won't know who the fuck they are! Because they don't have any, they're re-evaluating, they know, we all know, everyone's always known! Anybody's always known."

M: "I think people are breaking right through."

MJ: "Like what?"

M: "Like you! When you have an audience you're able to break through all the veneer and they really start releasing energy."

MJ: "There's a lot of energy, true, but it's so violent! That's what I mean about a veneer, it's total violence, that's the result! You can make total violence from vibration, that's all. No ideology! No no, no nothing. No anti. I mean, you might in their heads stand for that, but all it is is that. It's so, you know, 'Demonstration in Grosvenor Square', for what? But I mean, I don't really put it down, I think it's a gas! I think that all the things we've said are wrong about it, but when it really comes down to it, to get people out of their seats is like difficult enough in this country. You've got to start at the beginning and you've got to see your vision right through to the end admittedly. There must be people that see the vision to the end and there must be people who get people that see the vision to the end and there must be people who get people out of their fucking seats! I'm not really getting to it, I'm going round it, I'm not sure, that's why I said I don't like talking about it because the . . . path to enlightenment is, Miles?"

M: "I don't know."

MJ: "I don't know, but there are so many people that do say, and they're so fucking wrong. I mean, you can see!"

M: "The ones who do know don't ever say it."

MJ: "They definitely don't say it. Or they just carry on with what they're doing and you never know. That they're . . ."

M: "To see everyone so messed up makes people want to help each other solve their problems to some extent."

MJ: "Yes, but you must be careful of messing with people until you're sure of yourself."

M: "You do something in the meantime."

MJ: "Yes, you find out about them. You can be negative too, that's good too. It's not good just to be negative; you can be very negative because that's a great help. You can see through things. You never really know how people are looking, or what for. How they break things up and how they see them, but it's difficult to be constructive. Because to be constructive in a political manner is just a farce, because you know it's all the same. I mean, the communist revolution in this country would sit in the House of Commons, you know, and the House of Lords probably. You know that that can't be . . ."

M: "How about the other ways? Artists have a huge effect."

MJ: "Yes, they don't know what it is, though, because they don't understand their audience, because you can't, you can't. How can you understand a worldwide audience? Of God knows how many million people. Each so different! Like, how different is a person in Asia to an American college student? I mean, they're so different, man! And they're not even from one age group any more, they start at eight and they go to thirty. I mean, it's not the same. The screaming teenagers were all little girls wetting their knickers, but that's not true any more! No. How can you expect a pop singer to analyze his audience or his effect or anything? I mean, you can generalize vaguely."

M: "Not the audience but the effect?"

MJ: "You don't know what the effect is. The effect on stage is different to the effect on record. You can see what the effects on stage are, but that's all . . . I always think that's more superficial than the effect you have when somebody plays it at home. Because you get more into their head, because it's a different scene."

M: "When you record, other aesthetic considerations come in?"

MJ: "Weird kind of aesthetic things. It's got so weird because people keep talking about it. And you've got this incredible sort of pulling, which is between 'Pop music is rubbish and it's fun and it's here today and gone tomorrow' which it should have, or should it? Ha ha ha! But you know what I mean?"

M: "Probably about 5% will last as great music."

MJ: "It's all music."

M: "So was classical music."

MJ: "Yeah! It's become weird expression. It's just folk music, I think, just exploited folk music. But it's still folk music because it's so easy to . . ."

M: "The art form of this generation."

MJ: "It is an expression because it's so changing now. D'you know what I mean, because people are coming out of the people all the time. It is a lot of folk music, it isn't all folk music, whatever folk music is, but I know what it is." [laughs]

M: "Being so expensive an art form, I would think it gets censored by the big companies."

MJ: "Probably the least censored art form . . . as far as mass art form as a total mass thing. It's not a painting for instance, you can paint what you fucking like! But you're not necessarily going to have it reproduced 10,000 times. I think it's probably the least censored, because it's the least understood. Because they can't see it in pictures, you can censor a film, and you can miss it, and you can miss what you should have censored in their head you know. It's weird, they always get the wrong end of the stick, nearly always. You can totally confuse everybody on that level. I don't think there are censors at all because if you get into anything they never understand it. If it's just sexual you get it censored, that's the only way. But it's still less than in the movies really, but nobody really writes sexual pop songs, like really, like they write sexy novels. You just don't write songs like that. I don't know why, to my knowledge. I mean, I don't. And I don't care to. There wouldn't be anything wrong with it. They won't not put it out. They might not play it on the radio, but that doesn't make any difference because you can always put it on an LP which they don't play on the radio anyway necessarily, yet still millions of people hear it. There's no censorship involved with it. I mean, you can say anything you want."

M: "What about commercial considerations? Do you consider whether it will sell or not?"

MJ: "Long pause! The only time I think about whether a record will sell or not is when we make a single. Then you don't actually make a single, you make six or seven records, or we do, and somebody says, 'That's good for a single.' They mean, 'If you put that out, more people will like that than any of the others.' You haven't recorded it for them, you've just done it. It's one of the things you've done, and yet you think it's easily understandable. You might say, 'The lyrics are simple,' or 'It's good to dance to' but it's still the same as the others, it's still one of them, well it has something you can whistle, and you think, 'Oh well, that's your single!' That's your consideration for the market. Your other considerations for the market are why you're doing that in the first place, in that particular form, why you chose that form. Because pop music's become a very malleable form. You get pop music that's into electronics and jazz and just music, you know it's just music."

M: "Which direction do you think you're going in?"

MJ: "I dunno! Oh, I really I don't know! I never know till we get there. It's really how you feel. It's like the reflection of what you feel, which is why it's so groovy. Last year we felt so freaky and so uptight and 'orrible, we just made very freaky records, half of which we never released even, they were so strange. They just weren't any good. They were great to do once, but we couldn't bear listening to them more than six times. Now it's much more together."

M: "Are you influenced by what other people do?"

MJ: "Oh yes! Influenced by everybody all the time. Probably less influenced than we were, by anybody. The only people that interest me are people that write and they quite often don't write pop songs. I can't even remember their names half the time, but everything influences you, really. Musically we made the form, it's very simple, it's really simple.

"Our last disc wasn't a unit because one never knew if you were going to be in jail, so we never knew whether to book sessions. You didn't know who was going to be there. But this album's been done in a space like a month and a half. The whole lot, a single and an album, yeah. Which we're halfway through now. And we should finish off by the end of next month, so it's all in two months, you see. It is a reflection of a much smaller time period, so it's much more the same and it is much more of a unit because all the songs, they all sound the same. It's very much more together. It's very basic, but it isn't backwards, it doesn't sound like Rolling Stones or anything like that. I think they're very good, they fit together, they work much more."

M: "Much of your work is descriptive of people."

MJ: "Yeah, I've made them about people, the single's called 'Jumping Jack Flash', and he's a person, and the other side is called 'Child of the Moon' and she's a person . . . they're all people. There's one called 'Mr Gorilla Man', he's a person, and there's one called 'Parachute Woman'."

M: "That's a nice way to work."

MJ: "I didn't think of it like that. I just looked at the list afterwards and saw . . . they're all about people. So I thought, 'Well I'll tell you what I'll do, I'll make them more or less like that so when the album's finished, they'll all be people really.' D'you know what I mean? It's such a haphazard art form! Because it's not a product of any technical, it's not eleven years of intensive study. And one's always aware of that limitation, so it's a total throwaway."

M: "Are you aiming at technical improvement?"

MJ: "Yes, but I don't really think I will. Brian will get into electronics. I'm more interested in writing. I'd like to be a very good writer of songs. It's a very weird medium, actually, because it's so incredibly compressed."

M: "A lot of people think that modern pop lyrics are the only valid form of poetry these days."

MJ: "But that's not true, you know, a lot of it is very good verse, and is easily as good as popular verse in the last century. And more people will hear it. Some of it is probably very, very good, but it's not the best verse that's being written or the best poetry."

M: "Dylan stands up very well."

MJ: "Oh yeah, Dylan stands up. There's very few modern poets I like that I've read, that I've picked up at Indica Bookshop that have been anywhere near as good. I mean most of them aren't even as good as the Byrds' songs. I decided to go round every bookshop looking for modern poetry, and I tried to. I asked for . . . Where was it? And they sort of looked very depressed and said, 'It's all such rubbish!' and it is, most of it, it's not very good, and it's not very modern. It always reminds me of 1950 rather than now, it always makes me feel like a child because it reminds me of rationing or something."

"JUMPIN' JACK FLASH"

Sean Egan

When "Jumpin' Jack Flash" appeared on 24 May 1968 (1 June in the States), it marked a gap of five and a half months that was the longest ever known between UK Stones releases. The tribulations through which the band had gone of course made such a breather understandable but, there again, perhaps the Stones were banking on the idea that those two-monthly manifestos were ceasing to lose their importance, as demonstrated by the fact that the indisposed Bob Dylan's complete absence from the release schedules from mid-1966 to the end of 1967 had not affected his popularity one iota. If so, they were correct: with their comeback single, the group turned in a bravura performance which returned them to the top of the charts. The disc was the Stones' first UK no. 1 for two years and reached no. 3 in America.

Down the years much has been made, including by the Stones, of "Jumpin' Jack Flash" being a return to their roots. Yet – "Little Red Rooster" excepted – there had never been a Stones single like it in either spirit or tone. The one-time blues purists had long surrendered to the pop principle, even if it was a pop grittier than almost anybody else's. There is nothing about "Jumpin' Jack Flash" that seems to assume a pop demographic. Rather, it is as though in their fifth year as a recording outfit the group had suddenly realized that the fourteen-year-olds who had bought "I Wanna Be Your Man" were now leaving their teens and could stand – maybe even desired – something more mature. "Jumpin' Jack Flash" – an extrapolation of the devilish blues of Robert Johnson and Charley Patton – is the first adult Stones song.

The lyric is about a man born in a crossfire hurricane to a toothless, bearded hag. He is schooled with a strap across his back and proceeds to endure an existence that washes him up, leaves him for dead and makes him collapse to his bleeding feet, crumbs of a crust of bread his only sustenance. Ultimately, he is crowned with a spike right through his head. That each verse of wretchedness is tailed with a chorus that maniacally insists, "But it's alright now, in fact it's a gas!" doesn't alleviate this nightmarish vista. It's astonishing to think that such tortured visions were kicked off by the comical scenario of the huge feet of Keith Richards' yokel gardener Jack Dyer creating a noise on the guitarist's gravel driveway one morning that startled Jagger.

The music accompanying this extraordinary lyric is not quite so radical – something that would be pretty much impossible in light of the fact that this was surely the most ferocious and unforgiving lyric ever to appear in the charts – but is not far off: the single was surely the hardest rock yet to top the UK hit parade. The thin, resonating guitar line that begins proceedings certainly creates a contrast with the baroque strains wafting from their flower-power records, as does Watts' no-nonsense flat drumming. With a "One-two!" from Mick, the track then settles into its famous lurching riff, one that Wyman claims he authored and worked on with Jones and Watts before Jagger and Richards co-opted it for their purposes. Despite the earthiness, there is a tinge of exotic colouring in the form of liquid guitar lines. Maracas add an extra sonic layer for the final verse. In his vocal, Jagger picks up the gauntlet thrown down by his own lyric with his most intense and dark performance yet. Amazingly, Richards claims there are no electric guitars on "Flash", merely acoustic guitars played though a cassette recorder's distorting speaker.

That the B-side, "Child of the Moon", is of *Satanic Majesties* vintage is evident from its lilting music and mystical words. However, in this new recording, the band give it a darker and more substantial feel, marrying that scattershot celebratory tone of the previous album with something more in keeping with their blues roots. Much discussion has stemmed from the fact that some releases have placed the letters "rmk" in parentheses after the title, the favourite theory centring on the fact that Allen Klein's daughter Robin Mary Klein was born around the time of its release, her star sign of Cancer making her a child of the moon. Jody Klein – son of Allen – has mysteriously exhibited nervousness when asked to explain . . .

Michael Lindsay-Hogg directed two promotional films for "Jumpin' Jack Flash", one a straightforward live rendition, the other far from straightforward in which Mick is daubed in warpaint, Keith is distant behind shades, Brian is in grotesque quasi-blackface and garish sunglasses, a pancaked Bill is even more lugubrious than usual and a made-up Charlie looks like a louche transvestite. The Stones now resembled less opponents of convention than envoys from Satan. The sight was genuinely disturbing. It was also exciting: Jagger's prancing, preening, mindless dancing towards the end sees him developing the unique style that would make him the greatest frontman rock has ever seen.

BEGGARS BANQUET

Sean Egan

UK release: 6 December 1967; US release: 7 December 1967

Produced by: Jimmy Miller

Charts: UK no. 3; US no. 5

Tracklisting:
Sympathy for the Devil
No Expectations
Dear Doctor
Parachute Woman
Jig-Saw Puzzle
Street Fighting Man
Prodigal Son
Stray Cat Blues
Factory Girl
Salt of the Earth

Jimmy Miller had not had too great an influence on either side of the "Jumpin' Jack Flash" single, the first Stones product to bear his producer's credit, but for the half-decade from *Beggars Banquet* (spelt without an apostrophe) onwards he had a huge impact on the band's sound. Although the Stones had always had an ally in the studio in the shape of Oldham and simpatico ears and hands in the shapes of engineers like Hassinger and Johns, Miller was all those things and more. A "proper" producer as well as a musician (he drummed on a few Stones cuts), his understanding of their music and his ability to translate their visions into reality is evident in what used to be called the grooves of what used to be called the records made by the Stones in this period, one that most consider their peak.

Brian Jones barely appears on *Beggars Banquet*. Unknown to the wider public, over the previous year his process of disintegration had accelerated. In late '67 he was given a twelve-month prison sentence for cannabis possession and allowing his home to be used for drug taking. This was reduced following an appeal – and a night in jail – to three-years' probation. Another bust followed in May 1968 that seemed certain to result in custody, but the judge's palpable scepticism of the police evidence led to a fine. By this time, though, the police harassment had served to turn Jones from a strutting dandy into a humiliated, emasculated wreck – that and the nagging pain of having to work with the man involved with the woman he considered his own. He was also weighed down with the knowledge that his conviction jeopardized the Stones' ability to tour America and therefore his usefulness to them. The car that the Stones' office sent to Jones' house in Sussex to pick him up for studio sessions as often as not returned empty. On the photograph on the sleeve of "Jumpin' Jack Flash", Jones is placed prominently, standing in front of his colleagues, smiling as he holds a drink in one hand and what is clearly intended to resemble a devil's fork in the other. Yet although he can be heard on brass and Mellotron on "Child of the Moon" and (according to Wyman) plays guitar on "Jumpin' Jack Flash", he was already on his way out of the band.

America got a tantalizing taster of *Beggars Banquet* on 31 August 1968 when "Street Fighting Man" b/w "No Expectations" was released as a single there. In a year that had seen the streets of the Western world erupt into riots in which the young were demanding liberal reform, calling for the end of the Vietnam War or expressing somewhat more undeveloped grievances about the existing order, the very title of the A-side was incendiary. Accordingly, many US stations declined to play it, with Chicago – host to a Democratic National Convention that had descended into violent chaos – particularly sensitive. One listen to the lyric would have dispelled the illusions of those who assumed from the title, the original picture sleeve of a demo (quickly withdrawn) and the rabble-rouser reputation preceding the Stones that it incited rioting. But what straight was going to bother analysing the song words? We'll never know whether the no. 48 peak position was the result of the bans/non-playlistings, but more likely is that this roaring, raucous track was too difficult to be chart material.

The parent album should have appeared in September but hit a snag when Decca refused to release it in the band's chosen sleeve, which featured the album title, artist credit, tracklisting and various juvenile and bawdy pieces of humour scrawled on the wall of a filthy toilet in Los Angeles. The stand-off rumbled on in the music press for the rest of the year, with the record company naturally being cast as totally uncool breadheads. It wasn't until 1976 and the publication of Roy Carr's LP-sized book, *The Rolling Stones: An Illustrated Record*, that the public got the chance to see for themselves the preferred sleeve in full size and full colour. With the fleeting moment in history in which it would have been a valid broadside against the straights who were terrified by rudery long past, the artwork was now simply vulgar and childish. The replacement sleeve, an elegant white invitation card with a gold border, did far more justice to the contents, although – here we go again – it couldn't help looking imitative of The Beatles' minimalist white sleeve for their eponymous double-album released just three weeks previously. Inside the fold-out sleeve, the Stones were seen at a table in medieval costume. The customary scaling back of design occurred after the initial printing, the adoption of a single sleeve banishing the banquet picture to history. Eventually the entire cover art would be thus "disappeared", with the Stones' dubious original being preferred on ABKCO releases.

The two songs on the "Street Fighting Man" single had given US fans a pretty accurate idea of what the new album contained, even if the A-side was subsequently given a new vocal track and tweaked instrumentally for later single pressings and its appearance on the LP. To British fans in a disconnected world, the non sequitur that *Beggars Banquet* constituted in relation to their previous recordings would have been something of a shock. It was not exactly an entire album of songs as uncompromising as "Jumpin' Jack Flash" but it wasn't far off. There was nothing pop about *Beggars Banquet* whatsoever. Additionally, the overwhelming timbre of the album is surprisingly acoustic, with only two tracks boasting unequivocally rock instrumentation. This was layered, measured, subtle, unsweetened fare, much of it brilliant but all of it of an adult sensibility.

With the tone of '68 being one less of We're-All-One than You-Against-Us, the Stones here attempted to at least indicate that they knew – to use their argot – where the campus stone-throwers were "at", even if they did not get in step with them. "Jig-Saw Puzzle" and "Street Fighting Man" are tracks in which they explore the burning issues of the day – albeit from a notable distance – and "Factory Girl" and "Salt of the Earth" are effectively displays of solidarity with society's powerless, even if they are hardly socialist anthems. Jagger said in more than one sixties interview that he was not a socialist, so he can't be accused of trying to portray himself as something he isn't. That the Stones' were anti-authoritarian rather than leftist doesn't make them toytown rebels. In fact, many would argue that anti-authoritarianism has forged greater changes to society and alleviated more suffering and injustice than economic systems predicated on the redistribution of wealth. However, it is rather interesting that though much has been made of the Stones awkwardly adopting the trappings of love and peace on *Satanic Majesties*, much less has been written about their similarly unconvincing adoption of something approaching protest on this album.

The opening track took popular music where it had never been before. In the context of today where every two-bit heavy-metal band purports to be in league with Satan, "Sympathy for the Devil" may not appear remarkable. However, in 1968, though the Western world was increasingly secular, the Church and its assumptions still held vast sway, especially in America. A song whose narrator adopted the role of the Antichrist was taboo-shattering. Although there is an element of Jagger gleefully living up to the image of the Stones as the nemesis of supposedly decent society, he is far too intelligent a man to simply throw together some provocative slogans. His song is based on the classic novel *The Master and Margarita* by Mikhail Bulgakov and he accords his lyric thought and craft worthy of its literary roots.

An opening of tablas and devilish yelps and grunts surprisingly augers not a maelstrom but a polite narrator who requests you allow him to introduce himself. He does eventually reveal his name to be Lucifer but not before imparting the information that he is the author of many of the world's misfortunes. The track is propelled by a brawny bass line, played by Richards. Over six and a half mid-tempo minutes, the increasingly frenzied narrator boasts of a catalogue of blood-drenched horrors ranging from Jesus Christ's execution to the Russian Revolution to the blitzkrieg. One particularly noteworthy line marks Jagger out from the gormless likes of Black Sabbath downwards: which other songwriter pledging devotion to the devil would be so literate and educated as to state, "And I lay traps for troubadours who get killed before they reach Bombay"?

The intensity rises almost unnoticed, with a slight stepping up in pace, the introduction of maracas and the arrival of delightful cum maddening "Woo-woo!" backing chants. By the close, we are indeed approaching the situation of maelstrom. The instrumental break could not be more apposite: a guitar solo from Keith that sounds as if his strings were made out of barbed wire – aflame. So unlike his usual staccato instrumental break is it that one would literally not believe this virtuoso performance was his if he had not been seen executing it in Jean-Luc Godard's late 1968 movie *One Plus One*, also known as *Sympathy for the Devil*, in which footage of the Stones constructing and perfecting this track is juxtaposed with abstract dramatic vignettes.

In contrast, "No Expectations" is a ballad of utter righteousness. The narrator is being escorted to the station, where he is to depart from a lover whom he will – through no choice of his own – never be seeing again, a matter he accepts with humility despite his heartbroken state. Richards' strummed acoustic guitar, Jones' slide and Nicky Hopkins' delicate piano make for an utterly beautiful creation and one whose subtle charms would have been befuddling to Stones fans a few years before.

"Dear Doctor" is a song out of left field, the lament of a member of an American white-trash family being forced into a marriage of which he wants no part – only to realize he is devastated when his Southern belle skips town on the day of the nuptials. It is rendered in outrageously over-the-top style, including a mass singing of the rising, exclamatory line endings and a falsetto Jagger impersonation of the vanished bride. Despite this, the band's country blues stylings are lovingly authentic. It being uptempo, horny and riff-driven, one might think "Parachute Woman" would be an opportunity for the Stones to fall back on the electric sound with which they had always felt most comfortable, but though Keith executes some great, keening electric lines, his acoustic rhythm work is just as prominent. The track has deep texture: with such touches as a muffled, indistinct yell, a switching from brittly echoing to dampened drums, the blurring of rhythm guitar and an echo that makes guitar lines resemble a vapour trail, Miller is engaging in one of his noted production tricks in creating something bigger than the sum of its parts with the smallest, most unexpected elements.

"Jig-Saw Puzzle" is a sort of variant of "Sittin' on a Fence", though this time the neutrality the narrator is trying to adopt relates not to matters romantic but to the political conflicts raging around him. He notes tumult and juxtaposition of privilege and each time shruggingly returns to his jigsaw puzzle. His vision lurches from a bishop's daughter jealous of an alcoholic tramp she imagines to be less outcast than she to a ruthless gangster who is a loving family man with his children to the differing personalities in a rock band to a final descent into surrealism in a depiction of the Queen slaughtering grandmothers disgruntled about their pensions. This approximation of social commentary feels absolutely forced where it's not banal. It's clear that Jagger (Richards having never evinced the slightest interest in politics) is anxious to assert that he has something to say about current events – and equally apparent that he doesn't. This all wouldn't matter too much if it was accompanied by the musical excellence evident everywhere else on the album, but the tune is as boring as the lyric is trite, meandering like an aural shopping list, with only the dialogue that Richards' cawing guitar lines create with Mick's voice commanding much interest. Matters are compounded by the fact that the band's conviction that this is an epic statement requires it to run over six minutes.

That side two opened with "Street Fighting Man" is unfortunate, for we are presented with the second consecutive track in which Jagger demands to voice his take on the current climate only to reveal that his perspective is uncertainty bordering on apathy. Hearing the calls for "palace revolution" in Chicago, Paris and Rome, Jagger can only offer that in sleepy London town the "game to play is compromise solution" (the ungainliness of that line compounding its emptiness), leaving him only with the option of singing in a rock 'n' roll band. This torpor is perhaps deserving of laidback instrumentation. Fortunately for the sake of listenability if not appropriateness, the Stones provide something more galvanizing, with Jagger virtually shouting the melody line against ringing guitar riffs, rattling piano and booming, clipped drums.

Robert Wilkins was a bluesman who got religion, hence his 1929 recording "That's No Way to Get Along" being retooled by him in 1964 as "The Prodigal Son". The Stones didn't just drop the definite article in their first cover version for over three years but also jettisoned seven minutes of the Reverend Wilkins' template, a feat partly achieved by ramping up the tempo. Richards hones in on a recurring guitar figure and makes it the central motif in a supple-wristed performance that must be one of the guitarist's greatest ever. Jagger turns in an authentic vocal that is a million miles removed from his boyish pretensions on early Stones records. An absolute treat of a recording.

The second of the brace of electric freak-outs on *Beggars Banquet* is, like the first, one that plays up the Stones' outlaw image. "Stray Cat Blues" sees the narrator enticing into his bed a fifteen-year-old and suggesting that she get her friend to jump in with them. A track that sounds absolutely creepy today, at the time it was in the spirit of a generation reacting against what they considered to be the arbitrary rules of their hung-up elders. It was also a sentiment emerging from the mouth of a man yet to experience concern over the welfare of his own female progeny. The ambience is exquisitely menacing, a brutal bottom end propelled by Watts' relentlessly sizzling hi-hat overlaid with cat's-claw guitar.

"Factory Girl" is a matter-of-fact depiction of proletarian life in the spirit of the kitchen-sink dramas that had latterly become fashionable in cinema. It is brief (just over two minutes) and lovely, with mandolin and more of Richards' fine acoustic work draping Jagger's complaints about his feet getting sodden as he awaits the arrival of his unskilled worker girlfriend with a broken purse. The track's milieu makes it a natural lead-up to the closer, "Salt of the Earth". At close to five minutes, the final track is clearly intended as another grand statement, something underlined by Richards and Jagger alternating vocals on the first two verses as though this were some sort of state-of-the-union address in relay formation. The song was clearly intended to be perceived as a political declaration in its celebration of hard-working people, the lowly of birth, the common foot soldier, uncounted heads, "ragtaggy people", those more than averagely susceptible to cancer or polio . . . Richards recalled, "I think I came up with the title of that and had the basic spur of it, but Mick did all the verses." Jagger is as awkward as he ever is on such territory: he has no programme for improving the lot of these people and can only implore us to raise our glasses and to spare a thought for them. Additionally, there is a rather peculiar bridge in which he seems to acknowledge ambivalence about the workers, confiding that when he looks into faceless crowds implicitly comprising of such people, "They don't look real to me, in fact they look so strange."

Yet for all its vagueness, the track has pathos. Not only does Jagger manage to inject some crack-voiced emotion into his confused philosophizing but the music is elegant and exciting, building from a tranquil opening into a quicker, cymbal-splashed middle section before spiralling into a triple-time finale. The Watts Street gospel choir – overdubbed at Sunset Sound Studios, Los Angeles, where final mixing took place after initial recordings at Olympic – provide a heavenly gloss.

More important than the album's commercial success was that it reasserted the Stones' gravitas after a calendar year in which they had released two uncharacteristically un-gritty and spotty albums. The swagger of its tone, meanwhile, effectively asserted they were unbowed after the assault on them by their country's Establishment.

"HONKY TONK WOMEN"

Sean Egan

Although *Beggars Banquet* was a rebirth for the Stones, their new life would be in a different form.

The parting of the ways with Brian Jones might not seem that big a deal from the perspective of today in the light of the band's subsequent long life and the documenting in multitudinous Stones biographies and interviews that he was a declining force in the group in any event. However, in 1969 it was a scenario that those not cognizant with the fact that he barely played on *Beggars Banquet* found pretty much unthinkable. That Jones had always been the most beautiful Stone – attractiveness being a far more important requisite for band members then than it is today – was only the half of it. He was also a key part of the Stones' image as both important musicians – his multi-instrumental skills were widely known and discussed – and icons of articulate rebellion. To the fans, he was no less adored and central than Mick and Keith regardless of the latter pair's profoundly greater importance in the process of the band's compositions. The Stones were therefore taking something of a risk on 8 June 1969 when, after a mixing session at Olympic, they visited Jones at his home and delicately sacked him. (Wyman didn't form part of the party that made the trip because he hadn't been needed at the mixing session.) Perhaps the mega-confidence instilled in Jagger and Richards by the millions of records their songs had sold over the past four years militated against that fear of risk. The move was certainly reasonable, though: the band were anxious to revitalize their career after two years off the road and Jones had made himself a passenger. For the other members his travel-restricting drug bust may have been a case of there-but-for-the-grace-of-God but the recollections of Dave Hassinger

– who stopped engineering Stones records as far back as 1966
– indicate that Jones had been a sulky and disruptive presence
in the studio for at least three years. Charlie Watts – always the
most good-natured of the band – later described the dismissal
as, "The worst thing so far that I've ever had to do."

Jones was offered severance terms far more generous than
might have been expected even factoring in the guilt engendered
by jettisoning the man who had shared both the Edith Grove
poverty and prosecution and imprisonment ordeals. He was told
he would receive a pay-off of £100,000 – an astronomical sum
for the day – plus £20,000 per year as long as the Stones existed.
One journalist, Terry Rawlings, has put forward a theory that
Jones had registered and therefore owned the name The Rolling
Stones. With the likes of John Lennon and Eric Clapton buzzing
around Jones, perhaps it preyed on the rest of the band's minds
that this man who was always popular with his fellow musical
luminaries would simply take the name away and form a new
Rolling Stones with a stellar line-up. Then again, maybe the
motivation for the pay-off was simple humanity.

A new Stones fronted by Jones, Lennon and Clapton is, of
course, a proposition intriguing beyond belief, but it resides in
an alternate universe. In our own universe, while Jones did
have discussions with various celebrity musician friends – and
rehearsals with more obscure ones – in the final weeks of his
life, plans for a group (super or otherwise) never came to frui-
tion. On 3 July 1969, less than a month after the sacking that
was announced to the press as an amicable separation due to
musical differences, Jones was found dead in the swimming
pool of his home.

The Stones had been recording with what would be his
replacement even before Brian's sacking. Twenty-year-old Mick
Taylor – who had been playing with John Mayall's Bluesbreakers – was brought in to embellish a couple of tracks on which
the band were working, "Live with Me" and "Honky Tonk
Women". So assured were his performances – especially on the
latter, which he transformed from a country number into a
raunchy rocker – that he was offered a permanent (if provi-
sional) gig. He was born on 17 January 1949 and brought up in
Hertfordshire. Although his guitar skills were unimpeachable,

he did not have the multi-instrumental talents of Jones, while a charisma even in the same ballpark as his predecessor was rendered out of the question by his diffidence and ordinary looks. Many would have been the Stones fan and observer of the music scene at the time wondering whether this was an equal or wise exchange.

The release of "Honky Tonk Women" on 4 July 1969 (the following day in the States) would have gone some way to assuage such doubts. It can be theorized that its release was completely overshadowed by Jones' death on the day before. Equally, it can be plausibly suggested that the record sailed to no. 1 on both sides of the Atlantic on a tidal wave of confused sympathy. What's not in doubt is that it's a very good record.

Although the song changed drastically after its origins as an acoustic track begun by Richards during a holiday that he, Jagger and their ladies took to South America, something that didn't was the title phrase, one that Richards later admitted was "banal". However, the dummy vowels and consonants for which he never came up with a replacement sounded natural enough to the public. Nor did the public ever exhibit any particular concern about the fact that the two-line chorus doesn't rhyme. Although the track is archetypal rock raunch, there is something languid about it. A cowbell starts proceedings in a curiously understated way and is succeeded by lumbering drum-work. A swaggering guitar riff begins but maintains that non-urgent tone. The lyric is a sex travelogue in which the narrator is the passive partner with heavy-duty ladies he meets in Memphis and New York. The instrumental break finds a brass section peculiarly reduced to an indistinct smudge. However, the band recover to produce more taut, suggestive rhythms before bringing the song to an explosive close.

It's possibly pushing it to state that the Mick Taylor era audibly starts here – he was barely in the group – but equally undeniable that "Honky Tonk Women" has some of the hallmarks of much of the music of his time in the Stones. The lethargic but simultaneously insistent riff, the sexual frankness (Mick baldly refers to getting "laid") and the vaunting tone pave the way for the decadent sound that the Stones made their own over the course of the next half-decade.

The flipside "You Can't Always Get What You Want" was even more extraordinary and some noted at the time that they felt it should have been the A-side. Although the Stones had always put quality cuts on their B-sides, that this epic should be relegated to that status seemed to herald jaw-dropping riches on the album to come.

A long-scheduled gig at London's Hyde Park on 5 July to introduce the Taylor line-up to the public was, of course, as overshadowed by Jones' death as "Honky Tonk Women" had been but also, like the record, boosted by it: an estimated half a million people turned up to see a rebirth that was so news-worthy that London's *Evening Standard* newspaper published a souvenir edition headlined "Stones in the Park", which gave its name to a Granada TV documentary that followed the group on the day of the gig and interviewed the fans who filed in to see them. This documentary itself generated a tie-in magazine (three shillings). That the Stones' performance was somewhat ragged probably mattered little to the attendees basking in the sunshine and the presence of huge stars: they were charged no entrance fee.

Through the Past, Darkly (Big Hits Vol. 2) – a weird compilation title once again unexplained – was released in the UK on 12 September 1969 and, with a slightly different tracklisting, the following day in the States. That it was dedicated to Jones might suggest a product whose impetus was to wrap up the pre-Taylor era, but the photo session for the cover – in which Jones featured – was apparently arranged specifically for this record. If the rumour is to be believed that Jagger told Jones if he did not turn up for the photoshoot he was out of the band, then the decision to sack him came at quite a late stage.

The cover manages the difficult feat of making Jones look unattractive, but then he is pulling half a "Nanker". His colleagues are similarly straining to make themselves ugly as they press their faces against glass. The cover (which was hexagonal-shaped in the UK) saw the band looking very different from how they had appeared the last time they were depicted on the front of an LP two years previously. That young men in the Western world had become ever more hirsute over the course of the sixties was primarily down to The

Rolling Stones' example, with of course an acknowledgement of The Beatles' pioneering in that area. It had originally been shocking enough that their hair covered their ears and their foreheads. Now their tresses tumbled about their shoulders. Within two or three years, as long hair became a more stylized matter with the "moulded" look and the feather-cut, it would no longer be shocking or even particularly a sign of rejection of orthodoxy. In '69, though, it looked scandalously caveman-like. The fact that – overwhelmed by a young generation imitating their idols – employers were beginning to have no option but to allow such a look on their premises indicated that, in one sense at least, the Stones and their peers had won a battle of values with the old order.

Rob Chapman's massive Mojo *cover feature was timed to coincide with the thirtieth anniversary of Brian Jones' death. More important than that synchronization, though, is the fact that it was published in the days when some magazines thought nothing of treating their readers to an article running to fully 14,000 words. That and Chapman's diligent research and by turns poignant and hilarious turn of phrase make for a comprehensive overview on* The Rolling Stones' *tortured genius.*

THE BITTTERSWEET SYMPHONY

Rob Chapman

First published in *Mojo*, July 1999

Chances are, regardless of where or what location you grew up in, there's a couple of types you've known at one time or another. Firstly, there's our resident Lothario – let's call him Vinnie – a little mad, bad and dangerous to know. The local tearaway. Vinnie's name often crops up in the same hushed breath as "back seat of a car", "knickers round her ankles", and "had to go away for a while until the heat died down".

Then there's this other guy. Let's call him Cedric. Bespectacled. Quiet. Nervy rather than nerdy. Disconcertingly distant, as if he's forever entertaining some private joke in your presence. Invited you round to his house one day and you wondered why he was so intent on playing you his dad's record collection, until it dawned on you that these obscure discs in their thick cardboard sleeves by black artists you'd never heard of weren't his dad's at all. They were his and he seemed to know every note, every nuance.

Brian Jones was both of these characters. And a few others besides. A complex and bewildering bunch of multiple personalities, a man who panhandled the Cheltenham Delta and then upped and left for London, where he conceived and founded the biggest rock 'n' roll group of all time. A short guy with broad shoulders and a little-Welsh-bull chest that tapered down to a skinny waist, a bum like two boiled eggs in a hand-kerchief, drainpipe legs, and matching Achilles heels. How many contradictions can one frame take?

As a child he indulged in that most harmless of activities, bus-spotting. He also had a proclivity for staging car crashes with his Dinky toys and igniting them with lighter fuel. He carried those contradictions through into adult life. A softly-spoken, drinking, smoking, womanising Narcissus with a psychosomatic condition (asthma). A strutting, intense egotist with a gentle, shy smile that played across his face whenever the TV camera lingered long enough. A musical purist blessed, or cursed, with pop star looks. Eulogised by many. "Brian Jones, with his puffed-up Pisces, all-knowing, suffering fish eyes. Brian always ahead of style. Perfect Brian," as Lou Reed put it in *Fallen Knights And Fallen Ladies*, his elegiac 1972 essay on rock deaths. Demonised by just as many. "He was always nice to me," says Charlie Watts, "but he was not very liked, Brian. Stew [Ian Stewart, off-stage Stones pianist] just couldn't stand him. Bill [Wyman] never got on with Brian. Not Bill's fault. Brian's fault entirely." And misunderstood and misrepresented, it seems, as often as he was maligned.

The whole "Is it a boy or a girl?" thing starts with Brian Jones. He was the first heterosexual pop star to wear costume jewellery, off-stage and on. At the first of several drug-bust trials in 1967 he wore a navy blue Mod suit with bell-bottom trousers and flared jacket, large floppy blue-and-white spotted tie and Cuban-heeled shoes. As you do. "He was the definitive, quintessential pop star," says Nick Kent. "He looked as good as any of the women in the '60s like Verushka or Francoise Hardy or Nico. And he did it himself. He didn't get a bunch of designers. It wasn't 'Brian Jones dressed by . . .' It was self-presentation. That was his art."

And it all went so terribly wrong. In 1962 he had a head full of the blues and a heart full of hope. By 1967 he had a ward-robe full of Chelsea velvet and Marrakesh silk. But by the summer of 1969 the blues was merely a distant, fading bottle-neck note, the dandy clothes were crumpled in unwashed, hashburned heaps, and Brian Jones floated face down in a swimming pool.

Brian was a bright kid. Nine O levels. Two A levels. Obvious university material. But, with a perverse intransigence that would become a hallmark of his short life, he took a series of menial jobs instead – everything from coalman to clerk – which exasperated his parents beyond endurance. It annoyed them even more when he was sacked from most of these dead-end occupations for petty pilfering. But the thieving didn't upset them half as much as when Brian kissed the girls and made them cry. And got one of them pregnant; she was 14. And then another; she was married. Then they packed him off to Europe, "until the heat died down".

"When I was 15 a bunch of us used to sneak into Sunday afternoon pictures at the Cheltenham Regal, when it was supposed to be adults only," says Pat Andrews, Brian's girlfriend from 1961 to 1963 and then mother-to-be of his third child, Mark (whose other Christian name, Julian, he shares with all Brian's sons, in honour of one of his heroes, tenor saxophonist Julian "Cannonball" Adderley).

"One of the guys in our little group said he had a friend who'd been away for six weeks and had just come back from Germany and Scandinavia. He said he'd lost track with his friends and had no girlfriend and seemed a bit low." Pat agreed to meet Brian on a blind date in the Aztec coffee bar. "I don't know why they called it the Aztec," she laughs. "It has fishermen's nets and candles. But it did have a jukebox. I'd arranged to meet him in this alcove. I didn't want my friends seeing him in case he was frumpy and looked like Abbott and Costello. He had beautiful golden shiny hair which you could see in the darkness, but he was wearing this tweed suit which put me off. But when we talked he was so different from all of the other Cheltenham boys. He wasn't after a quick grope. You could actually have a conversation with him."

In the re-telling of the Brian Jones story his birthplace is constantly caricatured as a Regency rest home for retired majors and assorted nobility. Charlie Watts still subscribes to this view: "He was a pretentious little sod. He was from Cheltenham. Does that sum it up? An English boy from

Cheltenham." "He started off by being a clarinet player in a trad band," affirms Mick Jagger. "In a provincial West Country town. Very provincial."

That's not how Pat Andrews remembers it. "There were plenty of dancehalls. Five cinemas, including the Gaumont where the Stones played. During the war there'd been two airforce bases nearby. My older brothers used to get lots of American magazines and records from them. There was always a big jazz following in Cheltenham. In the '40s it was all bebop: Thelonious Monk and people like that would come and play. At the town hall it was all Kenny Ball and Johnny Dankworth. Then they opened up a place called the Barbecue, and it was always full of beatniks from the art college."

Brian was already proficient on saxophone, clarinet, guitar and piano when Pat met him. He had played trad jazz with people twice his age in local bars, in the quaintly monikered Cheltone Six, and had now progressed to an R & B combo called the Ramrods. "He was very modest at that time," says Pat. "He said he played a couple of musical instruments, tinkered around – he made it sound more like a hobby – but he didn't push it. He didn't start playing properly 'til he met Alexis."

When Alexis Korner's Blues Incorporated came to town Jones immediately bonded with its talismanic leader. Seeking out the right people was a hallmark of his intuitive enthusiasm right from the start. It was Brian who would later pester Giorgio Gomelsky to let his new outfit play at the famed Station Hotel, Richmond. "We all went back to the coffee bar after the gig and Brian plonked himself down in front of Alexis," remembers Pat Andrews. "This kind of thing must have happened to Alexis hundreds of times, but Brian started telling him how much he loved the blues and what he played. He went home and got his guitar and went back and played for Alexis. Alexis was so taken by him that he gave him his address in London and said come up and stay."

Paul Jones, a fellow blues obsessive, was at that time playing parties around Oxford with the splendidly named Thunder Odin's Big Secret. "I'd just bought a 78 from the late '50s by Thunder & Lightning called 'Santa Fe Blues'. Lightning was Lightnin' Hopkins. Thunder was Thunder Smith, who never made it as big as Lightnin' Hopkins," he laughs. "I met Brian at an Alexis Korner gig in the Ealing Jazz Club in 1962. We jammed together at a few parties in Oxford. I asked Brian if he would come and play guitar in my band but he said, 'I don't really want to be in a band unless I'm the leader.' Brian wasn't so good at that stage that I couldn't afford to be without him so I got another guitarist. A few months later Brian said he was moving to London and forming a band and would I like to be in it? I said no. I told him, I don't think we will ever be able to make enough money from playing this kind of music to make a living from it, and in any case I've just got a job with a dance band. I'm just going to do blues as a hobby!

"Brian was more enthusiastic about the immediate future than I was – and a bit more perceptive, too."

After a few reconnaissance visits to the capital, Brian moved up permanently early in 1962. Pat, with six-month-old son Mark in tow, followed him soon afterwards. Dingy flats and dead-end jobs came and went as Brian pursued his mission. Alexis Korner was busy building a Trojan horse for R & B within the trad jazz enclave; just about anybody who would ever be anybody on that scene would sit in with his band, including Mick Jagger and Keith Richards. Charlie Watts was drummer with Blues Incorporated at the time.

"Alexis introduced me to Brian and we went off back to his flat," he remembers. "Bloody 'orrible thing, with one of the girls he was living with and was pregnant by him. He used to have short hair like Gerry Mulligan, blond, pushed forwards, and he used to wear thick-fur crew-necked sweaters. He played bottleneck guitar and loved soprano saxophone – his big heroes were Sidney Bechet and Elmore James. He used to play harp quite well, too, which not many people did then." Brian, with Alexis Korner's blessing, eventually convinced Charlie Watts to join his fledging outfit. "Brian saw in Charlie what he had in abundance and demanded from any musician: commitment and idealism," Bill Wyman later noted.

It was Brian who placed a Musicians Wanted ad in *Jazz News*. It was Brian who auditioned future members, named the band after a Muddy Waters song, and assertively defended his callow crew when the purists gathered round to sneer. Not that Brian wasn't a fundamentalist himself. His R & B was Muddy Waters, Sonny Boy Williamson, Howlin' Wolf, Elmore James, John Lee Hooker. He had to be convinced, by Keith Richards, that Chuck Berry wasn't just pop. In fact, potential Stones guitarist Geoff Bradford walked out over this very issue.

"I first saw Brian at the Ealing club playing with Paul Jones as interval guest with Alexis Korner," says early Stones member and Pretty Things founder Dick Taylor. "I was there with Mick and Keith and we were most impressed. He was playing an acoustic with a pick-up on it and his slide playing was extraordinary. It didn't take long to get talking with him and it wasn't long before he in turn heard Jagger sing and poached him for his band. Mick took Keith along which prompted Geoff Bradford and Brian Knight to walk and myself to get drafted in."

When the Stones toured with Bo Diddley the following year, such was Brian's reverence that the band dropped their Bo Diddley covers. Like The Beatles, the Stones occasionally had to pretend they played trad just to get a gig. Indeed, at their first big showcase, the Third Richmond Jazz Festival in August 1963, they played bottom of the bill to the likes of Terry Lightfoot and Acker Bilk. But within a year the Stones' brand of raw R & B had blown trad out of the water, and much else besides.

"A school friend's father was the promoter of gigs at the Sophia Gardens in Cardiff," remembers Nick Kent of his Damascene conversion as a 12-year-old in February 1964. "He got me backstage to meet them. Johnny Leyton was topping the bill. Jet Harris was on there. Their day was done. They weren't going to last another year. It was the changing of the guard culturally; the Stones just took that place. We had front-row seats and girls in the third row were threatening us with their stilettos. Backstage, Brian was clearly the leader. The others were sulking around but Brian was smiling and talking to all the girls."

The Rolling Stones' self-appointed leader had the musical acumen to back up his promotional skills. He "worked out" blues harp, "worked out" slide, "worked out" the Bo Diddley beat, and later the dulcimer and sitar like they were mere maths equations. Ginger Baker told Laura Jackson in her book *Golden Stone* how, during an early rehearsal with the fledgling Stones, he and Jack Bruce had played complicated patterns which completely succeeded in throwing Jagger. Jones had to go over to the singer and shout 1-2-3-4 to show him where the beat was.

Pat Andrews also witnessed this early musical maturity first hand: "They were rehearsing in the Bricklayers Arms. Mick Avory or Carlo Little was on drums, I can't remember who. Dick Taylor was there and Brian Knight, too. They were doing this song and Mick was playing the harmonica. Brian was never the kind of person who would turn round and say, 'You're rubbish.' He just pulled his harmonica out of his pocket and said, 'Mick, I think you should play it this way.' I'll never forget the look on Mick's face. It was like, 'Oh, shit. What else can this guy do?'"

"Brian at that time had a certain amount of moodiness about him but also a brilliant sense of humour and enthusiasm," says Dick Taylor. "He was very encouraging about my bass playing which was nice as I only started to play the bass in order to work with the band and was quite unsure of my own ability on it. Both Keith and myself had a lot of respect for his musical abilities, which were quite a bit ahead of our own. We, and Mick, tried to steer things a bit more into the Chuck and Bo areas than maybe Brian wanted."

"He was very diligent," remembers Paul Jones. "Once he got into something he wanted to do he went for it. I used to play harp in first position all the time. I wasn't good at bending notes. I could only really do the Jimmy Reed top end stuff. It was Brian who showed me quite early on how to do cross harp and other positions."

Working out instruments like they were logic puzzles was one thing. Charlie Watts, versed in the ways of the jazz apprentice, doesn't necessarily think this made him a great musician. "Brian was one of these people – Ronnie's the same – if you left him in a room with an accordion, he'd play you a song in about two hours flat. He has a natural ability with an instrument. But they get fed up with it halfway through. He'd play dulcimer for a year and be very good on it, and it'd be on a lot of our records, 'Lady Jane' and all those, but then he got fed up and that was it. He could play the Mellotron, he could play this, he could play a bit of that. He could have been very good if he'd have stuck at any of it."

"Brian did have the ability to pick up things," agrees Jagger. "He was a clarinet player, then he played the guitar, and then he liked to dabble on the piano, then George Harrison played the sitar, so he had to try and learn, and so on." So was this multi-instrumentalism worthy of the plaudits? "No, not really," says Charlie Watts. "He's eulogised but he's not John Coltrane. He was not what people thought he was, and he was not a wonderful player." Watts' view is that he is remembered more for being "the first one on a lot of things. And that is special you know." But even this comes with qualifiers: "He wasn't the first one on slide. But he was the first one that people saw on telly." Watts also claims that, despite the way that Brian's slide toughened up their version of "I Wanna Be Your Man" ("We played it like an Elmore James song instead of like the bloody Beatles"), Jones's ex-associate Geoff Bradford was actually a better slide player.

"Geoff was marvellous," agrees Paul Jones, "but he would not have been right for the Stones. It wouldn't have been the Stones with me in it either. Even Ian Stewart would have spoiled that image. Brian's playing on 'I Wanna Be Your Man' may have been rudimentary – everything about that record was rudimentary. But the thing for me, and always will be with the Stones, was 'Rooster Blues' ['Little Red Rooster']. Of all the wonderful things that they ever did, to get a slow blues to Number 1 on the UK chart was the most astonishing achievement of all."

Jagger is equally unequivocal in his assessment. "He picked up this Elmore James guitar thing which really knocked me out when I first heard him play it, because I'd never heard anyone play it live before – I'd only heard it on records. And it was really good. He really had that down and he was very exciting. The sound was right. The glissandos were all right. There was a really good gut feeling when he played it in the pub. And that translated all the way up to 'I Wanna Be Your Man' – on this really not very good pop song, suddenly there was this really hot . . . I mean, you can play that stuff and it can sound like crap. It's all to do with getting the right tone out of the guitar and the amp, which in those days was relatively difficult to do – you didn't have all these boxes to make it up for you. No, he was good at that, he definitely was."

"Mick and Keith absolutely idolised Brian at the beginning," says Pat Andrews. "They'd never met anybody like him, but I also think from a teenage point of view there was a lot of animosity because they thought they were streetwise. I think it was to do with Mick and Keith being from Dartford, trying to be London lads, and then there's this hick from Cheltenham, charming, really good-looking, talented, well-educated, knowledgeable – I think it put their noses out of joint."

In December 1962 Bill Wyman enlisted in what he referred to in his autobiography *Stone Alone* as "this itinerant unit of starving, sullen, lapsed scholars and amateur music makers", and the classic Stones line-up was complete. By this time Brian, Mick, and Keith were sharing a flat together in Edith Grove, Chelsea, and concentrating full time on their music. Charlie Watts was a regular visitor: "It used to be hilarious all day. We used to get up at about three in the afternoon, just play records all day. And Brian used to be really funny in those days. Obsessed with R & B and promoting The Rolling Stones." Brian dipped his hand into cash registers and stole food to pay for band rehearsals and equipment during this crucial period. He would later elicit resentment when the other Stones discovered that he was paying himself an extra £5 as "leader of the band".

Kathy Etchingham, later Jimi Hendrix's girlfriend, first met Brian in 1963 in Peter Cook's Establishment Club and hung out with him at all the regular London watering holes: The Cromwellian, The Bag O' Nails, The Speakeasy. "A group of us used to go down to The Scene Club off Windmill Street and watch The Who when they were still The High Numbers – Brian, me, Angie Burdon, Georgie Fame and his girlfriend Carmen. We used to drop purple hearts and dance around like nobody's business. Brian never danced, of course – Jimi never did either. Too cool."

"Most of the time Brian was pretty cool," Pat Andrews agrees. "But he was a bloody liar and an opportunist as well." She and Brian had lived on sandwich-spread and steak and kidney pies through the dark days. Pat was bringing up their baby in damp flats while Brian worked at, and got sacked from, a series of grotty jobs. "Mick used to come round with Vesta packet meals. That was like eating at the Ritz," she laughs. But by early 1963 their relationship had deteriorated and she returned to Cheltenham. "He got involved with a lot of girls and people seemed to think I didn't know about them," she says stoically, "but nine times out of 10 he would tell me about them. You have to remember that he was practically thrown out of his house when he was 17. He was trying to survive. Wages weren't good. Girls would come round and bring Brian food. He was a bit of a gigolo, really." And his infamous jealousy? "I only really witnessed that twice. Once when I went to buy a drink and this guy spoke to me completely innocently. I'm very polite and if someone speaks to me I speak back. Brian didn't say a word until we got outside and then he went absolutely berserk. Another time I was working at the laundry and I got a bonus and bought myself a skirt and a top. He went berserk again and asked me how I got this bonus and what did I do to earn it. I know he had mood swings but I think they were more to do with his insecurity than anything else. You've got to remember where he was coming from. Demonstrative love was not the norm in his family."

"He carries a lot of luggage, we used to say," comments Bill Wyman in *Stone Alone*, referring both to the bags that always appeared under Brian's eyes at the merest hint of excess, and more metaphorically, to the emotional and psychological burdens that seemingly forever weighed him down. "He was always terribly paranoid," agrees Kathy Etchingham. "It didn't just start. He was paranoid when I first met him. Not as badly as later on but it was always a trait." Charlie Watts also subscribes to the view that Jones's problems were deep-rooted, and that fame merely accelerated their growth. "He got worse. He drank more. He took loads of drugs, when nobody knew in those days what they'd do to you. He was young. He got very big-headed."

At one point Jones borrowed some gold cufflinks from photographer Dezo Hoffman and promptly gave them to Bo Diddley. He also borrowed a bunch of rare blues singles from Long John Baldry. Baldry never saw them again; Brian had given them to photographer Nicky Wright: "He came around and thrust this bag into my hand – 'Here you are, here's a present for you.' Inside were all these wonderful records – Howlin' Wolf, Lightnin' Hopkins, John Lee Hooker. Twenty years later I realised they belonged to Long John Baldry when I read a magazine interview where he mentioned he'd lent a stash of Chess records to Brian, and never got them back! By then someone had stolen them from me, too."

"Brian could be sweet – he was intelligent, would listen to your conversation carefully, and was very charming. But," Nicky continues, "he could also seem totally psychotic and schizophrenic. We were coming back from Folkestone one night about nine o'clock, sometime in 1963, and had stopped to look for something to eat. We found a fish shop, but it was closed. We banged on the door and this chap came to the door and told us, 'We've switched everything off, the fat's cooled down, we're closed.' No one argued until I shouted, 'This is the Rolling Stones!' This little husband and wife were really sweet, and said come in and sit down while we see what we can do. So everybody's ordered their fish and chips, steak and chips, and it takes quite a long time while they heat up the fat or whatever. Finally they bring it to the table. Keith's happily eating away, so are the others, then Brian tries a forkful, and starts complaining: 'I don't like this! It's soggy! I can't eat this!' He stands up, takes this bottle, and squirts ketchup over the table and knocks his food on to the floor. It was heartbreaking – there's this couple thinking, 'Great, it's The Rolling Stones', then this happens."

"My best friend hated him, could've killed him," says Charlie Watts. "He was a scheming little bugger. And then as we got more famous he became more conscious of himself. He became sadder and more obnoxious at the same time. But to be fair to Brian, a lot of his problems with people might have been because he wasn't that healthy. He was a great catalyst, though, especially at the beginning."

"He was such an ambitious young man, so determined, long before the Stones ever were," confirms Paul Jones. "He was always dressed sharp. When he met people he would intensely concentrate on the conversation; that was very different to how he later became: very vague and self-concerned."

"I've been really shocked at some of the things that people have written about Brian. It's like they hated him or something," says Kathy Etchingham. "I was really miffed when Bill Wyman wrote in his book that I was one of Brian's critics. He used me as an example to show that other people hated Brian, as well as himself. What he said in his book was totally untrue."

Rolling Stones fan club secretary Shirley Arnold is another of those offering only positive testimony. Rooting through drawers and cupboards in her south London flat she proudly shows me mementos of her past association with the band; one of Brian's stage outfits, a red velvet frock coat, a little blue Dinky toy Commer pick-up truck and a carved wooden cutlery holder that Brian brought back from Morocco: a thank-you for all the fry-ups Shirley had cooked him when he'd been up all night getting wasted. "It's probably the only thing that came out of Cotchford that got to the person it was meant to get to," she says poignantly. Shirley used to go and see the Stones at Ken Colyer's Studio 51 on Sunday afternoons early in 1963. "They were doing all the old rhythm and blues stuff like 'Cops And Robbers' and 'Roll Over Beethoven'." One day, down at the front in the crush and the heat, she fainted and was passed over the heads of all the punters and into the dressing room. "Bill said the fan club's not that together. Would you like to run it?" It was a chance encounter that brought Shirley Arnold into the inner sanctum. "I was working in the city for a fiver a week. They offered me seven. I said I'd have done it for free. There was never any bitchiness in those early days within the band," she claims, "never anything that I thought was nasty."

Cast your eyes over those early publicity shots. They look remarkably prescient: Bill, the shrewd, slightly older guy; Charlie, looking like what he always was and forever will be, a jazzer who thought he'd give this pop lark a go; Keith looks like he's got potential, as soon as he grows into that demeanour;

Mick, undeniably enthusiastic and undeniably gauche, too. And who's this one on the end? Dressed in white slacks and black polo neck, and already sporting a hairstyle that every band from The Byrds to The Yardbirds will aspire to over the next three years: there's yer pop star, mate.

"Brian, I'd met socially in 1964, before I met the Stones," says group photographer Gered Mankowitz. "At that time he was very charming, very polite, and well-mannered. A lovely man. Andrew Oldham liked the photos I'd done of Marianne Faithfull and asked if I'd do The Rolling Stones. In visual terms Brian was the strongest. On that first photo session that became the *Out Of Our Heads* cover he is in the foreground with his blond hair glowing, while Mick, always the leader on-stage, is right at the back. Brian's hair was coiffured, shaped, and pretty long, but he didn't just look shaggy like The Pretty Things or Them. It was groomed. Extraordinarily so for that time, when I think back."

"I don't think we'd have got where we are if he hadn't been at the helm at the beginning," says Charlie Watts. "But I think he wanted to be the lead singer. Well, of course, he wasn't. He wasn't a singer at all. His breathing would never allow him to be. And he wanted to be leader, and he wasn't a leader."

Gered Mankowitz saw the power struggles that were starting to develop within the band. "Remember that the lighting at concerts in those days was relatively crude, and there would just be a spotlight on the main singer. It might just manage to swing over if there was a guitar solo but otherwise the singer was the only one who was consistently lit." The few surviving early *Top Of The Pops* clips bear this out. As they mime their way through that month's hit record the camera focuses almost exclusively on Mick. On the rare occasions that it picks out Brian, stage left, he often appears to be disenchantedly gazing up at the studio monitors, already seemingly disillusioned with the pop route. As if to say, "How can you mime the blues?"

"The thing about Brian is that he wanted so much to be the leader of the band," confirms Jagger, "and when you try too hard to do something you quite often fail. He was so jealous of everybody else: that was his personality failing." Did he feel threatened by you? "I guess so. The thing is that singers always get more attention than anyone else, even if they're not very good. And Brian really didn't like that. He thought he should get more attention.

"But," Jagger stresses, "he was quite fluid in the way he talked. He was quite a good communicator at the beginning, though it was in a kind of slightly schoolmaster-ish way. But he did communicate, which was really needed then, because people didn't quite understand what it was all about." In the early days Brian was the self-appointed conscience of the band, the R & B evangelist writing earnest letters to the pop and trade press and to BBC producers. Within two years that entire *raison d'être* had been usurped by Top 10 singles, and light entertainment impressionists doing Jagger's monkey walk and big lips on prime-time TV. Keith, also with an initial awkwardness, visible on those early televised appearances where he is not averse to the odd self-conscious mop-top shake of the head, gained confidence both through live performance and his burgeoning songwriting partnership with Jagger. Arguably it was this factor alone that irreversibly upset the subtle dynamic of the early Stones, edging Brian out of the limelight.

When Andrew Loog Oldham first came on the scene (becoming the band's co-manager with Eric Easton in 1963), Brian passed him off as an old Cheltenham pal on Giorgio Gomelsky who himself had designs on managing the group. "Brian stepped up and said he was the leader," Oldham remembers. "When they came to the office first, it was Brian and Mick who appeared. Brian was an important power in the Stones while he could play. Once he'd stopped trying and decided to play rhythm guitar that was it. Brian was basically the manager of the group until Eric and I were. When a real manager comes along you've got to assume that some people can handle the loss of power and some can't. Within a short time of Eric and I signing the Stones for everything, they were coming to us direct. He'd lost his power. In *Charlie Is My Darling*, the film I made, he said he wouldn't be around at 27. That seemed to be a big age with him. He was self-destructive."

Gomelsky was promptly erased from the picture. Fame isn't so much fickle as ruthless, and its path, then as now, was littered with those whose faces simply didn't fit. Just ask Pete Best. And just ask Ian Stewart, who was relegated from bona fide Stones member to roadie in one fell swoop just because he didn't look the part. It was Loog's arrival that effectively hastened the demotion of Brian Jones, too. It was Loog who decided six was too many band members. More crucially it was the Stones manager who threw Jagger and Richards together as a song-writing team. And as far as songwriting goes, three's a crowd.

Jones, for his part, quickly decided that Loog was an embarrassment. This manifested itself at an early recording session when it became clear that, for all his Spectoresque aspirations, the teen Svengali didn't even know what a mix was. Unfortunately for Jones, Loog was the image spin doctor par excellence. It was Loog who came up with "Would You Let Your Daughter Marry A Rolling Stone?" It didn't help that a Rolling Stone had kids of his own.

"They had done a photo shoot on the steps that led down to the river at Battersea Park," remembers Pat Andrews. "There was this little crèche where you could leave kids and we'd left Mark there and gone on the water chute. When we came out of the park Brian was carrying Mark on his shoulders. He was so happy that day and he'd got some money so he said, 'Let's go and buy Mark some clothes.' The next day Brian said Andrew had called him into the office and told him he mustn't be seen with Mark again. Brian got very upset by this. After all the hard work he'd gone through he wasn't going to be told that he couldn't walk through the park with his son."

"Oh yes, Andrew wouldn't have agreed with that," confirms Shirley Arnold. "The children were there but Brian couldn't acknowledge them. In those days it wasn't the thing to be married or have children. Look at John Lennon. Charlie and Shirley had to keep their marriage quiet as well."

At the height of their pop fame in 1965 the Stones appeared on the Christmas edition of *Ready Steady Go!* miming hilariously to Sonny & Cher's "I Got You Babe". Brian in his pomp played Sonny to Cathy McGowan's Cher. By now he was well used to playing a part. But when they performed live on the programme it was Mick that the girls tried to mob, not Brian.

The onset of fan hysteria only heightened the tensions. Gered Mankowitz remembers the mayhem of the Stones' second tour of the USA that year: "Travelling TWA Ambassador class. Allen Klein whisking us through customs. Girls screaming at Mick. Girls pounding on the limo roof." There was a fair bit of partying with the elite as well. "Dylan doing everything in reverse to us. Wearing a mohair suit and then putting on jeans to go on-stage." It was on this tour that Mankowitz first saw signs of Brian's behavioural problems. "Signs of his disturbed personality were quite clearly manifesting themselves. At some point he just disappeared. Just walked out of the limo and disappeared. It was announced that he was ill but he'd just vanished."

"At the time I left the Stones everybody was still getting along just fine," remembers Dick Taylor. "But that was at the start of the Edith Grove period. We didn't see much of each other 'til he lived in the basement flat of the house The Pretty Things had in Belgravia. By then Brian had changed quite a bit: the more paranoid side of his character was a lot more evident. Which wasn't to say his humour didn't still come out, but it was just darker, and the drink and drugs certainly emphasised his mood swings."

Nicky Wright photographed the Stones for the sleeve of their self-titled debut album, which knocked *With The Beatles* off the top spot in May 1964 (the first time the Fabs had lost pole position in the LP charts in nearly a year). Even as Brian's band were challenging the hitherto unassailable Moptops, the man himself was cracking. "I had a chalet in a little place called Whitehill in Hampshire, near Borden Army Camp," Nicky Wright recalls. "Brian used to come down there in his Humber Hawk for peace and quiet, often to escape these girls' fathers. We'd hide his car in the woods in case any of them came looking for him. He had a string of girlfriends and a succession of babies. He was like a tom cat, really. In the summer of 1964, he'd come down to my chalet, and seemed rather out of it on something or other. As the evening drew on and whatever it was wore off, he was getting more and more morose, complaining about how he wasn't being listened to. Suddenly, standing in this tiny kitchen, he said, 'I'm fed up – this will show all of them,' took a knife, and slashed it across one wrist. My brother Patrick was standing by the kitchen door, and as he saw Brian doing this, he punched him clean on the chin, and Brian went out like a light. His wrist was just scratched, there was no serious damage."

Brian's cry for help that night didn't end there. Patrick Wright takes up the story: "He threw himself out of the ground-floor window in a futile attempt at committing suicide. We hadn't the faintest idea where he had gone. My brother rushed down to the police station and said rather apologetically to the policeman, 'Please don't tell anybody, but I've got Brian Jones staying at my house and he's fallen out of a window and we can't find him.' This roly-poly old-fashioned policeman came up, and we found this figure lying in the gorse bush beneath the window."

Nicky: "My father, very much of the old school, came over to see what all the fuss was about. Ever so politely Brian said to him, 'I'm awfully sorry, Mr Wright; I've been such a cunt.' Next morning I went upstairs, rather apologetically, to take Brian a cup of tea. He was all sweetness and light then, cheerful and happy."

Patrick Wright recalls another of Brian's visits to the Whitehill chalet: "He would come down with Linda [Lawrence] and a box of fanmail. She was pregnant by him and he would sit there opening his fanmail from teenage girls who wanted to go to bed with him or meet him in Epping Forest. He would say, 'Do you think I should do this one, Linda?' She would sit there looking absolutely distraught. She obviously loved him a great deal but he was callous: a nasty little man, really vicious and unkind." A few months later, in early 1965, Brian returned to the chalet with Linda and baby in tow. "They started having this argument, and their baby started crying," Nicky Wright remembers. "Suddenly he lost his temper, grabbed the baby from her, she started shouting at him, and he opened the window, and held it out of the window by one leg, upside down, saying, 'Shut the fuck up!' I ran over and pulled him away. It was shocking. He had absolutely no control over himself at all."

"I don't really want to pop-psychoanalyse Brian," says Jagger before rendering as astute and expansive account of his former colleague as he's ever given. "He wasn't really good material to be in the pop business. He was too sensitive to every real slight and perceived slight; just over-sensitive to everything. And then when he started taking drugs that became more and more exaggerated. I think he was a shy person – and shy people in show business put themselves at risk. Shy actors have to drink before they can act. I've seen shy singers who take drugs before they go out." (Ironically, Shirley Arnold had earlier said to me, "The amount of people in the industry I've seen who have to have a line of coke before they could go up and talk to Mick . . ." Readers who want to double the irony quota are referred to Tony Sanchez's book *Up And Down With The Rolling Stones*.)

"It's mostly to do with the fact that some people are born shy," continues Jagger. "You see children of the same age, of the same parents or similar background, and some children are very shy and won't come out. Remember when you were a kid? There was always the one that wouldn't go into the circle for Pass The Parcel or they wouldn't go in the Dancing Statues. Well, Brian was probably one of those children. Those people are very bad material for show business because they're not like some other people, like myself or the more extrovert people. We have a shy part, of course, and don't want to make a fool of ourselves, but it's completely overshadowed by an extrovert nature. You take the knocks and you can deal with it. And you're still out there doing it. But Brian wasn't really like that, and there are a lot of other people like that, and they try and handle it by drinking, or being rude, and they suffer. They're basically in the wrong business. They have to alter their personalities to be what they perceive they want to be.

"He just wanted to be in a blues band," summarises Jagger, "and didn't really think it was gonna be show business. Perhaps the biggest ambition he thought of was playing the Marquee on Thursdays. That was the end of it."

At the end of the famous, oft-shown concert footage of rioting fans at the Royal Albert Hall in 1966, Mick and Keith are nearly torn limb from limb and are lucky to get off the stage. Jones suddenly lurches into picture, teeth bared and bent double with unhinged laughter as Richards tries to hold on to his guitar. It's the same manic response you see at the end of the "Have You Seen Your Mother, Baby" promo film with the Stones in drag, all managing to keep a straight face except Brian, who dissolves into another unsettling cackle.

"There was a two-year period when the audience were louder than us, all screaming teenyboppers," Keith Richards remembers. "Brian had this terrible joke of playing 'Popeye The Sailor Man' in the middle of anything because it didn't matter, nobody could hear shit anyway. I'd be walking past him on-stage and I'd hear [sings] *da-da-da da da da da* all the time. For Charlie I think that was the most frustrating time. He was a serious musician, a jazz drummer, and all of a sudden he's playing to a load of 13-year-old girls wetting themselves and Brian's doing 'Popeye The Sailor Man' and it was, 'Whatever happened to the blues?'"

What Brian was doing instead was schmoozing at Andy Warhol's Factory and bonding with Bob Dylan. "Because of the world he got into, he knew a lot of people long before we did," says Charlie Watts. "Jimi Hendrix was one, and Bob Dylan was a friend of his. A lot of people liked him and admired him. Now whether they liked him because he was a Rolling Stone or whatever I don't know. He became more of a celebrity than a great musician."

"The phone bills were massive," remembers Shirley Arnold. "He'd be on the phone to Dylan for four hours from the office." Dylan would tease Brian about his paranoia, telling him that he was the Mr Jones of "Ballad Of A Thin Man". "Look at how much cred McCartney gets now that history, quite rightly, has put it straight that he was the most avant-garde Beatle, hanging out with artists on the London scene," says Jones's biographer Terry Rawlings. "Well, Brian was hanging out with Arthur C. Clarke, checking out the Spear Of Destiny and the Holy Grail and all that business. That's way out there as far as I'm concerned."

"Brian knew Kenneth Anger very well, and lots of people like that," confirms the unflappable Charlie Watts. "I didn't really know them that well, but I've met them. I was never interested in that world and I never came from it. A night out for me was going to the Flamingo. I'd see Georgie Fame more than I'd hang out with that lot. But you've only got to look at the bloody Palladium tape with us on there with him with the hat on. I mean that's how out there he was."

In 1964 the Stones had filled out the obligatory "Life Lines" section for *NME*. In time-honoured fashion they all lied about their ages. Under "Biggest Break In Career", Brian entered "Break with parents". Under "Husband And Wife's Name" he wrote, "Husband Stew and he works in a glass furnace". Under "Brothers And Sisters' Names" the entry read, "Sister half Moroccan named Hashish".

"He was ahead of the game in many ways," points out Gered Mankowitz. "He was experimenting more and earlier than the others with drugs, with instrumentation in music, and with the way he was living his life. I don't remember anyone else in the band getting visibly out of it, but Brian did. One time on tour he rang me, asking me to go up to his room. He said, 'I've got two tabs of acid, I thought maybe you'd like to share it with me.' I said, Brian, you know I don't do acid. He said, 'Oh right. OK, I tell you what I'll do. I'll take both of them and you write down everything I say.' I said, 'Er, no I don't think so'."

Brian was also the first Rolling Stone to check out the burgeoning West Coast scene. Keith Altham, who interviewed Brian for *NME* in 1966, remembers him playing experimental free-form tapes that he was working on. "We just sort of laid back and listened to what they were doing in Frisco, whereas Brian was making great tapes, overdubbing," Keith Richards told *Rolling Stone* in 1971. "He was much more into it than we were. We were digging what we were hearing for what it was, but that other thing in you is saying, 'Yeah, but where's Chuck Berry?'"

As Brian's cultural antennae became more finely tuned than his bandmates', the darker side of his personality started to manifest itself more clearly. "It was always there, you just picked up on it more as time went by," says Mankowitz. "You dismissed a lot of things as vagaries of the moment but as I spent more time with him I started to note a pattern. On one or two occasions in clubs he just snapped when he considered some journalist or fan was pushing him too much. In one place he just put a glass in someone's face. Unhesitatingly. It made

you wary of him. There was an instability to him. When he was
on form he was an incredibly important, crucial part of the
band. When he was off form he let everybody else down. One
time I saw Ian Stewart grab Brian in the wings as they came
off stage and shake him and say, 'What are you doing? You're
playing like a piece of shit.' It infuriated Ian and it frustrated
everybody else. Brian wasn't only not bothering. He was
making a joke about it."

And playing "Popeye The Sailor Man" where once he
would have played Elmore James licks.

Much of the debate about the decline of Jones as a musical
force within The Rolling Stones seems to hinge upon his role
during the band's classic pop period from '65 to '67: that
richly prolific purple patch spanning "The Last Time", "Satisfaction", "Get Off Of My Cloud", "19th Nervous Breakdown",
"Paint It Black", "Have You Seen Your Mother Baby", *Aftermath* and *Between The Buttons*, which culminated in the
Sunday Night At The London Palladium performance of "Let's
Spend The Night Together" – Brian replete with costume
jewellery, frock coat and bipperty-bopperty hat – and the
band's subsequent refusal to join the other acts on the podium
for the show's cheesy showbiz finale. This was the period when
what Marianne Faithfull calls their "blend of blues mythology
and King's Road noblesse oblige" was at its most synchro-
nised, and Jones the texturalist was at his peak.

"Brian was a sensitive person and that translated into his
playing," says Jagger. His marimba on "Under My Thumb",
sitar on "Mother's Little Helper" and "Paint It Black", dulcimer on "Lady Jane" and "I Am Waiting" are more than mere
musical embroidery. Sometimes the contribution is simplicity
itself, merely repeating the vocal melody on "Lady Jane" or
running up and down the Eastern scale on "Paint It Black",
but Jones's multi-instrumental finery is integral; it is the making
of all these songs. And for those who care about these things,
it is possible that the haircut he sported around the time of
"Paint It Black" is the finest that ever adorned a pop star.

In one of the most telling episodes in *Faithfull*, her autobiographical collaboration with David Dalton, Marianne describes
the moment in the studio when Jones first plays on recorder

the beautiful lilting pastoral melody that would eventually become "Ruby Tuesday". Richards picks up on it and starts shaping it on the piano. Jones tells him that it's a cross between John Dowland's "Air On The Late Lord Essex" and a Skip James blues. "Brian wanted everyone to say, 'That's great Brian, wonderful! Good work!'" says Faithfull. "But of course nobody did." When it was released, as the flip side to "Let's Spend The Night Together", "Ruby Tuesday" carried the standard Jagger–Richards songwriting credit. When they performed it on TV, Jones and Richards were sat together at the same piano stool, accentuating their physical and musical closeness. They would never be that close again.

It was in the autumn of 1965 that model and actress Anita Pallenberg had first attached herself to Jones. They soon merged into one straw blond boy-girl, same hair, same clothes, same penchant for experimentation. "He was besotted with her," says Kathy Etchingham. "I met Anita last October at an art exhibition in Notting Hill and she seems very embittered about it all. I introduced myself to her and said I'd been a friend of Brian's. She just guffawed and said, 'Yes, he had lots of friends.'"

"He fell in love with someone who was just too tough to be broken by him. That's the secret of that relationship," surmises Nick Kent. "It was his misfortune to fall in love with someone as free-spirited as her. That really was his karma in a sense. The way he treated women so badly. He found more than his match in Anita."

Ask Jagger, after all this time, if Pallenberg was a good influence on Brian and the Stones vocalist laughs uproariously. "No," he says. "No, she wasn't." Jones and Pallenberg's intense affair burned itself out in Morocco. After one fight too many Anita ran into the consoling arms of Keith Richards. "Keith and Brian had this very odd relationship, which was very peculiar," says Jagger, distancing himself. "All of it was very strange and I didn't get involved because I was outside it, you know, I was in another place completely, and it wasn't particularly healthy." Jagger had Marianne Faithfull as soulmate, bedmate, and fellow astral traveller during this period. Jones, on the other hand, started to come apart at the seams.

"The drugs were still quite private then," says Gered
Mankowitz. "You didn't go round the streets with a joint. I
remember one time when we did, thinking it was pretty daring.
Andrew pushed it sometimes, asking a policeman for a light
for his joint in Newcastle in 1966 when we were doing the Ike
& Tina Turner tour. But there were no drugs backstage in
those days because there were always police outside the door."

But bad karma was beckoning. Reality fades with every
retelling of a familiar story, and just as we occasionally have to
be reminded how different the Stones looked or how raw they
sounded in the early '60s, it's also worth re-emphasising how
the establishment brought all its weight to bear in its attempts
to crush the band in 1967. This was an era when the *News Of
The World* could run an item about London's UFO club under
the headline "I Saw Couples Injecting Reefers", and when a
leading police chief could tell Jock Young in his classic sociological study *The Drug Takers* that the hippies were flea-ridden
and made his skin crawl. Detective Sergeant Norman Pilcher
(the "semolina pilchards" of John Lennon's "I Am The
Walrus"), who would arrest Brian, was charged with corruption and blackmail during the seedy '70s.

First came the systematic raids on highly symbolic targets,
like the UFO club, and Dandie Fashions, a boutique frequented
by both the Stones and Beatles. Then there was the famous
News Of The World exposé of February 1967, where Mick
Jagger allegedly told a reporter, in suspiciously unhip Fleet
Street argot, that he "had sampled LSD" but that he didn't
"go much on it now that the cats have taken it up". The *News
Of The World* got one minor detail wrong. They identified the
wrong Stone. It was Brian being indiscreet in a dark nightclub,
not Jagger. The Stones singer issued a writ. Too late. The
machinery was in motion. Acting on a Fleet Street tip-off, the
police decided to call in on Keith Richards' Redlands pad.
And the rest is history: Wormwood Scrubs, *Times* editorials
about butterflies being broken on wheels, and enduring urban
myths about Mars bars.

After Jagger and Richards' convictions and subsequent
release on appeal, the Stones singer was whisked off to ITV's
World In Action for a tête-à-tête about the generation gap with

Times editor William Rees-Mogg, former Home Secretary Lord Stow-Hill, Jesuit Father Thomas Corbishley, and the Bishop of Woolwich (a summit organised by a 23-year-old TV researcher name of John Birt). Meanwhile, as Bill Wyman reports, "it was sad to see Brian scuffling for cash from the Stones office".

Jones, of course, was the real butterfly broken on a wheel. After unsuccessfully pursuing Mick and Keith, the police turned their attention to Brian. Jagger and Richards seemed to add a further armadillo layer to their rebel armour after their bust; Brian visibly diminished after his. Alexis Korner, who saw him during the summer of 1967, was shocked at the decline: "He looked like a debauched version of Louis XIV. That's when I realised that acid-taking can cause casualties." The promotional film for "We Love You" recorded in July of that year was banned by the BBC, not for its allusions to the trial of Oscar Wilde, but because in the few brief glimpses of him Brian looks absolutely shit-faced. In fact, he had sneaked out of psychiatric hospital to attend the session.

His debilitated condition didn't stop him adding some inspired spiralling multi-layered Moroccan brass at the tail-end of the track. Neither did it stop him contributing some deft orchestral touches on the Mellotron to *Their Satanic Majesties Request*, most notably on "2000 Light Years from Home". Brian's North African-influenced embellishments of woodwind and percussion are all over that most maligned of Rolling Stones albums. Not bad for a bloke rumoured by this time to be ingesting LSD by the bucket load and drinking brandy from a pint glass: "Even when he was in the most appalling state they could still prop him up and stick a recorder in his mouth and he could make music," notes Gered Mankowitz with amazement.

It might be fanciful to suggest that, like Lenny Bruce, it was "an overdose of police" and not a swimming pool that ultimately killed Brian Jones, but it's undeniable that the weeping, sick man who appeared in the dock throughout 1967 and 1968, forced to listen to humiliating psychiatric reports about his "condition", was now a shadow of his former self. At the June 1967 Monterey Pop Festival, Jones wandered about as

the high priest of hip, introducing Hendrix on-stage like some
alternative toastmaster revelling in his patronage. But such
appearances offered only brief respite from the drug-busts,
the paranoia, and the legions of liggers.

"I'd go round there when he was in a bad way and cook him
breakfast," remembers Shirley Arnold. "He'd phone up and
say, 'Get some money from the petty cash', and I'd go round
with eggs and bacon. There'd be all these people in the flat, all
these hangers-on, passed out. It was a shambles. There'd be
someone in the bath passed out. Then I'd cook breakfast and
go to find Brian and he'd have passed out again. I'd sometimes
think, 'Something will happen, he'll kill himself if he carries on
like this.' One morning he was sitting in the kitchen watching
me as I was cooking. He thought it was all quite amazing that
I could do all this. He was saying, 'One day, Shirley, I'm going
to get it all together. I'm going to get married and have it all
together.'"

Kathy Etchingham also found herself having to play surro-
gate mum. "He'd phone up in his little boy voice and go, 'I'm
in a terrible mess over here. Can you come over and help me?'
I used to go over and clean his place up. The sink would be
piled up with dishes. Crud all over the place. He'd be meeting
a girl that night and wanted the place clean before the girl
came over. But at least he owned up about it. Then one day he
phoned up and said he had this girl there and he couldn't get
rid of her and could I come over? It was four in the morning
and he sent a taxi for me. When I got there he said, 'Sit on my
knee', and I had to pretend to this American girl that he was
with me. Eventually she got the message and left. Next day he
was busted and some dope was found. He absolutely blamed
this girl. Swore that it was her but I know it wasn't. She definitely had the hots for him but it was his dope. It was on the
table. We were smoking it."

At the second of his court appearances in October 1967,
Brian (said by his psychiatrist to be "potentially suicidal")
wore a pin-striped charcoal-grey Savile Row suit with flared
cuffs, a blue-and-white polka dot tie, and a white frilly lace
shirt. This, in an era when high court judges routinely had to
ask what a T-shirt was, let alone how to inject yourself with

reefers. Brian was given a custodial sentence for possession of a minuscule amount of hash, again reduced on appeal to a fine.

"He was regularly so stoned in the studio that he would just nod off," says Gered Mankowitz. "The band would send out for food about two o'clock in the morning and I saw Brian just fall head first into his duck à l'orange. It was very sad and it showed a weakness which began to get picked on. When they put him in the soundbooth at Olympic and he had to be propped up with cushions it was really sad and awful but in the control room we were all laughing and joking about it. I don't think we knew how else to deal with it. Nowadays there would be clinics and counsellors but nobody had written the textbook then on how to deal with a rock casualty. There wasn't a manual. There was a lack of concern all round. Nobody rallied round. You ran out of sympathy for him." "Perhaps in these slightly more enlightened days, dealing with personality disorders and drug problems ... I mean, everyone knows about it now," adds Jagger, "but I don't think in those days there was such a lot of understanding about."

"We were in the Maddox Street offices. They'd left Andrew [Loog Oldham] by then and [Allen] Klein was on the scene," says Shirley Arnold. "Jo Bergman had been brought in from California to run the office. Brian was paranoid and he didn't take to Jo. He thought she was just catering for Mick, but Mick was the businessman. He was the one that was coming into the office and attending the board meetings. This was '68 and Brian wasn't even attending recording sessions, and when you did see him he looked so tired."

"He wasn't showing up," confirms Charlie Watts. "And you know what happens when people don't show up – you do without them. And then when you do without them, suddenly they're not needed. And then it was a decision. Shall we get somebody else?"

"They wouldn't record anything that he'd written and he wanted to do other things," says Shirley Arnold. "I was never sure what it was but he wasn't keen on the way the music was going. He didn't think the Stones should be moving in that direction." "People say because he wasn't writing songs he compensated by playing every musical instrument going – but he did write songs," claims Terry Rawlings. "Shirley Arnold knew he was writing songs. There's been lyrics found since. I just don't think they got a chance to be heard." David Dalton: "Much later on Andrew Oldham showed me some lyrics Brian had written. It was this very repetitive, very generic blues thing. There was no resonance at all. The guy just couldn't write lyrics."

Whatever the merits, or otherwise, of his lyrics, there's plenty of evidence to suggest that Brian has been written out of history in other ways. "There's a great scene in that Doors movie where they get taken into the inner sanctum of Andy Warhol's Factory," recalls Terry Rawlings. "Brian is in there at the time and he's the one who fucks them off! But they leave him out of the movie. He fucked all those bands off. This is the man who burped in Frank Zappa's face. Zappa is trying to be this far-out dude, trying to outgross Brian, and Brian just burps in his face and walks away."

"People who didn't feel threatened by him got on well with him," notes Kathy Etchingham. "Jimi didn't feel threatened by him and Brian adored Jimi, really respected him. Jimi got a copy of *John Wesley Harding* and wanted to cover 'I Dreamed I Saw St Augustine', but thought it was too personal to Dylan, so he decided to do 'All Along The Watchtower' instead. Jimi phoned Dave Mason and Brian Jones and asked them if they'd like to come and play on it. They came round when we lived in Upper Berkeley Street. Brian could hardly get through the door with this huge sitar. We all piled into this taxi to go over to Olympic Studios – Jimi, me, Dave Mason with this big, I think it was his 12-string, guitar, and Brian and this enormous sitar, sitting like contortionists in this taxi. I remember my feet up on Dave Mason's legs in that taxi. That's the kind of thing you don't forget."

A lot of what has been written about Jones's diminishing talents as a musician just doesn't add up. Someone as suppos- edly washed up as he was wouldn't have been capable of putting together the *Pipes Of Pan At Joujouka* album, a project entered into with all the anthropological fervour of a Samuel Charters or Alan Lomax. Jones's doctoring of the primitive tapes, made on a simple 4-track, is proto-dub masterpiece – something the Stones themselves belatedly recognised when they used the Master Musicians Of Joujouka on the *Steel Wheels* LP in 1989. Neither would a dribbling basket-case with his marbles in his socks have been capable of writing a stunning Cannes-entry film score for Volker Schlondorff's *A Degree Of Murder*. Jimmy Page plays guitar, Nicky Hopkins piano and Kenny Jones drums. Brian Jones plays every instrument he'd ever picked up and got a tune out of. Around this time he also played alto sax on The Beatles' "You Know My Name" and, although few discographies credit him, is probably on "Baby You're A Rich Man" as well.

But for all this innovative extra-curricular activity it was becoming increasingly clear that The Rolling Stones were carrying a passenger. The big screen evidence is up there for all to see in the Jean-Luc Godard film *One Plus One*, with bleary Brian propped up in his corner as "Sympathy For The Devil" evolves without him. In the video for "Jumpin' Jack Flash" he looks like a waxwork effigy of himself. During the sessions for "You Can't Always Get What You Want", a legendary and brutally telling interchange, duly witnessed by Jack Nitzsche, occurred between Jagger and Jones. "What can I play?" says Jones. "I don't know. What can you play?" replies Jagger. On *The Rolling Stones' Rock And Roll Circus*, Jones had faded to silence, his broken wrist necessitating Keith Richards to double up on lead and rhythm guitar on just about everything. And let's not even speculate on what the assembled Lennon/Clapton/Richards supergroup version of "Yer Blues", with its "I feel so suicidal, just like Dylan's Mr Jones", will have done for Brian's paranoia. On *Beggars Banquet* his playing – what little there is – is sober and respectful. Apart from some nice sitar touches on "Street Fighting Man" he is becoming spectral within his own band.

"We carried Brian for quite a long time," says Jagger. "We put up with his tirades, and his not turning up for over a year. So it wasn't like suddenly we just said, 'Fuck you. You didn't turn up for the show, you're out.' We'd been quite patient with him. And he'd just gotten worse and worse. He just didn't want to be in it. He didn't want to come out of this rather sad state."

Nick Kent: "The guy was in a car driving himself at 150 mph at a brick wall, wasn't he? Drugs really did for that guy. They really sliced him up. There were a lot of people who wanted to help him but there were a lot of people who were too cool. Jagger and Charlie were very concerned. They could have fed stories to the press that he was unstable and just got rid of him but they didn't. They were considerate."

Ultimately a decision had to be made. When it emerged in early 1969 that the Stones couldn't tour the States because of Jones's drug convictions the inevitable loomed. "I think he knew, in a way," says Jagger of the final split. "He was quite philosophical about it." Was it a hard thing to do? "Really hard. But it was either that or just going on with someone that was just not functioning. I mean, he was in a really bad state. We couldn't have survived with Brian. He was too ill to play. It was sorrowful."

"I'm sure it nearly killed him when we sacked him 'cos he'd fought so hard to put it all together at the beginning," states Charlie Watts. "It was a huge void in his life, especially being young. If he'd have made 60 million dollars, if he'd had that cushion . . . He had a little bit, but not what people think. But he was very young, you know, so there was a big space of nothing."

Jones had filled that big space of nothing some months earlier by purchasing A. A. Milne's old house at Cotchford Farm in Sussex. He inherited Keith Richards' chauffeur, Tom Keylock, and a motley crew of cowboy builders and their free-loading mates. It was here in an atmosphere of subterfuge and bathos that the final acts of Brian Jones's life were played out. "There was Tom Keylock at the top and it all went out in tiers," says Terry Rawlings. "There was a network of drivers, builders, labourers. The same guys who were working on Redlands. All working class, all in their thirties, all taking as many liberties as they could, borrowing his Rolls-Royce. Seeing him swan around with dolly birds in this beautiful house, there's bound to be resentment."

"The quality of the people who were working as minders and chauffeurs for the Stones wasn't all that it could have been," notes Gered Mankowitz. "I don't think they were great human beings and I don't think Brian was well served at all. It's a pretty horrible job anyway to be a servant. And to see this young bloke with so much going for him, beautiful women, money, fantastic cars, and there he was fucking up and here's the minder having to pick him up, clean him down, put him to bed, or extricate him from some problem. Once you lose respect for the person you're working for I don't think you're going to do your job very well."

"He used to be a lot of fun in the early days," emphasises Charlie Watts. "But when that all went you were left with this rather ill, totally paranoid bloke, worried about his image. But having said that, the period when he died he lived near me in Sussex. I used to see him quite a bit on the way home from the studio and got very close to him again. But then, you know, I was never any threat to him. I didn't play guitar for a start, I was not a singer – both things that he wanted to do – I was not a writer. I was a drummer and if he'd have asked me to play on a record I'd have played with him."

Jones had made tentative unspecified musical plans. Mitch Mitchell, John Mayall, Stevie Winwood, and Alexis Korner had all been down to see him and reported that he was in good spirits and eager to resurrect his career. He had also eased off the substances, too. The Stones, meanwhile, had more pressing concerns, breaking in new guitarist Mick Taylor and rehearsing for their forthcoming free concert in Hyde Park on Saturday, July 5.

"He'd phoned me on the Tuesday before Hyde Park," remembers Shirley Arnold. "After it was announced that he was leaving he was concerned about what the fans thought. I'd said I was sending the post down to him. He was telling me that he was getting things together with Alexis Korner and everything was looking fine. Mick was always asking, 'Have you heard from Brian today?' He was genuinely interested in his welfare and what he was doing. Brian asked me if I'd go and work for him and would it make it awkward with the band? I'd said I'd never leave the office but I'd always help him. He sounded fine. I put the phone down and wrote him a two-page letter telling him what I'd said to him on the phone, that I'd always be there for him."

The following night Shirley was woken in the early hours by the phone ringing. Through the drowsy haze of half-sleep, she recognised the voice of Tom Keylock's wife, Joan. She was saying something about the pool: "Brian hasn't come out . . ." What do you mean?" said Shirley. "He's probably just wandered off somewhere." If only.

"It was dreadful, that next morning in the office," says Shirley Arnold. "Charlie was crying. Mick couldn't speak. I hadn't been to sleep. I got a mini-cab to work at seven o'clock. Driving through the West End and seeing the newspaper signs: 'Brian Jones drowns.' I opened the office and the first phone call was from Yoko Ono to say how sorry she and John were. Then Alexis phoned. Charlie was the first to arrive. He was in such shock that he just walked through into the boardroom without saying anything and sat there crying." It was also Charlie that laughed sardonically at Brian's funeral, when, as the cortege progressed through the crowded streets of Cheltenham, a policeman saluted. "I was surprised when he died," says Charlie. "He was actually getting his house together. He'd be showing me round there and he'd be painting all these walls. In those days purple walls were quite in. It was like one of Jimmy Page's homes, very nouveau."

As far as could be ascertained, Brian had gone for a late-night swim in Cotchford's outdoor heated pool. Those that were present, builder Frank Thorogood, his friend, nurse Janet Lawson, and a friend of Jones, student Anna Wohlin, all gave witness statements. None of them quite tallied. There were significant discrepancies regarding precise details of who was where and doing what when Brian, allegedly alone, went for a midnight swim. Conveniently or otherwise, nobody else was by the pool side when Jones somehow plunged to his death. In his statement Thorogood said he had just popped indoors for a cigarette.

The coroner recorded a verdict of death by misadventure: the cause of death, drowning. The post mortem revealed that both the liver and heart of the deceased were grossly enlarged due to long term alcohol abuse. Although the pathologist's urine test revealed traces of "an amphetamine-like substance", and "diphenhydramine . . . present in Mandrax", Jones's body contained no barbiturates and none of the opiate derivatives consistent with the use of hard drugs. An inhaler had been found at the pool side, leading some to suspect that Jones had suffered an asthma attack, but Pat Andrews never once saw him use his asthma pump, "not even when he got upset after arguments with his parents". Shirley Arnold says she never saw him have an asthma attack either. "Keith says it as well. He never saw him have one." Dr Albert Sachs, who carried out the post-mortem, saw fit to point out that "in death from an asthma attack, lungs are light and bulky", which they hadn't been in Brian Jones's case.

"I assumed he was stoned – he'd been an accident waiting to happen for several years," says Gered Mankowitz. "I wouldn't be surprised if it was accidental death but I don't believe it was murder. I don't see a motive, but Brian solicited resentment. These builders he employed, seeing this bedraggled, longhaired, sozzled pop star. They just thought, 'Fucking wanker.' He probably aggravated somebody. I think there was probably some horseplay that got out of hand. 'I'll teach the little fucker a lesson,' that sort of thing."

Mick Jagger remains totally sceptical about theories that Jones was murdered. "Oh please!" he says dismissively. "I wasn't there. I only know what everyone else says. I have no theories. I only know what I was told at the time, which seemed perfectly reasonable." That he was drinking and that it was an accident? "That all sounded very much par for the course. But who knows what happened? I never questioned it at the time. It sounds all a bit, 30 years after the event, like someone trying to drum up some sort of book or something."

The intrigue over Jones's death has indeed spawned a mini-industry of books. "I think he was definitely killed but I don't think he was meant to die," says Terry Rawlings, whose *Who Killed Christopher Robin?* is, along with Laura Jackson's *Golden Stone*, one of the few credible and painstakingly researched attempts to get to the bottom of what went on that fateful summer night. Rawlings' case hinges on an apparent deathbed confession made by Frank Thorogood to Tom Keylock in 1993. Subsequently, BBC's *Crimewatch* featured the case and new leads were followed up but the case remains unsolved. When Tom Keylock was contacted recently for further verification, he declined to comment, citing a contractual obligation to a forthcoming Brian Jones biopic.

Many of those interviewed for this feature had a "don't put my name to this, but . . ." theory on what went on in the murky waters of Cotchford. Conspiracy theories have continued to resonate down the years. Central to many of these is the idea that there was a party at Cotchford that night and many more people were present than has previously been acknowledged. "I've heard from Amanda Lear that she had been invited to a party at Brian's house and he'd sent a car to pick her up," says Pat Andrews, "but on her way she'd suddenly decided that she was going to see Salvador Dalí instead. So she stopped at Gatwick and sent the car back to Cotchford and got on a plane. She said to me that if she could ever change anything that would be it." Then there are the loony theories. Allen Klein ordered it. The Stones ordered it. Everyone but the badgeman on the grassy knoll seems to have had a hand in it.

"Obviously I don't know what happened but the thing that makes me suspicious was the way people acted afterwards," says Pat Andrews. We comb over the familiar territory. Jones's personal belongings being ransacked from Cotchford. His clothes being burnt. "His bedclothes were burnt, too," she says. "All I do know is that the police didn't do a proper job." Sussex CID continued to treat the death as suspicious, even reopening lines of inquiry six months after Jones drowned, but nothing came of them.

"For a long time everybody was just in shock about it all," says Shirley Arnold, "but I remember much later Keith getting really pissed off and saying 'What the fuck were they burning his clothes for? Why?' But analysing who was there and where they went isn't going to bring him back, is it? It's not going to take the sadness away."

Like Mick Jagger, Charlie Watts remains resolute that there was nothing sinister about the death. "I think he took an overdose. In England it's very rare to have an outdoor pool. The steam would be rising from it and I think he took a load of downers, which is what he used to like, drank, which he used to do and shouldn't have done, 'cos he wasn't strong enough to drink. And I think he went for a swim in a very hot bath. I don't see why you'd bother [murdering him]. He was worth more alive than dead. If you were going to screw him or whatever you'd try and be his manager. Quite honestly, I don't think he was worth murdering. And I don't mean that in a nasty way. I mean he was not that important to murder. Particularly at that time. He was very frail and a rather sad figure. And in a way, maybe if he'd have lived another 20 years he'd have got worse. He'd have been shuffling down the King's Road, you know, a shadow of his former self. Which is horrible. It's better he went how he did. 'Cos we wouldn't be doing this article if he hadn't."

"It's all very sinister and eerie," maintains Terry Rawlings. "There's some very dark corners of the whole story that you can't go into, stuff that I could never have put into my book, how it was done, how it was covered up. The policeman who inherited the original investigation was forever saying to me, 'Your book got pretty close to it but the stuff I could tell you – which I can't – is a book in itself.' But it will all come out eventually."

"The thing I came away with from having read those books was how little drugs were in his system the night he died," says Nick Kent. "And drowning in a swimming pool? I mean, c'mon! It's not like it was in the ocean. It's hard not to think that there was no foul play involved. Keith did an interview in Paris a while back where he said he agreed with the [*Who Killed Christopher Robin?*] book."

"I've seen Brian swim in terrible conditions, in the sea with breakers up to here," Richards told Robert Greenfield in a marathon *Rolling Stone* interview in August 1971. "I've been underwater with Brian in Fiji. He was a goddamn good swimmer. He could dive off rocks straight into the sea." Of his death Richards' response was, "such a beautiful cat, man. He was one of those people who are so beautiful in one way, and such an asshole in another. 'Brian, how could you do that to me, man?' It was like that." Richards has, however, retracted much of that over the years, most famously in a somewhat cathartic *Q* magazine interview in 1987. "I don't think honestly you'll find anyone who liked Brian," he says. "He had so many hang-ups he didn't know where to hang himself. So he drowned himself." In the middle of acknowledging that "I nicked his old lady" and Brian's penchant for "beating chicks up", Richards also finds time to resurrect the hoary old tale from the early days about Jones paying himself an extra £5 as leader of the band. "They still seem to dwell on that after all these years," says David Dalton. "It's incredible." Some dark memories obviously still rankle with Richards.

"When they were rehearsing for the Bridges Over Babylon tour in Toronto, Ron Wood got hold of a couple of Brian's old guitars – the 9-string and the 12-string Teardrops," claims Terry Rawlings. "Ronnie puts one on and he's going, 'Yeah, fucking great. Keith look at this . . .' Keith turns round, goes, 'Take that fucking thing off.' This is last year. Even now, y'know, after all this time."

"I think the highlight of Brian's life wasn't playing in a band that was idolised, it was meeting his idols," says Pat Andrews. "I think he cherished that more than standing in front of screaming girls. He had great respect for his fans, that's why there are so many letters around from Brian because he always answered his fanmail. But I do think he was looking for something else other than adulation."

"My ultimate aim in life was not to be a pop star," Brian Jones says in Peter Whitehead's documentary, *Charlie Is My Darling*, filmed as the Stones toured Ireland in 1965. "I enjoy it – with reservations – but I'm not really satisfied, either artistically or personally."

"He was bright, articulate, gifted, a shining star, but he was a flawed human being," says Gered Mankowitz. "It was pretty sad from '66 onwards and it was a sad end to a sad life. He was very unfulfilled. He had problems and there was nothing anybody could do about them, least of all him."

If "sad" and "sinister" are the only two choices on offer it's a pretty squalid testimonial to a young life that only five years earlier had been so full of promise. At the Hyde Park free concert, which became a requiem mass for Brian, thousands of butterflies were released and Jagger read from Shelley's *Adonais*.

After the loss of their founder the Stones descended into a little darkness of their own. "It was a very dark band anyway," says Jagger of the "Sympathy For The Devil" period. "The band's always been a very dark band." Still? "Yeah, I think so. Definitely." At the end of 1969, at the Altamont Speedway track, they opened another box, but instead of butterflies out flew the Furies. Mick Jagger stood centre-stage, impotently pleading with the Hell's Angels to be cool while his fans were having their faces smashed in with pool cues. Satanic role-playing came face to face with real evil and was found wanting. Somewhere in the melee, nemesis came crashing down on the head of 18-year-old Meredith Hunter as he moved towards the stage, pointing a gun. Just a shot away.

Meanwhile Jimi, Janis and Jim were waiting in the wings ready for their turns on the sacrificial altar. But in Brian Jones the '60s already had its first rock 'n' roll martyr.

Additional interview material: David Sinclair (Mick Jagger and Charlie Watts), Mark Hagen (Keith Richards), Johnny Rogan (Andrew Loog Oldham) and Paul Trynka (Nicky Wright).

LET IT BLEED

Sean Egan

UK release: 5 December 1969; US release: 29 November 1969

Produced by: Jimmy Miller

Charts: UK no. 1; US no. 3

Tracklisting:
Gimme Shelter
Love in Vain
Country Honk
Live with Me
Let It Bleed
Midnight Rambler
You Got the Silver
Monkey Man
You Can't Always Get What You Want

Let It Bleed marked an important milestone: the first time The Rolling Stones' new album was better than The Beatles' latest.

It starts reasonably well: "Gimme Shelter" is quite possibly the greatest recording in the history of rock. This four-and-a-half-minute blast of foreboding (spelt "Gimmie Shelter" on some early pressings) is the "cosmic blues" that Led Zeppelin's music was hailed as but rarely succeeded in being. The track starts tip-toe fashion with some tentative electric picking from Richards. A guiro or "scraper", gentle drum-work, female vocals, a second guitar and piano are incrementally added before, with a skitter of drums and a flare of distortion from Richards' amp, the storm breaks, the band erupting into a sound that is a musical juggernaut, at the head of which is

Jagger howling that a storm is threatening his very life and that fire is sweeping the streets. He is dramatically joined on a chorus that tells us that war is just a shot away by the banshee-like Merry Clayton. The instrumental break sees gigantic mouth harp slash across the broiling landscape followed by similarly colossal guitar lines. Jagger and Clayton then play off each other at an even higher level of intensity, Jagger bellowing her a cry of encouragement and Clayton screaming, "Rape, murder – it's just a shot away!" The third verse is less extreme (it could hardly be more) by virtue of the fact that the narrator offers hope, telling us that love is just a kiss away.

Some feel that the track perfectly sums up the sense of trepidation abroad at the end of a decade that had seen too many overturnings of verities and certainties to be able to assimilate or contextualize. Others have suggested that the song reflected the turmoil in Richards' mind in a period in which he was fearful that he might lose Anita Pallenberg to Mick Jagger: it was rumoured that they had conducted an affair on the set of the film *Performance*, in which they were both starring. In his 2010 autobiography *Life*, Richards rather shrugged off the Anita–Mick affair ("I didn't expect to put any reins on her") and revealed that the song was rooted in nothing less mundane than a London downpour. Of course, it's all of little consequence compared with the music, which will long outlive the memory of whatever served as its stimulus. "Gimme Shelter" is a perfect, blemish-free performance.

The credit "Woody Payne" against "Love in Vain" on early album pressings puzzled some. It was, in fact, a sometime pseudonym (perhaps forcibly imposed by publishing corruption) for Robert Johnson, whose *King of the Delta Blues Singers* was pressed as dearly to Richards' bosom as his copy of *Chuck Berry's Greatest Hits*. "Love in Vain" was to appear on *King of the Delta Blues Singers Vol. II* the following year, but the Stones had clearly heard the bootleg that had recently appeared of the previously uncollected Johnson recordings on which it featured and got their version out smartly. It's rather a pity that their craft did not match their promptness. "Love in Vain" fails in every way that "Prodigal Son" succeeded. Jagger drawls almost buffoonishly, Watts thumps his skins in a manner completely inappropriate for such a lovelorn tune and guest Ry Cooder's mandolin solo is limp. Only the sweet acoustic opening and the overall tone of vulnerability prevent a total disaster.

"Country Honk" underwhelms for a different reason. The track – whose slide work is Mick Taylor's only contribution to the record aside from "Live with Me" – is an acoustic version of "Honky Tonk Women". Although its country stylings are more in the manner of how Richards originally envisaged the song, it feels "off". We will never be able to forget the version we heard first (or, if not first, then more). The band enter into the project wholeheartedly, altering the first verse to have the narrator sitting nestling a jar of beer in Nashville rather than meeting a bar-room queen in Memphis and Jagger executing appropriately understated singing (proving he could have done it on the previous track if he'd wanted). However, in addition to that insurmountable impression of the band stamping over their own sacred ground, there is the issue of Byron Berline's fiddle. Overdubbed when the band were adding the last touches to the record in the States, it grates on the ears. And while the Stones were no doubt not even thinking about this, very unfortunately the reworking puts one in mind of the fact that the previous year The Beatles had similarly issued an acoustic version of a song already famous in an electric arrangement ("Revolution").

Following those two below-average acoustic tracks, the side is brought to a close by a brace of songs that are little more than attempts to play up to the band's outlaw image. "Live with Me" and "Let It Bleed" are both cuts whose lyrics rely for their power on the listener's knowledge of the Stones' history. The band's attempts therein to tweak the nose of straight society would have been exhilarating for the young in 1969. Today, with the Stones' sociopolitical import a thing of history and many of the hypocrisies and injustices alluded to in their lyrics either swept away or reinforced by consensus, the songs are dated. This particularly applies to their mild obscenities and endorsement of sexual licence. With blue language and blue movies now commonplace, their posturing comes across not as the daring provocation it once was but common-or-garden smut.

Even the very title of "Live with Me" was a throwing down of the gauntlet when unwed cohabiting couples were frowned on by parents, the media, the Church and (probably most problematically) landlords. It also had a special resonance in light of the fact that Jagger was known by the public to be shacked up with Marianne Faithfull, a mother of one who was still married to her estranged husband. A genuine fury may have lain behind it. In October 1968, it was announced that Faithfull was pregnant with Jagger's child. The brutal values of the generation in power were perfectly summed up by the fact that the Archbishop of Canterbury responded to the happy news by asking people to say prayers for Faithfull. (She later miscarried.) However, Mick squanders his moral high ground as he delights in painting from his "I got nasty habits" opening onwards a picture that is merely cartoonish, taking in a score of hare-brained, locked-up children and furiously fornicating servants in a chaotic household. Musically, the track is a brawny rocker with thumping piano and a sax solo from Bobby Keyes. The title track is simply a litany of debauchery. The first verse sees the narrator use an obvious vagina metaphor (parking lot) and make a reference to cocaine. Verse two finds him discussing ejaculation. By verse three, a stabbing in cahoots with a junkie has taken place. Dismemberment is then gleefully discussed – by the narrator victim. Several of these developments seem the result of no more thought than what constituted the easiest rhyme. It's like an aural version of the type of cartoon strips to be found in the underground press of the time. That said, although today even a schoolboy might be too embarrassed to savour the subversion of expectation involved in discussing "creaming" rather than "leaning" on someone, the track has aged better than the preceding cut. Despite its obvious origins as a response to the times, its ribald frivolity would have validity – if hardly gravitas – in any era. It's also more musically substantial than "Live with Me", even though far looser in structure: there are many moments of pleasure to be gleaned from Richards' keening guitar, Watts' bullish drums, Ian Stewart's barrelhouse piano and even Jagger's jackass singing.

Side two opens with a track that has dated in a whole other way. It now seems unbelievable that the fact that "Midnight Rambler" is clearly the anthem of a rapist and a murderer

raised few moral qualms at the time of its release. Then, elevat-
ir.g such evil-doing to heroism simply seemed something on
the same continuum as the growing penchant for non-
judgemental motion pictures. Just as the refusal of the film
Bonnie and Clyde (1967) to condemn its criminal protagonists
in black-and-white terms was less an endorsement of their
actions than a denunciation of the Hays Code that had for so
long obligated filmmakers to show the world not as it was but
how certain moral guardians would wish it to be, so "Midnight
Rambler" was another way for Jagger and Co. to stick two
fingers up to the starch-collared overseers of broadcast art.
Although the lyric can still make us shift uncomfortably
despite knowing those mitigating circumstances, there is nothing but pleasure to be gleaned from its music, which is weighted
with delicious dread. A bluesy nocturnal creep, "Midnight
Rambler" sees Richards' splintered guitar tussling with Jagger's
agitated mouth harp over the course of nearly seven minutes
of dramatic swells and respites.

After his cameos on "Something Happened to Me Yesterday" and "Salt of the Earth" as well as innumerable harmony
lines, Keith finally gets a full vocal showcase with "You Got
the Silver". He acquits himself well and surprisingly confi-
dently, doing justice to a beautiful, Romany-flavoured
ballad. The song climbs the scale in intensity from a croon-
ing voice-and-guitar opening to a middle section that glides
on delicate organ work to an uptempo, desperate climax,
but throughout Richards' adoration of his clearly capricious
lover is touching.

Having provided a variety of tone on the album via the
introduction of Richards' pleasantly reedy voice, the Stones
ratchet up that varying effect with the timbre of "Monkey
Man", which has a widescreen gloss more to be expected of a
cinema soundtrack than a rock record. Wyman sets up an
atmospheric aura with vibraphones, an instrument often heard
in suspense films. Jagger's lyric doesn't really chime with this
sophistication, or perhaps plays off it: it seems half a series of
in-jokes between him and Faithfull (the assertion that he was
bitten, gouged and gored by a boar and the comparison of
himself to a sack of broken eggs certainly seem to be the sort

of stuff that would chime with nobody but an intimate) and half more of his living up to Stones caricature (he even sardonically states he hopes "we" are not "a trifle too satanic"). This time, though, the music is too strong to be a fatality of such silliness. Particularly impressive is the elegant and leisurely (a minute and a half) instrumental break.

The album closes almost as impressively as it began with "You Can't Always Get What You Want". The already lengthy five-minute B-side of "Honky Tonk Women" turned out, amazingly, to be a cut-down version of the real thing. Here, it is a seven-and-a-half-minute extravaganza. The London Bach Choir provides an unexpectedly angelic, a cappella rendition of the first verse. One wonders how many of them understood what the word "connection" meant in the context of a number about a man watching in despair as his junkie lover disintegrates before his eyes. The presumably related philosophy of the title phrase can be interpreted as either admirably stoic or tragically resigned. It's possible that the Stones never created any more beautiful a section of music than the passage involving an acoustic guitar working in tandem with a mournful French horn that follows the Bach Choir introduction. Jagger sets the scene of disillusion and dissolution in a heart-meltingly enunciated first verse. An attendance at a demo and a meeting at a store with the mysterious Mr Jimmy in subsequent verses also give rise to the narrator musing that line of philosophy before a final verse in which the drug-addled woman is portrayed as less tragic than predatory. By this time, the song has long metamorphosed from melancholy to funky, with Jagger yelling his lines across a backdrop of sweeping keyboards, supple electric guitar, pulsating congas and soulful female vocals. In all of this, the repeated poised swells of the voices of the London Bach Choir work amazingly well. A quartet of outside helpers deserve a doff of the cap: Jack Nitzsche assisted with the arrangement, Al Kooper was responsible for the French horn and some keyboards, Rocky Dijon provided the exotic percussion and Jimmy Miller – as if his inspiration and ideas from behind the mixing desk were not enough – played drums after Watts couldn't master the rhythm he suggested.

The title of the album, of course, came from the track of that name, but the line doesn't appear – quite – in its lyric. It's clearly an allusion to The Beatles, whose "Let It Be" single did not appear until the following year but was known to be a component of their troubled "Get Back" film/album project (which indeed ending up being renamed *Let It Be*). Though apparently non-malicious, bringing up the Fabs was apposite in the circumstances. Conversations with most musicians will unearth the sentiment – apparently sincere – that although they acknowledge that art can be competitive, it is not competitive in a hierarchal sense: recording artists are anxious to make quality records, not to be considered the top of the tree. Despite a period in the early seventies when Jagger – in a particularly bitchy phase – was wont to slag off The Beatles, the two bands were genuinely friends. In their rarefied roles as pop's aristocracy, they enjoyed providing each other the support and empathy no other human beings really could. Yet the very ego that drove the two bands, and especially their respective songwriting axes, must surely have engendered some small feeling of wanting to outdo each other. Despite the Stones' consistent incremental development, they could hitherto never boast of having done that on a consistent scale. The occasions of their stealing a march on The Beatles had been restricted to the occasional single. Album-wise, the Fab Four had always seemed to have the upper hand.

Whatever the qualities of the first three Stones albums, they largely comprised covers when The Beatles were predominantly self-reliant from the get-go. Although the Stones had made a breakthrough on that score with *Aftermath*, it was released in the same year as The Beatles' dazzling *Revolver*. The very thought of *Satanic Majesties* bearing comparison to the Fabs' *Sgt. Pepper*, meanwhile, was laughable. And while *Beggars Banquet* was a fine album, The Beatles seemed to win the war of '68 simply by overwhelming the consumer with the sprawling "White Album" – this victory, almost by default, exacerbated by the fact that even the accomplishment of the Stones' comeback single, "Jumpin' Jack Flash", was made to seem small in the shadow cast by the Fabs' astonishing "Hey Jude"/"Revolution".

With *Let It Bleed*, the Stones finally broke that duck.

Although by no means a perfect album, its often magnificent music and its apocalyptic visions and sweeping soundscapes made *Abbey Road* – The Beatles' offering that year – seem a little lightweight, both musically and most certainly philosophically. Rumours were already abounding that The Beatles would not survive the decade they had in large part shaped, but should that long-standing Beatles v. Stones debate enter the seventies, for the first time it seemed that it was not a sure thing that the Fabs would continue to win on points.

Let It Bleed's cover art was as quasi-disturbing as some of the album's contents, featuring a record spindle bizarrely stacked with a plate, a tape canister, a tyre, a pizza, a clock and a prettily decorated cake made by a pre-fame Delia Smith. Early pressings came with a free 19 x 21-inch colour fold-out poster of the group.

The LP was released earlier in the States to take commercial advantage of the band's US tour of 7 November–6 December 1969. It was not by any means conducted on the massive scale of future outings, but this was the first Stones tour to be a recognizable version of the efficient, businesslike campaigns of today rather than the almost haphazard and snatched series of dates that had characterized their previous road work. The live circuit had changed much since they had last presented themselves to a concert audience (Hyde Park excepted): rock was beginning to be recognized as a valid business and promoters were starting to show concern for the sound quality and the comfort of audiences. Audiences themselves were also beginning to show concern about such things: no longer were they there to scream through the set. Another noteworthy aspect of the tour was the Stones' evident realization of just how much money they could generate from performing. The counterculture to whom they were figureheads were dismayed at the steepness of their ticket prices. The theory has long been that it was because the Stones were taken aback at denunciations in the likes of the then-alternative *Rolling Stone* that they were prompted belatedly to arrange a free show at the end of the tour. If true, this pricking of conscience backfired horribly. The concert at the Altamont Speedway in California on 6 December was no epiphany like the Monterey or Woodstock festivals, nor a pleasant day in the sunshine like the Hyde Park concert. It being the case that it would have been totally uncool for the Stones to request the police maintain order at the gig, which featured them and Santana, Jefferson Airplane, The Flying Burrito Brothers and Crosby, Stills, Nash & Young, they asked the local Hell's Angels to fulfil the task. However, the London Angels who had policed Hyde Park were toytown compared with the California mob, and much petty violence and harassment of concert-goers ensued, aggravating a crowd already unsettled by the distribution of a bad batch of LSD. That said, the perception of the Angels being the racist murderers of teenager Meredith Hunter is simplistic, and not just because of the not-guilty verdict reached in a subsequent trial. Stones tour manager Sam Cutler has said that however brutal the Angels were, they may have saved Jagger's life when they sprang into pitiless action as a visibly drug-crazed Hunter reached for a gun that, contrary to some reports, was loaded.

The whole nightmarish day was postulated by some (not all of them conservatives) as confirmation that the people whose values the Stones' generation were seeking to supplant with their own might have been right all along. The event (from which the scheduled Grateful Dead fled) seemed almost designed to mock Jagger's pronouncement beforehand that it would "create a microcosmic society which sets an example to the rest of America as to how one can behave in large gatherings". The fact of the concert happening in the last month of the last year of the sixties gave opportunity to symmetry-minded journalists to announce the end of the dreams wrapped up in that decade. It also gave some of them an excuse to vengefully suggest that the band had been singed by the fires of hell around which they had lately been provocatively dancing, with the really lazy ones repeating the line (some to this day) that the band had been playing "Sympathy for the Devil" at the moment of the unfortunate Hunter's demise (it was "Under My Thumb").

The tour had been filmed for a documentary by the Maysles brothers, who in the form of *Gimme Shelter* (released exactly a year after Altamont) got a somewhat more drama-filled end product than they could ever have imagined.

DECCA AND KLEIN BLUES

Sean Egan

The fact that on the bottom of the spindle on the sleeve of *Let It Bleed* there rested a vinyl album, upon whose label was clearly visible both the Stones' and the album's name, suggests the LP was intended to be issued sans additional lettering but that the record company couldn't resist plastering "Rolling Stones" and "Let It Bleed" at the top beside the Decca logo. Pretty soon, the band would not have to put up with such crass imperviousness to artistic intent. The Stones now owed one album and one single A-side to the label whose corporatism had repeatedly rubbed them up the wrong way, after which they would be free to sign to the highest and most solicitous bidder.

The Stones fulfilled their single obligation by delivering into Decca's possession a tape of new songs deliberately of such low fidelity as to be unusable, to which was appended a little ditty that was unusable for different reasons: although it is a cleverly written, minimalistically atmospheric (with just Jagger on vocals and guitar) and intensely sung twelve-bar, "Cocksucker Blues" is the lament of a rent boy trawling London for trade and explaining his experiences in profane detail. Retitled "Schoolboy Blues", it became part of the 1972 play *Trials of Oz* but its only commercial release has been as a bonus single on the eighties German box-set, *Rest of the Best*, that was quickly withdrawn.

In consideration of their outstanding album commitment, the Stones gave Decca *"Get Yer Ya-Ya's Out!"*. It has even been suggested that the Stones sanctioned the release of this live LP to counter the brisk sales of a bootleg featuring one of the concerts of their American tour that had appeared as soon as December '69. Titled *LiveR* [sic] *Than You'll Ever Be*, it was

180   *Sean Egan*

released by Trade Mark of Quality, the shady label who five
months previously had been behind the very first rock bootleg,
the collection of Bob Dylan material that became known as
The Great White Wonder. However, the only logical inference
from the fact that the Stones had gone to the trouble of recording the tour in the first place is that they always intended a live
album.

This text will not be detained too much by Rolling Stones
live product. Their ridiculous proliferation in recent years (in
the 1990s, the band released more in-concert albums than
studio efforts) is one of the dismaying hallmarks of their latter-
day prioritizing of commerce over art. They certainly don't
bear much critical scrutiny. *"Get Yer Ya-Ya's Out!"* – released
in both the UK and US on 4 September 1970 – is a little different in the sense of its exalted, if underserved, reputation.
Rolling Stone's adjudication that it was "the best rock concert
ever put on record" was possibly technically true: rock itself
was still only around fifteen years old and the concept of a
recorded document of a concert was correspondingly younger.
The album's drama-teasing "Midnight Rambler", for instance,
was in a different universe from other in-concert album high-
water marks like the contents of James Brown's *Live at the
Apollo*. However, it suffers from the same problems as any
other live recording. Live albums are essentially a pointless
exercise for anything but money-generating purposes. Nothing can replicate the atmosphere at a concert and nothing but
physical presence can compensate for a sound that will always
be flat compared with layered studio recordings. Then there is
the innate dishonesty of the exercise: no musician is going to
tolerate the wide dissemination of bum notes, out-of-tune
instruments and other imperfections common to live work, yet
once corrections are applied to the tapes in the studio, the live
concept immediately becomes meaningless, thus destroying
even the sentimental benefit of a souvenir for those who were
there on the night of the performance.

None of which prevented the public lapping up *"Get Yer
Ya-Ya's Out!"*. It topped the UK album charts and made no. 6
stateside. The bizarre title was actually taken from that of a
Blind Boy Fuller song. More puzzling is the cover picture of

Charlie Watts jumping joyfully in the presence of a drums-and-guitar-laden donkey. The album was the subject of the very first Stones release with bonus tracks when, in 2009 – two decades after the practice started and a few years after the demise of the compact-disc age that had kicked it off – ABKCO issued a deluxe four-CD edition with an extra disc of Stones performances, a disc of numbers from support acts B. B. King and Ike & Tina Turner and a DVD of Maysles brothers tour footage, accompanied by a thick booklet, all housed in a handsome box.

If the inverted commas/quote marks around the title of *"Get Yer Ya-Ya's Out!"* sought to turn a song title into a catchphrase it was ironic, for in fact the slogans that the album did bequeath were unintentional. One was Jagger's cheered remark at a Watts tattoo, "Charlie's good tonight, inee?" The other came from the start of their first gig at Madison Square Garden on 28 November 1969, when Sam Cutler excitedly babbled in his introduction that the Stones were "The greatest rock 'n' roll band in the world." By now, musical definitions and music itself had shifted since the early sixties, when the Stones had been anxious to emphasize that they were a rhythm-and-blues not a rock-'n'-roll band. Modern rock 'n' roll, or more increasingly "rock", was barely recognizable as having anything to do with either the R & B or early rock 'n' roll that numbered among its roots. It had also become an umbrella title for all rhythm-oriented white popular music. That part of the designation, therefore, was not a source of contention. However, although The Beatles had officially ceased to exist by the time the album was released, when Cutler bestowed that accolade upon the Stones the Fab Four were extant, not to mention The Who, Led Zeppelin and others who could plausibly lay stake to the claim. The Stones probably didn't dictate Cutler's intro – which sounds not only unrehearsed but almost half-hearted – but they effectively endorsed it by including it on the record. If The Beatles had not gone their separate ways, perhaps the phrase would never have taken off, but come 1970 "The greatest rock 'n' roll band in the world" took on a life of its own, adopted by fans and much of the press as The Rolling Stones' rightful title.

Less expensive to shake off than Decca was Allen Klein. The Stones had cause to regret that they had dispensed with Andrew Oldham, who nobody disputes had been both efficient and (post-drugs bust excepted) available. Klein was infuriatingly negligent and incompetent in the way he oversaw their affairs. The state of fury to which he regularly reduced the band was magnified by his frequent absences: a telephone call to his native New York from England in those days cost a small fortune. The alternative of telex was not only a staccato method of communication but their messages often went unanswered. More money had come the Stones' way as a consequence of their retaining Klein's services, but nothing like as much as should have. The 20 per cent of the Stones' income Klein was legitimately owed as their manager would have set him up for life, but he had the kind of mind ruled by dollar signs, not logic. The very rapacious instincts that led him to intimidate, humiliate and outmanoeuvre record companies on the band's behalf also led him illegally to deprive the Stones of money that was rightfully theirs.

Although he engaged in energy-sapping, finances-exhausting legal prevarication, not even Klein could force his unhappy clients to stay with him, even if their freedom came with the astonishing price of having to almost start the new decade from scratch. Part of the deal the Stones reached with Klein that allowed them to issue a press statement on 10 May 1972 that stated his company ABKCO no longer represented them was that Klein ended up with ownership of the master recordings of everything they had recorded during the sixties. Had the Stones not pretended that their following two studio albums *Sticky Fingers* and *Exile on Main St.* were exclusively recorded after they ceased to be his clients, Klein would have ended up with ownership of those, too. As it was, he managed to secure partial ownership of *Sticky Fingers* tracks "Brown Sugar" and "Wild Horses". The Stones never hired another manager, Jagger helming the band's affairs with financial adviser Prince Rupert Loewenstein.

The Stones – Mick and Keith especially – had the potential of future earnings from their existing catalogue and the prospect of an advance against royalties from their next record company, but their debts exceeded their immediately available assets. Their income tax had never been paid – they claim they had been promised it had been – and with a top UK tax rate of 93 per cent they could never earn enough to pay back that debt if they remained in Britain.

Accordingly, they became tax exiles. The concept was still new and those members of the public who were cognizant of it considered it to be wrapped up in greed and lack of patriotism. Accordingly, when the Stones announced in January 1971 that they would be leaving Britain, their publicist Les Perrin said that they were going to France not for the financial space it gained them, but because of their love of the country and its climate, plus an affinity resulting from its being the first continental territory in which they had achieved success.

The band arranged a "Good Bye Britain" tour that took place on 4–14 March 1971, five months after the end of a six-week European tour. The brisk trade in tickets despite their shocking twenty-shilling face value was not just due to the fact that the band had not toured their home country for four and a half years. Headlines had been increasingly asking the question of late, "Could this be the Last Time?" They had every reason to. Jagger had himself said, "I can't see myself doing all this when I'm 30. I'll draw the line, then." What seems a ludicrous statement now was a perfectly understandable sentiment then. Post-Elvis popular music was regarded as a medium for the young. Sinatra, Sammy Davis Jr and even Elvis could ply their trade despite their advancing years, but they had not nailed their colours to the mast of the sixties zeitgeist, which was so bound up in the virtue of youth that one of its tenets was Never Trust Anyone Over Thirty. Also lurking at the back of the band's minds might have been the spectacle of fifties rock 'n' roll idols, who stalked an undignified nostalgia circuit.

Perhaps it was these fears that prompted Jagger to sign up for two movie roles at the close of the sixties, *Performance* and *Ned Kelly*. He was good in the former, a dazzling if self-conscious depiction of an alternative side of London life then rarely spotlit by cinema in which he played a retired, androgynous rock star. He was not so impressive in the latter, a retelling of the legend of Australia's outlaw folk hero, although there were mitigating circumstances in the fact that it was a bad film overall and that his intended co-star Marianne Faithfull attempted suicide in their shared hotel room on the eve of filming, an event roughly concurrent with Jones' funeral. Had the release of *Performance* not been delayed until August 1970 by the movie studio's terror of the picture's sexual frankness, nudity and violence, Jagger's life might have turned out very differently. As *Ned Kelly* appeared first, he was widely ridiculed as a pop star overreaching himself. From then on, with the odd exception, he stuck to his comfort zone.

The producers of *Performance* thought they were getting a Stones soundtrack, but either due to the fallout from the Mick–Anita–Keith triangle or Richards' hatred of co-director Donald Cammell, they just got one song from Jagger (albeit credited to Jagger/Richards as per their business arrangement). "Memo from Turner" is at least top-notch. The instrumentation is surprisingly lumpen – Ry Cooder complements the Stones on slide – but Mick's lyric is a quite extraordinary litany of sexual perversity and violence replete with some deliciously grotesque imagery ("You're the man who squats behind the man who works the soft machine"). This catalogue of disgrace is the real deal and far more deserved space on *Let It Bleed* than some of his more cartoonish efforts in that area. It was released as a Jagger solo single in the UK in November 1970 and reached no. 32.

Although 1970 was a quiet year for the Stones insofar as they released no new studio product, they at the same time seemed to be everywhere, what with the releases of *Ned Kelly*, *Performance*, Godard's *One Plus One/Sympathy for the Devil* and the Maysles' *Gimme Shelter*. Perhaps Jagger took some crumb of comfort from the fact that all this activity, and this confidence in their box-office appeal, hardly indicated that moviemakers or the public were agonizing about the validity of the Stones' continuing existence, whatever their advanced age.

STICKY FINGERS

Sean Egan

UK release: 23 April 1971; US release: 30 April 1971

Produced by: Jimmy Miller

Charts: UK no. 1; US no. 1

Tracklisting:
Brown Sugar
Sway
Wild Horses
Can't You Hear Me Knocking
You Gotta Move
Bitch
I Got the Blues
Sister Morphine
Dead Flowers
Moonlight Mile

5 March 1971 saw the UK release of a new Stones album from Decca. With *Stone Age*, their former label had thrown together an LP that rivalled the worst American albums for arbitrariness. It consisted of album, EP and single tracks. That there were only three A-sides included and that they were by no means the top-selling Stones 45s ("It's All Over Now", "Paint It Black" and "The Last Time") might suggest a lack of cynicism, but the inclusion of four tracks never issued in the UK – "Look What You've Done", "Blue Turns to Grey", "One More Try" and "My Girl" – in turn suggests the opposite, as did the sleeve artwork. As if to demonstrate that the

corporation could deliver a "FuckYou" as emphatic as "Cock-sucker Blues", Decca commissioned a front cover with a graffiti design apparently intended to evoke the conflict between artist and label over the original *Beggars Banquet* jacket design. The band were incensed. A month before the compilation's release date, they took out full-page advertise-ments in all the British music weeklies effectively asking their fans not to buy it because, "It is, in our opinion, below the standard we try to keep up, both in choice of content and cover design." Their public outrage seems not to have worked: *Stone Age* made no. 4 in the UK charts and there would be several more fatuous Stones compilations from Decca over the following years, often timed to ride the publicity wave of a new Stones record or film.

The real Stones album of the year was *Sticky Fingers*. It was the inaugural long-playing release of their own label, distrib-uted by Warner-Elektra-Atlantic. Although The Beatles v. Stones debates had been rendered a thing of history by the Fab Four's demise, no doubt some Beatles fanatics were tartly observing that Apple had beaten Rolling Stones Records to the punch by three years.

The inaugural single release of Rolling Stones Records was "Brown Sugar" on 16 April 1971 in the UK and the following day in the States. While the American version had the normal one song on the flip – "Bitch" – the fashion of the day in Brit-ain dictated that it be a "maxi-single". Although the wisdom of squeezing an additional number on to seven-inch vinyl was audibly suspect – sound quality suffered – the British fans were presumably happy enough to be the recipients of a rough-and-ready version of Chuck Berry's "Let It Rock" recorded on the "Good Bye Britain" tour. The early pressings came in an extraordinary picture bag in which the band made the most in their poses of the fact that the sleeve of their immi-nent album featured a bejeaned man's crotch – complete with real zip – and backside. (Banned as too risqué in Spain, it was bizarrely replaced there by an unsettling design involving a woman's fingers in a just-opened can of treacle.)

The record's yellow label saw the first appearance of the lip-and-tongue image that was the band's new logo.

Befuddlingly, two different people – Ernie Cefalu and John Pasche – have come out with conflicting but equally plausible-sounding stories about having created it. Regardless of its provenance, the logo is superb. Without using the Stones' name, it instantly conjures them, or at least Jagger, as well as a certain lasciviousness that is the Stones' own. Although the logo was by definition an adjunct of the unavoidably increasing business-orientation of the group, that very lasciviousness prevents it looking corporate. It quickly and deservedly became the most famous logo in the history of popular music.

As for the actual song, "Brown Sugar" is where Jagger assumed a role as Richards' equal. Back in 1965, Allen Klein – evidently no pop consumer – had asked Oldham, "Andrew, who makes the records?" In replying, "Keith does", Oldham may have been doing nothing more than answering the question accurately if simplistically, but it still constituted an almost shocking dismissal of Jagger's lyrics and singing. Although he will always be behind Richards in sheer musicality – not least because he has many other interests than music – Jagger had by 1969 picked up more than just a few guitar chords from his colleague. "Brown Sugar" was naturally finessed by the Stones and probably Richards especially, but there is no dispute that the fine melody, famous riff and infamous lyric are essentially all Mick.

Adding to Jagger's woes when filming *Ned Kelly* Down Under in mid-1969 was the hostility towards his long-haired presence by a then very conservative country and outrage that a pom was presuming to play Australia's national hero. If there was one good thing to come out of Jagger's awful experience it was the traditional film set downtime that enabled him to begin strumming away on what began life as "Black Pussy". By the US tour at the end of '69, he was telling Stanley Booth that although he had nothing written down yet he had a few words in his head for a song "about a woman who screws one of her black servants". When the Stones came to record the track at Alabama's Muscle Shoals studio on December 1969, Jagger – according to the recollection of musician Jim Dickinson – simply wrote out the lyric he had spinning in his head in forty-five minutes.

By now the lyric was not about a woman screwing one of her black servants but more about a slaver taking his pleasure with a female in his charge. If it had been written in modern times it would seem a challenge to political correctness and even in 1971 it was eyebrow-raising to say the least. However, it's too cartoonish to be offensive, and Jagger is insulated from criticism to some extent by the plain fact that he is no racist. It also should not be forgotten that the song's sexual frankness placed it on the side of progressivism: the generation that had availed themselves of the contraceptive pill might now take pre-marital intercourse for granted, but they remained perturbing concepts for the age group in power. Also not to be underestimated, of course, are the quality of both words ("Lady of the house wondering where it's going to stop") and music (adorably scruffy and rousingly anthemic).

Although it begins and is underpinned by a brusque, staccato electric guitar riff, "Brown Sugar" is propelled by strummed acoustic guitar. Further evidence of nuance is the exotic percussion distinct to Muscle Shoals. Bobby Keyes executes a sax solo that is not only an instrumental break but a curtain-raiser for the second act: following it, a piano crashes in to intensify the atmosphere for a final and joyous verse. The track has a slightly awkward close, seeming to lurch on for a bar too long prior to its clean ending, although that is also consistent with that agreeable slovenliness.

Dawn's "Knock Three Times" kept "Brown Sugar" at no. 2 in the UK for three consecutive weeks, but the record did make it to no. 1 on the other side of the Atlantic. It was a mini-comeback and one possibly just as important as "Jumpin' Jack Flash". Although decades are perfectly understood to be artificial constructs, they still hold a spell for the human mind. "The end of the sixties" was not just a matter of calendar, it was a philosophical debate of the time. It prompted rumblings about how long the Stones could possibly keep going, an issue intensified by The Beatles calling it a day in 1970 and Bob Dylan having gone soft and domesticated. The idea of The Rolling Stones being a viable proposition in this new decade called the seventies was something with which even some sympathizers had a problem. There was no precedent by which people's points of view could be guided: no band had ever lasted this long and no musical act had continued to be "relevant", i.e. not nostalgia-peddling and not hived off to the sort of "all-round entertainer" area inhabited by Sinatra and Presley – where record sales mattered less than media presence – after such a lifespan. The artistic triumph and commercial success of "Brown Sugar" stated unequivocally that there was still a place for the Stones in the popular music firmament, and not a minor one either.

That its parent album made the same point was possibly even more important. That year, Richards expressed surprise that *Sticky Fingers* had sold more copies than "Brown Sugar". This man who had once been tasked with delivering a regular seven-inch manifesto was showing his age. Although such manifestoes might still be necessary for younger acts, for a band of the Stones' monumental stature, a single need now only be a means by which to promote an LP, purchase of which rising living standards had made possible for so many more people since the Stones had started out, a process accelerated by the fact that their original fans had long graduated from pocket money to a wage. Accordingly, having always insisted on a complete demarcation – at least in their homeland – between 45 and 33 rpm product, the Stones would henceforth fall into line with the new marketing approach of the music industry. "Honky Tonk Women" was not just the last Stones 45 of the sixties but also their final standalone single.

Sticky Fingers is an album that once again defies expectations raised by the Stones' reputation as a kick-arse rock-'n'-roll band. They certainly are that in places, but most of the songs are slow and several are ballads. The social commentary that had characterised parts of *Beggars Banquet* and (less overtly) *Let It Bleed* is not in evidence, although in one sense they continue where they left off: the sense of decay, ennui, resignation and chemical intoxication that laced "You Can't Always Get What You Want" abounds in these grooves. This was the music of decadent men, rich and idle enough to be utterly absorbed by their own romantic dramas and drug habits. By some bizarre form of osmosis – either that or simple coincidence – the music sounds as stoned as the lyrics, the instrumentation possessing a quality of raggedy lethargy despite managing to consistently remain brilliant. This even extends to the maladroit way the otherwise excellent Jimmy Miller mixes the guitar solos, rendering them as almost background noise instead of the traditional centrepiece. This is not to say that this or the fact that they were now domiciled in the exotic climes of the South of France made the Stones suddenly seem Establishment. Dirty, scruffy rock was still two fingers held up to orthodoxy. That and the audacious multiple drug references only four years after the Jagger, Jones and Richards drug trials marked them as rebels to the core, possibly the most influential in the world at the time.

"Sway" follows opener "Brown Sugar". Jagger plays rhythm on a track on which Richards doesn't appear. In contrast to the narcissism of the opener, "Sway" is a song of vulnerability. Although the lament that the "demon life" is what has him in its sway fits in with the LP's overall morning-after bleariness – as does the circular, woozy music – the narrator also movingly posits love as the solution to his ills. The country-inflected "Wild Horses" was started by Richards – melody and title phrase – as a song for Pallenberg at a time when she had just become the mother of his son Marlon and he was torn by the fact that he was required to go on tour. It was finished by Jagger, whose mind, it has been variously claimed, was distraught over the fact that his own lady had gone off with another man or was in a coma after taking her overdose in Australia, although he has denied the song has anything to do with Faithfull. The only flaw in this ballad of devotion is that it outstays its welcome: what starts as heart-melting becomes, over the course of more than five and a half minutes, tiresome. The song was chosen as the second American single from the album, issued on 12 June with "Sway" on its flipside. It effected the usual so-so chart performance – no. 28 – for a second single, securing less airplay because its release was not an event presaging the excitement of a new LP and fewer sales because so many people already had it on the album.

With the sprawling, strutting, grimy-riffed "Can't You Hear Me Knocking" the world gets what it didn't yet know was the apotheosis of the Mick Taylor years. Jagger is beseeching a woman by whose satin shoes, plastic boots, cocaine eyes and speed-freak jive he is intoxicated. The choppy, cranked-up riff that Richards maintains where he is not hammering out the vocal melody line is surely what made WEA include the rather nervous liner note wherein the listener was informed that the occasional distortion on the guitars was not a technical fault. Approaching the three-minute mark, the track turns from a song into a jam. As with *Aftermath*'s "Goin' Home", the band kept playing after the musician's indefinable but logical stopping point. Although the ensuing vocal-less, Santana-like four-and-a-half-minute "blow" is agreeable, it doesn't seem to have much to do with what has preceded it, featuring none of the motifs of the first act. Nonetheless, the track shows that the Stones could fit in with the musical fashion of extemporization and do it with far more visceral power than the bombastic likes of King Crimson or Emerson, Lake and Palmer.

Side one closed with an example of what was by now a Stones tradition: a cover that seemed designed to insist that they hadn't forgotten their blues roots. "You Gotta Move" was a Mississippi Fred McDowell the-Lord-takes-rich-and-poor-alike gospel number written with Gary Davis. The Stones produce a yowling performance with Richards on National Steel guitar and Taylor on slide.

Side two opens with a bang, "Bitch" being a fast-clipped affair with a dynamite brass riff. Bizarrely, radio stations that had no problem with giving "Brown Sugar" heavy rotation declined to play this song even though the bitch of the title is love, about whose senses-shredding qualities the narrator is loudly and often amusingly complaining. "I Got the Blues", as with the previous track, features sublime saxophone and trumpet contributions from Bobby Keys and Jim Price respectively, but otherwise the two songs are vastly contrasting. "I Got the Blues" is a sedate, grand and polished exercise in humility. The narrator is wishing his departed lover well in the arms of another, although not without evident pain, which itself seems manifested in an extraordinary shrieking organ solo from Billy Preston.

"Sister Morphine" is a Jagger/Richards/Marianne Faithfull composition, though Faithfull's credit for her (Mick says small) contribution was left off early pressings in a chivalrous act by Jagger and Richards to ensure that her royalties were not diverted to a manager with whom she was in dispute. Recorded before Mick Taylor joined the band, it features Ry Cooder on slide. To a gothic backdrop, the song explores the strange irony of the fact that patients in agony find inappropriate ecstasy in the drugs they are prescribed to alleviate their suffering. Miller does a sterling job, making Jack Nitzsche's piano sound like heavy chimes and adding the appropriate touches of echo on a spooky creation ("Why does the doctor have no face?").

Country star Gram Parsons (whose version of "Wild Horses" appeared before the Stones') would have been proud to put his name to "Dead Flowers", in which Dartford's finest execute country and western as if they were Nashville-born. Taylor picks a snaking guitar line and Watts and Wyman get that easy-rolling rhythm down pat. This being the Stones, though, it is country seen through a singular prism in a remarkably mean-spirited song that is a hate letter from a poverty-stricken drug casualty to a rich ex-beau.

The album closes with the six-minute, dreamlike "Moonlight Mile" – another Richards no-show – where Jagger articulates the age-old musician's road-weary complaint with some imagination ("Made a rag pile of my shiny clothes") to a backing that includes raindrop piano and sweeping strings and wind orchestration in possibly the most impressionistic Stones track ever released.

Decca, who could have had this magnificent album had they only treated the Stones like the valuable asset they were, were reduced on 25 June to the release of a maxi-single that played at 33⅓ rpm featuring "Street Fighting Man" on the A-side and "Surprise Surprise" – never issued in Britain before – on the flipside. They could have elected to include the different, shorter, US-only version of "Everybody Needs Somebody to Love" as the other track, but that would have taken nous or interest, the presence of the opener from *The Rolling Stones No. 2* indicating they had neither. The single made no. 21 anyway.

Decca cranked up their contempt for the consumer on 27 August 1971 with the release of *Gimme Shelter*. The album clearly sought to cash in on the UK release of the celebrated movie of the same name but carefully included a note stating that the contents had nothing to do with the Maysles' work. It featured half of the contents of the US-only *Got Live If You Want It!* LP but, as though drawing back in horror at the thought of serving a useful function for the Stones completist, Decca neglected to include the other half, instead throwing on the other side six studio tracks from 1968 and 1969 (including "Gimme Shelter") already available in Britain. The paranoia about the spite of "The Man" that was rife in this era can't help but seem justified in this case. There were enough purchasers to send it to no. 19.

A somewhat more worthy compilation appeared – in the US only – on 11 January 1972 in the form of *Hot Rocks 1964–1971*, technically the Stones' first double album even if it had nothing to do with them. Allen Klein won an injunction temporarily preventing London Records from releasing it on the grounds that it compromised a set he was planning of the same title and nature, but in the end it was issued via that label. It was a fine collection of music and right up to date, courtesy of Klein laying shared claim to "Brown Sugar" and "Wild Horses".

Rolling Stone *magazine partly took its title from the Stones (Muddy Waters' song and Dylan's "Like a Rolling Stone" being the other subjects of hat-tipping). It was appropriate then that in the form of Robert Greenfield's 1971 sprawling feature on Keith Richard (still no "s" on his surname) the magazine offered what was then and remains now the best interview with any of the band ever published.*

Greenfield spoke to Richards just before the sessions at Villa Nellcôte, the South of France mansion rented by the guitarist and family, that would ultimately result in the album Exile on Main St. *The way Richards has assumed the role of fans' favourite makes Greenfield seem prescient in interviewing him at a time when Jagger was far more the epitome of the Stones to the public but in fact he reveals, "I did not choose Keith. I was given the assignment by [*Rolling Stone *editor] Jann Wenner who had fixed it up with Marshall Chess [president of Rolling Stones Records]." Greenfield was lucky to acquire an in-depth interview at a point in time when Richards had not granted many and was therefore evidently eager to talk. Equally fortunate was the fact that events were still fresh in Richards' mind but at the same time were distant enough for him to have acquired perspective on them. What also can't be underestimated as a factor contributing to his candour is that celebrities like him were still flush with their liberation to be frank with the press: up until only four or five years previously, even the Stones had felt obliged to largely stick to show-business banality and decorum. Then there is the happy leeway that* Rolling Stone *granted the author in regards to length.*

Greenfield, though, makes his own luck. Richards doesn't always get his facts right (his voice did not first appear solo in the opening verse of "Salt of the Earth") and is economical with the truth about how Jones left the band (presenting it as a resignation). Moreover, that Greenfield is American creates a small problem. British antennae will occasionally twitch in suspicion of a mishearing (Keith almost certainly said "they're just old lags" rather than the printed "lads"). However, Greenfield teases out of the guitarist fine detail about the history of the band, the members' backgrounds and drug use never previously touched upon or imagined, and asks fairly tough questions about Altamont and potentially irresponsible drug references in Stones songs.

The published interview immediately created a lodestar that every future Stones biographer was able to employ to navigate through their story. Greenfield now says about Richards, "What surprised me was how completely open and honest he seemed in answering everything I asked him." Several thousand words have sometimes been excised from this much-circulated feature. This is a rare uncut reprint.

The argot – man, cat, bread, gas, scene, etc. – is dated but that goes with the territory in a snapshot of Richards at a point in time marking his full rooster-headed, bell-bottomed, scarf-trailing, drug-use-flaunting, iconic glory.

THE *ROLLING STONE* INTERVIEW: KEITH RICHARD

Robert Greenfield

First published in *Rolling Stone*, August 1971

Keith plays in a rock & roll band. Anita is a movie star queen. They currently reside in a large white marble house that everyone describes as "decadent looking." The British Admiral who built it had trees brought from all over the world in ships of the line, pine and cypress and palm. There is an exotic colored bird in a cage in the front garden and a rabbit called Boots that lives in the back. A dog named Oakie sleeps where he wants.

Meals are the only recurring reality and twenty-three at a table is not an unusual number. The ceilings are thirty feet from the floor and some nights, pink lightning hangs over the bay and the nearby town of Villefrance, which waits for the fleet to come back so its hotels can turn again into whore-houses.

There is a private beach down a flight of stairs and a water bed on the porch. Good reference points for the whole mise-en-scène are F. Scott Fitzgerald's Tender Is The Night *and the Shirelles' greatest hits. There is a piano in the living room and guitars in the TV room. Between George Jones, Merle Haggard, Buddy Holly, and Chuck Berry, Keith Richard manages to sneak in a lick now and then like a great acoustic version of "The Jerk" by the Larks one morning at 4 a.m.*

A recording studio will soon be completed in the basement and the Stones will go to work on some tracks for the new album, Mick Jagger having returned from his honeymoon. They will tour the States soon.

Most of it is in the tapes, in the background. Two cogent statements, both made by Keith, may be kept in mind while reading the questions and answers (which were asked and answered over a ten-day period at odd hours).

"It's a pretty good house; we're doing our best to fill it up with kids and rock 'n' roll."

"You know that thing that Blind Willie said? 'I don't like the suits and ties? They don't seem to harmonize.'"

What were you doing right at the beginning?

I was hanging out at art school. Yeah. Suburban art school. I mean in England, if you're lucky you get into art school. It's somewhere they put you if they can't put you anywhere else. If you can't saw wood straight or file metal. It's where they put me to learn graphic design because I happened to be good at drawing apples or something. Fifteen . . . I was there for three years and meanwhile I learned how to play guitar. Lotta guitar players in art school. A lot of terrible artists too. It's funny.

Your parents weren't musical?

Nah. My grandfather was. He used to have a dance band in the Thirties. Played the sax. Was in a country band in the late Fifties, too, playin' the US bases in England. Gus Dupree . . . King of the Country Fiddle. He was a groove, y'know . . . a good musician . . . He was never professional for more than a few years in the Thirties.

What did your father do?

He had a variety of professions. He was a baker for a while. I know he got shot up in the First World War. Gassed or something.

Were you raised middle class?

Working class. English working class . . . struggling, thinking they were middle class. Moved into a tough neighborhood when I was about ten. I used to be with Mick before that . . . we used to live close together. Then I moved to what they'd call in the States a housing project. Just been built. Thousands and thousands of houses, everyone wondering what the fuck was going on. Everyone was displaced. They were still building it and really there were gangs everywhere. Coming to Teddy Boys. Just before rock and roll hit England. But they were all waiting for it. They were practicing.

Were you one of the boys?

Rock and roll got me into being one of the boys. Before that I just got me ass kicked all over the place. Learned how to ride a punch. It's strange, 'cause I knew Mick when I was really young . . . five, six, seven. We used to hang out together. Then I moved and didn't see him for a long time. I once met him selling ice creams outside the public library. I bought one. He was tryin' to make extra money.

Rock and roll got to England about '53, '54, you were eleven . . .

Yeah. Presley hit first. Actually, the music from *Blackboard Jungle*, "Rock Around the Clock," hit first. Not the movie, just the music. People saying, "Ah, did ya hear that music, man." Because in England, we had never heard anything. It's still the same scene: BBC controls it.

Then, everybody stood up for that music. I didn't think of playing it. I just wanted to go and listen to it. It took 'em a year or so before anyone in England could make that music. The first big things that hit were skiffle – simple three chord stuff. It wasn't really rock and roll. It was a lot more folky, a lot more strummy. Tea chest basses. A very crude sort of rock and roll. Lonnie Donegan's the only cat to come out of skiffle. But we were really listening to what was coming from over the Atlantic. The ones that were hitting hard were Little Richard and Presley and Jerry Lee Lewis. Chuck Berry was never really that big in England. They dug him but . . . all his big big hits made it . . . but maybe because he never came over. Maybe because the movies he made like *Go Johnny Go* never got over because of distribution problems. Fats Domino was big. Freddie Bell and the Bellboys too; all kinds of weird people that never made it in America.

They loved the piano. Looking back on it, all the piano boys really had it together for England. More than just the cat that stood there with the guitar.

Did you start really playing in school then?

Yeah. It's funny going back that far. Things come through but . . . I'll tell you who's really good at pushing memories: Bill. He's got this little mind that remembers everything. I'm sure it's like he rolls a tape.

How things were at the start is something. It's when everybody's got short hair. And everybody thought it was long. That's the thing. I mean, we were really being put down like shit then for having long hair. Really. Now, people go into offices with longer hair. When I went to art school, people were just startin' to grow their hair and loosen up. You got in there on the favors of the headmaster. You go there and show him your shit, the stuff you've done at ordinary school, during art lessons, and he decides. You don't have to do anything apart from going to see him. He says, "You takin' anything? What are you on?" And you're about 15 or 16 and you don't even know what the fuck they do in art school. You have this vague picture of naked ladies sittin' around. Drawing them . . . well, I'll try that.

So you go there and you get your packet of Five Weights [cigarettes] a day. Everybody's broke . . . and the best thing that's going on is in the bog [toilet] with the guitars. There's always some cat sneaked out going through his latest Woody Guthrie tune or Jack Elliot. Everybody's into that kind of music as well. So when I went to art school I was thrown into that end of it too. Before that I was just into Little Richard. I was rockin' away, avoidin' the bicycle chains and the razors in those dance halls. The English get crazy. They're calm, but they were really violent then, those cats. Those suits cost them $150, which is a lot of money. Jackets down to here. Waistcoats. Leopardskin lapels . . . amazing. It was really "Don't step on mah blue suede shoes." It was down to that.

I really, literally, got myself thrown out of school. I was livin' at home but I had to go every day. When you think that kids, all they really want to do is learn, watch how it's done and try and figure out why and leave it at that. You're going to school to do something you wanna do and they manage to turn the whole thing around and make you hate 'em. They really manage to do it. I don't know anyone at that school who liked it or anyone my age who liked to be at school. One or two people who went to a decent school had a good teacher, someone who really knew how to teach. The nearest thing I been to it is Wormwood Scrubs [an English prison] and that's the nick. Really, it's the same feeling.

So you spent three years there and it was coming to degree time . . .

That's when they got me. It was 1958, they chucked me out. It's amazing – Lennon, all those people, were already playing. I hadn't really thought about playing. I was still just jivin' to it. I went straight into this art school, and I heard these cats playin', heard they were layin' down some Broonzy songs. And I suddenly realized it goes back a lot further than just the two years I'd been listenin'. And I picked up the nearest guitar and started learnin' from these cats. I learned from all these amateur art school people. One cat knew how to play "Cocaine Blues" very well, another cat knew how to play something else very well. There were a lot better guitar players at school than me.

But then I started to get into where it had come from. Broonzy first. He and Josh White were considered to be the only living black bluesmen still playing. So let's get that together, I thought, that can't be right. Then I started to discover Robert Johnson and those cats. You could never get their records though. One heard about them. On one hand I was playing all that folk stuff on the guitar. The other half of me was listenin' to all that rock and roll, Chuck Berry, and sayin' yeah, yeah.

And one day, I met Jagger again, man. Of all places, on the fucking train. I was going to the school and he was going up to the London School of Economics. It was about 1960. I never been able to get this one together, it's so strange. I had these two things going and not being able to plug 'em together, playing guitar like all the other cats, folk, a little blues. But you can't get the sounds from the States. Maybe once every six months someone'll come through with an album, an Arhoolie album of Fred McDowell. And you'd say: There's another cat! That's another one. Just blowin' my mind, like one album every six months.

So I get on this train one morning and there's Jagger and under his arm he has four or five albums. I haven't seen him since the time I bought an ice cream off him and we haven't hung around since we were five, six, ten years. We recognized each other straight off. "Hi, man," I say. "Where ya going?" he says. And under his arm, he's got Chuck Berry and Little Walter, Muddy Waters. "You're into Chuck Berry, man, really?" That's a coincidence. He said, "Yeah, I got few more albums. Been writin' away to this, uh, Chess Records in Chicago and got a mailing list thing and . . . got it together, you know?" Wow, man!

So I invited him up to my place for a cup of tea. He started playing me these records and I really turned on to it. We were both still living in Dartford, on the edge of London and I was still in art school.

There was another cat at art school named Dick Taylor, who later got the Pretty Things together. Mick found out – "Oh, you play?" he said to me. That's what amazed him. Mick had been singin' with some rock and roll bands, doin' Buddy Holly . . . Buddy Holly was in England as solid as Elvis. Everything came out was a record smash number one. By about '58, it was either Elvis or Buddy Holly. It was split into two camps. The Elvis fans were the heavy leather boys and the Buddy Holly ones all somehow looked like Buddy Holly.

By that time, the initial wham had gone out of rock and roll. You were getting "By The Light of The Silvery Moon" by Little Richard and "My Blue Heaven" by Fats, "Baby Face." They'd run out of songs in a way, it seemed like. England itself was turning on to its own breed of rock and rollers. Cliff Richard at the time was a big rocker. Adam Faith. Billy Fury, who did one fantastic album that I've lost. He got it together once.

One really good album. Songs he'd written, like people do now, he got some people he knew to play together and did it. His other scene was the hits, heavy moody ballads and the lead pipe down the trousers. They were all into that one.

To get back to Mick and I . . . He found out that I could play a little and he could sing a bit. "I dig to sing," he said, and he also knew Dick Taylor from another school they'd gone to and the thing tied up so we try and do something. We'd all go to Dick Taylor's house, in his back room, some other cats would come along and play, and we'd try to lay some of this Little Walter stuff and Chuck Berry stuff. No drummer or anything. Just two guitars and a little amplifier. Usual back room stuff. It fell into place very quickly.

Then we found Slim Harpo, we started to really find people. Mick was just singing, no harp. And suddenly in '62, just when we were getting together, we read this little thing about a rhythm and blues club starting in Ealing. Everybody must have been trying to get one together. "Let's go up to this place and find out what's happening." There was this amazing old cat playing harp . . . Cyril Davies. Where did he come from? He turned out to be a panel beater from North London. He was a great cat, Cyril. He didn't last long. I only knew him for about two years and he died.

Alexis Korner really got this scene together. He'd been playin' in jazz clubs for ages and he knew all the connections for gigs. So we went up there. The first or the second time Mick and I were sittin' there Alexis Korner gets up and says, "We got a guest to play some guitar. He comes from Cheltenham. All the way up from Cheltenham just to play for ya."

Suddenly, it's *Elmore James*, this cat, man. And it's *Brian*, man, he sittin' on his little . . . he's bent over . . . da-da-da, da-da-da . . . I said, what? What the fuck? Playing bar slide guitar.

We get into Brian after he finishes "Dust My Blues." He's really fantastic and a gas. We speak to Brian. He'd been doin' the same as we'd been doin' . . . thinkin' he was the only cat in the world who was doin' it. We started to turn Brian on to some Jimmy Reed things, Chicago blues that he hadn't heard. He was more into T-Bone Walker and jazz-blues stuff. We'd turn him on to Chuck Berry and say, "Look, it's all the same shit, man, and you can do it." But Brian was also much more together. He was in the process of getting a band together and moving up to London with one of his many women and children. God knows how many he had. He sure left his mark, that cat. I know of five kids, at least. All by different chicks, and they all look like Brian.

He was a good guitar player then. He had the touch and was just peaking. He was already out of school, he'd been kicked out of university and had a variety of jobs. He was already into living on his own and trying to find a pad for his old lady. Whereas Mick and I were just kicking around in back rooms, still living at home.

I left art school and I didn't even bother to get a job. We were still kids. Mick was still serious, he thought he was, everyone told him he ought to be serious about a career in economics, He was very much into it.

But Brian, he was already working at it. We said, "We're just amateurs, man, but we dig to play." He invited me up to listen to what he was getting together in some pub in London. It's then it starts getting into back rooms of pubs in Soho and places. That's where I met Stew [Ian Stewart]. He was with Brian. They'd just met. He used to play boogie-woogie piano in jazz clubs, apart from his regular job. He blew my head off too, when he started to play. I never heard a white piano like that before. Real Albert Ammons stuff. This is all '62.

A lot of these old cats had been playin' blues in those clubs for ages, or thought they were playin' blues. Just because they'd met Big Bill Broonzy at a party or played with him once, they thought they were the king's asshole.

Music was their love. They all wanted to be professional but in those days a recording contract was a voice from heaven, it was that rare. Not like now when you get a band together and hustle an advance. It was a closed shop.

Were you and Mick and Brian very strange for them?

That's right. They couldn't figure us out. Especially when I tried to lay Chuck Berry shit on them. "What are ya hangin' with them rock and rollers for?" they'd ask. Brian kicked a lot of them out and I really dug it. He turned around and said, "Fuck off, you bastards, you're a load of shit and I'm going to get it together with these cats." This cat Dick Taylor shifted to bass by then. We were really looking for drums. Stew drifted with us for some reason. I sort of put him with those other cats because he had a job. But he said no too. "I'll stick around and see what happens with you."

So we got another back room in a different pub. Competition. Not that anybody came. Just rehearsin'.

Stew at that time used to turn up at rehearsals in a pair of shorts, on his bike. His piano used to be by the window and his biggest fear, the only thing that really stopped him at piano, was the thought that his bike might get nicked while he was playin'. So every now and then when someone walked past his bike, he'd stretch up and put his head out the window and keep playin', sit down again and then he'd see someone else lookin' at his bike. Up and up, still playin'.

Were you playing electric then?

Yeah. With homemade amps, old wireless sets. It took a while longer to get the electric bit together. At the time we thought, "Oh, it just makes it louder," but it ain't quite as simple as that.

Brian was the one who kept us all together then. Mick was still going to school. I'd dropped out. So we decided we got to live in London to get it together. Time to break loose. So everybody left home, upped and got this pad in London, Chelsea.

Different Chelsea than now?

Edith Grove. World's End. That place . . . every room got condemned slowly. It was like we slowly moved till we were all in the end room. Every room was shut up and stunk to hell, man. Terrible. Brian's only possession was a radio-record player. That, and a few beds and a little gas fire. We kept on playin', playin', playin'.

Brian kicked his job. He was in a department stare. He got into a very heavy scene for nickin' some bread and just managed to work his way out of it. So he thought, "Fuck it. If

I work any more I'm gonna get in real trouble." Get into jail or something.

He only nicked two pound . . . but he quit his job and his old lady had gone back to Cheltenham so he was on the loose again.

Are you gigging?

We didn't dare, man, we didn't dare. We were rehearsin' drummers. Mick Avery came by, the drummer of the Kinks. He was terrible, then. Couldn't find that off beat. Couldn't pick up on that Jimmy Reed stuff.

Is everybody still straight?

It was very hard to find anything. No one could afford to buy anything anyway. A little bit of grass might turn up occasionally but . . . everybody'd dig it . . . everybody's turn-on was just playing. It didn't matter if you were pissed. That was it. That was the big shot.

Mick was the only one who was still hovering because he was more heavily committed to the London School of Economics and he was being supported by a government grant, and his parents and all that. So he had a heavier scene to break away from than me because they were very pleased to kick me out anyway. And Brian too, they were glad to kick out. From university for making some chick pregnant or something.

Brian and I were the sort of people they were glad to kick out. They'd say, "You're nothing but bums, you're gonna end up on skid row," and that sort of thing. Probably will anyway, but Mick was still doing the two things. Brian and me'd be home in this pad all day tryin' to make one foray a day to either pick up some beer bottles from a party and sell 'em back for thruppence deposit or raid the local supermarket. Try and get some potatoes or some eggs or something. I went out one morning and came back in the evening and Brian was blowing harp, man. He's got it together. He's standin' at the top of the stairs sayin', "Listen to this." *Whooooow. Whooow.* All these blues notes comin' out. "I've learned how to do it. I've figured it out." One day.

So then he started to really work on the harp. He dropped the guitar. He still dug to play it and was still into it and played very well but the harp became his thing. He'd walk around all the time playing his harp.

Is there anything going in London in terms of music then?

Alexis had that club together and we'd go down once a week to see what they were doing and they wanted to know what we were doing. "It's coming," we'd tell 'em. "We'll be gigging soon." We didn't know where the fuck do ya start? Where do ya go to play?

But you were living together, unlike Cyril Davies or the older blues musicians, because you were young and broke . . .

Yeah. Just Mick and myself and Brian. We knew Charlie. He was a friend. He was gigging at the time, playing with Alexis. He was Korner's drummer. We couldn't afford him.

One day we picked up a drummer called Tony Chapman who was our first regular drummer. Terrible. One of the worst . . . cat would start a number and end up either four times as fast as he started it or three times as slow. But never stay the same.

We did say, "Hey Tony, d'y'know any bass players?" He said, "I do know one." "Tell him come to next rehearsal." So we all turned up and in walks . . . Bill Wyman, ladies and gentleman. Huge speaker he's got, and a spare Vox eight-thirty amp which is the biggest amp we've ever seen in our lives. And that's spare. He says, "You can put one of your guitars through there." Whew. Put us up quite a few volts goin' through there.

He had the bass together already. He'd been playin' in rock bands for three or four years. He's older than us. He knows how to play. But he doesn't want to play with these shitty rock bands any more because they're all terrible. They're all doing that Shadows trip, all those instrumental numbers, Duane Eddy, "Rebel Rouser." There was no one who could sing very good. Also, they don't know what to play any more. At that point, nobody wants to hear Buddy Holly any more. He's an old scene already to the rock and roll hip circuit. It's that very light pop scene they're all into . . . Bobby Vee was a big scene then. You wouldn't dream of going to play in a ballroom. They'd just hurl bricks at you. Still have to stick to this little circuit of clubs, back rooms for one night, a shilling for everyone to get in. For people who didn't want to go to ballrooms, who wanted to listen to something different.

Most of these clubs at the time are filled with dixieland bands, traditional jazz bands. An alternative to all that Bobby Vee stuff. There was a big boom in that: the stomp, stompin' about, weird dance, just really tryin' to break the ceiling to a two beat. That was the big scene. They had all the clubs under control. That's where Alexis made the breakthrough. He managed to open it up at the Ealing Club. Then he moved on to the Marquee and R & B started to become the thing. And all these traddies, as they were called, started getting worried. So they started this very bitter opposition.

Which is one reason I swung my guitar at Harold Pendleton's head at the Marquee thing, because he was the kingpin behind all that. He owned all these trad clubs and he got a cut from these trad bands, he couldn't bear to see them die. He couldn't afford it.

But Alexis was packin' 'em in man. Jus' playing blues. Very similar to Chicago stuff. Heavy atmosphere. Workers and art students, kids who couldn't make the ballrooms with supposedly long hair then, forget it, you couldn't go into those places. You gravitated to places where you wouldn't get hassled. The Marquee's a West End club, where we stood in for Alexis a couple of times.

With Charlie drumming?

No. Our first gig was down at the Ealing Club, a stand-in gig. That's the band without Charlie as drummer. We played everything. Muddy Waters. A lot of Jimmy Reed.

Still living in Chelsea?

Yeah. We had the middle floor. The top floor was sort of two school teachers tryin' to keep a straight life. God knows how they managed it. Two guys trainin' to be school teachers, they used to throw these bottle parties. All these weirdos, we used to think they were weirdos, they were as straight as . . . havin' their little parties up there, all dancing around to Duke Ellington. Then when they'd all zonked out, we'd go up there and nick all the bottles. Get a big bag, Brian and I, get all the beer bottles and the next day we'd take 'em to the pub to get the money on 'em.

Downstairs was livin' four old whores from Liverpool. Isn't that a coincidence? "'Allo dahlin', 'ow are ya? All right?" Real old boots they were. I don't know how they made their bread, working . . . They used to sort of nurse people and keep us together when we really got out of it.

The cat that supported Brian, this is a long story. He came from Brian's hometown. He got 80 quid a year for being in the Territorial Army in England, which is where you go for two weeks on a camp with the rest of these guys. Sort of a civil defense thing. They all live in tents and get soakin' wet and get a cold and at the end they learn how to shoot a rifle and they get 80 quid cash depending on what rank you've managed to wangle yourself.

This cat arrived in London with his 80 quid, fresh out of the hills, from his tent. And he wants to have a good time with Brian. And Brian took him for every penny, man. Got a new guitar. The whole lot.

This weird thing with this cat. He was one of those weird people who would do anything you say. Things like, Brian would say, "Give me your overcoat." Freezing cold, it's the worst winter and he gave Brian this Army overcoat. "Give Keith the sweater." So I put the sweater on.

"Now, you walk twenty yards behind us, man." And off we'd walk to the local hamburger place. "Ah, stay there. No, you can't come in. Give us two quid." Used to treat him like really weird. This cat would stand outside the hamburger joint freezing cold giving Brian the money to pay for our hamburgers. Never saw him again after that.

No, no, it ended up with us tryin' to electrocute him. It ended up with us gettin' out of our heads one night. That was the night he disappeared. It was snowing outside. We came back to our pad and he was in Brian's bed. Brian for some reason got very annoyed that he was in his bed asleep. We had all these cables lyin' around and he pulled out this wire. "This end is plugged in, baby, and I'm comin' after ya."

This cat went screaming out of the pad and into the snow in his underpants. "They're electrocuting me, they're electrocuting me." Somebody brought him in an hour later and he was blue. He was afraid to come in because he was so scared of Brian.

Brian used to pull these weird things. The next day the cat split. Brian had a new guitar, and his amp re-fixed, a whole new set of harmonicas.

I guess the craziness comes from the chemistry of the people. The craziness sort of kept us together. When the gigs become a little more plentiful and the kids started picking up on us was when we got picked up by Giorgio Gomelsky. Before he was into producing records. He was on the jazz club scene. I don't know exactly what he did, promoting a couple of clubs a week. He cottoned on to us and sort of organized us a bit.

We still didn't have Charlie as a drummer. We were really lacking a good drummer. We were really feeling it.

All I wanted to do is keep the band together. How we were going to do it and get gigs and people to listen to us? How to get a record together? We couldn't even afford to make a dub. Anyway we didn't have a drummer to make a dub with.

By this time we had it so together musically. We were really pleased with the way we were sounding. We were missing a drummer. We were missing good equipment. By this time the stuff we had was completely beaten to shit.

And the three of you get on? Are you the closest people for each other?

We were really a team. But there was always something between Brian, Mick and myself that didn't quite make it somewhere. Always something. I've often thought, tried to figure it out. It was in Brian, somewhere; there was something . . . he still felt alone somewhere . . . he was either completely into Mick at the expense of me, like nickin' my bread to go and have a drink. Like when I was zonked out, takin' the only pound I had in me pocket. He'd do something like that. Or he'd be completely in with me tryin' to work something against Mick. Brian was a very weird cat. He was a little insecure. He wouldn't be able to make it with two other guys at one time and really get along well.

I don't think it was a sexual thing. He was always so open with his chicks . . . It was something else I've never been able to figure out. You can read Jung. I still can't figure it out. Maybe it was in the stars. He was a Pisces. I don't know. I'm Sag and Mick's a Leo. Maybe those three can't ever connect completely all together at the same time for very long. There were periods when we had a ball together.

As we became more and more well-known and eventually grew into that giant sort of thing, that in Brian also became blown up until it became very difficult to work with and very difficult for him to be with us. Mick and I were more and more put together because we wrote together and Brian would become uptight about that because he couldn't write. He couldn't even ask if he could come and try to write something with us. Where earlier on Brian and I would sit for hours trying to write songs and say, "Aw fuck it, we can't write songs."

It worked both ways. When we played, it gave Brian . . . man, when he wanted to play, he could play his ass off, that cat. To get him to do it, especially later on, was another thing. In the studio, for instance, to try and get Brian to play was such a hassle that eventually on a lot of those records that people think are the Stones, it's me overdubbing three guitars and Brian zonked out on the floor.

It became very difficult because we were working non-stop . . . I'm skipping a lot of time now . . . when we were doing those American tours in '64, '65, '66. When things were getting really difficult, Brian would go out and meet a lot of people, before we did, because Mick and I spent most of our time writing. He'd go out and get high somewhere, get smashed. We'd say, "Look, we got a session tomorrow, man, got to keep it together." He'd come, completely out of his head, and zonk out on the floor with his guitar over him. So we started over-dubbing, which was a drag cause it meant the whole band wasn't playing.

Can you tell me about Oldham?

Andrew had the opportunity. He didn't have the talent, really.
He didn't have the talent for what he wanted to be. He could
hustle people and there's nothing wrong with hustling . . . it
still has to be done to get through. You need someone who can
talk for you. But he's got to be straight with you too.

Was he in the business before the Stones?

Yeah, he was with the Beatles. He helped kick them off in
London. Epstein hired him and he did a very good job for
them. One doesn't know how much of a job was needed but he
managed to get them a lot of space in the press when "Love
Me Do" came out and was like number nine in the charts and
the kids were turning on to them and it was obvious they were
going to be big, big, because they were only third on the bill
and yet they were tearing the house down every night. A lot of
it was down to Andrew. He got them known. And he did the
same gig for us. He did it. Except he was more involved with
us. He was working for us.

He had a genius for getting things through the media.
Before people really knew what media was, to get messages
through without people knowing.

Anita: But Brian, he never got on with Andrew.

Keith: Never. I've seen Brian and Andrew really pissed
hanging all over each other but really basically there was no
chemistry between them. They just didn't get on. There was a
time when Mick and I got on really well with Andrew. We went
through the whole *Clockwork Orange* thing. We went through
that whole trip together. Very sort of butch number. Ridin'
around with that mad criminal chauffeur of his.

Epstein and Oldham did a thing on the media in England
that's made it easier for millions of people since and for lots of
musicians. It's down to people like those that you can get on a
record now. They blew that scene wide open, that EMI–Decca
stranglehold. EMI is still the biggest record company in the
whole fucking world despite being an English company. They
can distribute in Hong Kong. They have it sewn up in the Phil-
ippines and Australia and everywhere. No matter who you go

through, somewhere in the world, EMI is dealing your records. It's a network left over from the colonial days and they've kept hold of it.

Oldham made money for the Stones.

Yeah. I mean, God knows how much money has been made on the Stones name and how much of it has got through to us and how much got through to people along the way. Without mentioning any names but there is one guy I'm still going to get.

It's not money. It's like, what do you want? And how do you want to get it? And do you want to keep it cool? It's not simple, cut and dried. By the time it goes through all those people's hands they're pretty soiled those dollar bills. To work it out any other way, you have to end up like them to do it.

How long was Andrew involved?

From '63 to the end of '67. It still goes on though. I got a letter the other day about some litigation, Oldham versus Eric Easton, who was our first manager proper. Oldham was only half of the team, the other was Eric Easton, who was just a bumbly old Northern agent. Handled a couple semi-success-ful chick singers and could get you gigs in ballrooms in the North of England. Once it got to America, this cat Easton dissolved. He went into a puddle. He couldn't handle that scene.

Was Charlie drumming with you when Andrew first saw you work?

I'll tell you how we picked Charlie up. I told you about the people Brian was getting a band together with and then he turned on to us and he told those other people to fuck off, et cetera. Our common ground with Brian back then was Elmore James and Muddy Waters. We laid Slim Harpo on him, and Fred McDowell.

Because Brian was from Cheltenham, a very genteel town full of old ladies, where it used to be fashionable to go and take the baths once a year at Cheltenham Spa. The water is very good because it comes out of the hills, it's spring water. It's a

Regency thing, you know Beau Brummel, around that time. Turn of the 19th century. Now it's a seedy sort of place full of aspirations to be an aristocratic town. It rubs off on anyone who comes from there.

The R & B thing started to blossom and we found playing on the bill with us in a club, there were two bands on, Charlie was in the other band. He'd left Korner, and was with the same cats Brian had said fuck off to about six months before. We did our set and Charlie was knocked out by it. "You're great, man," he says, "but you need a fucking good drummer." So we said, "Charlie, we can't afford you, man." Because Charlie had a job and just wanted to do weekend gigs. Charlie used to play anything then – he'd play pubs, anything, just to play, cause he loves to play with good people. But he always had to do it for economic reasons. By this time we're getting three, four gigs a week. "Well, we can't pay you as much as that band but . . ." we said. So he said, OK and told the other band to fuck off, "I'm gonna play with these guys."

That was it. When we got Charlie, that really made it for us. We started getting a lot of gigs. Then we got that Richmond gig with Giorgio and that built up to an enormous scene. In London, that was *the* place to be every Sunday night. At the Richmond Station Hotel. It's on the river, Richmond, a fairly well-to-do neighborhood but kids from all over London would come down there on a Sunday night.

There's only so far you can go on that London scene; if you stay in that club circuit eventually you get constipated. You go round and round so many times and then suddenly, you're not the hip band any more, someone else is. Like the High Numbers, they took over from us in a lot of clubs. The High Numbers turned out to become the Who. The Yardbirds took over from us in Richmond and on Sunday nights we'd find we were booked into a place in Manchester.

Where are you recording now, with Giorgio?

Not with Giorgio. Eric and Andrew fucked Giorgio because he had nothing on paper with us. They screwed him to get us a recording contract. We were saying to Giorgio, "What about records?" and he didn't have it together for the record thing.

Not for a long time afterwards either. He was still very much a club man. We knew that to go any further and reach out a bit, we wanted to get off the club thing and get into the ballrooms where the kids were. It turned out to be right.

It was difficult the first few months though. We were known in the big cities but when you get outside into the sticks, they don't know who the fuck you are and they're still preferring the local band. That makes you play your ass off every night so that at the end of two hour-long sets, you've got 'em. You've gotta do it. That's the testing ground, in those ballrooms where it's really hard to play.

Stew is driving you around now?

Yeah, there was this whole thing, because for us Stew is one of the band up until Andrew. "Well, he just doesn't look the part," Andrew said, "and six is too many for them to remember the faces in the picture." But piano is important for us. Brian at that time is the leader of the band. He pulled us all together, he's playing good guitar, but his love is the harmonica. On top of that, he's got the pop star hangup – he wants to sing, with Mick, like "Walking the Dog."

Are you singing?

Naw, I was getting into writing then though. Andrew was getting on to me to write because he sussed that maybe I could do it if I put my mind to it.

What are some of the first things you wrote?

They're on the first album. "Tell Me," which was pulled out as a single in America, which was a dub. Half those records were dubs on that first album, that Mick and I and Charlie and I'd put a bass on or maybe Bill was there and he'd put a bass on. "Let's put it down while we remember it" and the next thing we know is, "Oh look, track eight is that dub we did a couple months ago." That's how little control we had, we were driving around the country every fucking night, playing a different gig, sleeping in the van, hotels if we were lucky.

A lot of it was Andrew's choice. He selected what was to be released. He was executive record producer, so-called. While we were gigging, he'd get that scene together. But remember then, it was important to put out a single every three months. You had to put out a 45, a red-hot single, every three months. An album was something like Motown – you put the hit single on the album and ten tracks of shit and then rush it out. Now, the album is the thing. Marshall has laid the figures on me and *Sticky Fingers* album has done more than the single. They're both number one in the charts but the album's done more than the single.

The concept's changed so completely. Back then it was down to turning on 13-year-old chicks and putting out singles every three months. That was the basic force of the whole business. That was how it was done.

That's another thing. Both the Beatles and us had been through buying albums that were filled with ten tracks of rubbish. We said, "No, we want to make each track good. Work almost as hard on it as you would work on a single." So maybe we changed that concept.

Still, we were on the road every night so there are probably a couple of tracks in there that are probably bummers because Andrew said, "Well, put that on." Because up until the Beatles and ourselves got into records, the cat who was singing had absolutely no control, man. None at all. He had no say in the studio. The backing track was laid down by session men, under the A and R man, artists and repertoire, whatever the fuck that means. He controlled the artist and the material. Bobby Vee or Billy Fury just laid down the vocal. They weren't allowed to go into the booth and say, "I want my voice to sound like this or I want the guitar to sound like this." The man from the record company decided what went where.

That's why there became longer and longer gaps between albums coming out because we got into trying to make everything good.

The first three albums are pretty close though.

The first one was done all in England. In a little demo studio in "Tin Pan Alley" as it used to be called. Denmark Street in Soho. It was all done on a two-track Revox that he had on the wall. We used to think, "Oh, this is a recording studio, huh? This is what they're like?" A tiny little backroom.

When we got into RCA in Hollywood, fuckin' huge Studio A, with Dave Hassinger engineering we said, "We can really do it here. It's all laid out. All you have to do is not let them take you over." Engineers never even used to work, man. They'd flick a few switches and that was it. The machinery was unsophisticated in those days, four track was the biggest there was.

Suddenly a whole new breed of engineers appears, like Glyn Johns, people who are willing to work with you, and not with someone from the record company. There are all those weird things which have broken up in the record industry, which haven't happened for movies yet. There are no more in between men between you and the engineer and you can lay it down. If you want a producer or feel you need one, which most people do, it's a close friend, someone you dig to work with, that translates for you. Eventually we found Jimmy Miller, after all those years.

Slowly and slowly, we've been finding the right people to do the right thing like Marshall Chess, like Jo Bergman. All those people are as important as we are. Especially now that we've got Rolling Stones records, with the Kali tongue . . . nobody's gotten into that yet, but that's Kali, the Hindu female goddess. Five arms, a row of heads around her, a sabre in one hand, flames coming out the other, she stands there, with her tongue out. But that's gonna change. That symbol's not going to stay as it is. Sometimes it'll take up the whole label, maybe slowly it'll turn to a cock, I don't know yet.

You going to put two pills on the tongue?

We're going to do everything with it, slowly. Don't want to let it grow stale. It's growing change. Got to keep it growing.

What was the first time Oldham saw the band?

It was in March, 1963. The next week he took us right into a big studio and we cut "Come On." We were always doing other people's material but we thought we'd have a go at that – "Oh, it sounds catchy." And it worked out. At the time it was done just to get a record out. We never wanted to hear it. The idea was Andrew's – to get a strong single so they'd let us make an album which back then was a privilege.

Were you still a London band then?

Completely. We'd never been out of the city. I'd never been further north than the north of London.

Was Andrew a change in the kind of people you had to deal with?

He faced us with the real problems. That we had to find the hole to get out of the circle of London clubs and into the next circle. Lot of hustle, a lot of blague.

Did you have an image thing already?

It's funny. He tried ... people think Oldham made the image, but he tried to tidy us up. He fought it. Absolutely. There are photographs of us in suits he put us in, those dog-tooth checked suits with the black velvet collars. Everybody's got black pants, and a tie and a shirt. For a month on the first tour, we said, "All right. We'll do it. You know the game. We'll try it out." But then the Stones thing started taking over. Charlie'd leave his jacket in some dressing room and I'd pull mine out and there'd be whiskey stains all over it or chocolate pudding. The thing just took over and by the end of the tour we were playing in our own gear again because that's all we had left. Which was the usual reason.

You weren't the socially "smart" band yet?

No. The Beatles went through it, and they put us through it. They have to know you. They've changed a lot too you know. A lot of them have gone through some funny trips. Some titled gentlemen of some stature are now roaming around England like gypsies and they've acquired this fantastic country Cockney accent. "Ai sole a fe 'orses down 'ere. Got a new caravan like and we're thinking of tripping up to see ..." But it's great.

It must have been amazing early on, when some young lord or some young titled lady would come to see you play?

Brian and I were really fascinated by them. They used to make us really laugh, from a real working class thing. It was so silly to us. It happened so fast that one never had time to really get into that thing, "Wow, I'm a Rolling Stone." We were still sleeping in the back of this truck every night because of the most hard-hearted and callous roadie I've ever encountered, Stew. From one end of England to another in Stew's Volkswagen bus. With just an engine and a rear window and all the equipment and then you fit in. The gear first though.

But to even get out of London then was such a weird trip for Mick and me. The North. Like we went back this year right, on the English tour, and it hasn't changed a bit, man. In the Thirties, it used to look exactly the same, in the middle of the depression. It's never ended for those people.

You're travelling alone?

Sure. Never carry chicks. Pick it up there or drop it. No room, man. Stew wouldn't allow it. Crafty Bill Wyman. For years we believed that he couldn't travel in the back of the bus or he'd spew all over us so he was always allowed to sit in the passenger seat. Years later, we find out he never gets travel sick at all.

Is the first album out?

No, we released two singles before the album. The first single was "Come On" with Muddy Waters' "I Wanna Be Loved" on the other side. We were learning to record. Andrew too. He'd never made a record in his life, and he was producing. Just to walk in and start telling people, it took guts. Andrew had his own ideas on what we were supposed to sound like. It's only been in the last few years with Jimmy that it's changed. The music went through Andrew then. He was in the booth.

Was there a period when it was all the same, just working, but you knew something was building?

It's weird. I can remember. You know it in front. Being on the road every night you can tell by the way the gigs are going, there's something enormous coming. You can feel this energy building up as you go around the country. You feel it winding tighter and tighter, until one day you get out there halfway through the first number and the whole stage is full of chicks screaming "Nyeehhh." There was a period of six months in England we couldn't play ballrooms any more because we never got through more than three or four songs every night, man. Chaos. Police and too many people in the places, fainting.

We'd walk into some of those places and it was like they had the Battle of the Crimea going on, people gasping, tits hanging out, chicks choking, nurses running around with ambulances.

I know it was the same for the Beatles. One had been reading about that, "Beatlemania." "Scream power" was the thing everything was judged by, as far as gigs were concerned. If Gerry and the Pacemakers were the top of the bill, incredible, man. You know that weird sound that thousands of chicks make when they're really lettin' it go. They couldn't hear the music. We couldn't hear ourselves, for years. Monitors were unheard of. It was impossible to play as a band on stage, and we forgot all about it.

Did you develop a stage act?

Not really. Mick did his thing and I tried to keep the band together. That's always what it's been, basically. If I'm leapin' about, it's only because something's goin' drastically wrong or it's going drastically right.

Mick had always dug visual artists himself. He always loved Diddley and Chuck Berry and Little Richard for the thing they laid on people on stage. He really dug James Brown the first time he saw him. All that organization . . . ten dollar fine for the drummer if he missed the off beat.

What was Brian like onstage?

He'd worked out these movements. In those days, little chicks would all have their favorites. Yeah, when you think the Rolling Stones magazine, the Beatles magazine came out once a month. Big sort of fan thing. It was a very old thing that one had the feeling had to change. All those teenyboppers.

It might have been a great last gasp.

Yeah, I think so. Chicks now maybe they feel more equal. I think chicks and guys have gotten more into each other, realized there's the same in each. Instead of them having to go through that completely hysterical, completely female trip to let it out that way. Probably now they just screw it out.

Was it innocent hysteria?

They used to tell us, "There's not a dry seat in the cinema." It was like that.

Were you being approached by the kids?

Yeah, I got strangled twice. That's why I never wear anything around my neck any more. Going out of theatres was the dodgiest. One chick grabs one side of the chain and another chick grabs the other side . . . Another time I found myself lying in the gutter with shirt on and half a pair of pants and the car roaring away down the street. Oh shit, man. They leap on you. "What do you want? What?"

You have to get a little crazy from that.

You get completely crazy. And the bigger it got, America and Australia and everywhere it's exactly the same number. Oh, we were so glad when that finished. We stopped. We couldn't go on any more. And when we decided to get it together again, everybody had changed.

Was it the same kind of madness in the States before it changed?

Completely different kind of madness. Before, America was a real fantasy land. It was still Walt Disney and hamburger dates, and when you came back in 1969 it wasn't any more. Kids were really into what was going on in their country. I remember watching Goldwater–Johnson in '64 and it was a complete little show. But by the time it came to Nixon's turn two years ago, people were concerned in a really different way.

Rock music as politics?

Who knows, man? I mean they used to try and put it down so heavy, rock 'n' roll. I wonder if they knew there was some rhythm in there that was gonna shake their house down. I used to pick up those posters down South that say, "Don't let your kid buy Negro records. Savage music. It will twist their minds." Real heavy stuff against a black radio station or black records.

Was it a big thing to finally see the black lifestyle in America for the first time?

It was a real joy. It was like I imagined but even better. Always a gas to see Etta James or B. B. King work for the first time. Some of those old blues cats. Wherever I go I still try and see whoever I can, I've heard is good or is still alive. I saw Arthur Crudup and Bukka White last time. Incredible.

We all went to the Apollo Theatre the first time over. Joe Tex and Wilson Pickett and the complete James Brown Review. Could never get over the fact that they were into that soul bag in '64. Those suits, those movements, the vocal groups. It became obvious then the spades were going to change their music. They were into that formal, professional thing, which is not half as exciting as when they just let it go. And music ties in with all the rest. Like a real rebellion against that soul thing. Like "Papa's Got a Brand New Bag." You were always told it was going to be heavy going up there, but it never was.

Actually, the first gig was in San Bernardino. It was a straight gas, man. They all knew the songs and they were all bopping. It was like being back home. "Ah, love these American gigs" and "Route 66" mentioned San Bernardino, so everybody was into it. The next gig was Omaha with the motorcycles and 600 kids. Then you get deflated. That's what stopped us from turning into pop stars then, we were always having those continual complete somebody hittin' you in the face, "Don't forget, boy." Then we really had to work America and it really got the band together. We'd fallen off in playing in England 'cause nobody was listening, we'd do four numbers and be gone. Don't blink, you'll miss us.

There was one ballroom number in Blackpool during Scots week when all the Scots come down and get really drunk and let it rip. A whole gang of 'em came to this ballroom and they didn't like us and they punched their way to the front, right through the whole 7,000 people, straight to the stage and started spitting at us. This guy in front spitting. His head was just football size, just right. In those days for me, I had a temper, and "You spit on me?" and I kicked his face in. It was down to the pressure of the road too. America to Australia to Canada to Europe, then recording.

You did some recording the first time over?

Yeah, at Chess, "Michigan Avenue" and "It's All Over Now" and "Confessing the Blues." Oldham was never a blues man, which was one reason he couldn't connect with us. But a lot of things like "Spider and the Fly" were cut at the end of a session, while some guy was sweeping up. "Play With Fire" is like that, with Phil Spector on tuned-down electric guitar, me on acoustic, Jack Nitzsche on harpsichord, and Mick on tambourine with echo chamber. It was about seven o'clock in the morning. Everybody fell asleep.

Did you meet Spector that first time over?

I think we met him in England before we even went to the States. We were still into the blues. Phil Spector was a big American record producer, kind of just another person that Andrew wanted you to meet. Although I really dug his sound, those records. Always wanted to know how he got such a big sound, and when I found out it was a 170-piece orchestra, OK. Jack Nitzsche was Phil's arranger and a very important part of that whole sound. It was Jack's idea of harmonies and spacing. But it's nice he's singing with Crazy Horse now. He couldn't stand to ... to even get him to play the piano you used to have to do a whole Jack number. It's great he's doing it.

Brian had some kind of genius for finding people, didn't he?

He did. He got us together ... Charlie, Mick and me.

He brought Nico to the Velvet Underground.

He was into Dylan too, very early on. He was the only one of us who hung out with Dylan for a bit. A lot of people know Brian that I don't know, that I didn't know knew him who come up and say, "Yeah, I knew Brian."

He was great. It was only when you had to work with him that he got very hung up. Anita could tell you a lot about Brian, obviously, because she was Brian's chick for a long time. Brian did have that thing for pulling people together, for meeting people, didn't he?

Anita: Mixing. Mix it. Mix it, Charlie. Fix it, Charlie.
Keith: We're just trying to figure out why Brian couldn't be with Mick and me at the same time. "Why can't Mick come in?" "No, no" he'd say . . . he was a big whisperer too, Brian. Little giggles . . . you don't meet people like that. Since everybody got stoned, people just say what they want to say.

Brain got very fragile. As he went along, he got more and more fragile and delicate. His personality and physically. I think all that touring did a lot to break him. We worked our asses off from '63 to '66, right through those three years, nonstop. I believe we had two weeks off. That's nothing, I mean I tell that to B. B. King and he'll say, "I been doing it for years." But for cats like Brian . . . He was tough but one thing and another he slowly became more fragile. When I first met Brian he was like a little Welsh bull. He was broad, and he seemed to be very tough.

For a start, people were always laying stuff on him because he was a Stone. And he'd try it. He'd take anything. Any other sort of trip too, head trips. He never had time to work it out 'cause we were on the road all the time, always on the plane the next day. Eventually, it caught up.

Right until the last, Brian was trying to get it together. Just before he died, he was rehearsing with more people. Because it happened so quickly people think . . .
Anita: They think he was really down. But he was really up.
Keith: And they also think that he was one of the Stones when he died. But in actual fact, he'd left. We went down to see him and he said, "I can't do it again. I can't start again and go on the road again like that again." And we said, "We understand. We'll come and see you in a couple weeks and see how you feel. Meantime, how do you want to say? Do you want to say that you've left?" And he said, "Yeah, let's do it. Let's say I've left and if I want to I can come back." "Because we've got to know. We've got to get someone to take your place because we're starting to think about getting it together for another tour. We've got itchy feet and we've got Mick Taylor lined up." We didn't really, we didn't have Mick waiting in the wings to bring on. But we wanted to know if we should get someone else or if Brian wanted to get back into it again. "I don't think

I can," he said, "I don't think I can go to America and do those one-nighters any more. I just can't." Two weeks later, they found him in the pool, man.

In those two weeks, he'd had musicians down there every day. He was rehearsing. I'd talk to him every day and he'd say, "It's coming along fine. Gonna get a really funky little band together and work and make a record."

Do you think his death was an accident?

Well, I don't want to say. Some very weird things happened that night, that's all I can say. It could have as well been an accident. There were people there that suddenly disappeared . . . the whole thing with Brian is . . .

Anita: They opened the inquiry again six months after his death.

Keith: But nothing happened. None of us were trying to hush it up. We wanted to know what was going on. We were at a session that night and we weren't expecting Brian to come along. He'd officially left the band. We were doing the first gig with Mick Taylor that night. No, I wouldn't say that was true. Maybe Mick had been with us for a week or so but it was very close to when Mick had joined. And someone called us up at midnight and said, "Brian's dead."

Well, what the fuck's going on? We had these chauffeurs working for us and we tried to find out . . . some of them had a weird hold over Brian. There were a lot of chicks there and there was a whole thing going on, they were having a party. I don't know, man, I just don't know what happened to Brian that night.

Do you think he was murdered?

There was no one there that'd want to murder him. Somebody didn't take care of him. And they should have done because he had somebody there who was supposed to take care of him. Everyone knew what Brian was like, especially at a party. Maybe he did just go in for a swim and have an asthma attack. I'd never seen Brian have an attack. I know that he was asthmatic. I know that he was hung up with his spray but I've never seen him have an attack. He was a good swimmer. He was a

better swimmer than anybody else around me. He could dive
off those rocks straight into the sea.

He was really easing back from the whole drug thing. He
wasn't hitting 'em like he had been, he wasn't hitting anything
like he had. Maybe the combination of things. It's one of those
things I just can't find out. You know, who do you ask?

Such a beautiful cat, man. He was one of those people who
are so beautiful in one way, and such an asshole in another.
"Brian, how could you do that to me, man?" It was like that.

How did you feel about his death?

We were completely shocked. I got straight into it and wanted
to know who was there and couldn't find out. The only cat I
could ask was the one I think who got rid of everybody and did
the whole disappearing trick so when the cops arrived, it was
just an accident. Maybe it was. Maybe the cat just wanted to
get everyone out of the way so it wasn't all names involved, et
cetera. Maybe he did the right thing, but I don't know. I don't
even know who was there that night and trying to find out is
impossible.

Maybe he tried to pull one of his deep diving stunts and was
too loaded and hit his chest and that was it. But I've seen Brian
swim in terrible conditions, in the sea with breakers up to here.
I've been underwater with Brian in Fiji. He was all right, then.
He was a goddamn good swimmer and it's very hard to believe
he could have died in a swimming pool.

But goddammit, to find out is impossible. And especially
with him not being officially one of the Stones then, none of
our people were in direct contact so it was trying to find out
who was around Brian at that moment, who he had there. It's
the same feeling with who killed Kennedy. You can't get to the
bottom of it.

Anita: He was surrounded by the wrong kind of people.

Keith: Like Jimi Hendrix. He just couldn't suss the assholes
from the good people. He wouldn't kick out somebody that
was a shit. He'd let them sit there and maybe they'd be thinking
how to sell off his possessions. He'd give 'em booze and he'd
feed 'em and they'd be thinking, "Oh, that's worth 250 quid
and I can roll that up and take it away." I don't know.

Anita: Brian was a leader. With the Stones, he was the first one that had a car. He was the first into flash clothes. And smoke. And acid. It was back when it seemed anything was possible. Everybody was turning on to acid, young and beautiful and then a friend of Brian's died and it affected him very much. It made it seem as if the whole thing was a lie.

Did he stop taking acid then?

Anita: No. He got further into it. And STP. DMT, which I think is the worst, no? Too chemical. The first time Brian and I took acid we thought it was like smoking a joint. We went to bed. Suddenly we looked around and all these Hieronymus Bosch things were flashing around. That was in 1965. Musically he would have got it together. I'm sure of it. He and Keith couldn't play together any more. I don't know what causes those things but they couldn't.

Was there a gap between Brian and the rest of the Stones because he had taken acid and they hadn't?

Anita: Yes, as far as I know, Mick took his first trip the day he got busted, in '67. Keith had started to suss, he saw us flying around all over the place. He started to live with us. Every time Brian was taking trips, he was working, making tapes. Fantastic.

He didn't dig the music the Stones were making and he really got a block in his head that he couldn't play with them. Now, he would dig it. He never really stopped playing. It was just so different from what they were playing, he couldn't play in sessions. I'm positive he could have gotten it together. Positive. He was just a musician. Pure, so pure a musician.

Keith: I remember once in Philadelphia some kids had picked up on an interview Brian had done with somebody, he'd used one of those intellectual words like "esoteric." And so, right in the front, these kids had big signs that said, "Brian, you're so esoteric." It had that aura. It was down to *Sixteen* magazine. Everything you did in America then, it could all be in *Sixteen* magazine.

It was a thing when the Beatles and the Stones came over on that first wave . . . in New York, they were on the radio all the time with Murray the K . . .

Ah, Murray. The fifth Beatle and the sixth Rolling Stone. Nobody realizes how America blew our minds and the Beatles too. Can't even describe what America meant to us. We first started listenin' to Otis when we got to the States, and picked up our first Stax singles. And Wilson Pickett. That's what's so amazing about Bobby Keys, that cat, man, he was there from the beginnin'.

If you come from the city, somehow you're aware of black music but if say, you're from Nebraska . . .

Nebraska. We really felt like a sore pimple in Omaha. On top of that, the first time we arrived there, the only people to meet us off the plane were twelve motorcycle cops who insisted on doing this motorcade thing right through town. And nobody in Omaha had ever heard of us. We thought, "Wow, we've made it. We must be heavy." And we get to the auditorium and there's 600 people there in a 15,000 seat hall. But we had a good time. The only thing that went down heavy there was a cop scene. It was then I realized what Lenny Bruce was talking about. We were sitting back in the dressing room. First time in Omaha in '64. Drinkin' whiskey and coke out of cups, paper cups, just waiting to go on. Cops walked in. "What's that?" "Whiskey." "You can't drink whiskey in a public place." I happened to be drinking just Coke actually. "Tip it down the bog." I said, "No man, I've just got Coca-Cola in here."

I look up and I got a .44 lookin' at me, right between the eyes. Here's a cop, tellin' me to tip Coca-Cola down the bog. Wouldn't be there if it wasn't for Coca-Cola. But that's when I realized what it could get into.

Lenny Bruce gave his life . . .

They really got him strung up. He must have read every lawbook. His last gigs were all Constitution and Federal law. In England, that's where they did him way back. They left him alone in America until the English bothered about him and when he went back, they threw the shit at him.

The same thing happened to Jerry Lee Lewis, man. He was ridin' on the crest of a wave until he came to England with his 13-year-old wife. The English busted him for it and said, y'know, "Get out of the country. This is scandalous." When he got back to the States he suddenly found out he couldn't gig any more, straight from being number one.

England's so strange. The way they've taken over the Stones, as "our" Stones and "good on ya, boys," for making it.

The English are very strange. They're tolerant up to a point where they're told not to be. You get to a point up there where somebody turns around and swings a little finger. They've had it in their hands so long, the power. They haven't been fucked since Cromwell, man.

Three weeks before I left, I was just goin' out my front door. Up screams a squad car. "Hello, Keith. How are ya, boy? All right? Let's roll up your sleeve, eh? Let us have a look at your veins. Not on the heavy stuff, are ya?" Just like that. "How's Anita and the baby? What's this? This smell like hash to you, Fred?"

In the States, you know the cops are bent and if you want to get into it, OK, you can go to them and say, "How much do you want?" and they'll drop it. In England, you can drop fifty grand and the next week they'll still bust you and say, "Oh, it went to the wrong hands. I'm sorry. It didn't get to the right man." It's insane.

This whole Western Civilization would be fine if everybody works, if they did it right but they don't. They're all trying to fuck each other, behind each other's backs. The people in England think their police are the finest police force in the world. They don't even know, man . . . what goes on. If they were told, they wouldn't wanna believe it. What goes on in London. They'd turn the other way and pretend they hadn't heard.

The 1967 bust was arranged, wasn't it?

The *News of the World* got hold of someone who was working for us. I think it was the cat who was driving me, at the time. They knew we were going to be down there at a party. Really, just something I'd done a million times before and I've done a million times since. I simply said, "Let's go down to my place for a weekend." It just so happened we all took acid and were in a completely freaked out state when they arrived. They weren't ready for that.

There's a big knock at the door. 8 o'clock. Everybody is just sort of gliding down slowly from the whole day of sort of freaking about. Everyone has managed to find their way back to the house. TV is on with the sound off and the record player is on. Strobe lights are flickering. Marianne Faithfull has just decided that she wanted a bath and has wrapped herself up in a rug and is watching the box.

"Bang, bang, bang," this big knock at the door and I go to answer it. "Oh look, there's lots of little ladies and gentlemen outside." He says, "Read this," and I'm goin' "whaa, whaa." All right.

There was this other pusher there who I really didn't know. He'd come with some other people and was sittin' there with a big bag of stash. They even let him go, out of the country. He wasn't what they were looking for.

When it came down to it, they couldn't pin anything at all on us. All they could pin on me was allowing people to smoke on my premises. It wasn't my shit. All they could pin on Mick was these four amphetamine tablets that he'd bought in Italy across the counter. It really backfired on them because they didn't get enough on us. They had more on the people who were with us who they weren't interested in. There were lots of people there they didn't even bring up on charges.

Because you were young kids with a lot of money or because they saw you as leaders of some kind of movement?

Both. First, they don't like young kids with a lot of money. But as long as you don't bother them, that's cool. But we bothered them. We bothered 'em because of the way we looked, the way we'd act. Because we never showed any reverence for them whatsoever. Whereas the Beatles had. They'd gone along with it so far, with the MBEs and shaking hands. Whenever we were asked about things like that we'd say, "Fuck it. Don't want to know about things like that. Ballocks. Don't need it." That riled 'em somewhere.

It came from quite a way up, that thing. It was CID.

Was the bust physically heavy?

No. It might have been. But we were just gliding off from a 12-hour trip. You know how that freaks people out when they walk in on you. The vibes were so funny for them. I told one of the women with them they'd brought to search the ladies, "Would you mind stepping off that Moroccan cushion? Because you're ruining the tapestries." We were playin' it like that. They tried to get us to turn the record player off and we said, "No. We won't turn it off but we'll turn it down." As they went, as they started going out the door, somebody put on "Rainy Day Women" really loud. Everybody must get stoned. And that was it.

What usually happens is that someone gets busted, the papers have it the next day. For a week they held it back to see how much bread they could get off us. Nothing was said for a week. They wanted to see. Unfortunately none of us knew what to do, who to bum the bread to and so went via slightly the wrong people and it didn't get up all the way.

Mick can tell you how much. It was his bread. Quite a bit of bread.

Eventually after a couple of weeks the papers said the Rolling Stones have been raided for possession. The first court thing didn't come up for three months. Just a straight hearing. That was cool. The heavy trial came in June, about five months after. It was really startin' to wear us out by then. The lawyers were saying "It seems really weird, they want to really do it to you."

I didn't play it that way anyway. When the prosecuting counsel asked me about chicks in nothing but fur rugs, I said, "I'm not concerned with your petty morals which are illegitimate." They couldn't take that one.

The rumor that there was an orgy going on was part of the thing too, wasn't it?

Nobody was in the state for an orgy, man. They should have come some other times, they would have really . . . They tried to make it seem as bad as they could. So OK, here come the sentences. Mick and Robert Fraser, who was another cat who got done, already been in the local jail for two days, waiting. They'd already been found guilty. They were waiting for their sentence until they'd gone through with my one. Mick gets three months for those four amphetamine pills. They give me a year, for allowing people to smoke in my house.

Now Wormwood Scrubs is a 150 years old, man. I wouldn't even want to play there, much less live there. They take me inside. They don't give you a knife and fork, they given you a spoon with very blunt edges so you can't do yourself in. They don't give you a belt, in case you hang yourself. It's that bad in there.

They give you a little piece of paper and a pencil. Both Robert and I, the first thing we did is sit down and write. "Dear Mum, don't worry . . . I'm in here and someone's workin' to get me out, da-da-da." Then you're given your cell. And they start knockin' on the bars at six in the morning to wake you up.

All the other prisoners started droppin' bits of tobacco through for me, 'cause in any jail tobacco is the currency. Some of them were really great. Some of them were in for life. Shovin' papers under the door to roll it up with. The first thing you do automatically when you wake up is drag the chair to the window and look up to see what you can see out the window. It's an automatic reaction. That one little square of sky, tryin' to reach it.

It's amazing. I was going to have to make those little Christmas trees that go on cakes. And sewing up mailbags. Then there's the hour walk when you have to keep moving, round in a courtyard. Cats comin' up behind me, it's amazing, they can talk without moving their mouths, "Want some hash? Want some acid?" Take acid? In here?

Most of the prisoners were really great. "What you doin' in here? Bastards. They just wanted to get you." They filled me in. "They been waiting for you in here for ages," they said. So I said, "I ain't gonna be in here very long, baby, don't worry about that."

And that afternoon, they had the radio playing, this fucking Stones record comes on. And the whole prison started,

"Rayyyyy!" Goin' like mad. Bangin' on the bars. They knew I was in and they wanted to let me know.

They took all the new prisoners to have their photographs taken sitting on a swivel stool, looked like an execution chamber. Really hard. Face and profile. Those are the sort of things they'll do automatically if they pick you up in America, you get fingerdabs and photographs. In England, it's a much heavier scene. You don't get photographed and fingerprinted until you've been convicted.

Then they take you to the padre and the chapel and the library, you're allowed one book and they show you where you're going to work and that's it. That afternoon, I'm lyin' in my cell, wondering what the fuck was going on and suddenly someone yelled, "You're out, man, you're out. It's just been on the news." So I started kickin' the shit out of the door, I said, "You let me out you bastards, I got bail."

So they took me to the governor's office and signed me out. And when it got up to the appeal court, they just threw it out in ten minutes. This judge had just blown it. I mean, he said things to me while I was up there that if I'd caught him by himself I'd have wrung his neck. When he gave me the year sentence, he called me "scum" and "filth," and "People like this shouldn't be . . ."

Was the bust some kind of confirmation of things you already knew?

Yeah. It kind of said, "OK, from now on it's heavy." Up till then, it had been show biz, entertainment, play it how you want to, teenyboppers. At that point you knew, they considered you to be outside . . . they're the ones who put you outside the law. Like Dylan says, "To live outside the law, you must be honest."

They're the ones that decide who lives outside the law. I mean, you don't decide, right? You're just livin'. I mean your laws don't apply to me, nobody says that, because you can't. But they say it. And then you have to decide what you're going to do from then on.

It was the summer too. You had just started to turn on to acid.

Yeah, we had picked it up in America in '66, on that last tour in the summer and we came home and just laid back and started to get it on. We had been working for a long time without stopping, without thinking for a long time. For three years. The bust ended it. We knew it was going to be heavy. We split England about a week after the bust.

Keith: We just carried on down in Morocco for a while. Soon after then it's "You have to come back to England to speak to the lawyers." Slowly you start to straighten out again.

Anita: Mick was on his first trip at the bust.

Keith: I'm not sure. I know he took a lot more after that.

Was "Between the Buttons" cut after the bust?

No, that was done after the American tour. The album that was done while we were waiting to go in and on trial was *Satanic Majesties*. It was made in between court sessions and lawyers with everyone sort of falling apart. I ended up with chicken pox. At the appeal, when I got up, I was covered with spots, man. It was too much. It was the last thing, they couldn't take it. They couldn't even get me into court because I was diseased.

Flowers was put together in America by Andrew Oldham, just to put something out because they were begging for product. In fact, all that stuff had been cut a year or so before and rejected by us as not making it. I was really surprised when people dug it, when it even came out. Andrew was kind of getting pissed off with us by then because we were getting stoned and been busted. It hung him up that he couldn't carry on hustling because he didn't know if we were going to jail or what. And we kept saying, "Andrew, Andrew . . ."

I remember "Dandelion" as a single in the States in flower power summer.

With the other side, "We Love You" with the sound of the jail door. We didn't have a chance to go through too much flower power because of the bust. We're outlaws.

But there's a time in everybody's life when they come out, when they bloom and it was just about then for the Stones.

Keith: Brian was like that at Monterey.

Anita: He was on STP at Monterey.

Did he come back from there with a lot of things in his head?

Keith: Yeah, he did.
Anita: With a lot of STP.
Keith: He changed . . . because we changed around Brian, Anita, and I. We had that whole thing in Morocco and that kind of blew Brian too, on top of everything else. The thing I've forgotten about was when we were in court waiting to hear if there was to be bail before the real trial, that's when they busted Brian, man. They had it timed down to the minute. When we were actually in the fucking courtroom up in London, an hour and a half drive away, they were going into Brian's house to do him so that the papers would come out with "Rolling Stones Keith Richard and Mick Jagger on trial for this, meanwhile Brian Jones just been found with this" – so they could lay that on. "Well, they must be guilty."
Anita: They were going to come down and see us . . . and we called from Brian's house and said, "Don't bother. The cops are here."
Keith: "Don't come down. We'll come up." Unbelievable. It's really weird because people think of England as far more tolerant and genteel than America but when they laid that one on us, when they want to lay it down, they can be just as heavy. They just don't carry guns, that's all.

But some good came out of it. There was a rally and Release grew up around it.

Sure. The thing that shocked the cops was *The Times* coming out in our favor. *The Times*! *The* tabloid of the Establishment came out and said, "Why are you trying to break a butterfly on a wheel? What is this? What have they done?" The *Times* people, they're the ones that can absorb, see? They're the ones who can say, "You're just a butterfly. Let's just keep you a butterfly and leave it at that."

To talk about the music then, with Brian into acid before anyone and having been to the West Coast, was there a reluctance to play just rock and roll?

There was a point where it was difficult to do that. People
would say. "What you playin' that old shit for?" Which really
screwed me up 'cause that's all I can play. We just sort of laid
back and listened to what they were doing in Frisco whereas
Brian was making great tapes, overdubbing. He was much
more into it than we were. And we were digging what we were
hearing, for what it was but that other thing in you is saying,
"Yeah. But where's Chuck Berry? What's he doing?" It's got to
follow through. It's got to connect.

*The feeling that a lot of people had first in '69, that they didn't
want to work for other people, do you think that might have rubbed
off on the Stones?*

With the Stones though, you're always involved in that other
scene, that financial scene. Another heavy trip. But it's more
under control now. I mean ask John Lennon and Paul
McCartney if we aren't more together than they are with it.
They're not. Because it's a very hard thing. You can get it any
way you want it, but it's who gets it for you, and how much do
you want? For doing what?

I don't want to go to America and be called a capitalist
bastard because of what the tickets cost. In '69, I didn't know
what the tickets were costing. You just go and play some music
and when you get there you find out and you're in the deep
end already.

What were you paying in '66 to see us? Because I don't
want to make the prices so high that there is a whole stratum
of kids that can't afford to see us. They're probably the funki-
est kids, you know? They're the ones that would come and dig
to see it and have a good time at doin' it too.

Like in Poland, in Warsaw in '67. Nearest thing to that Long
Beach riot I ever saw.

You did a concert in Warsaw?

Man, fantastic. We get there, behind the Iron Curtain, do the
whole bit, all very uptight. There's Army at the airport. Get to
the hotel which is very jail-like. Lots of security people about,
a lot like America. And it gets even more like America as it
goes along. We're invited by the Minister of Culture, on a

cultural visit, and we're playing in the Palace of Culture. We get there to do our gig. We go on "Honksi-de-boyskj, boysk. Zee Rolling Stones-ki."

And who's got the best seats in the house right down front? The sons and daughters of the hierarchy of the Communist Party. They're sitting there with their diamonds and their pearls . . . and their fingers in their ears. About three numbers, and I say, "Fuckin' stop playin' Charlie. You fuckin' lot, get out and let those bahstads in the back down front." So they went. About four rows just walked out. All the mumma and daddy's boys.

Outside, they've got water cannons . . . the only scene I ever seen near it was when we tried to get out of the Long Beach Auditorium in 1965 when a motorcycle cop got run over and crushed. Exactly the same equipment, man. Deployed in the same way. All the cops had white helmets and the big long batons. Exactly the same uniforms.

There were 2,000 kids that couldn't get in because of the sons and daughters. They wouldn't have had a riot there if they'd let the kids in. Only later I found out Poland is one of the most corrupt countries in the world.

There can't be many bands that have been played behind the Iron Curtain.

I always figured the Beatles were perfect for doing that. They were perfect for opening doors. But somewhere along the line, they got heavy. They wanted to be the ones to actually do it. They copped all the goodies for doing it. Sure enough.

When they went to America they made it wide open for us. We could never have gone there without them. They're so fucking good at what they did. If they'd kept it together and realized what they were doing, instead of now doing "Power to the People" and disintegrating like that in such a tatty way. It's a shame.

The Stones seem to have done much better in just handling success.

Anita: As far as I can see, it has always been a question of the Stones being from London and the Beatles being from Liverpool.

Keith: Maybe, because you're not English you can see it that way. It's true enough that the Beatles' first obstacle was to get out of Liverpool and get into London. We kicked off in London so it was no hang-up. Brian knew about those problems because he came from a provincial town in England. He had to conquer London first, that was his thing. He felt very happy when he made it in London, when we were the hip band in London.

For Mick and me, it didn't mean a thing, because it was just our place. We thought "Well, at least we've got a foothold in our own fucking town."

Do you and Mick still write now the way you used to then?

Well, I haven't seen him for a couple weeks because he went and got married, but basically yes. We do bits that we hear and then we throw them all together on a cassette or some- thing, and listen to it. Mick writes more melodies now than he used to.

The first things, usually I wrote the melody and Mick wrote the words. It's not gotten like the Lennon–McCartney thing got where they wrote completely by themselves. Every song we've got have pieces of each other in it. The only thing in *Sticky Fingers* I don't have anything to do with is "Moonlight Mile," 'cause I wasn't there when they did it. It was great to hear that because I was very out of it by the end of the album and it was like listening, really listening. It was really nice. We were all surprised at the way that album fell together. *Sticky Fingers* – it pulled itself together.

How about "Satisfaction"?

I wrote that. I woke up one night in a hotel room. Hotel rooms are great. You can do some of your best writing in hotel rooms, I woke up with a riff in my head and the basic refrain and wrote it down. The record still sounded like a dub to me. I wanted to do . . . I couldn't see getting excited about. I'd really dug it that night in the hotel but I'd gone past it. No, I didn't want it out, I said. I wanted to cut it again. It sounded all right but I didn't really like that fuzz guitar. I wanted to make that thing different. But I don't think we could have done, you needed either horns or something that could really knock that riff out.

With "Satisfaction," people start to wonder what certain phrases mean like "smoke another kind of cigarette."

A lot of them are completely innocent. I don't think that one is. It might have been. I don't know if it was a sly reference to drugs or not. After a while, one realizes that whatever one writes, it goes through other people, and it's what gets to them. Like the way people used to go through Dylan songs. It don't matter. They're just words. Words is words.

There was a time when for the Beatles and us . . . Dylan was another punch in the face. Someone said, "You've got to look outside what you're doing." He was someone else who was working hard but . . . good musicians too, that cat always picked 'em. Robbie Robertson . . . Kooper.

Al Kooper's a gas to play with. We cut a version of "Brown Sugar" with Al Kooper, it was a good track. He's playing piano on it at Bobby Keys', and my birthday party which was held at Olympic Studios. A lot of people came; Eric's on guitar. We wanted to use it 'cause it's a new version but there's something about the Muscle Shoals feel of the album one, that we got into at the end of the last American tour. Charlie really fills the sound and it was so easy to cut down there. We do a track a day there which is amazing. If you've been playing every night you can record quickly.

That's why we all moved . . . people say, "Why the south of France?" It's just the closest place where we can relax a bit and then record. That's why we're all living in the same . . . to transfer all that equipment, I hope it's worthwhile.

After you came back to England from the first or second American tour, did you have some kind of acceptance, were you starting to get respectable?

Still came across some opposition. It wasn't that complete acceptance that the Beatles had. Always being kicked out of our hotel for not being dressed properly or something.

How is it that the Stones are banned from essentially every hotel in Manchester?

It's from years ago. They're so ridiculous with their little rules. For us to arrive at a place at 3 o'clock in the morning and be told we couldn't have anything to eat or that the drink cupboard is locked, immediately it's "Wadda you mean?" You're off a gig and you've been traveling for five hours and you've been doing it every day for a year. Eventually, they just ban you and night porters put up their bars when they hear you coming.

The funniest thing that happened like that was the court case for peeing in the gas station. That was just in that period, when the Rolling Stones were real big biggies. One night coming back from a gig in North London, Bill Wyman, who has this prodigious bladder, decided he wanted to have a pee. So we told the driver to stop. The car is full up with people and a few other people say, "Yeah, I could get into that. Let's take a pee." So we leap out and we had chosen a gas station that looked closed but it wasn't. There they are, up against the wall, spraying away.

And suddenly this guy steps out. And a cop flashes his torch on Bill's cock and says "All right. What you up to then?" And that was it. The next day it was all in the papers. Bill was accused and Brian was accused of insulting language. Because what they did them for was not peeing but for trespassing.

All these witnesses come up. "There he was, your Honor, he was facing the wall, and well, he was, uh, urinating."

How about the wall of the toilet for the corner of Beggars Banquet?

Anita, Mick and I found this wall. Barry Feinstein photographed it. It was a great picture. A real funky cover. The fight they gave us – we dug in our heels. They really wouldn't budge. It stopped the album from coming out. Eventually it got to be too much of a drag. It went on for nine months or so.

It was like them saying, "We don't give a shit if your album never goes out." After that, we knew it was impossible and started looking around to do it differently. The main thing about having your own label is that you're not solely confined to putting out Rolling Stones material. If we come across anyone else we like or any other thing we dig that people are saying, we can put it on record. It doesn't all have to be our product. Somebody said they got hold of some tapes of Artaud explaining a few things. That would be great to put out.

Did the Stones sign a film deal for five films when Oldham was handling things?

I think there was definitely a film clause. We were part of Andrew's hangup. One of the first things he put out in the English press were that talks were going on for the Stones to appear in their own full-length feature movie. Just to make people keep their ears open a little more. It never got together.

Later on we paid for *Only Lovers Left Alive*, which is a book. I haven't read it for years. It seemed corny then but . . . it was quite a heavy book, some nice things in it. We saw some very straight English film directors about it and they really put us off. Their concept of how it should be. Them trying to turn us on to it really turned us off it.

Would you want to make a movie?

It would just have to happen. I couldn't think about going into it. Mick wanted to do something and nobody was together enough, he didn't have a band together enough to do anything and he felt he'd like to learn about films. There was only one way he could do that. And after, we understood more about the movies because he went through a whole movie.

What do you think of Performance?

I thought it was a great movie. There were a lot of things in there. It was heavy, I mean Donald Cammel is heavy, he wrote it. We've known him since '65 or '66. Anita and I went back to England for that, we hadn't been living there. I mean they did that movie in '68. In the fall.

Donald had so many hassles getting it out. They kept making him re-edit it, I don't know how many times. It was the last film Anita did before Marlan [Marlon].

Did you go to Rome to write that album?

No, to Positano, south of Naples. We'd been there before. We knew the place vaguely and someone offered us their house there. It was empty, barren, very cold. Huge fires and we just sat and wrote. Did "Midnight Rambler" there, "Monkey Man" and some others.

Do you think Let It Bleed *is the Stones' best album?*

I haven't heard it for a long time and I believe things like "Midnight Rambler" come through better live, because we've extended it more. Sometimes when you record something you go off half-cocked because maybe you haven't ever played it live. You've just written it and you record it. From then on you take it and keep on playing it and it gets different. I remember I was into 12-string bottlenecks then.

That song is Mick way out on his persona, isn't it?

Usually when you write you just kick Mick off on something and let him fly on it, just let it roll out and listen to it and start to pick up on certain words that are coming through and it's built up on that. A lot of people still complain they can't hear the voice properly. If the words come through it's fine, if they don't, that's all right too because anyway they can mean a thousand different things to anybody.

But the song's almost psychotic isn't it?

It's just something that's there, that's always been there. Some kind of chemistry. Mick and I can really get it on together. It's one way to channel it out. I'd rather play it out than shoot it out.

People come to Stones concerts to work it out.

Yeah, which in turn has been interpreted as violence or "a goddamn riot" when it's just people letting it out. Not against anybody but with each other. That rock and roll thing, even when it was young, those songs created a domestic revolution. When the parents were out, there were all those parties. Eddie Cochran and all those people, they created some kind of thing which has followed through now and is being built on.

Like "Street Fighting Man"?

The timing of those things is funny because you're really following what's going on. That's been interpreted thousands of different ways because it really is ambiguous as a song.

Trying to be revolutionary in London in Grosvenor Square. Mick went to all those demonstrations and got charged by the cops.

The basic track of that was done on a mono cassette with very distorted overrecording, on a Philips with no limiters. Brian is playing sitar, it twangs away. He's holding notes that wouldn't come through if you had a board; you wouldn't be able to fit it in. But on a cassette if you just move the people, it does. Cut in the studio and then put on a tape.

Started puttin' percussion and bass on it. That was really an electronic track, up in the realms.

Some songs, with a 16-track, I don't really need all that. It's nice to make it simpler sometimes. "Parachute Woman" is a cassette track.

"Salt of the Earth"?

No, that's studio. Mick's words, but I think I was there for a bit of them too. I'd forgotten about that actually. Nearly all Mick, that one. Funny year, '68, it's got a hole in it somewhere. Coming out of the bust and other stuff . . . I was in L.A. for a couple months.

When did you start to meet with Alan Klein?

Andrew got Klein to meet us, to get us out of the original English scene. There was a new deal with Decca to be made and no one really knew, everyone wanted to know about it, in a business we'd never thought of. Who's actually making the money. He was managing financial advisor for Donovan and the Dave Clark Five, Herman's Hermits, who were all enormous then.

The first time we met was in London. The only thing that impressed me about him was that he said he could do it. Nobody else had said that. The thing that he really wanted was the Beatles and the Stones together, to have them both. He did it. But as he picked one up, he dropped the other. A juggling act. Then he didn't get Paul either, which was a real fuckup, coming at such a time that it really did them in. In a way, he was probably the last straw in the whole thing for the Beatles. To be set against each other in things like that is such a downer. To have to go through that court thing that they did in London.

Did the Stones decide together to go with Klein?

I really pushed them. I was saying, "Let's turn things around. Let's do something." Either we go down to Decca and tell them to do it with us . . . which is what we did that very day with Klein, just went down there and scared the shit out of them.

You originally signed a two-year contract with them?

Yeah, in '63. He did a good job, man. Andrew told us that Klein was a fantastic cat for dealing with those people, which we couldn't do. Andrew knew he didn't know enough about the legal side of it to be able to do it. So we had to get someone who knew how to do it or someone who'd fuck it up once and for all. Then it would be up to us to deal with him.

Andrew had gotten together his own label and we had the feeling that he had what we wanted and could go ahead and do his own stuff. He was no longer that into what we were doing and we weren't sure what we wanted to do, because of the busts. He didn't want to get involved in all of that, so it seemed the right time. It just fell apart.

Did it feel like an end to anybody?

It did to Brian, thinking about it. Not to me. I just sort of picked it up again. I think Brian felt that was it. He was really a sensitive cat, too sensitive, the thought of going back on the road really horrified him, in '66 when we last saw America it was 45s and teenyboppers and in three years it established a completely different order. What a change in America, just amazing.

And he was OK on that last tour?

Yeah, we were all very stoned. The last gig was in L.A. We came back to England with pockets full of acid. In '65 you hardly saw any grass. By '66, it was becoming common. It was still a spade trip before that, a spade laid it on you and it was a pleasure to get a joint. It was one of those turn-ons, like when we get to America, we'll get joints laid on us if we get a spade act with us.

Apart from a visit to New York in '67 to do the cover for *Satanic Majesties*, which we constructed in a day, and a couple months in '68, I was there just before the Convention . . . the only contact I had was the underground press and whatever came through.

Were the Springfield going in L.A. then?

Jack Nitzsche had told me about Neil Young and I had seen the Springfield in a club in New York in '66. Hendrix too, at Ondines. He was fantastic. Doing Dylan songs and "Wild Thing" in a club with a pick up band. Fantastic. One of those cats you just knew you were going to see again. He was like Brian too. We were on the European tour when both Jimi and Janis died, so I didn't really get into it till I got back, a few months later.

Did it scare you?

Not really, because I don't feel as fragile as those people.

You live in the same world.

Yeah, but they were very vulnerable. Like Brian was. He really got it all off on stage and he didn't want to fuck with anybody after. I didn't know Jimi that well, but he had a lot of people hangin' 'round that he didn't need and that's what screwed Brian. We're talking about people I really didn't know that well, so I can only relate it to Brian.

Did you do a lot of traveling in the years when the Stones didn't work as a band?

Went to Morocco for quite a while. I drove down through Spain. It's incredible. It's like getting stoned for the first time to go through the Casbah. Mick and everybody ended up there because it was after the bust. Everybody sort of ran. Met Achmed down there, Anita had known him from before, when she went with Brian, but then in '67 he was just getting his thing together . . . he had this beautiful little shop and he'd tell all these incredible stories, and he made this incredible stuff. I haven't been there for two or three years and I keep meaning to go back.

It was quiet in Tangier then. Just a few American kids. Brion Gysin was there too. That cat who wrote *The Process*. Weird. I'm expecting him down here, with Burroughs, they're talking about *Naked Lunch* and trying to get it together for a movie.

How did that picture of the band in drag come about?

There was a big rush for "Have You Seen Your Mother, Baby?" Jerry Schatzberg took the picture and Andrew ordered a truck-load of costumes and Brian just laid on me this incredible stuff. He just said, "Take this." We walked down from Park Lane in that gear and we did the pictures. It was very quiet, Saturday afternoon, all the businesses are shut but there's traffic . . .

Wearing high heels?

Yeah, and the whole bit. Bill in a wheel chair. It took a while to get this picture and going back, what do you do? Do you take half the stuff off and walk back . . . or do you keep it on? Anyway, I'm thirsty, let's go and have a beer. We all zip down to this bar. Hey, what voice do you do? We sat there and had a beer and watched TV and no one said anything. But it was just so outrageous because Bill stayed in his wheelchair and Brian was pushing him about.

Do you like that record?

I loved the track of it. I never did like the record. It was cut badly. It was mastered badly. It was mixed badly. The only reason we were so hot on it was that the track blew our heads off, everything else was rushed too quickly. Tapes were being flown . . . and lost. It needed another couple weeks. The rhythm section thing is almost lost completely.

Along with "Stupid Girl" and "Under My Thumb" and other songs of that time, there's a real down-on-chicks feeling in it.

It was all a spinoff from our environment . . . hotels, and too many dumb chicks. Not all dumb, not by any means but that's how one got. When you're canned up – half the time it's impossible to go out, it's a real hassle to go out – it was to go through a whole sort of football match. One just didn't. You got all you needed from room service, you sent out for it. Limousines sent tearing across cities to pick up a little bag of this or that. You're getting really cut off.

Of course, there was still "Lady Jane."

Brian was getting into dulcimer then. Because he dug Richard Farina. It has to do with what you listen to. Like I'll just listen to old blues cats for months and not want to hear anything else and then I just want to hear what's happening and collect it all and listen to it. We were also listening to a lot of Appalachian music then too. To me, "Lady Jane" is very Elizabethan. There are a few places in England where people still speak that way, Chaucer English.

Brian played flute on "Ruby Tuesday."

Yeah, he was a gas. He was a cat who could play any instrument. It was like, "there it is, music comes out of it, if I work at it for a bit, I can do it." It's him on marimbas on "Under My Thumb" and mellotron on a quite a few things on *Satanic Majesties*. He was the strings on "2000 Light Years From Home," Brian on mellotron, and the brass on "We Love You," all that Arabic riff.

How about "Goin' Home"? It was one of the earlier jams to be put on a pop album.

It was the first long rock and roll cut. It broke that two minute barrier. We tried to make singles as long as we could do then because we just like to let things roll on. Dylan was used to building a song for 20 minutes because of the folk thing he came from.

That was another thing. No one sat down to make an 11 minute track. I mean "Goin' Home", the song was written just the first two and a half minutes. We just happened to keep the tape rolling, me on guitar, Brian on harp, Bill and Charlie and Mick. If there's a piano, it's Stew.

Did you record during those years you didn't gig?

A lot of recording, and getting together with Jimmy Miller in '68 or late '67 when we started *Beggars Banquet*. It's really a gas to work with Jimmy. We'd tried to do it ourselves but it's a drag not to have someone to bounce off of. Someone who knows what you want and what he wants. I wouldn't like to produce, there's too much running up and down, too much legwork.

John Lennon said that the Stones did things two months after the Beatles. A lot of people say Satanic Majesties *is just* Sergeant Pepper *upside down.*

But then I don't know. I never listened any more to the Beatles than to anyone else in those days when we were working. It's probably more down to the fact that we were going through the same things. Maybe we were doing it a little bit after them. Anyway, we were following them through so many scenes. We're only just mirrors ourselves of that whole thing. It took us much longer to get a record out for us, our stuff was always coming out later anyway.

I moved around a lot. And then Anita and I got together and I lay back for a long time. We just decided what we wanted to do. There was a time three, four years ago, in '67, when everybody just stopped, everything just stopped dead. Everybody was tryin' to work it out, what was going to go on. So many weird things happened to so many weird people at one time. America really turned itself round, the kids . . . coming together. Pushed together so hard that they sort of dug each other.

For us too, we had always been pushed together . . . not bein' able to get hotel rooms. Even now, it's one of the last things I say, you never pull that thing . . . that you're a Rolling Stone. I like to be anonymous, which is sort of difficult.

How long did Satanic Majesties *take to cut?*

It wasn't meant to be that ambitious, it just got that way. It must have taken nearly all of '67 to get it together. Started in February and March and it came out in November.

The design was yours?

Michael Cooper was in charge of the whole thing, under his leadership. It was handicrafts day . . . you make Saturn, and I'll make the rings. I forget the name of those people, those 3D postcards. Thing is, everyone looks round on that one. They take pictures at slightly different times and distances and they're put together and the heads move but after it gets scratched you don't really see it any more.

People always ask, "Are John and George in there?" I don't even know, I'd forgotten if they're all in there. They are all in there. And Paul and Ringo.

And who else?

Lyndon Johnson and Mao . . . We just started. . . we had to put a stop to it. We were getting the whole of *Sergeant Pepper* in there, just for the hell of it. It was gettin' late and Michael finally got Saturn suspended . . . It was really funny . . . we should have done a gig that night.

Hidden things like that . . . like Paul is dead.

Ohhhhh. We were in L.A. when that came down. Just playing before the tour started. It's incredible. I've never heard the things they say are on the albums. I've read about it but I've never gotten into it enough to sort of try and slow down a track. Somebody should make a tape of the whole thing and lay it down. All those connections and pictures. But the thing is, he's alive.

It's a weird kind of paranoia. To think that people are working on you that way.

"2000 Light Years From Home". Were you into reading science fiction then?

Not so much. We got into a lot of those English eccentrics. People finding out all about these magnetic lines. We hung around a lot with John Michelle, wandered around England a few weekends, and he showed us obvious things. I mean, bloody obvious. He's into the pyramids in Egypt. There are an awful lot of straight professors who are aiding in that thing. Michelle's incredible. I haven't seen him for ages. He's the sort you never see for years . . . and then he pops up.

And all those flying saucers kept appearing. A whole rash of them in England. There was one right near my place that two cops had seen. We all rushed out to a village about fourteen miles from my place. They'd seen it and chased it and lost it.

The whole story got lost and you never heard any more about it, but two cops around our way, man, were really spaced out.

Is that where "God ride the music" comes from?

There was a cat in America, Charles Foot, who collected useless information, about levitating plates with violin notes. I don't know where he is now either.

Where did the title Beggars Banquet *come from?*

It comes from a cat called Christopher Gibbs. Mick laid it on me but it was Christopher who arrived at that mixture. Although we had all been throwing around "Tramps' Mushup" or something. On the same idea. We wanted to do the picture, that idea came first, the beggars thing came first. "Sticky Fingers" was never meant to be the title. It's just what we called it while we were working on it. Usually though, the working titles stick. Mick was very into that tattered minstrel bit then.

Did Let It Bleed *have anything to do with* Let It Be?

Not a thing. Just a coincidence because you're working along the same lines at the same time at the same age as a lot of other cats. All trying to do the same thing basically, turn themselves and other people on. "Let It Bleed" was just one line in that song Mick wrote. It became the title . . . we just kicked a line out. We didn't know what to call that song. We'd gone through "Take my arm, take my leg" and we'd done the track. We dug that song so . . . maybe there was some influence because *Let It Be* had been kicked around for years for their movie, for that album. Let it . . . be something. Let it out. Let it loose.

Do you sing for the first time alone on that album?

Please. My voice first appeared solo on the first verse of "Salt of the Earth." We did the chorus together, me and Mick. If I write a song, I usually write it all but it's difficult. Somebody's always got their finger in there. I thought I wasn't on "Moonlight Mile" but the last riff everybody gets into playing is a riff I'd been playing on earlier tapes before I dropped out. "Wild Horses," we wrote the chorus in the john of the Muscle Shoals recording studio 'cause it didn't finish off right.

Does it have to do with Marlan's birth?

Yeah, cause I knew we were going to have to go to America and start work again, to get me off me ass, and not really wanting to go away. It was a very delicate moment, the kid's only two months old, and you're goin' away. Millions of people do it all the time but still . . .

How about earlier stuff like "Paint It Black"?

Mick wrote it. I wrote the music, he did the words. Get a single together.

What's amazing about that one for me is the sitar. Also, the fact that we cut it as a comedy track. Bill was playing an organ, doing a takeoff of our first manager who started his career in show business as an organist in a cinema pit. We'd been doing it with funky rhythms and it hadn't worked and he started playing it like this and everybody got behind it. It's a two-beat, very strange. Brian playing the sitar makes it a whole other thing.

There were some weird letters, racial letters. "Was there a comma in the title? Was it an order to the world?"

How about "Get Off My Cloud"?

That was the follow-up to "Satisfaction." I never dug it as a record. The chorus was a nice idea but we rushed it as the follow-up. We were in L.A. and it was time for another single. But how do you follow "Satisfaction"? Actually, what I wanted was to do it slow like a Lee Dorsey thing. We rocked it up. I thought it was one of Andrew's worse productions.

"Mother's Little Helper"?

In those days, Mick and I were into a solid word-music bag unless I thought of something outstanding, which could be used in the title or something. I would spend the first two weeks of the tour, because it was done on the road, all of it was worked out . . . an American tour meant you started writing another album. After three, four weeks you had enough and then you went to L.A. and recorded it. We worked very fast that way and when you came off a tour you were shit hot playing, as hot as the band is gonna be.

*"Nineteenth Nervous Breakdown," "Have You Seen Your
Mother, Baby," "Mother's Little Helper," they're all putting
down another generation.*

Mick's always written a lot about it. A lot of the stuff Chuck
Berry and early rock writers did was putting down that other
generation. That feeling then, like in '67. We used to laugh at
those people but they must have gotten the message right away
because they tried to put rock 'n' roll down, trying to get it off
the radio, off records. Obviously they saw some destruction
stemming from . . . they felt it right away.

The Mayor of Denver once sent us a letter asking us to
come in quietly, do the show as quietly as possible, and split
the same night, if possible. "Thank you very much, we'll be
very pleased to see you in the near future." I've got that letter
with the seal of Denver on it. That's what the mayors wanted
to do with us. They might entertain the Beatles, but they
wanted to kick us out of town.

Part of the Stones image is sex trips.

Yeah, on our first expedition to the United States we noticed a
distinct lack of crumpet, as we put it in those days. It was very
difficult, man. For cats who had done Europe and England,
scoring chicks right, left, and center, to come to a country
where apparently no one believed in it. We really got down to
the lowest and worked our way up again. Because it was
difficult.

In New York or L.A., you can always find something in a
city that big if that's what you want. But when you're in Omaha
in 1964 and you suddenly feel horny, you might as well forget
it. In three years, in two years, every time you went back it
was . . . the next time back it was like, it only took someone
from outside to come in and hit the switch somewhere.

Did you have guys trying to hustle you?

Yeah, in America we went through a lot of that. In France and
England too, not groupies as such, they have some concrete
reason for being around. They work for a radio station, they
contribute to some obscure magazine. It's hard to suss if they

want to know what's going on or if they just want to be around for a second-hand thrill. Out of just being around.

Unlike the Beatles, the Stones, and Mick in particular, have always had the uni-sexual thing going.

Oh, you should have seen Mick really . . . I'll put it like this, there was a period when Mick was extremely camp. When Mick went through his camp period, in 1964, Brian and I immediately went enormously butch and sort of laughin' at him. That terrible thing . . . that switching around confusion of roles that still goes on.

Anita is something very special for the Stones.

It's because she's an amazing lady. She's worked with Mick, Mick and I work together . . . she's an incredible chick. She found us, through Brian. A long time ago. She's been involved in it all . . . Anita . . . yeah . . . there are some people you just know are gonna end up all right. It's really nice. That's why we had Marlan . . . because . . . we just knew it was the right time . . . we're very instinctive people. He's traveled around, though, even before he was born, to Peru. We found out in South America she was pregnant.

What was South America like?

I really like to go to places I know nothing about. Brazil is an amazing place, aside from the amazing hangovers from the Spanish thing that run it. North of Rio it gets really primitive, and Mick's been there a couple times.

But even Rio, man, on New Year's, on the beach practicing macumba. Whole place turns into . . . thousands of thousands of people living in shacks on hills and every time they knock one down, three or four new ones pop up . . . an even more incredible city is Sao Paulo. Which is, in the south, as fast as New York, as speedy as that in tropical conditions, it pours down rain for ten minutes then the sun comes out and it's a hundred and twenty, and the place starts to steam. Millions of people rushing about . . . all for Coca-Cola. It's just like New York.

Lot of good guitar players down there. All over South America, it must be the most widely played instrument.

Did you get the earring in South America?

The one that's hanging there? Yeah. Not the hole. I bought the earring in Peru. I re-bent this one after I got into a fight . . . I mean that's why I say I never mention the Rolling Stones when I'm just going about my business. We had a car crash down there and settled it all and some little bureaucrat from the local harbor has to butt in so someone mentioned, "Oh, that's one of the Rolling Stones." Is it? Bang. Someone leaps in. Telephones flying. And when someone hits them back, it's pistols. "They've got a gun. Call the police." Mention the Rolling Stones and get a smack in the face.

I know what we did do in South America. Went to a ranch and wrote "Honky Tonk Women" because it was into a cowboy thing. All these spades are fantastic cowboys. Beautiful ponies and quarter horses. Miles from anywhere. Just like being in Arizona or something.

"Honky Tonk" is always the song that brings people up to dance, isn't it?

We've never known why. There's always been a few songs that do that. If they weren't dancing by then, you'd know you weren't getting it on. The guitar is in open tuning on that, I learned that particular tuning off Ry Cooder.

It's been said that the Stones brought him over for Let It Bleed *and ripped him off.*

He came over with Jack Nitzsche, and we said, "Do you want to come along and play?" The first thing Mick wanted was to re-cut "Sister Morphine" with the Stones, which is what we got together. He's also playing mandolin on "Love In Vain" or . . . he's on another track too. He played beautifully, man. I heard those things he said, I was amazed. I learned a lot of things off a lot of people. I learned a lot watching Bukka White play. He taught me the tuning and I got behind it.

He says you kept him in the studio with the tapes going and then just used some of his stuff and stole the rest.

If the cat . . . first of all, he was never brought over for the album, which is the main thing. He came over with Jack Nitzsche to get the music for some movie. He came by and we played together a lot, sure. I mean, he's a gas to play with. He's amazing. I wasn't there for a lot of it, but Bill and Charlie still talk about it. They really dug to play with him. I mean, he's so good.

I had already been into open tuning on *Beggars Banquet*, "Street Fighting Man." Just a different tuning. Those old cats are always turning a few machineheads. I learned a lot of things from watching Chuck Berry's hands on *Jazz On A Summer's Day*. It got shown a lot in Europe.

I remember Brian, Mick and I on the way to one of our first gigs stopped into a cinema because we had a few hours to kill to see this movie. I had a guitar with me in just a soft case. We had just gotten in on Chuck Berry's bit, which is what everybody wanted to turn on to, particularly. We were watching and walking and I tripped over this fucking guitar and smashed it to pieces. "Dyonnng" . . . it made this huge noise, strings going and wood splintering.

But you learned from his hands.

It was the only way to watch someone play then.

Tell us the interesting story of how you got your ear pierced.

Well, the cat who was doing it – a jeweler or he studied it – was on about 15 Mandrax. Very stoned. Doing it the good old-fashioned way. None of your anaesthetics and machinery. With a sewing needle and ice. Me next. Rubs the ice on and he's dodging back and forth. God knows how he managed to do it. And he just made it. It's right at the lobe.

I've always wanted a pierced ear. I made me first bottleneck and had me ear pierced the same night, with about fifteen of the Living Theatre and I was about the fourth ear. He did Anita's, too, at a special angle. By then he had another ten Mandrax and was completely out of it. Try it from the front. No, let's go at it from the back.

But a lot of people got their ear pierced that night, it was around the time of the Hyde Park concert.

That was June, 1969. You hadn't worked for two years but had you become better musicians?

No, you always get worse laying off, in one way. You get rusty. Which you can put right if you start playing together. None of us were worried about it. I learned a lot though. I played a lot of acoustic guitar. I did a lot of writing; I didn't use to but I dug to do it. I was writing in a different way, not for a hit single or to keep that riff going.

Everybody let their hair grow.

The thing is we were already getting so hassled with our hair like it was. You really weren't safe in some places. I've chopped it off now for the sun. It's usually long in the winter. You couldn't go into Omaha, you'd get the shit beat out of you.

We did a lot of things in those years, traveled, I hung around a lot with the Living Theatre when they were in Rome and London. They were still working on stage doing things which made the audience no longer an audience, which got them involved.

Did the Stones get more theatrical? "Midnight Rambler" is a piece of theatre.

It's all experiments. I know there are certain things you can do up there when the lights are on you. But the gas of it is when the whole place looks the same, when the house lights are up, when the stage then looks just as tatty as the rest of the auditorium and everybody's standing up. That's the real turn on. Not the theater, although that song's a gas, and I dig to play it. It's when the audience decides to join, that's when it really knocks you out.

You've only got to see a few people dancing, and I turn and watch, and play for them to dance to. It's like you can play for a body that moves. It's always them turning you on so that you can turn them on some more.

Was the Hyde Park concert scheduled before Brian's death?

It was. Don't forget, it was our first thing with Mick Taylor. We wanted to get Mick Taylor up on stage to be seen. We wanted to do something in London. And we wanted it to be free. Which is also a bastard. Because the two free things we've done have been that and Altamont. Both so totally different. People trying to pull that old riff on us, going there in armor. Maybe it was the wisest thing. So we went in an armored ambulance. Took about two hours to drive through the crowd. And we played pretty bad. Until near the end, 'cause we hadn't played for years. And nobody minded 'cause they just wanted to hear us play again. It was nice they were glad to see us because we were glad to see them. Coming after Brian's death, it was like a thing we had to do. We had that big picture of him on stage and it comes out looking like a ghost in some pictures.

Was his death still unreal?

It didn't hit me for months because I hadn't seen him a lot. The only time we'd see him was down at the courthouse, at one of his trials. They really roughed him up, man. He wasn't a cat that could stand that kind of shit and they really went for him like when hound dogs smell blood. "There's one that'll break if we keep on." And they busted him and busted him. That cat got so paranoid at the end like they did to Lenny Bruce, the same tactics, break him down. Maybe with Mick and me they felt, well, they're just old lads.

Mick read a poem for Brian at the concert.

He read something from Shelley. He wanted to do it for Brian. It's a tough thing . . . the first thing you've done on stage before an audience in two years. To get up and read a Shelley poem. He wanted to do it for Brian. He said it was necessary to make some sort of incantation.

And the butterflies . . . they were really nice. Biggest public gathering in London for over two hundred years. The last time they had a gathering that big in England, it started a people's revolt. Had to be put down with the dragoons.

You did songs from Beggars Banquet.

Yeah. It had already been out quite a while because we'd had *Let It Bleed* almost finished. We took it with us to the States where we met Bobby and Jim Price.

The whole Satan trip really comes out after Beggars Banquet.

I think there's always been an acceptance . . . I mean Kenneth
Anger told me I was his right-hand man. It's just what you feel.
Whether you've gotten that good and evil thing together. Left
hand path, right hand path, how far do you want to go down?

How far?

Once you start, there's no going back. Where they lead to is
another thing.

The same place?

Yeah. So what the fuck? It's something everybody ought to
explore. There are possibilities there. A lot of people have
played on it, and it's inside everybody. I mean, Doctor John's
whole trip is based on it.

Why do people practice voodoo? All these things bunged
under the name of superstition and old wives' tales. I'm no
expert in it. I would never pretend to be, I just try to bring it
into the open a little. There's only so much you can bring into
the open.

There's got to be people around who know it all, man.
Nobody ever really finds out what's important with the kinds
of government you've got now. Fifty years after, they tell you
what really went on. They'll let you know what happened to
Kennedy in a few years' time. It's no mystery. An enormous
fuckup in the organization, a cog went wrong, and they'll say
who did it. But by then it won't matter, they'll all be dead and
gone and "Now it's different, and in this more enlightened
age . . ."

*"I shouted out who killed the Kennedys." Does that thing hold for
Mick too, or is it more a show business thing?*

Mick and I basically have been through the same things. A lot
of it comes anyway from association and press and media
people laying it on people. Before, when we were just innocent
kids out for a good time, they're saying, "They're evil, they're
evil." Oh I'm evil, really? So that makes you start thinking
about evil.

What is evil? Half of it, I don't know how much people think of Mick as the devil or as just a good rock performer or what? There are black magicians who think we are acting as unknown agents of Lucifer and others who think we are Lucifer. Everybody's Lucifer.

Does that produce things like Altamont?

As I said, I particularly didn't like the atmosphere there by the time we went on. After a day of letting some uniforms loose, what can you expect? Who do you want to lay it on? Do you want to just blame someone, or do you want to learn from it? I don't really think anyone is to blame, in laying it on the Angels.

If you put that kind of people in that kind of position . . . but I didn't know what kind of people they were. I'd heard about the Angels but I haven't lived in California and San Jose, I have no contact with those people. I don't know how uncontrolled they are, how basic their drives are.

But when the Dead told us, "It's cool. We've used them for the last two or three years, Kesey cooled them out," I was skeptical about it but I said, "I'll take your word for it. I've taken everybody's word for it up till now that they know what they're doing when they put on a show." You have to accept that for a start, that it's gonna be together when you get there or else you never get to any gigs. Few ripoff promoters in the Midwest though . . .

Who put the Angels in that position? Specifically.

Specifically? . . . we asked the Dead basically if they would help us get a free concert together. First we had this idea we want to do a free concert and we want to do it in Frisco because that's where they do a lot of free concerts. Who do you ask and who's done more free concerts than anybody – the Grateful Dead. It's very nice, man, we hung around, talked about lots of things, played a bit. They said this is how they done it and this is a big one and they think they can get it together.

It comes down to how many people can you put together. In India they're used to that many people turning up for a religious occasion. But this was not a religious occasion and also it was in the middle of the fucking desert, in California with freeways. We were so hassled. We were in Muscle Shoals, trying to make a record. Meanwhile they're going through all these hassles with people saying, yeah, you can set up a stage and put up all your equipment and then saying, "Fuck off." We'd been going through it throughout the whole tour, man. "Golden Gate Park, yes it's on. No no. City officials say no." Then they pack across the Bay.

We're still in Alabama, into making records. And so we have to take people at their word. We have to trust them. And they could do it, and they did. But it wasn't their fault they didn't have enough time to think about the parking or how people are going to get there or the johns or the . . . they thought of them to a certain extent but nobody knew exactly how many people were coming anyway. Then you get there and what a fucking place, man. Well, let's just make the best of it.

I went out there the night before Mick. Mick went back. I stayed there. I just hung around, met a few nice people. It was really beautiful. That night before, everywhere I went was a gas. People were sitting around their fires, really cool, getting high and I ended up in a trailer and woke up when it was about a hundred and ten degrees inside.

Were you there when Mick got hit?

I was there the whole fucking day in that trailer. Also, it's the last gig. Do this and we go home. So everybody is in sort of that final mad rush. We'd done this incredible flight from New York to West Palm Beach and sat on the tarmac in the plane for nine hours at LaGuardia, in New York while they got it ready. We got to the gig eight hours behind schedule, after a helicopter flight. We got on at four o'clock in the morning. Below zero. And that was the last gig of the tour proper.

Those kids waited all night to see you.

They were great. Such a sight. That place wasn't much better than Altamont. Everyone was frozen stiff. We got it on for a bit but everybody dug it. It was a gas. By the time we finished and got back to the hotel on the beach, dawn was coming up, the sun was warm and we went to Muscle Shoals.

When did you first feel things might turn out badly?

The Airplane's gig. When I heard what they done to Marty Balin, they're gettin' out of hand. It's just gonna get worse, I thought, obviously it's not going to get better. Nothing's gonna cool them out once they start. What a bummer. What can you do? Just sit tight.

Did you consider not going on?

Can you think what that would have caused on top of getting all the people to the place? Talk about one cat getting killed . . . on top of that, everybody was very sensitive. America suddenly seems to have developed this hyper-sensitivity to life and death that I'd never seen them concerned with before. I never saw them concerned when a cop got crushed at Long Beach.

I don't care who it is. Some Angel or whatever . . . the underground suddenly leaps up in a horrified shriek when some spade hippie gets done, which is a terrible thing, but they never got uptight if some cop got done. Some cop, he's probably on extra duty, and he gets crushed at a pop concert. That one really brought me down. I could never believe it ended up in the 15th page of the *Herald-Tribune* or whatever it was called. That sort of thing makes you want to stop. I don't demand sacrifices at this stage of the game.

What information were you getting at Altamont as to what was going on?

Ah, it's obvious, man. Maybe they'll do me the next time I go there, but they were out of control, man. The Angels shouldn't have been asked to do the job. I didn't know if the Angels were still like Marlon Brando had depicted fifteen years before, or whether they'd grown up a little or if they're still into that "don't touch my chromework" bit. All right. Someone else should have known that. If they didn't, then the Angels kept it very well hidden for a long time.

Who should have known? Sam Cutler?

Sam Cutler was with us all the time, man.

Ronnie Schneider? John Jaymes?

They should have known. I think the Dead should have known. Rock Scully should have known, I think. He didn't. I spoke to him, we all spoke to him and he trusted those cats, man, to do just a good job of keeping the stage clear of people so no plugs'll get pulled out and no chaos would ensue. Somewhere along they flipped.

The people look very very stoned in "Gimme Shelter."

People were just asking for it. All those nude fat people, just asking for it. They had those victims' faces. That guy was pathetic. Most of this I've seen from the movie, same as anyone else. Most of the people who've seen what went down at Altamont have caught it from the movie. When I was there, I just heard a bit, I never actually saw anything flying till we went on.

What did you see when you went on?

The usual sort of chaotic scene.

Did you wait purposely until it was dark to go to heighten the effect?

Oh man, I'd been there 24 hours, I couldn't wait to get out of that place. It was fuckups, the beatups, the chaos, our people telling us not to go on yet, let the people cool down a bit. Those campfire sessions, they always go on longer than expected anyway.

What happens when you come out on stage?

Perfectly normal. Go into "Jumpin' Jack Flash." It felt great and sounded great. I'm not used to bein' upstaged by Hells Angels – goddammit, man, somebody's motorbike. I can't believe it. For a stunt. What is the bike doin' there anyway, in the fourth row of the fucking . . . it would have looked better up on stage and it would have been safer too.

So the cat left his bike there and it got knocked over so that was the first one. "Oh dear, a bike's got knocked over." Yes, I perfectly understand that your bike's got knocked over, can we carry on with the concert? But they're not like that. They have a whole thing going with their bikes, as we all know now. It's like Sonny Barger. "If you've spent $1,700 . . ."

Well, if that's what you want to get together, that's fine but I really don't think if you leave it in front of half a million people, you can't expect it to not to get knocked over.

What if someone tried to do your guitar? They'd get punched out very quickly, wouldn't they?

I don't kill him, man. And I don't get five hundred buddies of mine to come down and put their boot in too. I don't have it organized to that extent. If someone tries to do my guitar, and I don't want it to be done, it's between him and me. I don't call in Bill Wyman to come in and do him over for me, with one of his vicious ankle-twisters or Chinese burns.

I didn't see any killings. If I see any killing going on, I shout "Murder." You dig, when you're on stage you can't see much, like just the first four rows. It's blinding, like a pool of light in complete darkness, unless someone out there lights up a cigarette. All you see is lights out there. If someone strikes one or shines one. Since all this went on 10 or 15 rows back, the only time we were aware of trouble was when suddenly a hundred cats would leap in front of us and everybody would start yelling.

But you stopped playing right after the stabbing and Sam Cutler went to the mike for a doctor.

Someone asked for a doctor, yeah. Half of our concerts in our whole career have been stopped for doctors and stretchers. How much responsibility for the gig are you going to lay on the cat who's playing and how much on the cat that organized it? Rolling Stones' name is linked with Altamont, it wasn't our production particularly. Our people were involved but they were relying on local knowledge.

There were all these rumors flashing around. "There's a bomb gone off and 20 people have been blown to bits, man." You say, "I think you got it wrong, man, I'm sure you got it wrong." 'Cause you've been hearing crazy rumors all day, that you're dead, as ridiculous as that. By the time you're in California and you've gone through a whole tour and you've heard all those rumors that seem to go round and around and around . . . you don't believe anything. I don't believe anything at the end of an American tour ever.

Mick seemed to know something was going on, he tried to cool it out.

The same as Grace Slick tried earlier. "Be cool, be cool." For all the control one can have over an audience, it doesn't mean you can control the murderers. That's a different thing, man, you can't make someone's knife disappear by just looking at him. Somehow in America in '69 – I don't know about now, and I never got it before – one got the feeling they really wanted to stick you out.

Like at the Rainbow Room press conference. So ridiculous, cats asking what to do about the Vietnam War. "What are you asking me? You've got your people to get that one together." And they're asking you about everything, about your third eye . . . it's very nice. But you can't be God. You can't ever pretend to play at being God . . . Altamont, it could only happen to the Stones, man. Let's face it. It wouldn't happen to the Bee Gees and it wouldn't happen to Crosby, Stills, and Nash.

Except that they were there and it didn't make a difference.

Were they? I heard they were in some airport and didn't come, all those rumors. The wisest people I saw were Jerry Garcia and Phil Lesh in that movie: "Those Angels beatin' the shit out of people? I ain't goin' in there." I don't blame the Dead for not working. I just wish they . . . ah, it's too late. Maybe what saves the whole thing is making a movie about it and showing what went down and maybe a little less belief in uniforms.

Does the money from that film go to Meredith Hunter's family?

I don't know, man. As far as I know, the Maysles, the cats who made it, told me that the premiers in various cities have been to help street clinics . . . I don't know about the Meredith Hunter scene because it's all litigation. It's all lawyers.

I've never met his mother. They should get something from somebody. Because . . . I don't know. I get like Charlie when I get down and think about it. The cat was waving a gun, man, and he looked very spaced out.

But the gun was unloaded.

Tell it to Wild Bill Hickok, man.

How did John Jaymes get to the Stones?

Ronnie Schneider we'd known. He's Klein's nephew but he broke away from him. He's a smart cat. I dig Ronnie. He'd been on a lot of tours with us handling business and hung around with us. He was the only cat we knew in '69 who could handle the Stones tour that everybody knew, that we could leave to get on with it till we got there.

How Jaymes got in, I don't know. First met him in L.A. I don't know the whole riff that goes down there. Just like I don't know the whole riff about America, who organizes it all. Occasionally, they show up. Leave it at that. They laid some good shit on me, those people.

The story is that Jaymes had ex-narcos who did heavy numbers on the Stones.

He was an ex-narco.

And he had bodyguards . . . were you being held prisoner?

Oh no, man. It's nice . . . I get the riff, I get the riff. No, there was some paranoia among the organizational people about Uncle Alan. It comes down to the . . . uh . . . the Jewish trade unions and the Italian trade unions, y'see. There are these two trade unions. And they just love to fuck with each other. And it was down to family connections, as far as I could see. And I just wanted to get on with the tour,

And Jaymes' people were going to protect you.

No, in the crew, there were street cats, Chip Monck's crew, very together cats. But there were stories of things being dropped on their heads from unusually high places and weird coincidences. Just things I hear. You never know if it's the truth or rumors. Everyone gets paranoid. There's a lot of other peoples' paranoia beside your own, which you can probably cope with. How many strings can you pull at once? Twelve is my maximum . . . six is my speciality.

But no one liked Jaymes, did they?

Ah, on the last American tour we did in '66, you never expected to meet anyone you liked. All you expected to meet were

assholes and maybe laugh at them, and that's where the whole
cynical thing really was fed. Being left adrift with the editor of
Sixteen magazine for two days. Or having the prizewinner of
some schnooky competition in Iowa to have lunch with. I think
once in Harrisburg, Pennsylvania, we did wind up with the
Mayor and his daughter in the civic banqueting hall.

She escaped intact?

I think Brian let rip with a few golden oldies. I know we ended
up in the supermarket across the road, buying records.

What were the concerts on the tour like before Altamont?

I remember enjoying them. There's always a bummer. It was
probably West Palm Beach. You could enjoy the people for
hanging around that long but it was too fucking cold to play
properly and we tried to do the whole show . . . too fucking
cold. A bummer. After Madison Square Garden, came out of
three shows there to freeze your balls off in a Florida swamp.
We always get 'em.

It was the first time you saw that America.

It was the first time we played it. Mick and I had been to L.A.
in '68, the Strip every night, I dug what was going on there.
Brian and I popped over a few times in '67 incognito. Went
over in December '66 with Brian. Down in Watts a lot. Very
stoned. We got so out of it we wanted to go back and do some
more. Without having to play a gig every night. It was the only
place we knew where to score, man.

And then Mick and I went in '68 to mix down *Beggars
Banquet* with Jimmy and stayed for two months. Hung out
with Taj and the Burritos. Went to the Palomino a lot. I think
England has such a high standard in heavy drugs. Well, the
system for junkies was beautiful. It's fucked up now because
it's a halfway thing. They really had it under control. It depends
how you want to see junk.

It's two years since I've been to America, which is the
longest period ever I'm away. I hear stories. You hear how
that junk thing is getting heavier and heavier. I been through
all that. It depends how you want to see it. There's a lot of

Chinese shit around. That's all I can say. That's another one of those rumors.

You get young kids as junkies in the cities.

You know what it does. It's on the wrong end. They should turn on to it when they're 60. All these old ladies down here, learn a lesson from these old chicks. For a start look at its effect on a nine-year-old. Say he kicks when he's 15. More than likely he'll only be 10 or 11 when he's 15. His voice will break suddenly. Puberty is delayed.

But these old ladies, they leave it alone, then start hitting morphine and horse and they don't feel things like lumbago and arthritis and the plague or old age and things like that. They live to 90, 105. It's a particular Europe trip. Old rich people.

If you're going to get into junk, it stands to reason you should . . . for a start, in guys particularly, it takes the place of everything. You don't need a chick, you don't need music, you don't need nothing. It doesn't get you anywhere. It's not called "junk" for nothing. Why did Burroughs kick it, after 25 years? He's thankful he kicked it, believe me.

How about for making music?

People have offered me a lot of things over the years, mainly to keep going. "Work ya bastard. Take one of these." I've tried a lot of shit. I don't even know what it is. I personally think . . . it depends if you're ready. Same with alcohol. You should find out what it does. If you don't know what it does and you're just putting it in, for the sake of it, you're a dummy.

What it does depends on what form you take it in. Some people snort, some people shoot it. You tell me what it does. The Peruvians, they chew it, and that's the trip. You can buy it in any grocery store and you eat it with a hunk of limestone and it just freezes you . . . at 11,000 feet it's hard to breathe anyway. Those cats have 47 per cent more red corpuscles than us lowlanders. Huge lungs, and they're chewing it all the time. You buy it along with your eggs and your lemons. It depends how you take it.

People also say the drunker you are, the better you play.

All those things are true. The first time you go out every time roaring drunk, after five years you're a fucking wreck. And you still might think it's a gas, but you're making it for yourself, which is cool, but people are coming and paying and you're not turning them on, you're only turning yourself on. And you don't know.

What works for you?

It used to be booze. It used to be this . . . I try not to get behind anything for too long any more because . . . I've been hung up on things. I've got to travel on, I've got to be onstage, I don't want to be hung up carrying all those things with me. When I go through, I go through clean. I'm a clean man.

Again, about Hendrix . . .

I don't know if someone sold him some bad shit or what. These days they're selling stuff, it's no longer cut with talcum powder and sugar, its cut with caustic soda, or with Ajax. England is a very healthy place in a way, or was, because they fucked it and they're gonna let the big boys in now for sure. They're blowing it by the way they're handling the drug situation. People will go somewhere else to look for junk and buy bad shit.

Once things get into powders . . . Arthur Machen wrote a story about white powder back in 1909 . . . a guy takes more and more white powder until one night he turns into a blob and drips through the ceiling. Since then I haven't touched a white powder if I don't know what they are. Even if it's for the runs.

You, though, are in a unique position. People listen when you sing, and Sticky Fingers *is a heavy drug album, one way or another.*

I don't think *Sticky Fingers* is a heavy drug album any more than the world is a heavy world. In 1964, I didn't used to run into cats in America who'd come up to me and say, "Do you want some skag? Do you want some coke? Do you want some acid? Do you want some peyote?" And then go through all those initials and names. Now you have trouble avoiding them.

People who think you're ready to finance every drug smuggling expedition in the world. "Hey listen, I'm not interested. You got the wrong idea." The cats that are into it are into it because they're good at . . . they've taken their chances at it. They're not doing it for nothing, it's either they're getting their rocks off or they're into it for bread. A lot of cats get their kicks going through customs. So what, man?

How about a 12 or 13-year-old kid who buys Sticky Fingers *and that's the first time he hears about cocaine, or he finds out that "Brown Sugar" has another meaning?*

Well, I didn't find out that "Brown Sugar" had another meaning . . . we wrote it in '69. And as far as I can tell they weren't calling it brown sugar then.

Cocaine?

Horse, in some places. Apparently what they get in L.A., it's light brown with brown lumps in it. I don't know where that stuff comes from or what it is. These people don't know what they're getting. If you don't know what you're getting, you don't know what you're putting into yourself. And if you don't know that, you're a dummy. Nobody would eat meat with maggots crawling out of it but people will shoot up some shit they don't know about.

Don't take my example. Take Jimi Hendrix. Or not. Depending on where you are and how you feel. Who says you've got to live threescore and ten years? There's only one source of information I know that says that, and even that doesn't say everybody's got to make it. Everybody can't make 70.

Do you want to make 70?

I can't even imagine what it's like, to be 70. When I was 20 I couldn't imagine what it would be like to be 28.

Can you imagine 30?

It's only two years away. I don't know, not really. Thirty still seems like a real trip to me. And I know 33 is a real trip: 33 is a year.

When Christ was crucified . . .

Everybody who reaches 33, goes through some weird things.

About Sticky Fingers . . .

I mean, though there are songs with heavy drug references, as people have pointed out to me. Me being completely unaware of the situation. They're all actually quite old, which maybe indicates that we were into those things a couple of years ago, three years ago. Maybe we recorded it 20 years ago, man, you know.

I mean, people, you can't take a fucking record like other people take a bible. It's only a fucking record, man. Goddamn it, you know, you might love it one day, you might hate it the next. Or you might love it forever, but it doesn't mean to say that whatever it says in there you've got to go out and do, you've got to go out and say.

There's no rules, you know. When it was teenybopper time one just despaired anyway. I mean, what was the relevance of it.

What did it all mean?

Yeah. Suddenly you're a pop star. Well, you do that because you know pop stars only last two years anyway. So you go through it: "Oh, you know, I'll be that for a bit." The thing is that things change along with it.

You understand that hardly anybody especially in America—

I thought that also along with it had changed that sort of bull-shit, that authority. The establishment has its fingers on show business in this way that in fact it comes out through the mouth of justice itself. "Since you are an idol of millions you therefore hold special responsibilities."

In actual fact, you don't. There's only him that says you do. You don't shoulder any responsibilities when you pick up a guitar or sing a song, because it's not a position of responsibility.

Some people try and reflect it, don't they? Crosby, Stills, Nash and Young? The song, "Chicago" – like that.

Good topical stuff.

Which sells records?

Certainly. Mayor Daley's a good target. And there's a million Mayor Daleys in America. Why have a go at one? Sure he's a cunt, you know, everyone knows he's a cunt. But there's a million hiding behind. Last time I was in L.A. I met the old lady that owns most of those head shops in the Strip, man. She's got a little home in Beverly Hills, she's rolling, you know. She's made a packet, man, and she gets those little hippies to work in there. And it's a front, man. It's all a fucking front. There's another Mayor Daley.

I mean, who knows where they are? How many times can you use those words – justice, freedom. It's like margarine, man. You can package it and you can sell that too. In America they have a great talent for doing that.

And so, as I was saying, just because it's on a record doesn't mean that you have to take it for what it is. The cat could be lying, you know, at the end of the record, you know, maybe they cut the tape off and he said, "Oh, I'm sorry, I'm lying. You know, I'm just fooling you." But they just happened to edit the tape there, you know. "I'm putting you on."

Maybe Dylan said at the end of "Visions of Johanna" – oh, I don't know, which is a very personal thing – but maybe he said it at the end of some of his earlier stuff: "But I don't give a fuck," at the end of "Blowin' in the Wind" or "That's up to you," maybe said that.

But they just, by the time somebody gets to a record anyway, they've got to realize that even our records have gone through the hands of some of the straightest people you could ever meet. Nearly all the Rolling Stones records – you know this is the first album that hasn't – have gone through this very straight English private fucking company, man. They're the people that are really giving it to you. It's not us that are giving it, we're giving it to them.

Because that's the only way you can get records out, and they're giving it to the people. So really it's coming from them anyway. I mean, we went through a lot of hassles with them, but it's not like straight from us to you. It's always going through the hands of somebody, and the thing is to try and get those hands into the same sort of sympathy. The music says something very basic and simple, man. Which, I don't know, exasperates. I mean, look at Richard Nixon and then look at your average young cat in the street, or some Indian cat. It's all there, you've only got to look at what's in front of you. And that's all we've ever been trying to do. Not trying to tell people where to go or which way to go because I don't know. We're all following. I mean, it's all going to happen. It's all coming down.

And to us it might seem, oh, world population. Before there were newspapers and radios and TV you wouldn't hear about that . . . You would never hear about that plague in India or Bengal that they're having and the cholera thing. If you was living in Wales at the time of the great plague in London you probably wouldn't get to hear about that until five years after it happened. And so, something like world population, you wouldn't even know about it.

Depends how worried you want to get about everything. I mean, how can you worry about world population, whose problem is that? You tell me.

Everybody feels they ought to do something about it. If you know the facts. On the face of it, it sounds scary. But after a while it always splits into two things, one side is "Oh, in ten years there's going to be so many people on the earth and you not going to be able to do this, that and the other" and the other says, "Oh yes; it's going to be terrible for them, but it's going to be all right for us."

And then there's "Oh, the world's growing too much food and they're just throwing it all away, enough to feed the world five times over is being thrown into the Atlantic Ocean": and the only reason it's not getting to the people that need it to stay alive is either because they don't want to afford the cost of transporting it to those people or they want those people to die anyway. I mean, what about that tidal wave in Pakistan, man? Quarter of a million in one night.

No way to understand it. On the face of that, what kind of music are you writing?

I'll just keep on rocking and hope for the best. I mean that's really what in all honesty it comes down to. I mean why do people want to be entertainers or do they want to listen to music or come and watch people make music? Is it just a distraction or is it a vision or God knows what? It's everything to all kinds of people. You know, it's all different things.

OK, but the music's changing. "Can't you hear me knockin'" changed because of Bobby Keyes and Jim Price. "Moonlight Mile" is a change.

Yeah, it's a gas to play. It's a gas not to be so insulated and play with some more people, especially people like Bobby, man, who sort of on top of being born at the same time of day and the same everything as me has been playing on the road, man, since '56–'57.

He was on Buddy Holly's first record. I mean he's a fantastic cat to know, for somebody who's into playing rock and roll, because it's been an unending chain for him. The first few years that he was playing around man, I was just the same as anyone, I was just listening to it and digging it and wondering where it came from. And he was there, man. Bobby's like one of those things that goes all the way through that whole thing, sails right through it.

I didn't know it man, but we played on the same show as Bobby Keys in '64, first time we went to San Antone. San Antone State Fair, no, Teen Fair, San Antone Teen Fair, 1964. George Jones, Bobby Vee, that's who Bobby Keys was playing with, playing with Bobby Vee's backup band. I remember that gig, but I don't remember Bobby.

But the reason I remember San Antone so much is waking up and this is, I mean, a young English cat never been face to face with the realities of American life. San Antone was like one of the first places we hit after Omaha and L.A. L.A., Omaha, San Antone, you know, really right in there.

I put on the TV the first morning: "15 killed last night in a brawl down on the river Brazos" or whatever it is. I thought, "God, they're riotin' down here, what's going on?" "Is it a race riot, old chap?" Did you hear that? All these weird people with this English accent.

Turn on the TV next morning, 18 people killed last night and it slowly began to sink in, right, every night around 15 or

20 people get it done to them in San Antone, either Mexicans or spades or kids that go out. I mean in '65, I don't know if the locals are still up to it but in '64 they were very into spick hunting. You know, just go across the river on a Friday night and have a night, have a little chiv up.

I mean that's amazing. Why doesn't someone do something about that? That's what I used to think then. You know, that doesn't happen in my home town. It happens, one could find it, you could find it in any town, you could find it in my town, sure. But it wasn't *18 people* were dead the next morning, you know, and one could certainly get one's self chipped about quite easily.

You don't have to go very far to provoke, even in an English town, to get yourself done over, but 15 people dead, you know, 12 people, you know. If I'm exaggerating over the years, 12 people dead or whatever. But regularly every morning! I was there for about four or five days and every morning it was within two or three of 15. They're probably still going on now, man. I bet that morgue makes a fortune.

You going to start working on a new album here?

Yeah, right in me own basement, as it turns out. After months of searching I end up sitting on it.

How long has it been since Sticky Fingers *was finished? How long since the band recorded?*

We finished – when were the last sessions, man? Was I even there for the last sessions of *Sticky Fingers*? When did they finish it? February, January, March? Most of it was finished before the tour. And it was all finished, complete by the time we came here.

And it took over a year, did it?

Well, I mean, stretched out, the songs, one could say it stretched over two years, you know, because "Sister Morphine" comes from '68, although we cut it in early '69. Some songs were written awhile ago.

But Stones albums usually take a long time, don't they?

They've usually taken longer and longer.

Why is that?

Which really pisses me off. Because everybody's laid back a little more and everybody has other things, they do other things now, whereas when it was just a matter of being on the road and recording, that's all you did, you know, and that was it. And obviously you could do things much quicker that way.

But I mean, if we carried on doing it like that, we'd probably be doing it from wheelchairs already. Because you can't carry on at that pace forever. You know, you can do it in spurts, but I mean, even if you're young and a teenager, you get awfully drawn looking.

Do you reckon you could be doing more work than you are? More recording, laying down more tracks? You, personally?

Yeah, but you know, but you can't have weddings of the year and solo albums and you know, I mean, it's great fun.

You going to do a solo album?

No, I'm not going to do one. All I'm going to do is see if I've got enough things left over from Stones things that they don't like that I do, that I might want to put out at some time, but I'm not going to go and make an album.

Too much trouble or what?

I can't imagine doing it, you know? I can't imagine making an album just like that. I've never had an urge to be a solo. Maybe I can get together one song, two songs a year, that I really feel that I want to sing. And so I do it and I put it on the Stones album. Because it's cool. If I feel, if I become more productive, I'll just collect things. I'll just wait until I've got enough things.

Shit, man, I was just a hired guitar player when I started. Things grew out of that and I learned how to write songs just by sitting down and doing it. For me it seems inconceivable that any guitar player can't sit down and write songs. I don't see how a cat can play a guitar, really, and not be able to lay something down of his own in some way.

But that's the way I feel because I happen to be able to do it. For some guitar players it's inconceivable that nobody can play the guitar, you know, that anybody can't just pick it up just like that.

Because to them it's a second . . . you know. If it's sort of in you, and it's something that you've got together, it's simple, you can't explain it, it's easy. How do you write a song? It's fucking easy, man. I'll come back in a few minutes and lay one on you. But if you're one of these cats that sat down for fucking weeks and months and tried desperately to produce something and nothing ever comes out, it must seem like the greatest task in the world.

I mean, I've desperately tried to remain anonymous. The state the world is in today it's much more of an advantage to remain anonymous than it is to be identifiable or recognized.

As a musician?

Fucking Chuck Berry wrote "Let It Rock" under E. Anderson man, and it's one of the best things he ever did. And yet he put it out, you know he's got some tax publishing hassle, he puts it out under some middle name: Charles A. Berry, Edward Anderson, or whatever. He should have got recognition for it, and as far as I'm concerned he should definitely be recognized as the writer for "Let It Rock." Would the U.S. Internal Revenue kindly bear it in mind.

How do you feel about the music business?

How can you check up on the fucking record company when to get it together in the first place you have to be out on that stage every fucking night, you have to get out there every night in front of the people, saying here I am and this is what I do. You can't keep a check on it. Someone else is handling all that bread.

We found out, and it wasn't years till we did, that all the bread we made for Decca was going into making little black boxes that go into America Air Force bombers to bomb fucking North Vietnam. They took the bread we made for them and put it into the radar section of their business. We found that out, it blew our minds. That was it. Goddamn, you find out you've helped to kill God knows how many thousands of people without even knowing it.

I'd rather the Mafia than Decca. I mean, Mafia than the

CIA, man. But if you've got to be on that stage every night, there's no possible way of checking up on all those people.

Gram Parsons told me a great story about the Mafia. What they're really into now is growing tomatoes. Tomatoes is the only business in America that you can still get cash on the nail so that if you drive up with a truck load of tomatoes, you get money right off. So they have the whole tomato business sewn up.

Gram had an uncle who was growing a thousand acres of tomatoes and one day some guys came down in a limousine and got very heavy with him and said, "Why don't you switch to citrus fruits and leave the tomatoes to us."

Anita: Leave the tomatoes to us.

Keith: It gets so weird, one has to think about everything. I mean, they're running it. They're running America.

Anita: That's why in an interview with the *Daily Mirror* Keith said he was ready to grow tomatoes.

Keith: A subliminal message to the Mafia. "Come see me, I'm ready to grow tomatoes."

What is the conjunction of show business and crime?

A lot of money in entertainment. The criminal element is there for the bread. And where there's crime, there's cops. They're both in the same business, right? Who else deals with crime but criminals and cops? They're the only two that are hung up on it.

Anita: And Italians.

Keith: Anita's seen it all, from another viewpoint. I mean, I'm always in the middle. I've heard incredible Rolling Stones stories I know nothing about. I don't know if I was asleep in my room or . . . why did I miss out on that one?

EXILE ON MAIN ST.

Sean Egan

UK release: 26 May 1972; US release: 22 May 1972

Produced by: Jimmy Miller

Charts: UK no. 1; US no. 1

Tracklisting:
Rocks Off
Rip this Joint
Shake Your Hips
Casino Boogie
Tumbling Dice
Sweet Virginia
Torn and Frayed
Sweet Black Angel
Loving Cup
Happy
Turd on the Run
Ventilator Blues
I Just Want to See His Face
Let It Loose
All Down the Line
Stop Breaking Down
Shine a Light
Soul Survivor

The Rolling Stones never did much with their own label. Although they evidently had fairly grand plans for it – in the early days it distributed a band called Kracker in some territories – in the end it became, beyond their own releases, merely a means by which to issue the product of a few selected friends. *Brian Jones Presents the Pipes of Pan at Joujouka* appeared in October 1971. Jones had prepared the Moroccan field recordings before his death – even the artwork was finished – but it was another project bogged down by the incompetence of Klein. The project having no significant commercial prospects, it was a sweet and sentimental gesture for the Stones to sanction its release on their own label. Ditto two solo albums by Wyman (in 1974 and 1976), and a series of albums by original Wailer and Richards' friend, Peter Tosh. Then there was *Jamming with Edward*, a bizarre release from February 1972 of *Let It Bleed* vintage in which Jagger, Wyman, Watts, Nicky Hopkins and Ry Cooder farted around in the studio in the absence of a Richards, who, according to Roy Carr, had taken a dislike to Cooder. The results are of the standard one would expect of such high-calibre musicians bereft of a purpose: often easy on the ear but not bearing a second listen. Jagger's buffoonish album sleevenotes ("As it cost about $2.98 to make the record, we thought that a price of $3.98 was appropriate for the finished product. I think that that is about what it is worth") exhibited a contempt for the consumer worthy of Decca.

Exile on Main St. – at least at first glance – seems to exhibit the same contempt: a grotesque freak-themed cover, scrawled annotation, a musky sound quality and the fact that it was recorded in Richards' basement didn't on the face of it add up to product of a professional standard, even if the album did initially come with twelve free postcards. That there was a whole double album of this stuff seemed further evidence of self-indulgence. For those offended by such, the occasional profanities in the lyrics – the first on Stones fare, although the risqué "COC" catalogue number prefix was a tradition begun on *Sticky Fingers* – added to the air of vulgarity and decadence, an air summarized by the affectedly lazy murmur by which Jagger opens the album. Adding to a suspicion of insubstantiality is the fact that there are no signature songs present, no iconic numbers like "Brown Sugar" whose quality are doubted by nobody. Some hate the album to this day as much as they did on its release. Others were simply disappointed with it. Yet many consider it The Rolling Stones' masterpiece. Greeted by mixed reviews, it still topped the charts on both sides of the Atlantic.

It should be noted that the story originally put about by the band that *Exile on Main St.* was exclusively the product of sessions at Nellcôte was a bending of the truth designed to throw Klein off the scent: there were prior sessions at Olympic and Jagger's country mansion Stargroves (as well as the traditional subsequent stateside overdub and mixing sessions). However, it is indisputably the case that much of the basic work was laid down in a hot, claustrophobic basement with bad acoustics, and it sounds like it. (This process was assisted by the Rolling Stones Mobile Studio, a van packed to the gunnels with top-flight recording equipment which many other top rock acts would hire from the group in the seventies.) Somehow, though, it works. *Sticky Fingers* had established that raggedy indolence is okay if you are effortlessly brilliant and the step the Stones take further in that direction here via a (not necessarily intended) murky atmosphere is in keeping with rock 'n' roll's baseness and menace. Moreover, ragged though the soundscape may be, courtesy of the presence of Nicky Hopkins, Bobby Keys, Jim Price and various female backing vocalists, it is also a lavish one.

Opener "Rocks Off" can serve as a microcosm of *Exile on Main St.* and the complicated relationship it creates with even its admirers. At first listen, it seems to lack drive, while the reduction of brass to bright glimmers beneath the cloudy sonic surface provokes frustration. Repeated exposure, however, unearths the pleasure of the pounding piano and the interesting incongruity of the fact that this is an anthem of impotence, while resentment at the low audibility of the brass dissipates at the realization of just how delightful is the little of it that can be heard.

"Rip this Joint" is a breakneck rockabilly number which in its two and half minutes takes in (and lovingly perpetuates) pretty much most of the rock-based American myths in which British war babies were drenched. Slim Harpo's "Shake Your Hips" was an extraordinary percolating record with a vocal performance punctuated by elongated warbles. The Stones'

rendition is nowhere near as good. This time their usual rein-
vention "thang" doesn't work, their slowing down of the tempo
and attempt to add a sense of atmosphere draining the song of
its original power. Moreover, the fact that the track fades both
in and out somehow gives it a feeling of insubstantiality, as
though it were a disposable wisp.

"Casino Boogie" features an interesting lyric, which, like a
couple of other places on the album, seems to refer to the
pregnancy ("Skydiver inside her") of Bianca Pérez-Mora
Macias, the beautiful Nicaraguan whom Jagger married on 12
May 1971. Not necessarily contradicting that theory is the fact
that Jagger and Richards later revealed that the lyric is a "cut-
up" wherein they appropriated author William Burroughs'
technique of randomly reassembling detached phrases. In any
case, the meaning does not matter too much, for the track has
a hypnotically syncopated, funky feel.

"Tumbling Dice" was the album's lead-off single, appearing on 15 April 1972 in the States and 21 April in the UK, with
"Sweet Black Angel" on the B-side. It seemed a most curious
choice to promote the parent LP. "Rip this Joint" was probably
a little too hardcore, several of the other rockers were either
not catchy enough or rendered airplay-unfriendly by profanities or ribaldry, and the band were not yet at the point where
they could countenance the release of a ballad as an album's
first single. Even so, surely they could have found a better
track by which to advertise the record than something whose
woozy, lurching, sloppily overdubbed, incomprehensibly sung
qualities are the very opposite of the concise, sharp, instanta-
neously catchy requisites of a single? The Stones' stature
– massively enlarged that particular year by the media blitz
preceding and accompanying their first American tour since
1969 – saw it make the upper reaches of the charts almost by
force, although interestingly even with that media blitz the
public could not be persuaded to send it higher than no. 7 in
the US and no. 5 in the UK. The same de facto process has
also made it a concert perennial. There are many songs on
Exile of far greater quality that do not enjoy automatic set-list
fixture status because they would not elicit the instant recognition that is the preserve of the onetime hit.

Having made all those points, it should be noted that "Tumbling Dice" is far from an unpleasurable recording. Jagger's lyric is barely audible between his affected gasps and drawls (lyric books insist he is saying "Baby, I can't stay" but it seems like "Baby, damn straight" to these ears). However, that which can be discerned is a clever litany of gambler's and small-time hood's phraseology. The music is a mid-tempo affair that seems to stagger under the weight of its overdubs – especially in the awkward opening bars – but is floridly compelling. As with several places on the album, the juxtaposition of the sonic gloaming and rich overdubs – in this case three-part female backing vocals – initially feels amateurish but is something one comes not just to accept but to love with repeated listens.

Side two of the original vinyl configuration was deliberately designed by the band to be an experience for late nights and other mellow occasions. It opened strongly with "Sweet Virginia". Although another example of the fact that they could never quite play country with a straight face (its joyous and hilarious chorus refrain is "Got to scrape the shit right off your shoes!", while references to hiding speed inside one's shoes is something of which Merle Haggard most certainly wouldn't have approved), there is an affectionate warmth to the piss-taking. An opening that sees Richards' and Taylor's acoustic guitar work combine with Jagger's mouth harp is blissful. Also lovely is Bobby Keys' sax break. "Torn and Frayed" hints at demons at work in the Stones' camp. "Who's going to help him to kick it?" asks Jagger/the narrator, which is not necessarily a reference to Richards – who, though in a happy relationship, a doting father and in possession of possibly the best job in the world, was now deep into heroin addiction – but more likely is. The circular chorus and similarly spherical guitar figure lend something of the comforting tone of a lullaby to this window on the grubby netherworld of show business.

"Sweet Black Angel" takes as its subject the travails of Angela Davis, a massively Afroed black American woman whose prosecution for murder on controversial "common enterprise" grounds became a cause célèbre in the early seventies. Jagger rather wastes the privilege of commentary conferred on him by America's lack of *sub judice* laws (Davis was acquitted the month after the album's release) with a polemic that neither seeks to explain the situation nor offers memorable phraseology in its generalized message of protest ("Now the judge he going to judge her for all that he's worth"). It's also written in a peculiar patois that some may even find offensive. Perhaps we shouldn't be too hard on the band in the circumstances of their first ever proper protest song, but it's to be doubted whether early-sixties Bob Dylan would have made the mistake of mentioning the subject's name in neither title nor lyric. However, that it's the thought that counts goes some way to generating goodwill, a task completed by the quality of the melody and pleasing acoustic guitar work. "Loving Cup" was debuted as far back as the July 1969 Hyde Park concert. It was worth the three-year wait. It is a superb creation right from its opening, ornate, Nicky Hopkins piano passage. The narrator prostrates himself before the lady of his desires, desperately demanding – in an operatic, drum-booming refrain – a metaphorical drink.

Having forgone a vocal showcase on *Sticky Fingers*, Keith returns to the mic with "Happy", the side-three opener that is an anthemic and touching declaration that he is content to spurn the flashier pleasures in life for the joy afforded by his partner. (With "All Down the Line" as its B-side, "Happy" became the album's second US single on 15 July 1972 and made no. 22.) "Turd on the Run" is a mean, greasy, quick-stepping blues. The lyric about a man literally trying to hold on to his rapidly departing lover is packed with comical imagery ("Grabbed hold of your coat tail but it come off in my hand"). With "Ventilator Blues", Mick Taylor gets his one and only songwriting credit on a Stones track. Knowing what we know now of the parsimonious and intricate way songwriting credits have been decided on Stones albums, it may even be the case that the Jagger/Richards/Taylor attribution means that he is responsible for the whole song and not just the snaking riff. It is an allusion to the stultifying, patience-fraying atmos-phere in Nellcôte's basement, where the heat was so intense that guitars spontaneously went out of tune and whose

awkward layout consisting of a long room with multiple separate bunkers inhibited freedom of movement and eye contact.
It sees Watts playing an ingenious rhythm on the off-beat and
swells of horns accentuating the drama of Jagger's wits-end
delivery. The track segues into "I Just Want to See His Face",
an odd cut similar to "Shake Your Hips" in its gossamer and
unresolved flavour. Although it is the rarest of beasts in being
an agnostic gospel song, it's innovativeness doesn't prevent it
being the slightest thing on the set. It's followed by arguably
the most substantial thing on the set in the shape of "Let It
Loose". A leisurely, sumptuous ballad that starts off caustically but also seems ecstatically to take in the October 1971
birth of Jagger's daughter Jade ("She delivered right on time"),
it has a clean, lustrous sound uncommon to the album. The
lack of clutter allows us to luxuriate in processions of elegant
brass, intricate alternating male and female gospel harmonies
and quavering lead vocals.

Side four opens with "All Down the Line", a railroad
anthem that is the apotheosis of the American myth in which
the album is saturated. As with so much of the LP, one is
initially dismayed by the apparent gap between intent and
achievement – it's not as rousing or as joyous as it thinks it is
– but, returning to it, the ear incrementally finds it better, as
though the brain, apprehending that all the required elements
are present and correct, begins to make allowances for those
elements being looser and untidier than convention dictates.
At the very least, the brass work is awesomely good.

This being a double album, the Stones extend their usual
insistence of their blues roots to two tracks. "Stop Breaking
Down" is their version of Robert Johnson's "Stop Breakin'
Down Blues". Unlike with their atrocious "Love In Vain", they
judge their retooling right, executing a stately if slightly overlong arrangement whose chief attributes are Taylor's winding
slide playing and Jagger's grungy harmonica. Just as in the ad
hoc style of the sessions "Happy" was knocked together by
Keith, Bobby Keys and Jimmy Miller, so "Shine a Light" was
recorded in the complete absence of Richards, Wyman and
Watts. Amazingly, what emerged is cut not from the same
ramshackle cloth as "Happy" but from the same big

production fabric as "Let It Loose". Although it apparently started life back in 1968 as Jagger's tribute to the disintegrating Brian Jones, it became here, after numerous recordings, a tender, gospel-flavoured song of concern for an insecure lover. It has an overall majesty, but several moments within it are extra special: Billy Preston's loud organ whoop after the line about turning one's head from every woman that one meets, the moment the drums (played by Miller) make their cushioned introduction, the delicate female coos that sound eerily like fluttering wings when Jagger refers to angels, the phased backing vocals . . . Throughout, Preston's agile piano, Taylor's slick, serpentine lead guitar and the collective voices of Clydie King, Joe Green, Venetta Field and Jesse Kirkland are aural ecstasy. The lyric boasts an instantly memorable catchphrase cum piece of philosophy worthy of the greatest gospel lyric or, indeed, pulpit address: "Make every song your favourite tune." One suspects that, had either "Shine a Light" or "Let It Loose" been chosen as the album's lead-off single, they would have jumped the barrier from status of obscure album track to signature song, the sort of which this album is supposedly bereft.

"Shine a Light" would have made a logical and lovely end to *Exile on Main St.* but in the spirit of one of rock's strangest works, "Soul Survivor" eccentrically fulfils the task of closer. A Kalashnikov riff propels a number that employs naval metaphors to summarize a troubled relationship ("You've got a cut-throat crew"). Although the rhythm seems stuck in the shallows, the track has an irregular charm – which description can also be said to apply to the whole album.

In May 2010, *Exile on Main St.* was released in a two-disc deluxe edition. The bonus disc consisted of ten cuts that were implied to be out-takes from the *Exile* sessions but, even though Charlie Watts' distinctive *Exile*-era clipped, splash-cymbal-heavy drum-work confirmed the basic tracks to be genuine, the overripe Jagger vocal mannerisms and other telltale anachronistic signs on at least half of them betrayed them as being the recipients of recent overdubs. Fans who had long treasured far worthier *Exile* offcuts on bootlegs could live with that. Not so easy to understand was the horrendous remastering to which the main disc was subjected: who would ever have thought that an album cloaked in primordial murk could be made tiresomely bright and glaring? It is strongly recommended that prospective purchasers who wish to hear this album should find issues previous to 2010.

The Stones toured North America from the first week in June to the last week in July 1972, criss-crossing the continent on a private jet decorated with the lips-and-tongue logo and enchanting huge crowds and armies of groupies. That celebrities ranging from Hugh Hefner (at whose Playboy Mansion they were guests) and Truman Capote (the acclaimed serious journalist, planning a *Rolling Stone* feature that never materialized) were keen to be seen within the Stones' orbit underlined how rock had moved since the band's career began from the bottom rung of the show-business ladder to the very top. As the longest-surviving group acting as spokesmen for their generation, there was nobody on a higher rung than the Stones, whose longevity was transformed by this tour from a fact almost approaching embarrassing to a cause for admiration by simple virtue of their demonstrable undiminished marketability.

Stevie Wonder opened for the Stones on a tour in which Jagger dispensed with the Satanic stagecraft that had been a feature of '69 but post-Altamont was suffused with too many bad vibes. However, he replaced it with something as outrageous in the form of a hyperactive, hip-wriggling effeminacy that at the time was both toe-curling and shocking. Meanwhile, Richards was by now the epitome of cool: mirror-shaded, draped in scarves and sporting a tangled black mane that was rapidly becoming the *de rigueur* rock hairstyle. An instantly iconic picture from the tour found Richards with head cocked sardonically beneath an airport customs sign reading "PATIENCE PLEASE . . . A DRUG FREE AMERICA COMES FIRST!" The rebel mien was further underlined when Jagger and Richards spent some time in custody after an altercation with a photographer, while the fact that they were sprung in order to prevent fans at that night's concert rioting indicated just what big business they were. The über-rebel, though, was now the father of two, Richards' daughter Angela having just been born. (The suggestion that her name was

Dandelion seems to have been more publicity stunt than anything else.) He was also the type of rebel who had little difficulty balancing his insistence on defying convention with being a nice guy: an incident filmed on this tour in which he nihilistically throws a television set out of a hotel window sees him insisting beforehand that he and his partner in crime check that there's nobody below.

A flavour of the tour's performances is captured in *Ladies and Gentlemen The Rolling Stones*, a documentary which splices songs from different gigs to create a mock concert. Directed by Rollin' Binzer and Stephen Gebhardt, it was released to cinemas in 1974. A flavour of what occurred behind the scenes is provided by *Cocksucker Blues*. Because this documentary by Robert Frank (designer of the *Exile* jacket) never achieved a formal release – the Stones, horrified at its contents, cooked up a fiendish legal agreement whereby it can only be shown at venues at which Frank or a nominated associate is present – that flavour was denied the vast mass of people. Bootlegs were inevitably manufactured, but in pre-internet times were much harder to distribute. Because of that, various urban myths have sprung up about the film, several started by Richards' ex-bodyguard Tony Sanchez in his book *Up and Down with The Rolling Stones*, such as the one about the scene in which Richards is injected with heroin by a groupie. Judging by Keith's glazed expression and by the proliferation of both drugs and willing young women in the film, no doubt something like that did actually happen on the road, but it's not captured here. The tour also led to a book, Robert Greenfield's *STP: A Journey Across America with The Rolling Stones*.

People who no longer had any association with the Stones made sure to exploit their raised profile that year. Decca released two further compilations. *Milestones* (18 February) was the usual fatuous mishmash of singles and album tracks. It being packed with hits, as well as magnificent album tracks, it understandably rose as high as no. 14. With *Rock 'n' Rolling Stones* (13 October), Decca tried to do something a little more high-concept. Unfortunately, their idea of an album that collected some of the Stones old-style rock-'n'-roll numbers was stymied somewhat by the fact that the Stones had never

played old-style rock 'n' roll. The closest they had come were
their many covers of the songs of Chuck Berry, who was really
an R & B artist but was always bracketed with Elvis, Little
Richard, Buddy Holly *et al*. Accordingly, six of the tracks here
are Stones versions of songs written by Berry or, in the case of
"Route 66", associated with him. The remainder of the twelve
cuts are R & B/blues, plus – because it was one of the hits that
hadn't yet featured on Decca's post-1969 Grand Sulk compilations – "19th Nervous Breakdown". The album could only
muster a chart position of no. 41. Over in the States, London
issued *More Hot Rocks (Big Hits and Fazed Cookies)*, a double
set of lesser-known Stones tracks, on 20 December, which
reached no. 9.

GOATS HEAD SOUP

Sean Egan

UK release: 31 August 1973; US release: 12 September 1973

Produced by: Jimmy Miller

Charts: UK no. 1; US no. 1

Tracklisting:
Dancing with Mr D.
100 Years Ago
Coming Down Again
Doo Doo Doo Doo Doo (Heartbreaker)
Angie
Silver Train
Hide Your Love
Winter
Can You Hear the Music
Star Star

After the money-spinning, plaudits-generating euphoria of the '72 American tour came a bit of a come-down for the Stones. Although they acquired kudos in January 1973 by playing a benefit concert for victims of a Nicaraguan earthquake, and although they embarked on a Pacific tour that took in Hawaii, New Zealand and Australia from late January to late February, there were also far less pleasant matters with which to deal. A planned live album recorded on the American tour was abandoned because Motown insisted on top billing for Stevie Wonder material. The album had reached as far as the cover artwork stage. Decca remained an irritant with regard to unauthorized, fatuous releases: 27 April saw them issue "Sad Day" (previously unavailable in the UK) as a single with "You Can't Always Get What You Want" as its *non sequitur* flip. (It failed to chart.)

Then, on 26 June, Richards was busted at his London house. The battery of offences with which he was charged – possession of cannabis, heroin, Mandrax and firearms – was not only mind-boggling but particularly dismaying for his colleagues because of legal, travel and financial problems currently being caused them by the chaotic, drug-strewn house he had kept at Nellcôte. A month later, Jagger turned thirty. Although that was a somewhat more foreseeable event, the reality of it once it did occur was sobering to many, possibly including Jagger himself. The disquiet it provoked was not just based on the normal "Where has it all gone?" ponderings of the ageing but was a result of the suspicion of seniority harboured by children of the sixties for whom older people had always been associated with injustice and intolerance. The milestone happened to coincide with a certain sour spirit in the air best summed up in the title of the 1971 Who song "Won't Get Fooled Again". As the world moved further into the seventies, many of the idealistic young – now not quite so young – were wondering what had really changed about the society they had found so unsatisfactory. Although Jagger, of course, could hardly be expected to take the burdens of a generation on his shoulders, some of this sense of disillusion transferred to him and the rest of the Stones.

Matters weren't helped by the substandard quality of the album they released in '73. Recorded in Jamaica, LA and West Germany, the first fruits of it were the single "Angie", released on 17 August in the UK and 28 August in the States. It marked the first time in Britain that the group had released a ballad on the A-side of a single. People knew they played slow love songs, of course, and did so rather well, but even America was not used to a new Stones album being heralded by music inimical to their hard-rockin' reputation. In a climate in which the antenna of the rock audience was finely attuned to any signs of selling out, such an act was a statement of having gone soft. "This is positively the most depressing task I've had to undertake as a rock writer," complained reviewer Nick Kent in the

New Musical Express. "This single is a dire mistake on as many levels as you care to mention. 'Angie' is atrocious . . ." From this distance, Kent's critique is unbelievably pompous and wrong-headed. At the time, though, shovelling so much import on to a record by a popular musical ensemble did not seem unreasonable, especially this particular ensemble. Kent's review pulsated with implicit discomfort at Jagger's embrace-ment of the bourgeois/outdated concept of marriage, the vast amounts of money being earned by the Stones, the decreasing sense of social commentary in their music, their increasing physical and spiritual distance from their geographical roots and their domestic fans, and their disinclination simply to step aside for younger bands like Slade and T. Rex, who – to give a sense of perspective – were themselves far enough into their chart careers as to soon be perceived as over the hill. To such people as Kent, a string-drenched ballad literally seemed a disavowal of the Stones' values, both musical and sociological, and a dismaying throwback to the anodyne, sentimental fare that had dominated the charts before rock had introduced sweat to popular music.

The fly in this ointment of outrage was the fact that "Angie" is a magnificent record, right from its beautiful opening acous-tic guitar passage to its finale, wherein the heartbreaking line, "They can't say we never tried", is capped by an orchestral flourish. The lyric – written by Mick to Keith's melody – is a work of surprising verisimilitude in which the narrator reasons with his titular long-term love that having exhausted their money and their hopes for a better life, it's time they went their separate ways. There's nothing vindictive or unpleasant about the song: this is the reasoned, torn, tender dialogue of real people, particularly people at the wrong end of their twenties who are apprehending (maybe for the first time) that romantic break-up doesn't have to involve attributing blame. Nicky Hopkins shadows the guitar figure on piano and in the instru-mental break takes over with a gorgeous solo against a mountainous backdrop of strings. Jagger's quavering vocal is slightly over-the-top – he is already moving towards self-parody – but is affecting nonetheless. The strings could also be said to be over-the-top – they could hardly make the track

more poignant – but their presence is not objectionable and, as
alluded to, is at times pleasing.

It's not known whether Nick Kent's demolition job was the
reason "Angie" only made it to no. 5 in the UK, but it was a
chart-topper stateside. It was also a huge hit in many countries
around the world and was many people's first Stones disc. It
was a "crossover" record that enchanted people who didn't
usually stray into harder territory than the likes of Johnny
Mathis.

It could even be argued that rather than serving to under-
mine their values, a record like this heightened whatever
influence the Stones had on society. Not only was it penetrat-
ing markets usually inaccessible to them, but a song that
showed they had a tender side proved that they were human
beings and made them – and by extension their values – less
frightening to non-rock consumers/straights/conservatives.
Incidentally, Jagger has denied the assumption that the song
was about David Bowie's then-wife Angela – a supposed icky
public flirting that may have informed some of Kent's ire –
while from Richards' recollection the song predated the
knowledge that his new baby was going to be a girl and the
decision to call her Angela.

The parent album's sleeve was shot by David Bailey for the
first time since *The Rolling Stones No. 2*. A lipsticked and veiled
Jagger looked like a Victorian lady on the front and Richards
like the wasted druggie he was widely known to be on the back.
One of the few remnants of the Jamaica sessions was the title,
Goats Head Soup, a delicacy on the Caribbean island. (The
title – no apostrophe – was not printed anywhere but the spine
of the sleeve.) The recipe was illustrated on a card insert, the
goat in question looking alarmingly alive as it stared at the
purchaser from a pot.

Those who agreed with Kent's assessment of "Angie" were
appalled by *Goats Head Soup*. So were many of those perceptive
enough to see the abundant quality of that single. It certainly
starts badly, with the first Stones song to merit the description
"self-parody". Although changes in society had drained
"Sympathy for the Devil" of its taboo elements over the course
of five years, it remained (and remains) a powerful piece of

music. The fact that "Dancing with Mr D." is like a cartoon version of "Sympathy for the Devil" has nothing to do with those taboo shifts. It has a forbidding riff but there is nothing vaguely threatening about its ambience or the lyric that discusses a graveyard meeting with the Grim Reaper and the agony of not knowing when he will strike. The overdubbing of a horror-movie female scream is risible even without the memory of that effortlessly threatening "Woo-woo!" chorus from "Sympathy". The vista conjured is little more menacing than that of "Monster Mash", an early-sixties comedy record by Bobby "Boris" Pickett & The Crypt-Kickers, whose tale of horror icons participating in a new dance ("It was a graveyard smash") coincidentally became a belated hit in the UK in the very month of *Goats Head Soup*'s release.

"100 Years Ago" is far stronger. Opening with a funky clavinet, it finds the group in nostalgic mood ("Don't you think it's sometimes wise not to grow up?"). The track has a slightly rambling structure, switching between mellow and urgent, although that's not particularly a fault: the contrast between the sections where Taylor – not for the last time on this album – executes lines of wailing virtuosity and the sleepy "lazy-bones" respite is pleasing. Keith's vocal showcase, "Coming Down Again", is a six-minute, downbeat exploration of a Richards household "domestic" whose traumas are – judging by the title and chorus refrain – worsened by his not having the means to alleviate pain of a different nature. Although it's tender in its own way, it is rather hard to feel sympathy for a narrator who admits he has been unfaithful but shrugs it off with the line, "Being hungry, it ain't no crime." And how are we supposed to take the self-pity of a vastly privileged millionaire in the throes of cold turkey? That a smoky saxophone solo complements the usual classy Nicky Hopkins piano part can't fully blind us to the fact that this track, more than any other, sums up the Stones' mid-seventies decadence. "Doo Doo Doo Doo Doo (Heartbreaker)" is the second Stones protest song, if a little more generalized than "Sweet Black Angel". Jagger denounces American horrors yet to reach the streets of Britain: ten-year-old junkies and children being gunned down by police officers. The song's odd title is a reference to its intricate soul vocal refrain, which glides exquisitely alongside a soaring brass section. The track became, on 19 December, the second US single from the album ("Dancing with Mr D." was the flipside) and made no. 15. "Angie" closes the side on a strong note.

The plodding, purposeless "Silver Train" (B-side of the "Angie" single) is a representative opener to side two. There are flashes of quality, such as Jagger's train-whistle harmonica and the bobbing bridge ("I'm going home on a southbound train with a song in my mouth") but it sounds like nothing more than the afterbirth of "All Down the Line". Rather worryingly, the band see nothing wrong with sequencing it next to "Hide Your Love", which is also a bluesy track so generic that it sounds like a glorified jam and is another cut with no momentum. And is that the applause of studio sycophants greeting its close? If so, including it is the height of hubris. "Winter" is similar to "Moonlight Mile" in its expansive vulnerability and use of strings. However, its sensitivity seems a little forced and it has begun to drag long before its five and a half minutes are up. "Can You Hear the Music" is almost exactly the same length as the preceding track and has a similar circular structure and similarly ornate adornment. The usual flashes of good playing that are inevitable in musicians of such rarefied ability are this time wholly inadequate, for this is a song that is explicitly a paean to the joys of popular music, albeit one that also addresses the mysteries of our purpose on earth. Many failed rock anthems from Danny & the Juniors' "Rock and Roll Is Here to Stay" to The Who's "Long Live Rock" to Led Zeppelin's "Rock and Roll" to The Byrds' "Born to Rock 'n' Roll" testify to how perilous is this territory. Sure enough this mediocre tune and uninspiring lyric are emphatically not the sort of stuff to prove the qualities upon which the subject insists. With the most painful irony, the whole enterprise communicates that the Stones – long among the most able practitioners of popular music – may be beginning to "lose it".

While Keith was keeping up his end of his responsibility to maintain the Stones' image as outlaws via his drug-related brushes with the law, Mick was doing his bit by writing what was originally called "Starfucker" and which held up the album's release by two months. "Star Star" – as it was ultimately retitled in response to WEA's objections – is a sort of obscene Chuck Berry anthem. Whereas Berry would celebrate love or rock 'n' roll, Jagger is either celebrating or condemning (it's never quite clear) a lady who delights in bedding famous men, differentiating herself in that crowded category by exotic tricks with fruit. It can't be denied that a lyric bristling with references to vaginal freshness and blow-jobs received by movie star Steve McQueen possesses a certain snap, crackle and pop, while the tune – though slightly too slow – manages what several tracks on this album fail to do in exploiting the virtue of marginal differentiation from beloved precedents while not sounding like a by-numbers job. There's no getting away, though, from the fact that this final flourish is the only cut approaching strong on the entire side.

There are good points to the album. Perhaps underrated is its different tone: it is more generous of spirit than usual, boasts oodles of virtuoso, treated fretwork that makes a change from that choppy Stones guitar signature and, in a step away from the usual rough-hewn Stones production job, it is unprecedentedly slick. It seeks in a modest way to encompass recent changes in black American music, specifically the way that the soul that had supplanted the band's beloved blues had now itself morphed into funk. Nor can an album containing quality cuts like "100 Years Ago", "Doo Doo Doo Doo Doo (Heartbreaker)" and "Angie" be lightly dismissed. However, this is often shockingly mediocre stuff by the Stones' exalted standards.

Jagger later recalled of the Stones' state of mind at this juncture, "I sort of remember the album *Exile on Main St.* being done . . . and after that going on tour and becoming complacent, and thinking, 'It's '72. Fuck it. We've done it.' We still tried after that, but I don't think the results were ever that wonderful." Perhaps it was inevitable. Human nature dictates that even the most driven artist will at some point lose his hunger to excel artistically. Some do so because their sense of self-worth becomes more bound up with romantic or family concerns, some because they have achieved a level of financial security that blunts the pursuit of money in which artistic ambition is often intertwined, some because they tire of repeatedly proving themselves and some because elements of their collaborative creative dynamic change. In the case of the Stones – for which read Jagger and Richards – it may have been all of those things. Mick and Keith were both now settled down with children and living their own separate lives (their respective partners did not like each other). That Jagger's life was that of a partying socialite and Richards' a smack-injecting homebody was something else driving a wedge between them. Meanwhile, their fleeing Britain – they had now left France but dared not spend too much of each tax year in the UK – had lessened their financial woes, thus reducing their motivation to apply themselves. Another classic album was not going to make much difference to the financial security of the two Stones who held the creative balance of power, wasn't going to make a huge difference to their feelings of self-worth, could hardly make them more celebrated than they already were and certainly wasn't going to make them live any longer. That *Goats Head Soup*, despite its manifold faults, was one of the Stones' biggest-ever sellers could only have reduced their creative drive even further.

Nobody knew this at the time – it was obvious the album was sub-standard but for all anyone knew it was a blip – but the golden age of The Rolling Stones was over.

IT'S ONLY ROCK 'N ROLL

Sean Egan

UK release: 18 October 1974; US release: 15 October 1974

Produced by: The Glimmer Twins

Charts: UK no. 2; US no. 1

Tracklisting:
If You Can't Rock Me
Ain't Too Proud to Beg
It's Only Rock 'n Roll (But I Like It)
Till the Next Goodbye
Time Waits for No One
Luxury
Dance Little Sister
If You Really Want to Be My Friend
Short and Curlies
Fingerprint File

By some legalistic miracle involving implied machinations this text will not essay for fear of libel, Keith Richards' punishment in October 1973 for his grand slam of drugs and firearms offences was a fine and a conditional discharge.

However, although the Stones' touring and earning potential had emerged unscathed, the guitarist was causing the band all sorts of headaches and traumas. The times when Jagger and Richards would bitch about the drug-related unreliability of Brian Jones must have seemed a long time ago to the singer. Lately, Richards had become – quite incredibly – far more of a liability than Jones had been. The anguish this caused the band was correspondingly more severe for, unlike Brian, Keith was unsackable. There are stories from this period of Jagger turning up at Mick Taylor's house literally crying tears of frustration. If true, one could hardly blame him. Although Richards made desultory attempts to clean up, the fact that he had beaten the law and cheated fate on multiple occasions seems to have caused him to acquire a sweeping sense of imperviousness. Stones engineer Andy Johns has recalled how on the very night of his legal let-off, a fire that jeopardized the life of Richards' children started in the guitarist's hotel room, with the obvious implications about its cause.

The Stones, though, kept on rolling. A European tour took place in September and October 1973. Their imperishable appeal had been underlined in '73, when the London label re-released the "Honky Tonk Women" single in the US and saw it sell pretty well, although curiously it was the B-side that charted, "You Can't Always Get What You Want" making no. 42 in June. In the UK, Decca issued yet another compilation but this one was for once marked by thought and care. Released on 5 October 1973, it consisted purely of tracks never previously issued on a UK Stones album: B-sides, EP tracks, "Surprise Surprise", a first UK release for "Congratulations" and even the rare *Saturday Club* version of "Poison Ivy". Of course, it was still a hodgepodge but in an age before well-researched, chronologically sequenced and lovingly annotated archive releases it was an unusually high-quality product and one very useful to the consumer in an era where it was not very easy to collate scattered tracks. Even the cover was clever: it exploited the fact that the picture bag of "Jumpin' Jack Flash" featured photographs on either side capturing the Stones in the same pose from front and back; the from-the-back shot appeared on the cover of an album Decca christened *No Stone Unturned*.

Towards the end of the same year, sessions began on a new Stones album at Musicland Studios, Munich, West Germany, although material cut in 1972 in Jamaica was revived, as was a song Jagger had cooked up in July 1973 at the home of The Faces' Ronnie Wood. Jimmy Miller was not on board for these new sessions, nor would he ever be again. Explaining the change, Richards later said that the Stones were disappointed with how *Goats Head Soup* had turned out and – when discretion had been worn down by the passage of time – that Miller had become increasingly unreliable via his heavy drug use. "Jimmy Miller went in a lion and came out a lamb," said Richards. "We wore him out completely. Jimmy was great, but the more successful he became the more he got like Brian." No doubt some in the Stones camp – and Miller himself – spluttered in incredulity when they saw such comments from Keith Richards of all people. It could be posited that a litmus test of whether Miller was responsible for the Stones' recent dip is the quality of the follow-up album. The result of that test would be inconclusive. Although an improvement, *It's Only Rock 'n Roll* was hardly anything to write home about.

Jagger and Richards' production *nom de guerre* "The Glimmer Twins" would now appear on Stones jackets. Mick and Keith hadn't made too good a fist of what had effectively been their previous production job – *Satanic Majesties* – and didn't acquit themselves spectacularly well here: their naïvety when it came to mixing engendered a certain muddy and congealed sound.

Guy Peellaert provided a cover painting that rendered the Stones as godlike figures being worshipped by classical-era women. There was no lettering on the front cover, but the title and "The Stones" adorn the classical venue's wall on the back in incongruously modernistic graffiti. Mysteriously, examples of such graffiti cropped up all around London at the point of the album's release. The Stones had commissioned Peellaert following the Belgian artist's infamous 1973 book, *Rock Dreams*. Of all the music stars he had depicted, Peellaert had the most fun with the Stones in the outrageous but philosophically representative poses. In one painting he satirized their perceived social threat by portraying Jagger as a transvestite and the others as Nazis as they relaxed in genteel surroundings in the company of naked, pre-pubescent girls. Because Peellaert reneged on a deal to hold off working for any other rock act, his far more outrageous image for David Bowie's *Diamond Dogs* (of Bowie as a man–dog hybrid with testicles showing) appeared six months before *It's Only Rock 'n Roll*. Being thus beaten to the punch by Bowie did the Stones no

favours when there was already a general perception that the
album was the work of ageing artistes anxious to hitch a ride
on the glam-rock bandwagon of which Bowie had been seen as
the driver, and which at any rate was creakingly nearing journey's end. The Stones' promotional film for the lead-off single
– "It's Only Rock 'n Roll (But I Like It)" – saw the band prancing around amid frothy bubbles in sailor suits and eyeliner.
Perhaps the construction put upon this was unfair: after all, if
the promo for "Jumpin' Jack Flash" had appeared at this stage,
exactly the same sham-glam interpretation could have been
made of it. They may have been able to plead innocence to
aping the glam rockers, but the Stones were unquestionably a
little desperate. Mick Taylor himself has said that one of the
reasons that this was his last album with them is because it
smacked to both him and his colleagues of self-parody.

That sense of self-parody started with that lead-off single,
released on 26 July 1974 in the UK (27 July in the States),
with "Through the Lonely Nights" as a by-now rare standalone B-side. The mysterious "Inspiration by Ronnie Wood"
line adjacent to the title was Jagger's way of acknowledging
the fact that he wrote it with The Faces' guitarist without
impinging on that inviolable Jagger/Richards Rolling Stones
compositional pact. (That Jagger gave Wood permission to
claim as solely his own their co-written "I Can Feel the Fire"
was hardly equitable recompense considering it was destined
for one of Ronnie's solo albums.) That Mick Taylor later said
"It's Only Rock 'n Roll (But I Like It)" was an attempt to
"write something in the classic Stones style" is somewhat
ironic in light of the fact that it's hardly a Stones track at all:
Taylor, Watts and Wyman don't appear on it. The basic track
features The Faces' Kenney Jones and Wood on drums and
acoustic guitar respectively, with Willie Weeks on bass. Richards added some electric guitar parts after a new version cut
by the Stones was adjudged not to have the compellingly
raggedy – one might even say "Stonesy" feel – of the original
demo. Despite it sounding Stonesy, it was also mid-tempo,
which would have been interpreted by some as a sign of a
band that had lost its energy and/or passion.

The lyric is addressed to a lover. That this lover is glacially disapproving of the narrator's rock pursuits is evident enough from the defensive title. The narrator is effectively accepting the diminutive but insisting that he likes the form in spite of its lack of worth. As rock anthems go, this is a pretty snivelling one and it didn't take a huge logical leap to conclude that this composition was addressed to Bianca, widely thought to be a rather snooty character from much more refined stock than her husband. A Mick Jagger publicly grovelling to his missus and furthermore seeming to take her (imagined) side in the debate about the validity of rock was a profoundly reduced figure.

In light of such second-guessing and brickbats from a non-musical angle, it must have been daunting for the Stones to write anything at all. Asking to be judged purely on their music – which, for the most part, they always had – was not unreasonable. On that count, "It's Only Rock 'n Roll (But I Like It)" is a good piece of work. Even despite that semi-apologetic tone, it works as a validation of rock, mildly anthemic and appropriately defiant of those crusty types who felt its invention had cheapened the culture. Jagger's mischievous vocal is nicely over the top, while Richards' guitar work has an attractively rasping, slurred quality. The arrangement – with its layerings of voice and guitar, considered musical lulls and call-and-response recitations of the chorus – is executed with all the slickness to be expected of pros who have been in and out of studios for at least two pop lifecycles.

"Through the Lonely Nights" is a ballad whose swirling guitar and crisply delineated drumming betrays its origins at the *Goats Head Soup* sessions. The lyric feels a little confused, with an allusion to the woman whom the narrator admits he misses being a prostitute never really pursued. The melody and instrumentation are pretty without ever being remarkable. In other words – the high production values aside – an archetypal flipside, except that the Stones never had made B-sides that sounded like it. This track would remain uncollected on album for over thirty years. The single's original picture bag featured another Guy Peellaert painting, this one of a sailor-suited Jagger shoving a giant-sized fountain pen into his chest.

The record just about achieved a respectable chart position

in the UK by becoming a top 10 record by the skin of its teeth (i.e. it made no. 10) but in the States it could only muster the sort of chart position normally the preserve of second singles from albums, no. 16. Somewhat unexpectedly, the song transpired to become iconic. Not only is it a singalong concert favourite but it provided a readymade, solidarity-inspiring slogan every bit as succinct and rousing as "The greatest rock 'n' roll band in the world".

The album opener, "If You Can't Rock Me", starts dramatically with an urgent drum roll and wailing Taylor lead guitar but doesn't live up to its intro. The lyric is not exactly profound: it finds a singer in a band looking out into the crowd from the stage for an interesting bed partner for the night. It has a certain musical energy, but a self-conscious one. Richards plays the unusually brawny bass. "Ain't Too Proud to Beg" is a cover of the Temptations hit written by Norman Whitfield and Eddie Holland. The Stones give it a piano-based muscularity for which Motown was not renowned. Released on 25 October as the album's second US single with "Dance Little Sister" on the flip – the first Stones cover-job issued on 45 since "Time Is on My Side" in 1964 – it made no. 17. "Till the Next Goodbye" follows "It's Only Rock 'n Roll (But I Like It)". It is full of in-jokes only fully penetrable to the couple depicted in its lyric, but this is a minor fault in a lovely ballad about the agony of separation.

The grand statement of "Time Waits for No One" ostensibly addresses one of the problems of a so far frivolous album. Its all-is-vanity topic was a surprising one considering how sensitive the age issue currently was for the band. The often formalized phraseology fits in with the very un-Stonesy musical elegance. There are exotic percussion noises and dreamy washes of keyboards and synth-replicated strings, but the heart of the song is Taylor's gilded guitar, which dominates the last third of the six-and-a-half-minute playing time. Although his fretwork is clearly the work of a talented man, it never truly takes off. This is symptomatic of an ambitious and thoughtful track that is never quite as good as one would wish it to be.

Side two opens with "Luxury", a reflection of Richards'

growing intertwined interest in reggae and Jamaica, where he maintains a home to this day. Doting dad Jagger shoehorns in a reference to his daughter in this lament of a man required to put his nose to the corporate grindstone to keep his family in comfort. The music doesn't attempt to be authentic reggae, instead representing it by a riff and Jagger's patois vocal within a rock arrangement. Either that or it does attempt to be authentic reggae and is completely ham-fisted. In that it's not clear which, we have a sign of the whole album's uncertain qualities, even if it does pass five minutes pleasantly enough. "Dance Little Sister" feels like another attempt to write an archetypal Stones rocker. Its rhythm is slightly leaden and its industrial-strength riff is unattractive. Who would have thought that the Stones would be more comfortable on ballad territory? "If You Really Want to Be My Friend" is another instantly likeable slowie. It also has something interesting and different to say. "Let me live it up like I used to do" is the narrator's plea to his beloved, whom from other lines it is clear is hated by his friends. Putting aside more speculation about Bianca, this is the best-produced track on the album, its aural polish heightened by the smooth tones of soul vocal group Blue Magic. In "Short and Curlies" Jagger chides a man that his woman has "got you by the balls". It's one of the only songs on the album that doesn't sound like it's not around a minute (or more) too long. However, that is not just attributable to its running time of under three minutes. Ian Stewart's prominent, sprightly piano is interesting in light of the fact that on this rolling blues the Stones sound comfortable in a way they rarely do elsewhere; it's like the old gang doing what they know best.

"Fingerprint File", is another side-closing grand statement of over six minutes. Its swirling, neon-lit soundscape, created by funky bass (Taylor), synthesizer (Wyman) and wah-wah guitar (Richards), is reminiscent of brooding seventies film soundtracks like that of *Shaft*. Jagger and Richards alternate vocals on a lyric that explores a concern new to the world: the sweaty paranoia induced by the knowledge of the proliferation of taps and bugs that the Watergate scandal in particular had highlighted. Jagger may also have got some inside gen on the FBI surveillance of New York-based John Lennon. Both its subject and arrangement are interesting but not only does the track run too long, the atmosphere is slightly suffocating. The excision of the spoken-word passages and pseudo telephone calls by a Jagger whose mannerisms and Americanisms are becoming more and more hammy could have made for a tight, sharp and bold performance.

Despite the relative failure of the lead-off single and the relative artistic failure of the album, *It's Only Rock 'n Roll* hit no. 1 in America and even though it was the first new Stones LP not to make no. 1 in their homeland since *Beggars Banquet*, its no. 2 UK placing was hardly something at which to sneeze. It gained some good reviews at the time, particularly from *Rolling Stone*, but you will find few today prepared to state that its merits are anything other than that of a good, minor work. This draining of initial enthusiasm is best summarized by the treatment of the album by the *Village Voice*'s Robert Christgau, who originally gave it a grading of A-minus in his famous "Consumer Guide" column but, when he revaluated it when compiling his reviews into book form in 1981, downgraded it to a B. Significantly, his original review had closed with the line, "This is definitely no *Exile* or *Let It Bleed*, but they haven't ever made a grade B LP, and there's no reason to pin the rap on this one. I don't think." That sign-off's betrayal of an attempt to kid himself was characteristic of the album's general critical reception (and indeed the reception accorded Bob Dylan's *Planet Waves* the previous year). The sixties generation were fervently – and, we now know, vainly – hoping that their idols would remain the powers they had been.

It's Only Rock 'n Roll is not a bad album per se. The craft and professionalism on display within its grooves mean that had it been the work of a new band, or even Slade, it would possibly even have been hailed as a fine piece of work. By now, the Stones were experiencing something that few other artists did when their work was evaluated: like Dylan, The Who and the ex-Beatles, their latest products were inordinately measured against their previous releases. Although this was galling for them it was also perfectly understandable, as was the fact that their new releases were being found wanting in this comparative process. A sense of deflation when the Stones' product was merely good was Fate's payback for their having created some of the greatest music ever recorded. In an industry like rock – where credibility and worth were still very much oriented around being young or at least fashionable – the critical knife was twisted further by those who queried the dignity of men their age continuing to do what they did and suggesting that they looked tired and irrelevant compared with younger acts. It being the case that they could never be young or new again, this was something to which the Stones would have to get used.

METAMORPHOSIS

Sean Egan

UK release: 1 June 1975; US release: 1 June 1975

Produced by: Various

Charts: UK no. 45; US no. 8

Tracklisting:
Out of Time
Don't Lie to Me
Some Things Just Stick in Your Mind*
Each and Every Day of the Year
Heart of Stone
I'd Much Rather Be with the Boys
(Walkin' Thru the) Sleepy City
We're Wastin' Time*
Try a Little Harder
I Don't Know Why
If You Let Me
Jiving Sister Fanny
Downtown Suzie
Family
Memo from Turner
I'm Going Down

Mick Taylor was not going to have to deal with this critical payback. At the end of 1974, he stunned The Rolling Stones by telling them he was leaving the band.

Wyman has said that they initially thought Taylor was

---

* Not originally included on the US version

bluffing and that he had indicated his desire to leave on other occasions. (He is reputed to have previously toyed with accepting an offer to join Free.) However, the unthinkable scenario of somebody voluntarily ditching "The greatest rock 'n' roll band in the world" (in legend if not prestige or sales) did indeed transpire.

Taylor has given a variety of reasons over the years for why he took this drastic action, among them the conviction that the self-parody of *It's Only Rock 'n Roll* presaged demise in any event, the frustration engendered by the inactivity of '74, which had been the first year without live Stones work since Taylor joined, and the fact that he had always somehow viewed the Stones as a temporary gig in the first place. One thing that hasn't been mentioned by Taylor but has been by others, including Tony Sanchez, Rose Taylor (Mick's wife of the time) and Anita Pallenberg, is a sexual relationship between the two Micks. If common gossip is to be believed, this would hardly be unusual for Jagger in that period, but it would potentially add a different complexion to Taylor's relationship with the band. Although some or all of these things may have fed into Taylor's feelings, according to the recollections of journalist Nick Kent the misgiving at the forefront of his mind was song-writing credits. In *The Dark Stuff*, Kent wrote of a meeting he had with Taylor in 1974: "he'd spoken excitedly about some songs he'd written with Jagger and Richards that were to appear on *It's Only Rock 'n Roll*. When I told him that I'd seen a finished sleeve with the song-writing credits and that his name wasn't featured, he went silent for a second before muttering a curt 'We'll see about that!' almost under his breath." Kent said that Taylor sounded more resigned than anything else and theorized that this was perhaps the problem: "He was too frightened to confront either Jagger or Richards directly, so he fumed in private about the miseries of being a junior partner in The Rolling Stones until he'd persuaded himself he ought to leave the group altogether."

Considering his vast talent and the fact that he was just twenty-six when he departed the band, Taylor's tepid post-Stones career is bewildering. A dynamite-sounding collaboration with ex-Cream man Jack Bruce sputtered out with no product released. Several years were wasted in a drugs torpor (ex-Mamas & The Papas kingpin John Phillips recalled Taylor telling him at one point in the seventies that he hadn't played guitar for two years). His one and only shot at the big time was a solo LP released in 1979. *Mick Taylor* is a slick record. There is the expected mellifluous guitar work but even more impressive – perhaps because it is not expected – is his singing, which exhibits a full-throated confidence few would have expected of the man who had been the shyest Stone. Yet, although a perfectly acceptable mainstream rock album, it lacked a sense of being special.

That the rest of Taylor's solo *oeuvre* mainly comprises perfunctory live albums is partly down to his bitterness over his lack of remuneration from the Stones: he has explicitly stated that he is reluctant to record when he received so little from some of history's biggest-selling works. Taylor's trouble – hinted at by Kent – is that he is too nice for his own good. His grievances about lack of reward are many: not only did he not receive credit for songs he had co-written, nor – according to him – sometimes mechanical-rights royalties for records on which he'd played, but some sources state that he has been cut out of the lucrative signing-on fee contractually due to each member on the now numerous occasions when the Stones' post-1970 catalogue has been licensed to a new distribution company. Yet despite promptings by those close to him to get what is rightfully his, he has not only never sued but has publicly insisted that a legal action is out of the question. This venality and dishonesty on the part of the Jagger/Richards axis – one that not only poisoned Taylor's time in the Stones' ranks but destroyed his potential once he had left – rather puts their grievances about Allen Klein into context.

The Stones were left in a bit of a quandary by Taylor's departure. They had already booked sessions in Munich. Having declined to cancel them once, Jagger, Watts and Wyman considered doing so when Richards failed to turn up on the first two days. Although he might have had his famously horrendous teeth fixed by this time, the cause of their rotten-ness clearly still existed in his life. When Keith did finally turn up on the third day, the quartet along with Nicky Hopkins knocked together some basic tracks. When they reconvened after Christmas, the band decided to combine the sessions with auditions for a replacement for Taylor. The result would be an album with a series of guests. A quite ridiculous but at the same time impressive series of stellar names made the trip to Rotterdam or Munich in the hope of joining the Stones' rarefied ranks, Jeff Beck, Rory Gallagher, Wayne Perkins, Harvey Mandel, Peter Frampton and Ronnie Wood among them. Even Jimmy Page made an appearance, although whether he would have left Led Zeppelin is a different issue. There are endless rumours and pieces of hearsay attached to this whole process. For instance, according to ex-Small Faces/ Faces keyboardist Ian McLagan, ex-Small Faces and Humble Pie singer-guitarist Steve Marriott would have got the job were it not for the fact that Jagger knew he was a better singer than he was. Meanwhile, Eric Clapton – who it seems may have been considered to replace Brian Jones back in '69 – has said he was surprised not to receive a call.

In the middle of all this, the Stones decided to tour America. Embarking on their longest jaunt so far in the world's biggest music market despite missing a member and despite having no new product to promote was bizarre, but perhaps the long lay-off had occasioned itchy feet. They were accompanied on the two-month "Tour of the Americas '75" that started on 1 June by Ronnie Wood. His position was a quite curious one: he was on loan from The Faces. This role was even more curious in light of the fact of how similar the two groups were: five-piece rock bands with charismatic lead singers. The Faces' 1971 hit "Stay with Me" was a dead ringer for the Stones, right down to its rampant misogyny. However, The Faces were in no way ersatz Stones: Rod Stewart was easily Jagger's superior as a singer and The Faces' collective beery, matey persona was actively hailed by some critics as a refreshing antidote to the Stones' drug-addled hauteur. At one point, The Faces had even seemed the successors to the Stones' Everyman mantel, although that point had probably passed with the departure of their original bassist and important melodic foundation, Ronnie Lane, in 1973.

During the tour, Richards was arrested yet again when a search of a vehicle found a knife and drugs. As usual, the charges somehow dribbled away to misdemeanour level. Perhaps this was in some way related to the fact that Richards claims that the FBI had arranged for him to receive top-grade heroin in order to avoid a scandalous, money-jeopardizing arrest when trying to score. Had the newspapers that were fulminating about the tour's giant inflatable penis and $10 ticket prices ("IT'S TIME WE EXORCISED THIS DEMONIC INFLUENCE OVER OUR CHILDREN!" screamed one headline) known about this, no doubt a national coronary would have resulted.

In order to have at least something vaguely new to capitalize on interest stimulated by the tour, on 6 June the band put out *Made in the Shade*, a thoroughly inferior compilation right down to its dull cover of a woman reclining on a sun lounger. There was nothing wrong with the contents but, hamstrung by Allen Klein's ownership of everything pre-1971, it was a "best of" that covered just four years of their illustrious career. They didn't even have the imagination exploitatively to throw on an unreleased track to snag the fanatics. Even so, it climbed as high as no. 6 in the States. In the UK it made no. 14.

The circumstances of a Stones tour and no new studio album were the perfect ones for Allen Klein's *Metamorphosis*, a compilation that only came into existence because Klein and Decca had the contractual right to exploit the Stones' discards from the sixties. Bill Wyman had assembled a tracklisting originally intended to be released as *The Black Box*, but Klein's avariciousness – he objected to the number of cover versions not on aesthetic grounds but because Jagger/Richards tunes would yield him publishing royalties – resulted in a compromise package. Half of the album is not even composed of Stones rejects but instead features demos played by session musicians with Jagger vocals – they were originally designed to attract cover versions. The album was issued in the UK by Decca, as per usual for such projects, but in the States this was the first Stones product to appear on Klein's own ABKCO label.

"Out of Time", of course, was the most successful Jagger/Richards "placing" of all. The version that opens this album is a hybrid of the Stones and Chris Farlowe, with Jagger singing over the orchestral backing track that would be used for the Farlowe hit. Jagger invests no less emotion than on the *Aftermath* cut but the rapid pace and female backing vocals rob it of that rendition's brooding vengefulness. "Don't Lie to Me" is the only genuine Stones cut on the original vinyl side one. Dating from June 1964 (i.e. it's an out-take from that drab *Rolling Stones No. 2* album), it's a rather perfunctory cover of a not especial Chuck Berry song. "Some Things Just Stick in Your Mind" is a yowling country number. The arrangement may include celebrated musicians like Clem Cattini and Jimmy Page, but it's meandering and unattractive. On "Each and Every Day of the Year", producer Oldham, deep in his Phil Spector period, gamely tries to make something of a gauche, melodramatic ballad with mariachi brass and piano glissandos. "Heart of Stone" is given an arrangement here in which genteel pedal steel vies with deafening electric guitar. "I'd Much Rather Be with the Boys" is the only song ever to be credited to Andrew Loog Oldham and Keith Richards. The narrator notes that his love has so soured that he would prefer to be with his mates. Although nothing special, it's an interesting lyrical angle and its frilly pop stylings, while hardly Stonesy, are whole-hearted.

The highly melodic "(Walkin' Thru the) Sleepy City" has a dense and rich arrangement more in keeping with a finished track than a demo. The ingénue tone that it shares with so many of these early Jagger/Richards tunes would make this almost laughable on a Stones album, but it's thoroughly enjoyable on its own terms. "We're Wastin' Time" is a mediocre country-inflected ballad with a waltz rhythm. It's one of the bizarre footnotes of the Stones' career that gap-toothed, mop-topped Liverpudlian comedian Jimmy Tarbuck issued this song as a single on Oldham's Immediate label in 1965. With its doo-doo-doo cooing, quick-stepping beat and infectious brass, "Try a Little Harder" is a feel-good confection and a worthwhile listen.

Side two comprises genuine Stones recordings of various vintage.

"I Don't Know Why" is a Stevie Wonder song that the artist wrote with Paul Riser, Don Hunter and Lula Hardaway. A *Let*

It Bleed out-take, it was of recent vintage when the Stones essayed it. Aside from some molten Mick Taylor guitar lines, their version is not remarkable but it does occupy a singular place in the band's history: this was the track on which the Stones were working when the horrific news came through to Olympic Studios that Brian Jones was dead. "If You Let Me" is of *Between the Buttons* vintage and instantly recognizable as such from the circular, fey, self-consciously breathless tone characteristic of that album. "Jiving Sister Fanny" is another *Let It Bleed* out-take. Although Taylor's larger-than-life guitar is a pleasing presence and the cut has a certain drive, its clipped R & B is over-generic. Listening to it, one is struck by the fact that many second-tier bands would have considered it a releasable product. Such conscientiousness in song selection is what differentiates the also-rans from the gods. "Downtown Suzie" could have been Wyman's second-ever contribution to a Stones album and indeed his first "proper" Stones track, as the rest of the group are fully involved with it. However, he withdrew it from consideration for *Beggars Banquet* and a subsequently overdubbed version from consideration for *Let It Bleed*. The chorus is infectious but the track as an entity is disjointed and Jagger's mockney delivery questionable.

"Family" is a *Beggars Banquet* out-take of a dark hue. Jagger's attacks the values of the family at a point in history where sexual liberation and anti-authoritarianism briefly made it seem a repressive set-up that needed to be questioned if not outright destroyed. Today, with the family less exalted (or perhaps more exalted as something irrevocably gone in its old form), it packs far less power than it would have if originally released, although its flat, morbid music in any case makes the issue moot. The "Memo from Turner" heard here is an earlier version than the one originally released and features the Stones augmented by Nicky Hopkins and Traffic's Steve Winwood and Jim Capaldi. Very different from the soundtrack version, its rushed pace, over-metallic guitar and glib vocal delivery are the perfect means by which to obscure the brilliance of Jagger's lyric. "I'm Going Down" is a *Sticky Fingers* out-take originally listed as written by Jagger/Richards/Taylor on the label of *Metamorphosis* but even that rare Taylor credit was withdrawn on the second pressing. This focus-lacking soup of a track closed a side that, soberingly, was not superior as a listening experience to the pseudo-Stones fare on side one.

The quality of *Metamorphosis* very much resembles a bootleg, right down to thrill turning to deflation; the excitement of being privy to a behind-the-scenes look at a band's music-making process turns into apprehension that there was a reason that the group had rejected the tracks. The bootleg ambience even extended to the fatuous title and cover art: the album's sleeve shows the six men so far to have been permanent Stones revealed to be giant-sized insects, an apparent allusion to Kafka's similarly themed story, "The Metamorphosis", although the reason for this literary reference is incomprehensible.

Two singles were released from *Metamorphosis*. "I Don't Know Why" b/w "Try a Little Harder" predated it (23 May 1975) and climbed to no. 42 in the US. "Out of Time"/"Jiving Sister Fanny" appeared on 12 August in the US and 5 September in the UK. Although the latter only managed to climb to no. 81 in *Billboard*'s Hot 100, it made a respectable no. 45 in Britain during a curious period in which there were four versions of "Out of Time" circulating on 45 rpm disc, the others being the re-released Chris Farlowe hit and versions by Dan McCafferty of Nazareth and Kris Ife.

The last thing anyone might have expected from Decca after the cynical ragbag that was *Metamorphosis* was a change in policy implicitly repudiating all the sub-standard Stones compilations of recent years. However, the label's Alan Fitter decided on a new approach. The result of this was an ambitious project called *The Essential Rolling Stones*. In the mid-seventies, the boxed set was a concept still in its infancy and – up until 1979's six-LP MCA collection *The Complete Buddy Holly* – it was a format restricted to the mail-order sector. Compiled with the assistance of *New Musical Express* scribe and Stones scholar Roy Carr, *The Essential Rolling Stones* was intended to be a three-album affair housed in a handsome case with an accompanying twelve-page booklet sold in normal retail outlets. The tracklisting included all the Decca UK Stones single A-sides and key album tracks. Many would have been delighted to receive this package in their stocking at Christmas 1974, its scheduled release period. Carr later wrote, "Test pressings were made, boxes ordered, text and photographs prepared, but as 'delicate' negotiations were taking place between Decca and ABKCO, the project was killed (allegedly at Klein's request) at boardroom level." Fitter disagreed, citing a lack of packaging at the pressing plant.

In the end, the project transmuted into *Rolled Gold: The Very Best of The Rolling Stones*, a double album released on 15 November 1975. Although it must have been soul-destroying for Carr and Fitter to see the original concept shelved after all their hard work, the set still managed to fulfil the original brief of encompassing all the British singles and most noteworthy album tracks up until the end 1969, especially on side four, where "Honky Tonk Women" heralded the formidable quintet of "Sympathy for the Devil", "Street Fighting Man", "Midnight Rambler" and "Gimme Shelter". An excellent introduction for the initiate, it spent fifty weeks in the UK chart, peaking at no. 7.

The reasoning behind Klein's apparent self-sabotage became a little more understandable on 21 October 1977, when *Get Stoned* hit the British market. A chronologically sequenced double-set with much the same rationale and contents as *Rolled Gold*, it pulled the rug from under the latter's feet, firstly by exploiting its ability to include 1971's "Brown Sugar" and "Wild Horses" and secondly by being licensed to a budget label, Arcade. Its quasi-crass title is a stark contrast to the classy handle given to the Decca set, while its cover of what looks like a giant plaster cast of Jagger's rubber lips, complete with the diamond stud he had recently had set into one of his teeth, lacks the quiet dignity of the *Rolled Gold* sleeve, which featured face shots against a black background. Despite its extra rewards, *Get Stoned* peaked one place lower in the UK album chart than had *Rolled Gold*, spending just fifteen weeks in its environs.

Story of the Stones was a 22 November 1982 double "best of" released by the most famous UK budget label of the era, K-Tel. It included some of the earlier singles spurned by the Arcade set but had its own drawbacks in being unable to include "Brown Sugar" and "Wild Horses", being non-chronologically arranged and being artless, excluding "Gimme Shelter" in favour of the likes of "Off the Hook" and "You Better Move On". This peaked at no. 24.

There would be only one more Decca compilation, *Slow Rollers*, a 6 November 1981 release that at least had a theme, even if shining a light on the tender side of "The greatest rock 'n' roll band in the world" might be said to be fatuous. In the spirit of all those old shoddy Decca compilations, some rarities were mixed in to entice those who already had most of the tracks, most notably "Con le Mie Lacrime".

As this live review demonstrates, the '75 Tour of the Americas marked a point where people suspected that the Stones were past their best but had no way of proving it – especially in the face of their fearsome live prowess.

IT ISN'T ONLY ROCK AND ROLL

Robert Christgau

First published in *Village Voice*, June 1975

My friend Anne Hill and I went to see the Rolling Stones in Toronto a few days before they got to New York. Our Row K tickets put us in the combat zone, with visual access blocked by less-privileged fans who'd fought their way to the forward aisles. So we stood up for most of a two-hour set in an un-air-conditioned hockey rink, packed in among dozens of human space heaters. It was tight like that. At one point I reasoned with a third-line forward who had edged in behind me by standing on his feet, and later I threatened to push a scrawny photographer off Anne's chair.

The hostility felt good, like the sweat – a survival mechanism that distracted me a little from the Stones but brought me closer to the reality principle, which is half of what the Stones are supposed to do. I experienced it as neither programmatic nor vindictive, just practical. I figure anyone who isn't willing to stand up for two hours doesn't deserve to see the Stones, especially on a free ticket. And I was jumping up and down quite a bit more than the sightlines demanded anyhow.

Later I had it from reliable sources that this show was the worst of the current tour, and I can believe it. It certainly wasn't transcendent. And yet there I was jumping up and down. For the simple truth is that the Stones never put on a bum show – they're transcendent when they're good and merely good when they're bad. If the guitars and the drums and Jagger's voice come together audibly in those elementary patterns that no one else has ever managed to simulate, the most undeniable rock and roll excitement is a virtually automatic result. To insist that this excitement doesn't reach you is not to articulate an aesthetic judgment but to assert a rather uninteresting crotchet of taste. It is to boast that you don't like rock and roll itself. For the Stones are the peak of the term.

For some reason (because this could be the last time? I don't know) the Stones' preeminence in their chosen field of endeavor seems finally to have earned them genuine respect in the world at large. Their music has achieved the third station of truth – first ignored, then denied, it is now taken for granted – as their image has softened, from satanic majesties down to playmates of Andy and Bianca into friendly Garden-variety celebrities. Tour One Post-Altamont, in 1972, was a time for recriminations both thoughtful and mindless in the press. This time, however, the Stones are presented not only as great professionals but as great professionals doing likable work.

The Stones, yes. Yes, we are told by Frank Conroy (a litterateur who also, the blurb says, "plays jazz piano professionally") and Joyce Maynard (who when she was younger was heralded as the youngest writer in the world) and Nik Cohn (whose history of rock loses much of its fine flash just when the music is getting serious), yes, this Rolling Stones music can be wonderful stuff. It makes Frank feel good right down to his socks; it introduces Joyce to sex and danger; it satisfies Nik's need for urgency and rage. They really like it, they do – but they don't go overboard. Conroy, who since he writes for the *New York Times Magazine* must know, determines that the Stones understand the zeitgeist no better than their audience. Maynard, who is into waltzing these days, concludes that they no longer speak for Her Generation. Cohn, who has been lamenting the brief half-life of supernovae for at least a quarter of his own, warns that they've become smug caricatures of their own uncouthness. The great Rolling Stones mind-fuck has ended if it ever really began, of that we are assured – it really is *only* rock and roll.

Well, perhaps it is. As Mick has noted in one of his more regrettable moments, time waits for no one. Like all of us, the

Stones are subject to history – the world's (Conroy's hustle),
their fans (Maynard's hustle), and their own (Cohn's hustle).
And they do seem to be wearing down a little. Their two most
recent albums, *Goats Head Soup* and *It's Only Rock 'n Roll*,
represent a nadir. It's hard to imagine the Stones even recording songs as tritely portentous as "Dancing With Mr D" or
"Time Waits for No One" or "Fingerprint File" five years ago,
much less releasing them or (as they do with "Fingerprint
File") performing them live. And even the peaks of these
albums – which I would identify as "Starfucker" and "If You
Can't Rock Me," respectively – simply don't match "Rip This
Joint" and "Sweet Virginia" and "Soul Survivor" and "Happy"
on *Exile on Main Street*, or "Bitch" and "Brown Sugar" and
"Moonlight Mile" on *Sticky Fingers*, or (God knows) "Gimme
Shelter" and "You Can't Always Get What You Want" on *Let It
Bleed* or "Street Fighting Man" and "Salt of the Earth" on
Beggars Banquet. Lists compiled by other Stones fans might
differ, but not their conclusions; relatively speaking, the two
latest LPs are forgettable stuff.

But that is only relatively speaking, for even at their most
perfunctory the Stones remain, at least so far, the peak of the
form: what's more, it's relative to their late work, all recorded
well after what observers like Maynard and Cohn regard as
their apotheosis. However passionate and urgent the music of
the Stones' early years (say *The Rolling Stones Now!*) and
middle period (try *Aftermath*) continues to sound, it is simply
not as rich and powerful as the work of their supposed decline.
Even proceeding from the common supposition that the
middle period extends through *Let It Bleed*, with the decline
beginning at Altamont (now almost half a career behind them,
by the way), we are left with *Sticky Fingers* and *Exile on Main
Street* on the saggy side of the dividing line. Joyce Maynard
says *Sticky Fingers* is the last Stones album she bought, and I
understand why – it was confusing when it came out, trifling
with decadence just when a lot of us were anticipating some
sort of apology or retribution. But listening to it now, a lot, I
think it may stand as their best album ever, with the competition coming from *Exile*, a two-record set so dense and various
that it is only after three years that I'm finally beginning to feel

some fatigue with it. Joyce could do worse than trade in some waltzes for a copy.

All this opinionizing is intended to remind you that the Stones are real Artists with an Oeuvre that relates to the well-known Zeitgeist. Such aestheticism is unorthodox for me – I like to locate music culturally, at its intersection with society – but it does get down to what I value about the Stones. It is a little obtuse, after all, to downgrade a rock group because rock culture itself has become so pluralistic and unfocused, hence decreasingly relevant – especially when the rock group has done much better than most with the available options. When Joyce Maynard declares evenly that she has outgrown the Stones and Nik Cohn triumphantly records the indifference of some designated everypunk – when two people who should know better ignore the work to tell us that this group doesn't conform to their obsolescent notion of what rock and roll should be – they make it easier for a man-about-letters like Frank Conroy to misrepresent that work altogether, albeit with moderately kind intentions.

The Stones' music used to create the impression that it was for kids because the Stones were quite young and their manager steered them towards an audience of adolescent rebels. But now they are in their mid-thirties, what's left of the rebel youth culture has lost much of its credibility and all of its cohesion, and Rolling Stones songs like "Torn and Frayed" and "Soul Survivor" – in fact all of *Exile on Main Street* – are about growing old with rock and roll. This music is weary and complicated and ironic and buried in its own drudgery, with all the old Stones themes – sex as power, sex as love, sex as pleasure, distance, craziness, release – piled on top of the implicit obsession with the passage of time. But it rocks harder than ever.

For what distinguished such songs from the ambitious work of other mature groups is not just that the Stones can manage all the extra thematic involvements but also that they rock even harder while doing so. Their music has always attracted the smartest fans because it never let its own realism get it down. It insists that it is possible to think and act at the same time, and at its most transcendent it promises a plausible triumph to those who are listening at peak attention. That may not be the zeitgeist, which is looking pretty dreary these days. But it's a really terrific substitute.

We are all still thinking about aesthetics here, what you can get from the records that you need even more than you want. But as masters of their options, the Stones haven't given up on culture. Because the promise of rock and roll is one teenagers are readier to believe, the Stones still got the kids and there were plenty of them at the Garden for the New York opener. But the crowd was markedly older than the one in Toronto, it was also hipper, more affluent, and more Mediterranean. The cross-section felt like youth culture revisited. When Carola and I arrived at 8:20 the already fierce energy level was being whipped higher by some fancy lighting and the dozens of steel bands who had been hired to roam the arena in lieu of an opening act. It had been years since I'd been in such a galvanic mass audience. Gradually the steel bands centered in front of the mirrored pyramid that would unfold into a six-pointed star stage at showtime. The crowd wanted the Stones. When the steel bands began to play "Satisfaction" instead, there was some ominous booing. But the Stones arrived in the nick of time.

From the loge, I could consider the art of the Stones more coolly. I have my reservations. Jagger's hyperactive stamina, two hours of motion, is an athletic marvel, but his moves aren't getting any subtler or more organic and he's pouting too much. Billy Preston is the most actively offensive in a long line of less than worthy side musicians. The selection of songs could be subtler and more demanding. And perhaps because it was opening night in New York, they were working too hard. Not a great show.

But there is an aesthetic purpose to all this. The 1972 tour really did suggest retribution. It was careful and even friendly; "Sympathy for the Devil" was not performed, the spirit of the gentle, musicianly Mick Taylor permeated the proceedings. Taylor's replacement, Ron Wood of the Faces, is a raver with a guitar as dirty, technically speaking, as Billy Preston's organ, but a lot more bracing. And because the others are constant his spirit comes through. The Faces are arrogant, but not in

the majestic fashion of the 1969 Stones, and the bumptious-
ness of the Stones' 1975 show is reminiscent of their foolish
playfulness. Jagger's rubber voice has taken on some high trills
and a faintly tasteless Satchmo growl, and though I'm pleased
to report that he's kicking his inflatable penis more and caress-
ing it less, that dumb joke seems to epitomize his current
attitude. I was struck by a new move in which he rolled down
an incline like a little kid getting dizzy. He could stamp his foot
and say "We are too the Rolling Stones" and it would not be
out of character.

The climax of New York was "Sympathy for the Devil". All
the steel drums came out again and played so loud you not
only couldn't hear the words, you could barely hear his voice.
Was this statement deliberate? I wondered. But Eric Clapton
appeared and ripped off a stunningly filthy solo, the steel rang
on, and without intending to – I've never been too crazy about
"Sympathy for the Devil," which I regard as middlebrow – I
began to get a buzz of transcendence.

"Sympathy for the Devil" was a coup, a genuinely impressive reassertion of their old prerogatives, and I went away high.
When I consider it coolly, though, I think it's more than possible that they've peaked. But Anne and Carola, who had never
seen the Stones, each thought her respective show was the best
she'd ever seen.

I wonder what I'll think of them in 1978.

BLACK AND BLUE

Sean Egan

UK release: 23 April 1976; US release: 15 April 1976

Produced by: The Glimmer Twins

Charts: UK no. 2; US no. 1

Tracklisting:
Hot Stuff
Hand of Fate
Cherry Oh Baby
Memory Motel
Hey Negrita
Melody
Fool to Cry
Crazy Mama

When the Stones embarked on a five-week European tour on 28 April 1976, Ronnie Wood was officially and permanently a Rolling Stone. The announcement had been made on 19 December 1975 after the implosion of The Faces. His retention seemed to some a genuine reinvigoration of a lately wayward band. Mick Taylor had been as shy on stage as Brian Jones had been extroverted, but in the *NME* Charles Shaar Murray noted of one of the tour's gigs that the energetic, rooster-haired newcomer with a fag permanently drooping from his lips, "erodes Richard's previously obvious Number Two Son position". He also noted how "right" Wood's presence felt: "Messrs. Wood and Richard flanked Jagger, looking for all the world like a pair of diseased crows. They're a remarkably well-matched pair both eyewise and earwise."

The Faces' rupture had been caused by the departure from their ranks of Rod Stewart. Although Stewart's parallel solo career had been far more successful than that of The Faces since his 1971 smash "Maggie May", with his latest album, *Atlantic Crossing*, he had exhibited for the first time a reluctance to use The Faces – in whole or part – on his own work. Subsequently, his interviews were littered with put-downs of the supposed slovenliness of his ex-colleagues' playing. Yet despite this and the fact that Wood had set off on the road with The Faces just a week after the end of the Stones' massive Tour of the Americas, Stewart pushed the blame on Wood for The Faces' split, citing as one of his reasons for leaving the fact that Wood "seems to be permanently 'on loan' to The Rolling Stones". Nonetheless, it was obvious that Stewart's actions had released Wood from an agonizing moral dilemma. He hadn't wanted to be responsible for The Faces breaking up but was unable to resist the overtures of a band he admitted he revered. Idolatry was clearly in Wood's blood: in this period he proceeded to become an almost embarrassingly transparent disciple of Richards, teasing his hair in an identical manner and adopting his penchant for bell-bottom trousers. Sometimes one would have to look twice at a photograph to be sure which Stones guitarist was pictured.

Although nobody disputes his technical abilities, and although he enabled a return to the two meshing rhythm-guitar parts with which Richards had always been more comfortable than the rhythm-and-lead format necessitated by Taylor's virtuosity, Wood would seem to have been recruited to the Stones for social reasons as much as any. Wood's sense of humour gelled with that of Richards, who later said of the good-natured but sombre Taylor, "he doesn't know any Max Miller jokes!" It's highly doubtful that Wayne Perkins knows any Max Miller jokes either. Richards has admitted that the Alabama-born sessioner had just about got the job before Wood started playing with the group but that retaining the Englishness of the band was another factor in Wood's favour.

Some are of the opinion that the incorporation of Wood's staccato, chicken-scratch technique into a band that already had a guitarist with a style not a million miles from that description has been a bad thing for both Wood and the Stones. The delight both take on stage in the nobody-knows-who's-going-to-take-the-solo spontaneity of Wood's and Richards' interlocking styles is clearly genuine, but the arid lack of contrast between their guitar techniques on record has become ever more noticeable down the years. A bad thing for Wood alone is the paucity of songwriting opportunities his tenure in the Stones has afforded him, as exemplified by the "Inspiration by Ron Wood" he was magnanimously granted by the band for his major contribution to *Black and Blue*'s "Hey Negrita". Wood had been a prolific songwriter, mainly in collaboration with Rod Stewart, hitherto.

Wood stared at the public from the gatefold cover of the album *Black and Blue* (the deadpan expression of a man known for always seeming to have a smile on his face an apparent measure of his absorption into the big, bad Stones) but he appeared on only two of its eight tracks. The high quality of the playing of the applicants to be in the band makes it understandable that the Stones were reluctant to replace their solos, but the decision not to get Wood to record over their parts backfired on them: a feeling that taped auditions were being passed off as a Stones album was one of several things to provoke the accusation that *Black and Blue* was an ersatz product. Another was the fact that in "Fool to Cry" the album had been presaged on 8 April 1976 in the US (16 April in the UK) by a single that aroused even more contempt than "Angie" had among the aficionados: not only did it again seem to some soppy and anti-rock but it saw Jagger adopt a falsetto that was for many a risible vocal manifestation of his increasingly gratuitous, camp stage mannerisms. Fuel to the fires of indignation was the fact that it proceeded to be a hit (no. 10 in the US, no. 6 in the UK and a big seller in many other territories) on the back of sales from ballad-happy types who one suspected had barely heard of the Stones.

Then there was the grand air of decadence about the project: the album has a slightly menacing ambience and towering, brutal sound. The decadent air was added to by the fact that it had been eighteen months since their last album: the decreasing visibility of the rock aristocracy was becoming a seventies bone of contention. The promotional campaign worsened things. One billboard advertisement featured a bound and bruised woman declaring "I'm Black and Blue from The Rolling Stones – and I love it!" Five years before, it would have been received as just another manifestation of the Stones' trailblazing outrageousness and sexual frankness. The fact that the criticism surrounding it was coming not from reactionary old farts but from people on the left of the political spectrum indicated that the Stones had not moved with the changing times.

Above all, though, the album was affected by the disillusion of a generation of thirty-somethings who had all their adult lives nurtured the idea of the Stones as harbingers of social change and champions of the dissident. Although there was nothing within these grooves that could plausibly be posited as socially regressive or evidence of them defecting to the Other Side, there was also absolutely nothing here to which to cling as proof of the Stones enduring as a totem of a set of querulous values. *Sticky Fingers* had dripped with daring drug references and *Exile on Main St.* had been peppered with the likes of "fucking", "cunt" and "shit". The implicitly anti-authoritarian air of those records had not been so much in evidence on *Goats Head Soup*, but the kiss-off of persistent outrageousness that its final track had constituted went a long way to dispelling doubts. Even *It's Only Rock 'n Roll* had possessed a just-about-risqué song title in "Short and Curlies", and in any case nothing much about losing touch could be extrapolated from one album, even when set against a backdrop of Jagger's partying with lords, ladies and other folk one could never imagine listening to rock or being amenable to the values of its audience. *Black and Blue* boasted no drug references, no obscenities, no social commentary and no overt or covert hint that these artists were once considered a danger to everything held dear by society's institutions. The resultant feeling in the air was best summed up by *Creem*. "The heat's off because it's all over, they really don't matter any more or stand for

anything," Lester Bangs averred. "This is the first meaningless Stones album . . ."

All of that was aside from quality issues. After the way that
lukewarm reviews of *Exile on Main St.* had within a few years
transformed into a critical consensus that it was a masterpiece,
the Stones could forever take comfort in the idea that they
might one day be vindicated over an album greeted with disappointment. However, few others were going to be thus kidding
themselves. Not even the most ardent Stones loyalist could
pretend that *Black and Blue* (any more than *Goats Head Soup*
or *It's Only Rock 'n Roll*) might join *Exile* in the ranks of the
belatedly venerated.

That said, it was something of an injustice that even the
album's adventurousness was held against it. As alluded to by
the title, the record was the band's most pronounced embrace-
ment of black music since they had mutated from a
rhythm-and-blues outfit into a rock group more than a decade
previously. As well as reggae and jazz – which they had rarely
essayed previously – they were tackling the newer sounds of
funk and disco. Far from being hailed for venturing into novel
territory, the band were ridiculed for it by the very critics who
had condemned them for treading water on their previous two
albums. It was apparently presumptuous of millionaires and
the nigh middle-aged to seek to get down with young, impoverished trendies.

The sound of the record is clean and spacious, courtesy of
engineer Keith Harwood, who took over from Johns. It's also
sparer, although the idea that Wood's arrival coincided with
the departure of the brass that had diverted the Stones from
their rock roots is a myth disproven by the absence of horns
from *It's Only Rock 'n Roll*, on which he did not play. The
emphasis is on the drums, the emphatic mixing of Watts one of
the main reasons for the menacing timbre. There are only
eight tracks on the record but the apparent parsimoniousness
was illusory – the album ran to forty-plus minutes, short by
the Stones' recent standards but typical length for a rock
album.

Disco number "Hot Stuff" is clearly intended to be an
explosive opener but is more of a damp firecracker. Although

musical self-aggrandisement is a staple of the medium, when Mick drawls, "The music is mighty, mighty fine", he's striking off into the same hazardous territory as on "Can You Hear the Music". Rather than mighty, mighty fine, the track veers over its five-plus minutes from strangely hesitant to slickly assured and back again. Robbing it of any feeling of authenticity are Harvey Mandel's wiggly guitar workouts, which don't gel with the track's taut, rhythmic groove. Also problematical is the pompousness of Mick's lyric. There's no law that says somebody immodest of means can't express solidarity with the man in the ghetto, but Jagger's patronizing advice to the people of New York that he is aware they are going broke but "I know you're tough!" is grating. As the B-side of "Fool to Cry", the track charted at no. 49 in the States. "Hand of Fate" is straight-ahead rock but its Wild West scenario sounds as though it was inspired by Bob Marley's "I Shot the Sheriff". The archetypal genre slang ("I should have known it was a one-horse town") is enjoyable, but, as with the first track, the instrumentation sounds like it could have done with a few more run-throughs to shake the stiffness out of the band. Canned Heat's Wayne Perkins is the man playing guitar parts that are incongruously dazzling for the Stones this time.

"Cherry Oh Baby" was a 1971 Jamaican single by Eric Donaldson. A jerky reggae with spasms of organ, it relied for much of its charm on the abandoned, nigh-falsetto vocal of the artist. That and its brevity. The Stones manage to add a minute to the song but their version – one of the two Wood tracks – has begun to drag before that extra time is reached. Although the "riddim" is authentic enough, it is a little lumbering, while there is also the impression that afflicts much of this album – particularly side one – that the whole enterprise was recorded in a chilly barn. "Memory Motel" is a seven-minute epic that closed the first side of the album. It begins with some surprisingly good piano work from Jagger. Richards and Billy Preston pitch in on electric piano and synthesizer, while Wayne Perkins plays acoustic guitar and Harvey Mandel adds understated electric guitar. Mick and Keith alternate singing duties on a most curious lyric, a novelistic affair about a peachy, hazel-eyed, curved-nosed bar singer called Hannah with whom the narrator spends a night at the titular motel and who gifts him the song's reflective chorus after grabbing his guitar off him. The narrator can't get her out of his head as he embarks on a 10,000-mile, fifteen-state tour. Meanwhile the music is a high-gloss ballad crossed with half-hearted attempts at soul.

Reasonably good though much of side one is, only on side two do we get crackling, assured performances rather than concoctions that never quite sound like they are finished masters. The rock–reggae hybrid, "Hey Negrita", is a corker of an opener, combining a lyric spun out of a racially insensitive compliment shouted at Jagger's "old lady" with a vicious, splintered riff that should have got Wood a co-writing credit. Jagger is at his vocal best on stuff like this, whooping, hollering and growling the repartee between a man and a prostitute he can't afford. "Melody" also lends itself well to Jagger's penchant for the exaggerated and comedic. A playful number about a man who is maltreated and ultimately deserted by a fickle lover, it sees the band brilliantly embrace the idioms of jazz both musical (elastic rhythm) and lyrical ("I'm looking for her high and low like a mustard for a ham"). Jagger duets on the chorus with Billy Preston, who proves himself every bit as delightfully extroverted as the lead singer. He also, naturally, provides some excellent keyboards. An elegant horn interlude is the icing on the delicious cake. When playing the Jagger/ Richards "Melody" with his band the Rhythm Kings, Wyman has been known to introduce it from the stage as a song written by Preston. This is probably an exaggeration, although less so than claims by others that "Melody" is a rewrite of Preston's very mildly similar 1973 recording "Do You Love Me". However, the fact that the track carries the credit "Inspiration by Billy Preston" tells its own story. The keyboardist was not as sanguine about his lack of remuneration as was Wood over the identically credited "Hey Negrita".

"Fool to Cry" is a soulful, swirling ballad underscored by Jagger's electric piano in which Mick once again can't help shoehorning in a reference to his beloved daughter. The daddy who is being told he is a fool to cry in another verse is a man whose lover employs the fatherly term of endearment. One would say it's a most unusual recording for the Stones, but that description applies to just about everything else here. Vaunting bad-boy Jagger enunciating a track in which he – or at least the narrator – is posited as weeping about his problems, singing the chorus in a high pitch and intoning "I'm a certified fool" was certainly a new Stones experience that many found hard to stomach (the indigestion worsened by the fact that the narrator's problems were depicted as poverty-related and by the way the track feels a little too enamoured with itself). However, it's a sweet thing that leaves its refrain circling in one's brain. "Crazy Mama" closes the album with what some will have found a mercifully archetypal hard-riffing, anthemic Stones sound, although apparently in the spirit of the album's new horizons it's a somehow larger-than-life variant. Mick and Keith play all the guitar parts, while Jagger lets rip with a blustering lyric in which the narrator squares up to someone who has done him wrong, its repeated warning of a knee-capping in keeping with the album's threatening tone.

Black and Blue is a respectable album divided between a side that tries hard but doesn't always work and a side of consistent quality. Unfortunately, it was not received or reviewed on those musical terms but through the prism of the issue of whether it seemed to represent world-changing social upheaval or communicated something philosophically or politically profound. The Stones could hardly be blamed for the fact that it did none of those things. Part of the problem was that the world had already changed, and they were responsible for much of that change. For instance, no obscenity would be shocking any more because they had helped make society more informal and explicit by example. Meanwhile, even had they been minded to write songs of social commentary or rebel posturing, those critics who noted the omission of such things would surely be the ones questioning its seemliness for men of their age and means. The Rolling Stones were in an awkward place at an unresolved point in history, unable any more to be the rebel figureheads they had once been. That for the next few albums they would have to endure reviews – especially in more politically minded Britain – shot through

with disenchantment over their lost import was only the half of
it. The Stones were soon about to be shaken to their founda-
tions by a musical movement that would have been impossible
without their spiritual and musical example but whose practitioners held them in utter contempt.

Jonh [sic] Ingham was one of the first journalists to write about The Sex Pistols, the band who made a virtue of the fact that they despised what The Rolling Stones had come to stand for. In this snapshot of a moment eight months before the Pistols moved from cult to national fame, Ingham captures both the way the Stones' rebelliousness was spilling over into malevolent decadence and the increasing restlessness of writers who had once idolized them.

Ingham says that in its first appearance in May 1976 in British music weekly Sounds, *the article took a "very different form". He explains, "While the thrust and 90 per cent of the descriptions are as I wrote it, when it got published literally every reference to Keith's drug taking had been cut, and not with any finesse. The biggest change would be some of the stage descriptions – I wasn't bold enough to actually say that a lot of it sucked."*

AND SITTETH AT THE RIGHT HAND . . .

Jonh Ingham

First published on jonh-ingham.blogspot.co.uk, February 2007

April 29, 1976. Frankfurt, Germany: when I meet Dwayne he is busy crumbling golden-coloured hash from a thumb-sized block into a small, functional pipe. Like almost everyone in the first 30 feet of audience Dwayne is American and like them he wears an embroidered denim shirt covered with badges of his favourite groups, as though this hip uniform will offset his very short hair. Dwayne and his buddies are stationed at a local US Air Force base. Which one Dwayne won't say, because what he is doing is not only illegal but can get him court martialled. But hey! – we're about to see The Rolling Stones!

Dwayne is from a no-nothing town in a no-nothing state, where he'd be today if he hadn't been drafted. Fortunately, the Viet Nam War is over – his older brother went and a shadow came back, eyes permanently full of tracers and incomings.

Not that Dwayne has avoided carnage – he worked at the local munitions factory and one day a building blew sky high and to get out he had to scramble over some people who weren't so lucky. But in 1976 military service means a career opportunity instead of a place where every step really is a dance with Mr D and not an inane lyric.

Of course Dwayne's favourite Stone is Keith. He is: The Riff, The Rhythm, The Rebel Without Rules. Dwayne looks at me with eyes that have seen death and as the sweet Moroccan smoke pours from his lungs he says, "Hell I'm here for the same reason you are, right? Because they're the greatest rock and roll band in the world."

When we enter journalist Charles Shaar Murray's hotel room he is gluing together a generous joint. The contents of the mini-bar crowd a small round table and he gestures to the bottles in invitation. "We're on the road with The Rolling Stones!" Charles is doing the natural thing; the Stones' reputation is an undertow pulling us from the shores of sobriety, but he is willing to help us past the shallows and reefs to the outer depths because he is also playing that rockcrit game: I can get drugged up, hang with the stars, be a Rebel Without Rules, and still write a better story than you.

We drain the bottles and smoke the joints. Our Stones-view is clear: Keith is the world's most elegantly wasted human being – some of us even dress like we raided his laundry basket. Mick is a social-climbing hypocrite. The new album *Black and Blue* is the work of an oldies band – Charles has just mauled it in print. But that's OK, because they're The Rolling Stones. "We" are the UK's rock critics, the elite with Born To Analyse Rock & Roll tattooed on our arms. We sneer at hacks like those from the two London papers the *Evening Standard* and *Evening News*, who have been promised yet-to-happen interviews with Jagger and relentlessly shadow each other, neither wanting the other to get the scoop. We will get the story just by swimming in the depths.

Shortly after a purple scarf is placed on the drum podium the lights go down and the band walks out. A spot picks out Keith as he cranks up the intro to "Honky Tonk Women" and then BLAM! It's loud, it's awesome, it's the Greatest Rock and Roll Band In The World!

The band stands still, working the music, leaving Jagger out front to pout and swagger, shimmy and blow kisses and do all those Jagger things. The stage is a masterpiece in white, which the band slowly starts to use in their various stage roles of running, jumping, standing still. The sound is dreadful, at first all rhythm, then painful slabs of trebly guitar. Jagger works really hard at being Jagger, interspersed with showbiz *shtick* that we've never before seen in rock and roll: manhandling a dragon, fighting a huge blow-up penis that half-heartedly erupts from the stage floor, swinging on a rope. It's ok, but it doesn't look cool until you see it frozen in photos. Do the Stones think that playing the world's most dangerous music is no longer enough?

The old hits remind us why we're alive; the new, ordinary songs from *Black and Blue* pull us back from Olympus. Jagger talks to us, prods us – "C'mon Frankfurt!" – trying to find the magic thread in an off night, but he does it using a preposterous Negro accent and the unwanted thought creeps into view that, really, the singer is a bit of a tosser.

They end with the crowd pleasers of "Jumpin' Jack Flash" and "Street Fighting Man", played fast and messy. Then, in the midst of the noise is a huge out of tune twang and Keith is . . . let Charlie Murray describe it: "You know the riffs: that when Keith Richard comes into the room rock and roll walks in the door. Yeah, well rock and roll just fell on its arse." Mick looks back and with an *"oh dear"* expression minces over, swooping on the move to pick up the dropped plectrum and hand it to Keith, who is sitting with splayed legs, hammering away with his fingers.

We are ushered into Keith and Ron's suite – large, high-ceilinged, matching bodyguards at the door. In the centre an open flight case holds two Fender amplifiers. A cassette deck on top of one plays Furry Lewis, Robert Johnson, Burning Spear. In a corner Ron lounges on an ornate couch. Against the wall on the other side Keith holds court with a group of journalists and I kneel on the floor directly to his right. The chair looks like a throne and he's draped over it like discarded clothes, holding in his right hand a foot long slab of turquoise, flat on the upper surface and jagged on the underside. If he puts it down it will tip over and spill the contents of the flat side, which he's not going to because it holds what looks like a Himalayan range of cocaine. It's a dull, flat white powder – pharmaceutical cocaine, almost impossible to get, manufactured just down the autobahn in the Swiss laboratories of Merck AG.

While he talks he twirls a small square of neatly cut cardboard, using it to cut fastidious lines out from the mountain range and then, using a silver tube on a silver chain around his neck, casually snort them up between sentences. We're there for 30?, 45?, 90? minutes. In this room someone has pushed Time's pause button. So ask a question; Keith will answer.

"Too much technology makes it more and more difficult to record rock and roll properly *<snff!>* In Russia they spend so many roubles on black market records and there's a very big scene in South America but when you try to do a tour there there's so many problems *<snff!>* I miss singles but there's not a singles market any more *<snff!>* We never sat down to write singles, we sat down to write songs *<slice, chop, shape>* I never listen to white bands because white drummers don't swing, except for Charlie Watts."

While Keith talks the mountain range in his hand becomes a mountain, a hill, a bump, a dusty memory. Nothing seems to change: his speech remains slow and relaxed, his body flops like tomorrow's washing and he sounds coherent. Only the half-baked thinking betrays him. And just when you think, God he's boring, he'll say:

"I was reading a history of Bill Broonzy nicked from Hendon Library the other day *<chuckle>* and there was a little bit there where he said that if he were to put a band together again he'd have pot smokers instead of drinkers. They don't forget their notes and they're on time."

Suddenly there's a frisson of excitement. Another pile of cocaine is on the slab, Swiss Alps-sized this time (an appropriate metaphor given the persistent rumour that every six months he gets his blood changed there), and he's neatly parcelling out eight even lines. And there are eight people around him . . . Keith is going to get us high! Now if there's one immutable truth in this palace of self-centredness it's that Keith Richards is not going to share his drugs with a bunch of journalists and sure enough, as he *<snff!>* continues to talk he *<snff!>* casually snorts *<snff!>* all eight lines.

Charles ambles over, kneels on the floor and licks Rizlas. Of course Keith chats to his new friend, until Ron walks over to hold a card in front of him, on which is scrawled: "You're talking to Charles Shaar Murray." Keith stares at Charles, face growing cold as friend turns to nemesis.

With a show of boneyard teeth Keith challenges, "Your review was rubbish."

Charles calmly rubs thick crumbs of black hashish into the waiting Silk Cut. "I stand by what I wrote."

"You need to hear it again."

"That's ok, most of my friends think it's awful as well."

"You need to widen your circle of friends."

It's bizarre to watch this schoolboy bickering – a rock god trading insults with a critic. As if our opinions *mattered.*

Charles has a smoke and passes it to Keith. When he hands it to me it's a roach. Keith is defending *Black and Blue*, but no explanation can redeem it. Indeed, the story that it was assembled during 1974 and 1975 as an audition for guitarists to replace Mick Taylor damns it further. It's just released and it's already over a year old – rock and roll is about next week. Tellingly, the cover photo is by a celebrity *snapper-du-jour*, the first time the Stones have followed fashion instead of leading it.

For some months I have been following four urchins busy working out what rock and roll in the Seventies should sound like and this seems the right time to speak up. "Keith, there's a band in London called the Sex Pistols." He looks bored. "They think you're old and should stop playing and get out of the way." He jerks forwards, ultrasheen eyes glaring and just below the surface a volcano is erupting.

"Just let them try," he snarls, jabbing the joint at me. "We're the Rolling Stones. No one tells us what to do. We'll stop when we feel like it." Emotion spent, he sinks back into his throne, realises he's holding a roach and passes it to me.

Indefinably, a wave of charisma washes through the room. In the doorway stands Mick Jagger. He is stationary, hands on narrow hips, head slightly tilted and looking up, the King ready to acknowledge our worship. Only everyone looks up, thinks, "Oh right, Mick", and goes back to what they're doing. His shoulders slump and he stalks over to the couch. No one goes over to him. In our journalistic japery we've assigned the band roles like some cliché vaudeville gang; one critic had said earlier, "Who gives a shit what Mick Jagger thinks about these days?", and it seems to be true.

But we do care what Keith thinks and as he tells us he wipes his nose with a finger and scrapes it off on his trouser leg. A foot from my eyes, stuck to the corduroy, is a thick line of cocaine mixed with a little snot and for a mad punk minute I think of leaning forwards and with a quick "Excuse me Keith", snorting it. But manners prevail and I wonder how much more pharmaceutical-grade powder is lodged undissolved in his nose.

Charles is now on the couch sharing a joint with Ron while Mick broods next to them. Cutting through their talk come the distinct Jagger tones, now clothed in Cockney, "I fort your review was blaahdy stoopid." Charles ignores him and Mick repeats himself. Same result. Mick sulks, then gets up and talks to a mountainesque heavy, who in turn talks to a record company man and then it is announced: we must leave. Charles is now building joint number four and continues work while we're shepherded out. Keith follows.

"Jagger," he sneers with contempt, "wants to go over a few songs and change things around. But later on we'll go up to Billy's room. There's going to be a party."

He waits and chats while the joint is finished and the touch paper lit. Charles savours his work with a connoisseur's appreciation, watching the smoke exhalations, small-talking to Keith, having another draw, finally handing it to Keith, who opens the door, backs through it and with a cheery "See you later," waves the incriminating hand and shuts the door.

*   *   *

Three weeks later, the Stones start their first English tour since 1973. Driving to London after a show in Stafford, Keith drives his Bentley off the road. As the press jubilantly report, the police search his car, find "a substance", arrest and then release him on bail while forensics determine what it, "obviously a drug" according to the police, might be.

Their canter into London for six nights at Earls Court triggers press adulation. Hold the front page – Mick Is A Godfather! Mick Meets Princess Margaret! Every night sees a private party, from pubs to Sothebys. And Ron Wood has his salary held while Deltapad, a management company, sues Promotone Productions over causing Ron to breach contract by playing with friends. A few miles away in a crummy club, fifty people watch a scrappy group called the Sex Pistols work on a sound to change the world.

SOME GIRLS

Sean Egan

UK release: 16 June 1978; US release: 17 June 1978

Produced by: The Glimmer Twins

Charts: UK no. 2; US no. 1

Tracklisting:
Miss You
When the Whip Comes Down
Just My Imagination (Running Away with Me)
Some Girls
Lies
Far Away Eyes
Respectable
Before They Make Me Run
Beast of Burden
Shattered

On 4 June 1976, in the first week of a month-long European Stones tour, Keith Richards received the news that his son Tara – born in March '76 – had died of respiratory problems. When Nick Kent saw Richards and Pallenberg shortly afterwards, he found them so devastated that he later recalled, "I honestly never thought I'd see them alive again." That Pallenberg later admitted she was sure her drugs intake had caused the baby's death makes it all the more amazing that she and Richards – still responsible for the welfare of two other children – continued to be smack addicts. Also amazingly, the tour continued, and did so in triumph. Ticket demand for three planned shows at Earls Court, London, led to the number being doubled to six, while the tour climaxed with an extended gig in front of 200,000 at Knebworth Park, Hertfordshire. It was almost like the sixties again, with a Stones poster magazine appearing in newsagents and a documentary on the Knebworth concert airing on British TV. Another example of life rolling on for the Stones as usual was the upshot of Keith's latest drug bust – cocaine possession in May. In a day and age when such convictions, let alone multiple ones, often resulted in imprisonment, once again he was mysteriously landed with nothing more than a fine.

The Stones were talking of touring America, Australia, Japan and their home country during 1977. Meanwhile, they were coming to the end of their current distribution contracts. They decided to fulfil their obligations with a double live set, one side of which was to be recorded in the type of small venue their superstardom had long made impractical on a regular basis. Dates were arranged at the El Mocambo Club, Toronto. His convictions had ruled out an American venue, yet Richards was clearly less than contrite about the inconveniences to which his lifestyle was putting his colleagues: he failed to show for the first few days of rehearsals. The band despatched an exasperated telegram across the Atlantic reading, "WE WANT TO PLAY. YOU WANT TO PLAY. WHERE ARE YOU?" What happened next must have made them wish Richards had stayed put in Blighty as his chaotic, dazed, irresponsible, insane existence careened to its inevitable conclusion.

Richards and Pallenberg arrived in Toronto on 24 February. The Canadians welcomed Pallenberg by charging her with possession of cannabis, among other things. Three days later, the Royal Canadian Mounted Police raided Richards' hotel room and found in it cocaine, drug paraphernalia and enough heroin to warrant a charge of possession with intent to traffic. A comatose Richards had to be slapped around for half an hour before he was sufficiently awake to be formally arrested. On 4 and 5 March, the Stones played their two gigs at the El Mocambo and the recordings thereof betray nothing but good cheer and quality musicianship, but it was by now obvious that catastrophe was staring the band collectively and Richards individually in the face. The drug-trafficking offence with which Richards was duly charged – with possession of cocaine subsequently added – carried a maximum sentence of life imprisonment. Although nobody seriously anticipated that sanction being handed down, it seemed inconceivable that this time Richards' lawyers could magic up a paltry financial punishment. Exactly ten years after he had first been sent to prison for drug-related reasons, Keith was surely going back there, an event that could have nothing but fatal implications for the Stones. Jagger made some remarks to the press about carrying on with another guitarist should the worst happen, but assuming this wasn't bravado or flippancy – or indeed a manifestation of perfectly understandable fury at his colleague – he knew as well as any Stones fan that this was inconceivable. To some – like perhaps Lester Bangs – this whole affair might even have seemed a welcome way to bring the curtain forcibly down on a show that had run embarrassingly overlong.

Richards' $25,000 bail facilitated his putting some over-dubs on the El Mocambo tapes in a Canadian studio in the company of Watts and Wyman. Although Wood and Wyman were touchingly loyal enough to have scored heroin for Rich-ards when he was writhing in withdrawal pains in his Toronto hotel room, pretty soon they and the rest of the band had to leave him in Canada to return to their families and everyday lives. Canadian high society must have been glad to see the back of them for, unbelievably, the Stones had been enmeshed in an additional scandal while they were in the country, this one revolving around rumours that the wife of the Canadian Prime Minister Pierre Trudeau was having an affair with Jagger. The press had the right story but the wrong quarry: Margaret Trudeau – restless young spouse of a considerably older man – had the dalliance with Wood. It seems safe to assume that reaction to this in Establishment quarters was not bemusement that when the Stones were in town the best advice remained to lock up your daughters.

Richards was handed back his passport in mid-March, which saved him from having to spend eighteen months in a foreign country while the case ground through the courts. He was unexpectedly granted a visa by the United States, where he and Pallenberg underwent pioneering treatment to wean them off heroin and the Stones did more work on the live album. The semblance of things-as-normal made many begin to suspect – some with hope, others with disgust – that a custodial punishment for Richards was receding from the realms of possibility. Certainly the fact that Richards twice failed to show for court appearances without his bail being forfeited seemed to auger judicial laxity.

The live album appeared on 15 September 1977 in the States and on the following day in the UK. *Love You Live*, as the record was titled, was accompanied by the release to the press of a photo set that depicted the band members biting each other's bare flesh. Although there was nothing technically indecent about the shots, the sight of Wyman distending a nipple, Wood chomping on a toe, Richards chewing a belly, and so on smacked of homoeroticism at a time in history when the idea provoked disgust; the fact that this was overlaid with a veneer of sado-masochism made for something additionally unsettling. In 1977, unsettling people was in vogue, courtesy of punk, the first youth movement to exult not in looking good but in appearing grotesque, partly a function of the fact that the Stones' generation – and the Stones in particular – had made it very difficult for young people to succeed any more in their natural desire to shock. Naturally, the accompanying text in some of the newspapers that carried the photographs pointed out that the Stones might be getting on a bit but they could still teach those punks a thing or two about outrage.

The contents of the album were notable for two reasons. The first was that the Stones were now free to feature pre-1971 songs. The other was the side from the El Mocambo, which, though no doubt no more authentic than any other live recording, has an unusually intimate ambience. The four El Mocambo tracks were all oldies whose rights were owned by Chess, reputedly a lucrative farewell gift to Marshall Chess, who was leaving Rolling Stones Records after a seven-year stint. As with so many who had come into the Stones' orbit – Jimmy Miller, Nicky Hopkins, Mick Taylor, Tony Sanchez – he was departing depleted in spirit as a consequence of picking up or worsening a debilitating heroin habit.

Rolling Stones Records renewed their deal with WEA in the States but moved across to EMI in the UK. October found the Stones at the Pathé Marconi Studios in Paris. Times had changed since even the last time they had assembled to begin recording an album. They had long been used to brickbats from traditionally minded politicians and disapproving sections of the media, but over the last year they had become the recipients of regularly enunciated disdain from sources from which they could not ever have imagined it emerging: younger musicians and the rock press.

"They're knocking the Stones. The Stones are the Establishment to them." The delighted astonishment in this quote from EMI A & R man Nick Mobbs dates it specifically to October 1976, not long after his label had signed The Sex Pistols, the group who would come to be perceived as the leaders of the punk rock movement and who were voicing the criticism to which he referred. It was one thing for Lester Bangs to say the Stones "don't matter any more or stand for anything", but that anybody might posit popular culture's epitome of the rebel in such terms amounted to the unthinkable. It had been brewing for a few years but the Rubicon had been crossed. It wasn't just the Stones. Also soon targets of the Pistols and their followers' wrath were Rod Stewart, The Who, Led Zeppelin, Paul McCartney, Bob Dylan, Eric Clapton and anybody else responsible for the groaning inertia of the current music scene by dint of the fact that they had once made great records but were now issuing substandard product and/or music lacking the energy and rawness that once made rock unique. Contempt for decadence also filled the air: tax exiledom, singles released not as works of art in their own right but as a way to advertise albums, gigs played in hangars where the band resembled a group of ants to the people in the cheapest seats – in a fractious era where people were seeing their standard of living fraying, such things were no longer accepted as merely an aspect of the lovable extravagance that went with show business. Although the Stones were no more culpable than any other part of the rock aristocracy on these counts, their crimes aroused particular disgust because of what they had once stood for. Part of this process was the penchant of the young for outrage: sheer glee could be had by calling the Stones sell-outs and a bunch of old farts even if the name-caller didn't quite believe it. However, the Stones had provided handy ammunition when – in an age when republicanism was far more pronounced than today – they invited Princess Margaret backstage at their Earls Court gigs.

The entire atmosphere had changed almost overnight. The long hair that had so recently been a symbol of rebellion and which the Stones more than anybody on earth had popularized was now actively despised by the shorn, spikey punks as a symptom of the way alternative had turned corporate. Even the American accent in which Jagger – like all British rockers – sang because it had sounded cool was now deemed a mark of phoniness by the likes of The Sex Pistols, The Clash and The Jam, who, having decided to write about the problems affecting their own country, realized that it would be ridiculous to do so while drawling as if they came from a different land entirely. The music press rang with the insults of the punks and the bewildered "what's-not-to-love?" defence statements of the old guard.

That The Sex Pistols were the first in the musical community publicly to air the sentiment that the Stones were now Establishment may have been a matter of proximity. The four-piece came together via their habituating and in some cases working in the shop variously called Let It Rock, Sex and Seditionaries owned by Malcolm McLaren at 430 King's Road in Chelsea. King's Road was not only parallel with Cheyne Walk, where Jagger's and Richards' London homes were located, but it was still among the trendiest streets in the capital. Consequently, Johnny Rotten, Glen Matlock, Steve Jones and Paul Cook were used to seeing the Glimmer Twins around and about. It's doubtful that guitarist Jones brought up with Jagger or Richards when he saw them the fact that his surprisingly large and impressive guitar collection was partly the result of an audacious mid-seventies raid on the Stones' rehearsal space.

However, it has to be stated that providing the means by which to further their career was not the only musical bequest made by the Stones to the Pistols. Nobody the remotest bit interested in rock could fail to be in thrall to The Rolling Stones or their social or musical legacy. The Pistols were unusual among upcoming bands in not playing Stones songs, but the fact that they were even playing rock at all put them in debt to them. The Stones had become the template for what a rock band should look and sound like, something almost painfully obvious whenever a bright new prospect hoved into view. The Pretty Things, The Faces, Mott The Hoople, The New York Dolls and Aerosmith were just some of the many groups who – talented though all of them were – somehow seemed to aspire to nothing loftier than being almost as good as the Stones (being as good as "The greatest rock 'n' roll band in the world" obviously being out of the question, partly because such was their longevity that nobody could ever catch up with their legacy). Moreover, the Pistols were happy to acknowledge their debt to The New York Dolls, who though a fine band were almost laughably Stones-esque, right down to the remarkable physical resemblance of singer David Johansen to Mick Jagger and the remarkable physical resemblance (including heroin-related "wasted" air) of his guitarist colleague and songwriting foil Johnny Thunders to Keith Richards.

The Pistols' compositions of howling disaffection were by definition the grandsons of the first song in the rock canon to meet that description, "(I Can't Get No) Satisfaction". When the Pistols' behaviour started generating outrage, it was reported in terms of their being the new Stones or the inheritors of their bad-boy mantle, and, when the Pistols caused national fury with their profane language on a live teatime television show in December 1976, it marked just how much the Stones had changed society: it would have been career-destroying if any band had done it ten years before. Yet however important the Stones were to the Pistols even if by osmosis, there was no getting around the fact that the latter genuinely detested them and moreover that it was easy to understand why. The Pistols were themselves massively influential as leaders of a new musical movement, so the permission their contempt effectively gave other people to detest the Stones – or even, consistent with youth's delight in taking a stance unrelated to true feelings, pretend to detest them – was seismic.

During 1976, Jagger had come across as wreathed in a notable degree of ennui. The journalists who remarked that his demeanour suggested he was exhibiting fatigue at keeping the show on the road may have been projecting on to him their own incredulity and dismay at the Stones' almost paradoxical longevity, but some aspects of the singer's behaviour were definitely eyebrow-raising: "Boring, isn't it?" he enthused to a journalist at the end of a notably lethargic anecdote about the composition of "Memory Motel". Such comments certainly made the Stones' mid-seventies sluggishness begin to make sense. "General malaise," Jagger later said of the period. "I think we got a bit carried away with our own popularity and so on. It was a bit of a holiday period. I mean, we cared, but we didn't care as much as we had."

That had now all changed. Always a supreme egotist, Jagger clearly now felt he had something to prove to the disrespectful upstarts whose careers would not even have been possible without him. He arrived in Paris with a bunch of uptempo songs clearly inspired by the high velocity of punk. "The whole thing was to play it all fast, fast, fast," he later admitted. "I had a lot of problems with Keith about it, but that was the deal at the time." Richards was scathing. "Jagger believes punk is today, is now," he said. "For a band of the Stones' position to do that would have been ludicrous. It's fatal for the Stones to try that. What the fuck do we want to sound like The Sex Pistols for? What's the point of listening to that shit?" Richards, however, approached the sessions with just as much a sense of renewed purpose as his colleague, albeit for very different reasons. He later observed, "I'd been through the bust in Canada, which was a real watershed . . . for me. I'd gone to jail [*sic*], been cleaned up, done my cure, and I'd wanted to come back and prove there was some difference . . . some reason for this kind of suffering. So *Some Girls* was the first record I'd been able to get back into and view from a totally different state than I'd been in for most of the Seventies."

An additional reason *Some Girls* crackled with creativity

and purpose was Wood, and not just because the new boy must have relished the chance to sink his teeth into his first full Stones album. "I've written a bit with Mick, a lot with Keith wherever we've been," said the guitarist not long before the album's release. It stands to reason that the strength of the new songs was down to the fact that he lent a valuable compositional hand, even if nowhere on the sleeve or the label does it suggest any such thing. (Wood was just beginning to learn the painful lesson Taylor previously had.) The Stones also had a new engineer in the shape of Chris Kimsey and the bright, fresh, spotless sound he imparts is yet another thing that made the Stones seem as if their cobwebs had well and truly been shaken off. Even Watts seems to be intoxicated by the mission of renewal. Although obviously partly a consequence of the high-energy material, his drumming is absolutely blistering.

The first fruits of these sessions were the single "Miss You", released in the US on 10 May 1978 and 26 May in their home country. Right from the first moment, it was clearly a Stones record like none before. The thinner sound was almost shocking for a Stones track, but at the same time it was utterly modernistic and therefore helped stake their claim for a relevance that had lately been profoundly questioned. This relevance, though, was not a matter of aping the New Wave (although there would be plenty of that on the subsequent album). They had decided once again to essay the medium of disco, whose popularity had shot through the roof since *Black and Blue*'s "Hot Stuff" via the movie *Saturday Night Fever* and its mega-successful soundtrack. It was a type of music inimical to the punks, many of whom considered their favoured style to be tussling with disco for the very soul of popular music, as exemplified in 1979 by "Death Disco" by PiL, the band formed by The Sex Pistols' ex-frontman John Lydon. The Rolling Stones' brilliance saw them create a track that had all of disco's fun and infectiousness while side-stepping the spiritually banal and aurally suffocating faults it often possessed.

The song – mainly by Mick, as are many others on *Some Girls* – is about Jerry Hall, a statuesque Texan model who was the new love of his life following the rancorous break-up of his marriage. Having spent so much of the seventies trying to acquire financial security following the Allen Klein scenario, Mick lost it again when Bianca secured a pioneering big-bucks divorce settlement (although some caustically noted that the feminist principles supposedly motivating it didn't extend to Bianca dispensing with her husband's door-opening name). "Miss You" is a yearning expression of the narrator's desire to be with his absent love that is of an almost unprecedented vulnerability for the Stones.

Although not nearly as "pure" as "Hot Stuff", "Miss You" ends up sounding far more authentic. Whereas the former track had resembled the efforts of people nervously trying to find a groove in a musical arena they weren't even sure they had the right to inhabit, there is an absolute assurance and smoothness about this recording that makes even the anomalies sound natural. For instance, striding right alongside the four-on-the-floor dancer's beat is bluesy mouth harp. The track is also drenched in rock guitar, albeit in tunings that we have never heard from this band before.

"Miss You" is propelled by a pulsating riff which is presented to us in multiple forms, from Ian McLagan's electric piano to Sugar Blue's mouth harp to falsetto whooping from Jagger to the Stones' front-line's chanting. In a mid-tempo record of nearly five minutes, we are treated to a leisurely, wandering arrangement of swells and lulls featuring chants, singing, spoken word and a suitably agitated sax solo from Mel Collins. We also get quite possibly Jagger's finest ever vocal performance, which starts out in his by now quintessential buffoonish, gum-chewing mode but goes on to encompasses aching declarations of loneliness, barked desperation and whooping mocking of a friend who rings him with an offer of a meeting with Puerto Rican girls who are just "daaaayin to meet choo!"

It's a record as flawless in execution – right up there quality-wise with "Satisfaction", "Sympathy for the Devil", "Gimme Shelter" or any of their other iconic classic recordings – as it is astounding in concept, taking us right back to the sixties, when every new Stones record would sound unlike the previous one and yet still be unmistakably Stonesian by dint of sky-high quality.

"Miss You" stalled at no. 3 in the UK, although was kept off the top spot only by two of the year's most titanic singles, sales-wise, John Travolta and Olivia Newton-John's "You're the One that I Want" and Boney M's "Rivers of Babylon"/"Brown Girl in the Ring". In the States, the record topped the chart. The Stones were back, big-time. The crucial question was whether the parent album would maintain the quality. Released five weeks after "Miss You", *Some Girls* was housed in a striking, quasi-Day-Glo sleeve with cut-outs: sliding the inner sleeve enabled the purchaser to put different faces – some of female celebrities, some of the Stones – to different hair-dos. Eleven years after EMI insisted that The Beatles get clearance from all the living people depicted on the cover of *Sgt. Pepper*, the Stones made the mistake of not doing likewise here with the result that the objections of the likes of Farrah Fawcett-Majors and Raquel Welch meant an interim "Pardon our appearance" sleeve before a slight redesign. For the first time with a Stones album, a lyric sheet was included.

"Miss You" provided the opener. The fact that the second track, "When the Whip Comes Down", began with a cliché Rolling Stones sound signature – a blast of Richards' beloved Chuck Berry variant riffs – may have made many hoping for the maintenance of the single's quality groan. However, any fears that the band were about to sag into bad habits were instantly disabused in a track bursting with musical invention that moreover evidenced a new streetwise outlook thought forever beyond these rich boys. The result of Jagger being newly domiciled in a vibrant New York, its tale of a rent boy realizing that riches don't come without penalties in the Big Apple is deliciously edgy and profane. The music is big and bruising. While one misses the earthen thump of the Stones' rhythm section in the Taylor years – something that would never really return to Stones music – it is compensated for here by Watts' hyperactive drumming. The arrangement is pocked with little moments of improvisation (or pretend improvisation) and the types of musical tics (such as the section where the music pounds Boom! Boom! Boom! and Mick goes "Shh!") that bring one back for repeated listens.

The now *de rigueur* black vocal group cover is "Just My Imagination (Running Away with Me)". By tweaking the lyric and emoting, Jagger injects more vulnerability than was heard on the Norman Whitfield/Barrett Strong song that was a hit for The Temptations. This process is assisted by the band slowing down the groove. The tenderness is another trademark of an album where the Stones' customary hauteur is little in evidence.

The mid-tempo title track – like several cuts here – is an exquisite wall of swirling and intermeshing guitars: Richards, Wood and a rapidly learning Jagger all not only pitch in on *Some Girls* but tend to do so simultaneously, while never giving the impression of "too many cooks". Sugar Blue – who had been heard on "Miss You" – adds more top-notch mouth harp to an amusing erotic travelogue from Jagger, which aroused what-is-he-like! feelings from most but accusations of racism from some for its assertion that "black girls just want to get fucked all night". Side-closer "Lies" is probably the fastest track on the album but it is the only one of the uptempo tracks to sound overly self-conscious in its adoption of punk styles. A lyric that yowls about lies in "my papa's looks" and "history books" makes the mistake of assuming that powerful, uptempo, vital rock *ipso facto* must have a youthful perspective. Coming from a man daily tasked with encouraging his daughter to do her homework, it is unseemly and desperate. This probably wouldn't matter if the music was up to much, but it is a threshing machine of over-trebly guitar and whiny vocals.

Side two kicks off with a cut that is mercifully as spacious and relaxing as "Lies" is claustrophobic and irritating. "Far Away Eyes" is yet another example of the Stones' penchant for executing good country music at the same time as they are unable to resist mocking it. In outrageously cracker spoken-word verses, Jagger mocks the gullible flocks of the type of media preacher then just beginning to become big business. However, the choruses about the emotional salvation offered by the girl with "well, *you* know what kinda eyes she got" can't help but be tender and sweet despite themselves. Brian Jones must have been smiling from Cheltenham Cemetery at Wood's superb pedal steel guitar. The track was the flipside of the "Miss You" single (which in fact was a double A-side in the UK).

The transference of distribution rights to Rolling Stones Records in the UK enabled the band to have the singular pleasure of devising a new vulgar catalogue number prefix, CUN, to bookend WEA's COC, which was retained. However, it's doubtful whether, had they known of this evidence of the group's enduring mischievousness, the punks who complained of their latter-day lack of rebelliousness would have held their fire. "Respectable" is a song that explicitly addresses their disdain. "Well now we're respected in society" sneers Jagger, going on to claim that the Stones don't worry about the things that they used to be. The sarcasm-dripping, malice-bursting lyric seems to seek to refute the allegations of a band gone tame by taking in Keith's current legal problems and Wood's Canadian dalliance, as well as for some reason Jagger's ruptured marriage. It's all done to a snottily anthemic melody with a blistering pace, helped by Watts' finest performance on the album. The concoction showed exactly how men of the Stones' vintage could co-opt the velocity and attitude of punk without sounding risible.

"Before They Make Me Run" is one of the few cuts that are unequivocally Keith's. Perhaps significantly, it's also the only one that really adheres to the scruffily anthemic Stones tradition. While Jagger has, since the late seventies, always been the one to want the band to adopt new musical fashions and work with trendy producers, Richards has ended up being cast as the Stones traditionalist – dare one say conservative – something exemplified by his 1977 quote, "I don't think that Bowie or Johnny Rotten or all the Zeppelins are anywhere in the future let alone the present", a comment that suggests a viewpoint of what constitutes New Wave that basically encompasses anybody that started after the Stones. In the only track not mixed by Chris Kimsey, the more bottom-heavy timbre provided by Dave Jordan is another sonic ghost of the Mick Taylor era. The track chimes with what surrounds it, though, in the way it replaces swaggering with meditativeness. It is the most important and poignant vocal showcase of Richards' career. He is not just singing because it is primarily his song or

Some Girls 349

because his voice is the most suited: its heartfelt renunciation
of the druggie lifestyle that had caused him such misery could
simply not have been sung by Mick. "Gonna find my way to
heaven, 'cos I did my time in hell," laments the guitarist of the
lowlifes with whom his addiction had necessitated contact,
adding – in an allusion to his current legal problems and his
court-mandated detox – that he is going to walk away from
this demi-monde before he is forced to run.

Just as moving in its own way is "Beast of Burden". It was
traditional for the second American single from a Stones LP to
make a modest appearance in the top 20. For "Beast of
Burden" (b/w "When the Whip Comes Down") to climb to
no. 8 in the *Billboard* chart was extraordinary, a reflection both
of the band's renewed currency and the track's sheer loveliness. The lyric pleads with a hard taskmaster of a lover on a
bed of lilting, dreamy guitars. Jagger alternately growls and
coos a call-and-response with backing vocalists Keith, Ron
and his overdubbed self. (The mass harmonies are another of
this album's signatures, one that lends it a touching community spirit.) "Shattered'" fulfilled the moderately successful
role usually taken by the second US single: the Stones' first
ever third US single from an album made no. 31. (Over in the
UK, the first-ever second single from a Stones album was
"Respectable", also with "When the Whip Comes Down" on
the B-side, which made no. 23 on the back of a promo in which
the band crashed through the walls of a house and Mick and
Keith had noticeably shorter hair than had been usual the last
decade.) In its function as the closing track of *Some Girls*,
"Shattered" at first sounds odd, even disappointing, so out of
synch do its angular grooves and rapped lyric seem, set against
the polished, melodic fare that has preceded it. However,
repeated listenings reveal it to be a judicious parting shot, its
contrasting tone enrichening the album by adding an extra
dimension, just as "Mona (I Need You Baby)" did on the
debut LP back in 1964. In another track suffused with Jagger's
New York experiences, the singer passionately – even hysteri-
cally – lambasts the bitchiness, obsequiousness and gossip of
the Big Apple, even if we half-suspect he also loves those same
things. He also can't resist getting in a dig at punk, observing

of people dressed in plastic bags, "Some kinda fashion!" The
subject provides Jagger the opportunity to engage in the
cartoonish vocal gymnastics at which he excels. Two curious/
delightful elements are a Far Eastern-sounding guitar break
and a deadpan vocal refrain of "Sha-doo-bee", which Keith
and Ron are so assiduous in maintaining the more frenzied
Mick gets that it becomes hilarious.

Perhaps realizing that putting another *Some Girls* track on
the flip of "Shattered" in the US would mean that half the
album was now on single, which in turn would once more
propel them perilously close to the area marked "decadent",
the Stones offered a new song as the B-side, "Everything Is
Turning to Gold". Largely written by Wood in celebration of
the birth of his son Jesse (he gets a one-third writing credit
with the Glimmer Twins), it's a shuffling number augmented
by Mel Collins' saxophone and Sugar Blue's mouth harp that,
while not a classic, would have been a far preferable album
inclusion than the profoundly less sophisticated "Lies".

The album was quite remarkably the biggest-seller of the
Stones' long career to date. Good sales, though, had never
been something the band had difficulty achieving and probably far more satisfying was newfound respect. *Some Girls*
instantly joined the likes of *Aftermath, Beggars Banquet, Sticky
Fingers* and *Exile on Main St.* in the ranks of acknowledged
Stones classics. In securing such a wholly unexpected achievement, the Stones had proved to punks and other naysayers
their enduring musical validity. Moreover, they proved that
age could confer a layering of ability: *Some Girls*' songs had a
musical breadth and an emotional maturity beyond their
snotty, young detractors. A decade and a half to the very
month after their first record, The Rolling Stones were clearly
once more "The greatest rock 'n' roll band in the world".
Nothing, surely, could tarnish their reputation ever again.

A joint Bill Wyman and Charlie Watts interview may not sound like much of a coup, but that is what John Pidgeon's revealing 1978 feature transpired to be. At the time of its publication, the world had heard little from the Stones' rhythm section, let alone seen them speak with candour about inter-band relations and their satisfaction (Charlie) or frequent dissatisfaction (Bill) with their assigned roles. Valuable insights are also offered into the Stones' origins. Pidgeon recalls, "I'd been hanging out with the Stones for a few days, sleeping on the sofa in tour keyboard player Ian McLagan's suite. It occurs to me now that he fixed up for me to interview them – no publicists involved. Happy days."

THE BACK LINE

John Pidgeon

First published in *Creem*, November 1978

In a smoky cutting room on Sunset Boulevard, the entire history of rock and roll flashed before my eyes: Elvis, Chuck Berry, Buddy Holly, Little Richard, Jerry Lee Lewis, Fats Domino, Haley, Vincent, Cochran; and the high school heroes, all the Bobbys, Spector's girl groups and the beginnings of Motown, and the British Invasion, the Beatles and the Stones.

These last had long footage to themselves – Mick, Keith, Brian, Bill and Charlie – a reel of concerts, TV appearances, interviews, riots. I wasn't counting, but I don't recall more than a single shot of Bill Wyman, slow-faced, static, inscrutable, and Charlie Watts' solitary offering to an interrogatory mike: "Dunno."

And again, days but years apart, on a television show in London, a promo clip for a brand new track, "Respectable". It looked like Lindsay-Hogg. The group is playing in a bare white set; midway through the number Jagger goes for the wall with his guitar, the paper partition gives way, and Mick, Keith and

Woody wind up on the other side, falling about. Beyond the hole in the wall Bill and Charlie play on, and a look passes between them, a small glance, amused and almost paternally tolerant. Unspoken assent: *there* they go again!

Two images of The Rolling Stones, both real. The back line: undemonstrative, unnoticed, and a step away from the gallivanting Glimmer Twins. Coming on 16 years with the band and not a headline between them since Bill pissed on a filling station wall back in '65, yet when the Stones' story is finally written, the fact not the fiction, there'll be no truer chronicler than Wyman, an obsessive collector with an attic full of tangible memories, or Watts, a sketch of every hotel room he's stayed in tucked in his album.

The pair joined the band within a few weeks of each other, Bill in December 1962, Charlie in the new year, but their musical backgrounds were far apart. Charlie had been hanging around London's jazz fringes. "I came out of the school that never listened to rock 'n' roll, or refused to until I was about twenty-one. I was never really that good to play what you might term 'jazz', particularly at that time, so I just used to play with anyone really, which was mostly jazz people, but not on a very high musical level, not the best, though some of them turned out to be the best as time passed."

Then, through Alexis Korner, he drifted into the murky, uncharted waters of early British R & B. "When I first played with Cyril Davies in Alexis Korner's band," he recalled, "I thought, 'What the fuck is happening here?' because I'd only ever heard the harmonica played by Larry Adler, but Cyril was such a character, I loved him. But the rest of it! I didn't know what the hell was going on. Although I knew about playing a heavy backbeat, it wasn't like Chicago, which was what Cyril wanted. Now Alexis never did really front that band, so you had Dick Heckstall-Smith, then Jack Bruce, Graham Bond, Ginger Baker, an amazing band, but a total cacophony of sound. On a good night it was amazing, but it was like a cross between R & B and Charlie Mingus, which was what Alexis wanted.

"By the time I joined the Stones, I was quite used to rock 'n' roll. I knew most of the rock 'n' roll guys, people like

Screaming Lord Sutch, through people who played in bands
(like Sutch's pianist, Nicky Hopkins), though I never had any
desire to play it myself. But by the time I actually joined the
Stones, I was quite used to Chuck Berry and that, but it was
actually sitting up endlessly with Keith and Brian – I was out
of work at the time I joined them and I just used to hang about
with them, waiting for jobs to come up, daytime work – just
listening to Little Walter and all that, that it got ground in."

The southeast suburb of London where Bill spent his teenage years remained unaffected by the strange new sounds that
were reverberating through basement clubs less than a dozen
miles away on the other side of town.

"I'd been playing for just about two years and I had a couple
of bands in that time, formed from local kids, people I was
working with or lived round the corner. None of us could play
very well. All the local bands were playing Shadows stuff,
Ventures stuff, all those semi-instrumental groups, because
there were never really any good singers about. So most of the
bands had an echo chamber and a good lead guitarist who
could play 'FBI' and all that shit, and experiment and try and
play some American music, but it was always the wrong stuff
– it was 'Poetry In Motion' and 'Personality', all those things –
whereas the band I was trying to get together, we were trying to
play the R & B kind of American music that was coming over,
more like Little Richard, The Coasters, Chuck Berry, Fats
Domino, black artists, not the Pat Boones and the Bobby Vees.

"We weren't doing very well, playing youth clubs, doing
three or four gigs a week for almost nothing, and my drummer, Tony Chapman, answered an ad from Mick, Keith and
Brian in one of the music papers, and he came back the next
day and said, 'It's not bad actually, it's a very different kind of
music. I've made a tape copy and I thought you'd like to hear
it, because they haven't got a bass player either' – it must have
been after Dick Taylor split. So I listened to this stuff, and
there were about four or five Jimmy Reed tracks, and I thought
it was very interesting and unusual, and it gave me a weird
feeling to listen to it, but an excited feeling. But I thought, 'It's
so slow,' because we were playing uptempo semi-white, semi-
black stuff. So I said, 'All right, I'll go up.'

"So we went up there, and it was snowing and cold, to this horrible pub where there was a rehearsal hall, and nobody spoke to me for two hours. Mick said hullo to me when I arrived, and Stu [Ian Stewart], who was playing piano, was nice, but Brian and Keith never spoke to me until they found out I had some cigarettes, because they never had any money, so I bought them each a drink and we were all mates. They asked us to join, and our band wasn't doing so well, so we did, but after about three weeks they asked Tony Chapman, who wasn't a very good drummer, if he would leave, and asked Charlie if he would join permanently.

"I wasn't involved at all with the jazz thing that was going on in London, or even the R &B thing. I was more into rock 'n' roll, rather than the Korner thing, so the whole thing was very, very strange to me, and it was only Chuck Berry that held me in with the band for the first few weeks, because I knew all those Chuck Berry songs, and I knew Bo Diddley vaguely. I didn't know any of the blues people, but at least when they said, let's do 'Reeling and Rocking', I knew it backwards, and doing a blues on the bass was fairly simple anyway. It was just popular music that was being played by black artists instead of white, really, that was the difference, and we suddenly realised it was better."

Charlie already knew Mick, Keith and Brian from Alexis Korner's club in Ealing, West London, and had even caught their first gig – as the Roll*in*' Stones at the Marquee on Oxford Street. "There were a lot of people dancing," he recalled, "but all the usual crowd was saying 'Terrible!' But really they were very popular even then. The thing was – me included – the bands that were doing that stuff, like Alexis', were really eccentric old men. Now the Stones, the front line at any rate, were young, so there was obvious appeal for the kids who wanted to dance. Alexis' band was a joke to look at, but this lot sort of crossed the barrier. They actually were like rock stars, I suppose, but they could play."

Not, when he joined the band, that he could see any future in it; nor could Bill who, married and a father, didn't dare give up his day job. It was their ambitious young manager, Andrew Oldham, who granted them a degree of longevity, relegating the sixth Stone, Ian "Stu" Stewart, to roadie, bleaching the black out of their act for the studio, and moulding an image that made them whipping boys for the silent majority and hence heroes for a rebellious younger generation.

"He saw it as a bigger thing than I personally ever saw it as," Charlie admitted. 'He saw it as a product which he could promote. And I'm sure Brian and Keith at the time would sooner have played all Chuck Berry songs or Elmore James."

Bill agreed: "That was proven by the fifth single, [Willie Dixon's] 'Little Red Rooster'. We were still trying to play blues and get it across to the kids as an interesting music, but it was very hard. 'Little Red Rooster' worked, fortunately, but it could have been a disaster. Andrew didn't want us to do it. He wanted us to do some much more pop-oriented song. Every album we tried to put a few blues things on – 'Honest I Do' by Jimmy Reed, 'I Can't Be Satisfied' by Muddy Waters – we kept trying to get them in there, but Andrew was trying to get us to do Motown things like 'Can I Get A Witness?'. And he was right as well; he was more right than we were. But, of course, when Mick and Keith got into writing, the songs came out more like he was looking for. Andrew practically *forced* them into writing."

And it was the writing that clinched it, that enviable and prolific partnership of Jagger and Richards which has given the Stones immortality in a world of stillbirths and infanticide.

"*That*," Bill insisted, "and Keith's determination that the band will work and continue being a rock and roll band *and* a studio band. Because it could very easily have become just a studio band at the time of '67–'68, when the drug busts happened and we basically stopped going on the road, because there were so many problems doing a tour in England at that time. Every day we did a gig there was a riot. There were policemen injured, police dogs shot that went crazy, three hundred girls carried off – I mean *every* day. It just became impossible: police escorts, doors torn off police cars and ambulances, going down laundry chutes into hotels. It got mad, so we stopped touring because it was impossible to do shows. Gigs we were turning up to we couldn't get *in*, let alone play. And if we had've got in, we'd never've got out, so we gave up. And we could very easily have become a studio band, couldn't we, Charlie?"

"Yeah. Remember the one-and-a-half-number gigs?"

"Or the three bars at Birkenhead?"

"Walk on . . . da-da-da . . . off. We rarely finished a set."

"And it was only 25 minutes long anyway. Only seven or eight numbers, but we never got to the end of it. Never did a whole set for about two years."

"That's when I started practising again," Charlie said, stretching a memory of cramp from his fingers, "because we never played anything except in the studio. We never had time to play anything really."

"And the proof of that," Bill added, "is if you look at the records we recorded, for instance, at RCA in America and [Chess] in Chicago between about '65 and '68, hardly any of those numbers have ever been recorded live, because we hardly ever *did* any of them live. *Between The Buttons* and *Flowers* and *Satanic Majesties*, all those records right up until *Beggars Banquet*, we never performed them on stage really, because we weren't on the road that much. We did whole albums that we've never played any of the numbers on stage to this day, except maybe for the singles, like 'Let's Spend The Night Together' or 'Under My Thumb' or something like that."

The kind of chemistry that creates more than a dozen years of classic rock and roll hits, such as fuses the Twins, can be hard to live with. Not for Charlie, though. He's happy just to keep the beat. A taciturn prototype among rock drummers, the corners of his zip-lipped mouth plunge at the suggestion he's also the best. As proof he quotes praise for his playing on "It's Only Rock 'n Roll" or "You Can't Always Get What You Want". He didn't play on them.*

"That's why it's all bullshit when everyone says you're the best. If someone else can do the record and it's supposed to be you, how are you the best? If it was Max Roach, it would be fucking true, but when it's me, it isn't. Absolutely not true. That's why I don't believe all that crap. If people tell you how

---

* The Faces' Kenney Jones drummed on "It's Only Rock 'n Roll" and producer Jimmy Miller on "You Can't Always Get What You Want".

great you are, which in this business they always tend to overdo, and someone else did it, like on those things, it makes a joke of it."

What makes it for Charlie is not just good playing, but playing good songs. "If you haven't got a song to play, you can be just a good player, and you know how many good players there are – there's thousands of them, and some of them are *great* players – but if you've got a good song to play, if you've got a hit record, it's all part of one thing, it makes it seem ten times better than it actually is. To play 'Miss You' is really very easy, it's just four in a bar, it's even easier to play than a triplet, but it's a good song, so it works." Right. The way a heartbeat does.

Coaxing Charlie from behind his kit on stage is as likely as getting him out of his front door when he's off the road, and he's thankful for the front man who holds the eyes of the crowd. "I'd hate to be Mick," he admits cheerfully. "I'm glad to say he's promoted himself in that direction – always in the magazines – because it helps us. It's great for me, because I'd never do that. I hate that sort of thing. I'd hate to go on stage and walk about in front of everyone."

But if it all ended tomorrow? Poker face. "I'd just do something else."

And Bill? Well, Bill's happier now than he has been since 1966, but he's had his ups and downs in the meantime, even felt like quitting. Whereas Charlie has always been happy to leave the material to Mick and Keith, Bill has had ideas of his own from time to time, and you must have noticed how often B. Wyman has cropped up among the composer credits on Rolling Stones records.

"If I write a song and I think it could be good for the band, there's no way the band's going to do it, because firstly I can't sing the bloody thing to the rest of them or play the guitar as Keith might, to show them what it could sound like if it was done that way. I've got to pick up a bass to try to get a song across, or an acoustic guitar, which I can't play either – I can't play chords. I can't convey it to them, and Mick won't really try that hard to help you sing it, because he doesn't know it either, so it's pretty impossible unless I made demos or something at home and said, 'What do you think of this?' They'd probably say, 'Yeah, that's quite nice,' but they wouldn't record it.

"That was one of the things that disillusioned Mick Taylor, that he couldn't get involved with the writing of songs and be part of it. You *are* part of it, in fact, if you look at it that way: your name isn't on it, you don't get paid for it, but you *are* part of the song, because anybody can come up with a certain little thing that will make that song just a bit special.

"It's a very lucrative side of the business, and you can make an awful lot of money with songwriting and publishing, which goes two ways – record royalties, which we've all got an equal share of, go five ways, of course – so there is a vast difference. If the band brings in a million dollars in a year, there's obviously a vast difference in what Keith gets and what I get. Probably he gets five times more than me. I don't feel bad about that, because he writes the songs, but what does get me sometimes is *if* I had an idea for a song, I would like to be heard a little stronger than I ever have been. I'd like to be equally considered. Because I've worked on songs of Keith's in the studio – as the whole band have – seven nights, eight or twelve hours a night, to get from a riff into a great song, and if I had an idea for a song, and it *has* happened on occasion, I'd been given 20 minutes to experiment with it."

Thus the solo albums?

"Yeah, that and I was getting very frustrated in the band just being a bass player. Because, before, in the early days, the first three, four, five years, when Brian was in the band, he and I in particular, more than anyone else, would experiment with other instruments for overdubs and things. We would try to find glockenspiels and harps and marimbas and all that stuff, and we would use them. It was very much more interesting being able to experiment, like on 'Paint It Black', using organ pedals as well as bass. And it just ended up, after Brian left and Mick Taylor joined, and Nicky Hopkins came along, and then Billy Preston, and a horn section, there was nothing else to do but play bass on each number. And I wasn't interested in singing, because Mick and Keith were doing it all right, and they were also using back-up singers sometimes, and I found I was just playing bass on some numbers, that's *all* I was doing. And I got very bored.

"Before I did my solo albums I was getting to the point of thinking, 'God, I haven't got to go to another session again?' because they were so boring and such a downer. And you can't make good music like that. I was getting so depressed, I was thinking about leaving the band, because it was fun no more. It was becoming too strict, too bizarre, and incredibly heavy atmospheres and moodies, although the band has never really had a fight."

If his solo work purged him of these malignant frustrations, it was the recruiting of Ron Wood that patched whatever holes gaped in his friendship with Mick and Keith. If I was picking sides, *me* this is, I'd chose Woody for my team every time, because his ability to bring people together and keep them together and happy is rarer than fun at the dentist. Bill knows all about that.

"Woody's come along and, especially in the last year – I noticed it more than anything when we started recording for the new album – he's pulled both sides together, and I think he was the main reason for the band being so close and super-friendly suddenly in, say, the last nine months than we've been since, I don't know, '66 maybe. Really being able to talk to each other. I found great difficulty after a while in being able to communicate, basically with Mick and Keith. I never had a problem with Charlie, never had a problem with Mick Taylor or Brian, but Woody's really pulled us all in, because . . . I don't know, he talks to me the same as he talks to Mick and Keith and Charlie, and it's all very amusing and light-hearted – he's always laughing and joking – and he can always make you laugh.

"And there's such a great rapport going now between the band that people actually say to each other, 'You played great tonight!' – which we'd never say. That's never been said in twelve years. I've never been told *ever*, 'You did a great set tonight.' I've only ever been told, 'You were out of tune tonight.' If I play great, it's accepted, same with Charlie. If you play badly or something goes wrong, you get put down, so you never get that uplift, but Woody started to get that happening, and now everybody congratulates everybody, and it's 'Thanks for a great show!' We were all bumping into each other after the last show of the tour and everybody was saying to everybody else individually, 'Thanks for a great tour, man,' *thanking* each other for how good the tour was, and we'd never do that before. And I really got off on that. Woody's fabulous! He's made this band come back to life again."

Nowhere is that new life more apparent than on stage. In contrast to their previous outing, they've largely abandoned artifice, and the greatest hits which dominated the last set now sandwich a fat filling of cuts from *Some Girls*, itself proof enough for all but a handful of tired reviewers of renewed vigour and inspiration.

"We were all having such a great time in the studio," Bill explained, "so we never stopped really. We just worked and worked and worked. We were going to go there [Paris] for four or five weeks originally – middle of October till early December – six weeks with a break of a week in between, and we were still there in February, still having fun.

"Basically it was because we were really enjoying ourselves and we were getting things done and getting off on new songs, so we'd try a new one and then another new one. We've got lots of demos where we only did the song once, just to get it down on tape with some ideas – a guitar lick or bass run or something Charlie did – so we wouldn't forget it and we could refer back to it when we cut it properly. We probably finished twelve or thirteen songs and we picked those ten for the album, so there are two or three more that are finished now, about five or six that are near completion, and then there's a whole mass of stuff that are demos, no vocals, rough ideas, jams, an awful lot of material. We finished up with 96 reels of tape, where a normal band might use six, maybe, for an album."

Bill and Charlie both benefitted mightily from Mick's choice of Chris Kimsey as engineer (because of the bass and drum sound he gave Bad Company and Peter Frampton). According to Bill, he "got the best bass sound I've ever had, apart from an occasional track here and there, so immediately when you're listening back to something, a rough even, you get turned on because it sounds great anyway. You've only got to play it great then. Most of the time you can play what you consider one of your best songs, and it doesn't sound good because the sound isn't good, and it gets mixed in to all the guitars and the bass drum. He did get beautiful sounds for me and Charlie, and that inspires you and turns everybody on to your playing."

"It's easy," says Charlie. "If you've got a good sound, it's easy. There's no hassle. It wasn't like sitting there for an hour testing drums."

"We're bloody lucky, man," he adds. "We've signed a record deal three or four times, and each time we've had a fucking good single and a good album. We did it with Atlantic with 'Brown Sugar' and *Sticky Fingers*, and we've done it again this time."

It will surely be a while before those perennial harbingers of the Stones' end will have an excuse to prophesy the band's demise. As far as Bill, for one, is concerned, they'll last as long as they have fun.

"As long as it's worthwhile, as long as it doesn't become a drag and a bore and an obligation, and, as I said earlier, it was getting to be for me three or four years ago. Now I've got a new lease on life, a second wind, and it doesn't cross my mind ever to leave the band or that the band's going to break up. And touring, doing shows, getting on the road – Keith thinks that's the most important thing, and he's probably right. The most important thing for a band *is* to work on the road, and the more you work on the road the better you play and the better the next sessions gets and the next tour."

And the next. And the next. And the next and . . .

For those people who in the late seventies were claiming that The Rolling Stones' political credibility had been squandered, The Tom Robinson Band – who married their crunching hard rock to agitprop – were exhilaratingly fulfilling the promises the Stones had betrayed. Robert Christgau's 1978 article, while not hostile as such to a recently revivified Stones, offered an interesting contrast between the old and the new guard of rebel rock. It also, incidentally, answered that question about what Christgau would think of the Stones come '78 that he posed in the earlier article, "It Isn't Only Rock and Roll".

SOME GUYS

Robert Christgau

First published in *Village Voice*, July 1978

By mid-May, I knew what the big rock and roll event of the third week of June was going to be: Tom Robinson at the Bottom Line. Capitol/EMI had been preparing Robinson's assault on New York since last fall, when the Tom Robinson Band's first English release became an instant hit over there. "2-4-6-8 Motorway", it was called, and it earned its title for me by transforming a hectic Saturday-morning drive from the Pennines to London into a post-industrial epiphany. The football-cheer hook and marching-as-to-war beat of this robust car song were so English they made Johnny Rotten sound like Johnny Cash, but its rock and roll universality was as pure as Chuck Berry's. Just as important, Capitol was undaunted when their air radio classic barely dented FM in the States. There'd be others. The Sex Pistols were gone forever, but the company wasn't gonna bollocks this one.

I mention the Pistols because they're there. The only rock act signed by EMI in the eight months following the label's S.P. purge, the Tom Robinson Band was consciously postpunk

– not anti or un, post. I don't mean "power pop," either, although the single made plain their respect for the lucid arrangement, the articulated vocal, the catchy approach. I mean they knew they could risk simpler music than had been fashionable two years before because the punks got there first, and that the same went for a more militant social stance.

To EMI, this must have seemed even riskier, because rather than copping to the reactive politics of punk, Robinson expressed a positive ideology. Where Johnny Rotten might dismiss prejudice against blacks as stupid and disgusting, Robinson would identify it as racism and speak out against the abstraction. Not many rock and rollers go in for even such modest intellectualizing, not if they're attuned to the colloquial concreteness that puts the music across. But in the wake of punk Robinson could present himself as an activist and advocate who liked to think. He wanted to be a star, all right – he shared a manager with Pink Floyd. But his logo was an upraised fist, and almost every one of his songs had an overtly political theme – even "2-4-6-8", Robinson told interviewers, took its chorus from a gay rights chant and its verse from a flirtation between a male trucker and male motorcyclist.

Robinson's homosexuality is as straightforward as the rest of his radical identity. He's been out since 1971 or 1972, but only when he began doing volunteer work for London's Gay Switchboard did he really begin to get politics. A solicitor's son born in 1950 who spent his late teens and early twenties in a "school for maladjusted children," Robinson's political focus is backlash – the sort of backlash that's bound to get a gay who once believed coming out would solve his problems. "Glad To Be Gay", follow-up to "2-4-6-8", was on a live EP called *TRB-Rising Free*; it was a proud, sardonic singalong that revised a more cheerful coming-out song from Robinson's pollyanna days in the gay movement, and went top 20 in England, where crowds of hetero youths would lustily shout out the chorus. Many of the punks I talked to last fall singled out Robinson as a new artist they admired. He was saying what he believed.

The problem with this admirable coalition of punks, gays, and politicos was that it couldn't create a big rock and roll event by itself, because pop culture is supposed to reach beyond deserving interest groups. But rarely will any such interest group, much less three at once, enjoy the support of a major record company and – here's what was really special – a notoriously cautious "alternative" radio outlet. This last was WNEW-FM, and not just old reliable Vin Scelsa and new remarkable Meg Griffin, either – Scott Muni himself was a fan, beguiled by a chance to be hip, or by Robinson's cheerful charm, or perhaps by the music itself. In this year of Anita Bryant it was a shot in the arm to turn on the radio and hear Robinson's intelligent voice strafing homophobe hypocrites from the World Health Organization to your neighborhood queer-basher. Robinson's two nights at the Bottom Line sold out way in advance. I couldn't recall the last time a new performer with outfront politics had created such a stir. He wasn't just getting punks, gays, and politicos – he was getting real people. This was history.

Enter the Rolling Stones.

This hasn't been the best of decades for the Rolling Stones. Sure they've secured their once-controversial reputation as the greatest rock and roll band of all time-forming their own label, touring, triumphantly, even recording what many (including me) consider their greatest album, *Exile on Main Street*. Nevertheless, they've been going downhill for five or six years now, and despite reassurances from the big media and the balance sheet, they're worried. The mortality that haunts a former youth music is doubly dire for a narcissist like Mick, and even a cynic like Mick must entertain second thoughts about the company he's kept since hooking up with Ahmet and Bianca. If you play with decadence long enough, you start to decay – or at least your brain softens. When Jagger admitted to Jonathan Cott in *Rolling Stone* that recent Stones albums have "lacked direction," that's presumably what he meant.

On the other hand, maybe he just didn't want to come out and say they were shitty. After all, *Goats Head Soup* and *It's Only Rock 'n Roll* were not without redeeming cuts, even if these sound quite quirkish now, and while the dense rhythmic textures of *Black and Blue* haven't led anywhere, they were interesting enough in themselves. Last year's live album had its defenders, too. For me, though, *Love You Live* was where the Stones came audibly apart, starting with the very first bars – which happened to be from Aaron Copland's *Fanfare for the Common Man*, better than *Zarathustra* but not by much. This was lazy, unfocussed, desperately mannered music that like all arena rock attempted to make up in obvious gestures what it lacked in subtlety and feeling. The band itself was okay, despite occasional intrusions by Billy Preston and the inability of Ron Wood to fill solo space designed for the more accomplished if less personable Mick Taylor. But the old material sounded old and the new material sounded bad. There were no alternate arrangements that equaled, say, "Live with Me" on *"Get Yer Ya-Ya's Out!"* And for the most part Jagger was a disgrace. Once his slurs had teased, made jokes, held out double meanings; now his refusal to pronounce final dentals – the "good" and "should" of "Brown Sugar", for example – conveyed bored, arrogant indolence, as if he couldn't be bothered hoisting his tongue to the roof of his mouth. His cries of "oo-oo-oo" and "awri-" were self-parody without humor. This was an entertainer doing a job that just didn't get him off the way it once had, a job that got harder every time out.

Add to this dispassionate aesthetic judgment Mick's gossip-column activities and the explosion of young bands playing real rock and roll and you will understand why I didn't start marking up my calendar when the Stones announced a summer tour. A round of profit-taking just in case Keith got sent up for heroin, that was the way I figured it. Nor did I expect much of the accompanying album, not even after "Miss You" turned out to be one of those "Angie"-type slow songs that have been a strength of the mature Stones, and not even after the slow song proved fast enough to spawn a convincing 8:36-minute disco disc. The flip, after all, was Mick doing one of his hyper-conscious ethnic comedy routines, drawling on about "far away eyes" in an ignorant English takeoff on a Bakersfield redneck. This was before Jagger and Cott's searching, playful conversation was published, and I associated "Far Away Eyes" with a less savory interchange between Jagger and Jim Jerome of *People*. In the Jerome interview, done around the time *Love You Live* was released but only printed in last month's *Oui*, Jagger, drunk on sake, shifted emphases and accents and personas in a whirlpool of put-ons. This was the terminal irony of someone who had lost hold of his own cynicism, someone who'd been projecting images of self-knowledge/self-doubt for so long that the self itself had finally slipped away.

I got the new Stones album on a deadline Monday that left me so bushed I put on side two first, which is against my religion. The first cut was "Far Away Eyes", and as I lay there in a mild natural stupor I noticed that I liked it. I could hear Gram Parsons effects applied to Jagger's redneck protagonist, a gently waggish character gently conceived; there with humor in the sung, lyric chorus and pathos in the spoken, parodic verse. Then came "Respectable", the likes of which the Stones hadn't attempted since *Between the Buttons*, and a mournful Keith Richard feature that was almost as fast as "Happy", and a slower one that pleased even if it didn't impress, and an impressive riff song with a throwaway melody and a lot of funny throwaway rhymes about New York City. My God – I'd enjoyed every cut. I raised myself from the couch and turned the record over right away. After a hard day at the office, this is also against my religion.

I liked side one less – didn't think the mock stereotyping of "Some Girls", the album's signature piece, was funny or entirely mock – and found myself playing both sides all the time. It had been quite a while since a new record had cut so deeply into my professional listening time. I began to pay attention to rumors of local stops on a tour that wasn't scheduled to come closer than Philadelphia. But I didn't pursue them too hard. Whether these theatre gigs were strictly for the fans, as the Stones' friends reported, or strictly for the in crowd, as their enemies charged, I figured I'd get in without being pushy or I wouldn't get in at all. For the Ramones at CBGB or the 1976 World Series I have pulled rank and slept on line and contended with my fellow mob. But though I loved *Some Girls* – by then I was forcing my friends to sit there and listen, which hadn't happened with a Stones album since *Let It Bleed* – the memory that lingered from 1975 was of Mick scampering desperately up and down a malfunctioning stage ramp at the Garden, reduced from the epitome of live rock and roll to a fading decathlon champion who communicated by semaphore.

Nevertheless, something was going on here – the third week of June was upon me and my thoughts were not turning to Tom Robinson. Robinson's album, *Power in the Darkness*, was one of the competent-to-good musical endeavors *Some Girls* had displaced, but with an interview on tap I began playing it again. As product, it exemplified Robinson's penchant for good works, for in addition to a full 10-song LP it included a seven-song bonus record comprising "2-4-6-8 Motorway", *TRB-Rising Free*, and two B sides. "Glad To Be Gay", "2-4-6-8", and a music-hall number called "Martin" – about the rewards and ambiguities of male-to-male friendship – was each flat-out wonderful in its own way, and "Winter of '79" was in a league with "For What It's Worth", only much less coy. But musically the songs were rather foursquare, not clever enough for catchy pop nor unrelenting enough for hard rock, and Danny Kustow's guitar breaks sold even the guitar-break crowd short. The lyrics were foursquare, too, programmatic and preachy at their occasional worst and rarely suggesting that politics involves internal contradictions as well as oppression. Would the Clash or Arlo Guthrie ever dare simple-mindedness on the order of "If left is right then right it wrong/You'd better decide what side you're on"? Not in the world you and me live in.

Strangely enough, the person who complains hardest about that particular offense to reason is Robinson himself. This was a man who welcomed feminist complaints about condescension in "Right On Sister" out of sheer dialectical principle; his politics were so good he'd even outline his own limitations for you. Like me, he wondered in retrospect whether it wouldn't have been wiser to hold off "2-4-6-8" until a core audience had been consolidated, than take the world with a hit. And like anyone with a pinch of sense, he was of several minds about political songwriting, so that the usual conundrums lurked behind most of what he said: What's more important, to describe what you know or inspire effective action? Is it possible to inspire genuinely effective action if you write around the messier parts of what you know? Is it possible for a musician to inspire action in any case?

Robinson realizes that all he can achieve is bits of input, but he's also aware that bits add up, which is better than subtracting. He's proud of the huge Rock Against Racism rally that preceded electoral setbacks for the National Front, and humble about how hard it will be to organize against the more insidious reaction of the good old Conservative Party. So he remains of several minds. He regards "Winter of '79" – in which the epochal repression of that season is recalled from some further future as a hard but by no means (compare David Bowie, Black Sabbath) decisive or apocalyptic piece of history: politics is struggle, life continues – as his most satisfactory song. He hopes to write others of comparable complexity. But he doesn't want to go too far: "You become impotent as a songwriter, because you can't say anything clearly any more if you disappear up your own asshole worrying about it."

That was Tuesday. On Wednesday the Stones' p.r. people proffered one ticket for the Capitol in Passaic that night, and I stood up my wife to go. The show, scheduled to begin at 8, didn't go on until after 9, and I whiled away the interlude asking people how they'd come by their seats. I'd heard that many tickets had been sold in local bars and record stores, but, aside from the two guys whose buddy had happened to be in the Harmony Hut in Wayne when the sign went up, talked to no one who'd gotten in that way. Instead I found employees of Sound companies and college booking agencies, a mechanic at the Passaic police station, two kids who'd gotten theirs from a friend arrested on a drug charge, someone whose brother was "a big wheel", someone else who'd scalped an upfront pair from a ticket agent for "over $200", quite a few sticklers for reportorial courtesy, and record-bizzers fucking galore. The place was like a convention. I wouldn't say these weren't Rolling Stones fans, but I'd guess that their zeal was at least as questionable as mine and that, like me, many of the most zealous had been overexposed to live music. I had joined the in crowd at last, yet somehow I didn't feel honored.

Etta James's apologetic set did not improve my mood, and when the Stones opened with "Let It Rock" my ass was willing but my spirit weak. I stood because everyone was standing, and averted my eyes as Mick thrashed about in frenzied simulated stimulation. But I was sustained by the sight of sixth Stone Ian Stewart bashing his piano and re-bop king Charlie Watts beating his drums. Captured by Stewart's Johnnie Johnson barrelhouse riffs, I entertained my first doubts about the hardnosed media smarts that forced the blokeish-looking pianist to the sidelines of the group in 1963; analyzing Watts' driving, jazz-derived figures, I recognized my prejudices against swing in rock and roll. Listening to the music through those two guys was like discovering the two artisans who'd really put the cathedral together, and had Bill Wyman been better mixed, I'm sure he would have made three.

Cynics claim, no doubt with some justice, that the tour is basically high-powered promo for the new product, and for that I soon became grateful. Somewhat sick at heart, I had continued to contemplate Ian and Charlie through "All Down the Line" and "Honky Tonk Women" and "Starfucker", the throwaway rocker that survives as the most standard Stones standard since *Exile*, and which dropped the Passaic onlookers to their seats. But on the first song from *Some Girls*, "When the Whip Comes Down", the music lost its mechanical aura – through the next eight selections, seven more from *Some Girls* plus "Love in Vain", it gathered power and conviction. Suddenly Jagger seemed interested in what he was doing. It would be going too far to call it sincerity, but there was an ingenuous enthusiasm to his performance that I'd previously encountered only in a callower version on the early albums. By omitting "Some Girls", the one new lyric that demands an "ironic" reading, he remained consistent, projecting both anger and vulnerability with gratifying immediacy. Equally important, the guitar that he played on most of these songs contained him physically, kept his hands occupied so that he couldn't go looking for trouble while the band played on. Instead, his restless intensity was channeled through his vocal cords. At least on the new songs, the Stones were doing something new.

Carried forwards on this music, I rose with the crowd for a raucous "Sweet Little Sixteen" and was content to stay up through "Tumbling Dice" (although Mick was no Linda), "Happy" (although Keith was no Keith), "Brown Sugar" (vaguely offputting), and "Jumping Jack Flash" (a proper climax). The only major disappointment was the mumbled lyric on "Street Fighting Man", the encore, and while I stick with the judgment I returned to jealous acquaintances – "quite good" – I will add that this was the most revelatory of the eight Stones concerts I've seen.

Granted that I preferred the audience at the Palladium gig of five nights later – although a good many extra tickets from the WNEW postcard lottery were scalped by amateurs for a less than shocking median price of $40, at least they were scalped on the street to other amateurs. But perhaps because I was put in the loge with the goddam in crowd (Walter Becker left early, as did Hall, or was that Oates?; Paul McCartney stayed), not even my wife, who spent most of the concert diddybopping in the aisles, could make the show new for me the way the first one had been. The high spot actually preceded the Stones' set, when Mick did a dancey duet with new Rolling Stones Records signee Peter Tosh on the Temptations' "Don't Look Back", and I didn't get it when Jagger started waving his cock through his polyurethane pants – with both hands yet, what showmanship. Anyway, the third time through any set, drawbacks begin to come clear.

The second time had been Saturday at JFK Memorial Stadium in Philadelphia along with some 100,000 definitively amateur fans. My side location was about as far from the stage as the deepest reaches of Madison Square Garden, and a good half of the crowd was even worse off. I'm informed that the sound was quite adequate 40 yards downfield from the music, but where I was it was barely loud enough to qualify as rock and roll. Mick was once again held in check by the guitar, and the relative wit and elegance of his most hyperkinetic moves was put in perspective by the dull attitudinizing of Lou Gramm of Foreigner, the opener. This didn't matter much, though, and if it's true that Mick was feverish and off form that day, that doesn't matter either. Rock and roll can't be perceived through binoculars. The crowd was up well past "Starfucker" anyway, but they seemed to be flying on automatic pilot.

Meanwhile, the big rock and roll event of the third week of June proceeded apace, with WNEW preparing to broadcast Robinson's Thursday Bottom Line debut even as it cut its deal for the Stones tix. That night the club was jammed to the aisles with a crowd that was above all . . . straight, in the nonsexual sense. Even the record-bizzers were minimally flashy, and they fit right in with gays who were neither glitter queens nor short-haired neatnicks and punks with nostrils and brain pans intact and (I'm guessing) politicos who looked like schoolteachers and, of course, real people. Despite his sly, cheery, winning stage manner, Robinson couldn't conceal his nervousness. But this crowd didn't care. They hailed one protest song after another, and nearly went berserk when Robinson paid his respects to geography by substituting "New York police" for "British police" in the first line of "Glad To Be Gay". Nor were the record pros less enthusiastic than their fellow fans – I've heard lots of corporate applause, and this was different.

All this surprised me a little, especially the biz part, because my experience of bizzers is that their politics stop at the door to the A & R department. The rationalization, I'm sure, was that TRB is good old commercial rock and roll; as WNEW's Richard Near assured his listeners, "This is not political – it's a musical trip." But this time I think the realist was Vin Scelsa, who introduced Robinson with some heartfelt praise for songs about things that mattered, an approbation I'm certain this audience shared. For the pros, it was enough that (unlike the punks) Robinson espoused the principles of music that sells, even if there was only one "2-4-6-8" in his kit so far. Given that orthodoxy, their passion was inflamed by his desire to change the world. Maybe they were feeling scared, maybe they were feeling guilty, maybe they were feeling nostalgic for their own idealism, or maybe they had never abandoned that ideal-ism, but they wanted to help change the world.

Good for them, and so do I. Nevertheless, I couldn't escape the feeling that, spiritually, Tom Robinson was an exception-ally hard-rocking folkie. No matter what his principle, the words took priority. This wasn't necessarily because the musi-cal talent wasn't there – the key was that the band's conceptual inspiration was fundamentally verbal. Of course, the same was true of Elvis Costello less than a year ago, before the Attractions – a band identical in lineup and basic attack to the TRB – took over his soul. Maybe Robinson's new keyboard man, Nick Plytas, a veteran of a worthy post-pub group called Roogalator, can work a similar conversion, get something more explosive than those arbitrary rolls out of Dolphin Taylor and spur Danny Kustow to find licks as funny and sharp and spontaneous as his tough-guy stage poses. Robinson's got reason to believe.

Which leads us to the question: What was the big rock and roll event of the third week of June? My surprise answer: There were two. For music, Television at the Bottom Line Sunday, first set. Ficca and Smith are hardly Watts and Wyman, and Tom Verlaine is worlds from the singer Jagger can be – at the Palladium, the emotional twists from "Love in Vain" to "Beast of Burden" (that slower one that didn't impress me) to "Shattered" took on a resonance and directness that up to now Jagger has barely played with. But Television's syntheses promise a future the Stones can no longer imagine, and when their music comes together they're more exciting than the Stones, not only in theory but in the physical/psychological fact. For culture, though, I'll take the last four songs by Bob Marley at the Garden the following Saturday. It took us so long to escape the Stones' scene in Philly that four songs was all we caught, but maybe it was better that way, because it thrust us into the middle of a sweaty revelry that the most passionate Rock Against Racism event would be hard-pressed to approach. Not that swaying to "Kaya" will end war in Babylon – or begin it, if that's your analysis. But the biracial spontaneity of the crowd was a political event in itself.

The Stones and the TRB, however, also left me with wonderful memories, some of them preserved on plastic.

In the end, I didn't think the musical gains of the two Stones theatre concerts I saw justified their exclusivity, especially if debacles like Philadelphia are part of the deal. Better they should do like Bob Marley and settle for the Garden. But at least temporarily they seem to have sensed that irony is a perilous mode in this bitter time. It's significant, too, that they're not trying to write songs that will trigger new jumping-jack climaxes, because that mode seems less and less natural for them as well. There is a wonderful looseness to *Some Girls* that redeems (perhaps even requires) its sloppy solos and half-finished lyrics. The Stones aren't going to change the world any more, not even unintentionally, but at least they prove that a bunch of old pros can have fun. The TRB have their own future. After their show I went home to find words for the B plus I was finally convinced their album deserved. To my amazement, one song after another began to kick in for the first time. Not always real hard, and not without the problems I've explained, but enough. Good record. They may yet change the world, intentionally. Which would make that June gig a very big rock and roll event indeed.

EMOTIONAL RESCUE

Sean Egan

UK release: 27 June 1980; US release: 23 June 1980

Produced by: The Glimmer Twins, Chris Kimsey

Charts: UK no. 1; US no. 1

Tracklisting:
Dance (Pt. 1)
Summer Romance
Send It to Me
Let Me Go
Indian Girl
Where the Boys Go
Down in the Hole
Emotional Rescue
She's So Cold
All About You

Following the Stones' American tour on 10 June–26 July 1978, Keith Richards had to prepare to face a judge again in Toronto. By the time he did on 23 October 1978, all charges against him had been dropped except possession of twenty-two grams of heroin, to which he pleaded guilty. Of course, the fact that he had undergone therapy to rid himself of his enslavement to the drug counted in his favour (although his dilettante approach to being clean would have jeopardized that had it been known at the time). However, the penalty extracted of little more than a year's probation conditional on continued drug therapy made many jaws drop in the courtroom. The only other proviso attached was that Richards perform free concerts for the blind. This peculiar edict was supposedly the result of a blind Stones fan, whose safety on the road Richards had always taken trouble to ensure, petitioning the judge for mercy. That some reports suggested that the young woman in question was the judge's daughter – rather contradicting suggestions that she was a stranger who resourcefully found her way to the judge's home – raised a few eyebrows. Nick Kent suggested that rumours of $3 million "filtered through to the right people" was the solution to the conundrum of leniency. Some who felt they had decoded "Respectable" weren't surprised: replacing "president" with "prime minster" and "White House" with "24 Sussex Drive" in that song certainly puts a new spin on the parts that state the band are talking heroin with the president and that a certain little problem can be bent (and, come to that, on the references to the easiest lay on the White House lawn).

And with that revelation that the sword of Damocles was in fact a soggy noodle, much of the recent sense of urgency and mission around The Rolling Stones evaporated. They retreated from view for a while. When they returned, they were never the same artistic force again. As a commercial proposition, they went from strength to strength, but the fierce snatching back of aesthetic credibility with *Some Girls* turned quite astonishingly quickly into a complacency that ran far deeper than that manifested on the *Goats Head Soup/It's Only Rock 'n Roll/Black and Blue* doldrums trilogy.

In a way, one couldn't blame them. Not only were the Stones riding a wave of sales and acclaim, but their bête noire, The Sex Pistols, were now history, The Clash had been transmogrifying into the Stones (right down to guitarist Mick Jones' Richards-like thatch) and much of the rest of the punk movement was rapidly passing into history. The Stones' moment of credibility crisis was over. Moreover, it must have been hard for them to imagine they would be held to account again for letting their standards slip: *Emotional Rescue* broke all their previous sales records despite being the most flimsy album to which they had ever put their name.

The Toronto bust – whose legal papers required the proper spelling of Richards' surname – seems to have motivated the guitarist to insist on his previously missing "s". Although he had always signed autographs either way, now there was even an EMI memo effectively renouncing the Andrew Oldham-ordained change. Richards had rounded off 1978 by releasing his first solo record, the festive Chuck Berry number "Run Rudolph Run" backed with the Jimmy Cliff reggae song "The Harder They Come". The following year saw him engaged in more extra-curricular activity when he and Wood toured with the New Barbarians, two of their gigs as support to the Stones in his judge-dictated benefit concerts for the blind. Jagger was apparently a bit put out by the New Barbarians. Certainly one can read all sorts of things into the troubled relationship between him and Richards over the fact that the latter was happier to play second fiddle to Led Zeppelin in August '79, at the same Knebworth Fair the Stones had headlined three years previously, than work with Jagger. Richards, having awoken from his smack coma, had begun sticking his nose in the Stones' business affairs, which had been Jagger's exclusive preserve, much to the latter's disgust. Another factor in artistic underachievement was the fact that Ron Wood's drug prob-lems – freebase cocaine being his intoxication of choice – became as debilitating as had been those of Richards. Still, with WEA and EMI expecting product, new Stones work wasn't optional.

While awaiting this, EMI distributed a UK compilation called *Time Waits for No One*. Released on 1 June 1979, it compounded being circumscribed in having only post-Klein tracks from which to pick by electing mainly to go for non-single recordings. Not surprisingly, it did not chart and was swiftly forgotten. The same year saw a US-only release combin-ing the band's two disco tracks thus far, "Hot Stuff" and "Miss You". The form chosen was a twelve-inch single, then the vogue, especially in venues with a dancefloor. The extended "Miss You" featured lengthier mouth harp work from Sugar Blue than heard on the seven-inch single/album cut.

The Stones had recorded over forty basic tracks in Paris for the last album, so there was plenty of material left over for the next one but new sessions were also arranged in LA, Nassau and Paris. The final mixing sessions in New York (where Jagger,

Richards and Wood were all now domiciled) occurred twenty months after the first new recording sessions. The upshot of all this was a record that was inexplicably inferior to what a dregs-of-*Some-Girls* album would probably have constituted.

The bad news with *Emotional Rescue* starts with the fact that the "produced by the Glimmer Twins/engineered by Chris Kimsey" combination that was so exhilaratingly new and successful last time out inexplicably just doesn't work. The mix is tinny and insubstantial, with Charlie's drums particularly diminished. However, song selection is the main issue, with material lurching from very good to absurd but settling mostly in the range of mediocre.

Like the previous two albums, *Emotional Rescue* opens with a disco groove. With "Dance (Pt. 1)", Wood secures his second co-writing credit on a Stones record. That this is now precisely 50 per cent more credits than Taylor managed in all his time in the band may or may not be consolation to Wood for the fact that "Down in the Hole" – a track he claimed as his own in interviews – had the usual Jagger/Richards attribution. It may have appalled the rockist Stones fans in its glitzy emptiness – like much disco, it's a series of slogans with no emotional heart – but "Dance (Pt. 1)" is highly impressive in its authenticity, something aided by truncated flourishes of horns common to the genre. After that impressive start, the alarm bells start ringing with "Summer Romance". In a truly atrocious track, tired Chuck Berry-esque riffs accompany an uninteresting lyric lamenting an affair with a university student that didn't endure beyond the recess. Even the drums are mixed boringly. From the ridiculous to the pretty much sublime: "Send It to Me" is winning reggae with a dextrous melody and a smile-inducing lyric wherein the narrator states that he wants love from anyone – mother, sister, lover – and is willing to employ any mode of transport to put himself in its vicinity. Mick intones litanies of what he desires or is prepared to undergo, one of which culminates in a then-trendy reference to the film *Alien*. "Let Me Go" is more Chuck Berry-inflected sexual boorishness. Of course, some of the Stones' greatest music fits that description, but there is something about the thin sound and emotional banality that tips the whole thing over into plain irritating.

With "Indian Girl", sweet acoustic guitar and exotic Latin inflections seem to herald something interesting but the track soon develops into something categorically WTF?! The compelling subject – it seeks to explore the horrors then occurring in Central America – and lilting tune should make for something substantial, but between the hackneyed mariachi brass, references to "gringos" and Jagger's inappropriately playful singing, we never quite escape the feeling of a soundtrack to a lightweight film about the Battle of the Alamo.

Side-two opener "Where the Boys Go" is an anthem of working-class weekend brainlessness at a time when the celebration of such hedonism, and the mockney in which Jagger sings it, still had a smack of the rebellious. The subsequent securing of a permanent place in the media by chav culture has robbed such things of their charm, but in any case this is no "Salt of the Earth" but a cartoon made all the more risible by it feeling like an attempt to wrench back some street credentials from punks. That said, there's no denying that it's catchy and intoxicatingly sprightly. "Down in the Hole" is by far the classiest cut on the record. Sugar Blue mouth harp runs all the way through this haunting, atmospheric number. Jagger enunciates – brilliantly, anguishedly, soulfully – a condemnation of someone guilty of unspecified crimes but whom we infer is a Nazi simply via the line, "Bumming for nylons in the American Zone", which seems to place events in post-war Berlin.

The album was preceded – just – by the single "Emotional Rescue" b/w "Down in the Hole", released on 20 June 1980 in the UK and 23 June in the States. The A-side sounded bizarre on first listen, and to some extent still does. The track has some of the attributes of disco, particularly Wood's rhythmic, prominent bass riff, but its five and a half minutes – most of which Jagger sings in a mannered falsetto – are really musically uncategorizable. It sees a narrator cause distress to a lover and then rather cheekily offer consolation for such distress, even more cheekily positing himself in this action as a knight in shining armour arriving "on a fine Arab charger". It's one of the few tracks on the album whose production adds to rather than subtracts from the recording, with Watts' quietly brilliant drum work – resonating rimshots, pulsating bass drum, quietly inventive accents and pace-changing – particularly benefitting. Bobby Keys returns to blow some pleasingly smoky sax. One does wonder whether the cut would cross the line from impressive to likeable if Jagger dispensed with the Prince-isms. The single made no. 9 in the UK and no. 3 in America. "She's So Cold" was the second and final single in both the States and Britain (10 and 22 September respectively). Coupled with "Send It to Me", it made no. 26 stateside and no. 33 in the UK. A spare, rhythmic, vibrating rocker that sees the narrator lamenting the glacial properties of his lover, its surprisingly likeable, and if there arises a suspicion that it's a self-conscious attempt to purvey the classic Stones sound, the rejoinder instantly occurs that by now any uptempo, riffy number proffered by them would generate the same notion.

Keith's vocal showcase "All About You" is the album's second WTF?! side-closer. Lush saxophone and creamy guitars seem to promise something special, and perhaps the cut would indeed be that had not Richards executed such a couldn't-care-less vocal performance (apparently he cut his hand on a bottle of Jack Daniel's on the way to the studio). Richards' comment on his life in this vindictive kiss-off of a song, "Why must I spend mine with you?" made many assume he was referring to the now estranged Pallenberg, in whose bedroom a seventeen-year-old boy had recently shot himself in the head when Richards was absent in Europe. Richards himself said it was more about Jagger. Some, however, were less interested in the source of his ire than why he couldn't have returned to the vocal booth the next day with the benefit of a night's sleep and a plaster on his finger.

Emotional Rescue spent two weeks at no. 1 in the UK. In the States, it sat at no. 1 for a mind-boggling seven weeks. In the context of the album's lack of quality – and the stunning quality of previous albums by the band that hadn't done anything like as well – this type of success was preposterous. The tortured deliberations that marked the record's elongated gestation period (Wyman remembers Jagger and Richards shouting at each other over the track selection) render the Stones innocent of the charge of not caring about the product, even if the front

cover of thermo-imagery photographs of (what looks like)
Mick and Keith is thoroughly lazy. ("Lucky" early purchasers
got a thermo-imagery poster.) However, following a masterpiece like *Some Girls* with what is essentially half an album, and
a pretty banal one at that, would be disappointing at the best of
times but is crushing in the context of how deeply meaningful
a statement that aforesaid album had been. But then the Stones'
days of meaningful statements were over.

Two albums by other artists in this period seemed to carry
the torch that the Stones had abandoned. *London Calling* by
The Clash – released in December 1979 (January 1980 in
America) – displayed an all-encompassing musical vision
(including reggae, which, no doubt much to riddim-lover
Richards' chagrin, they tackled better than his own band ever
had). Moreover, the English New Wavers took the Stones'
dissidence a stage further: virtually every single track was
social commentary or an exploration of the street life with
which the Stones had lost contact long ago (Mick's New York
slumming notwithstanding). It was a work suffused with an
almost blush-making humanity. The fact that it bore a resemblance to *Exile on Main St.* in its double-LP format and card
inner sleeves with scrawled annotations prompted many to
make comparisons, postulating it to be an *Exile on Main St.* for
modern times. While *Exile* could hold its own with this record,
or any other, a juxtaposition of the Stones' latest album and
London Calling was a cringe-making measure of how far they
had fallen from what we will call, for the sake of expediency,
worthiness. *The River* by Bruce Springsteen (released in October 1980) was another double album with card inner sleeves
and contents that movingly and exhilaratingly addressed the
plight of the underdog and another record that made the
Stones seem loudly redundant.

Emotional Rescue made it clear that the Stones had nothing
profound left to say. *Some Girls* had created an illusion of relevance because there were a few streetwise songs and because
clued-in long-term followers could exult in ripostes like
"Respectable" and confessionals like "Before They Make Me
Run". With that stuff out of their system, the Stones were left
exposed as having no deep philosophical well on which to

draw, something already hinted at by *Goats Head Soup*, *It's Only Rock 'n Roll* and *Black and Blue*. To be fair, the Stones hadn't particularly changed – the world had. The social climate that had given the Stones importance over and above their art had now shifted. With society far, far freer than it had been in 1963, the Stones' image no longer communicated rebellion and relevance by default. Meanwhile, what quasi-political songs there were in their catalogue had now been drained of much of their resonance: the young record purchaser of 1980 could have no way of understanding what a totemic act issuing songs like "Satisfaction", "Let's Spend the Night Together", "Sympathy for the Devil", "Live with Me" or "Brown Sugar" had once constituted: the austere, disapproving world that had lent those creations their outlaw power was gone with the wind, leaving them merely as great listening experiences. The band hardly possessed the compositional armoury to write new songs as vital or politically charged as those cuts had once been. Jagger's and Richards' political leanings had never gone much further than a vague anti-authoritarianism. The subjects of love and sex essayed on *Emotional Rescue* were all they had left about which to write and any attempt to step outside that comfort zone could – as evinced by "Indian Girl" – go horrifically wrong. *Emotional Rescue* was the point where The Rolling Stones crossed over from any semblance of profundity to the status of good-time rock-'n'-roll band and there was nothing they or anybody else could do about it.

TATTOO YOU

Sean Egan

UK release: 28 August 1981; US release: 18 August 1981

Produced by: The Glimmer Twins, Chris Kimsey

Charts: UK no. 2; US no. 1

Tracklisting:
Start Me Up
Hang Fire
Slave
Little T & A
Black Limousine
Neighbours
Worried About You
Tops
Heaven
No Use in Crying
Waiting on a Friend

9 March (UK) and 21 March (US) 1981 saw the release of *Sucking in the Seventies*, yet another post-Klein Stones compilation. Like *Time Waits for No One*, its track selection was weird verging on stupid. Apparently arbitrarily, it only included stuff from the *It's Only Rock 'n Roll* album onwards, omitted obvious singles that would have enhanced its commercial chances (including "Miss You") and for no good reason shortened most of the cuts it did include. The only people one could imagine purchasing this mess were Stones diehards seeking the included rarity (the first LP appearance of "Everything Is Turning to Gold") and new tracks, one of which was a live

version of "When the Whip Comes Down", the other being "If I Was a Dancer (Dance Pt. 2)", a brooding variant of the upbeat Jagger/ Richards/Wood opener on *Emotional Rescue*. The US/"COC" release made no. 15 but UK/"CUN" did not chart. Incongruously, the Stones were gearing up for their biggest splash yet.

That their following album, *Tattoo You*, and the US and European tours promoting it were both commercial high-water marks for The Rolling Stones was something of a triumph, although not particularly one that it feels should be admired. The album comprised a bunch of overdubbed cast-offs and the tour groaned and squealed into existence via only the most supreme of efforts. The problem in both cases was outright hostility between the once brotherly Jagger and Richards: making a normal album was out of the question when they could not bear the prospect of being in a confined space with each other for prolonged periods, while Wyman, when discussing the tour with the band's financial adviser, was doubtful it would ever come about but felt that if it did it would be the band's farewell. Should that eventuality occur, Wyman had cause for feeling more secure about it than at any time previously. Although his seventies brace of solo albums on Rolling Stones Records had not set the world on fire, in the summer of '81 he became the first Stone to have a major solo hit when his delightful, self-deprecating single "(Si Si) Je Suis Un Rock Star" reached the UK top 20 and did well internationally. How thoroughly mean-spirited it was for Jagger and Richards, even in the midsts of a dearth of new material, to decline to find a place for such songs on the "new" Stones album.

Tattoo You's patchwork origination was the idea of Chris Kimsey who, cognizant of the Glimmer Twins' estrangement, pointed out the remarkably high quality of a basic track called "Start Me Up", a *Some Girls*-era rock re-recording of a Jagger/ Richards number originally essayed as a reggae during the *Black and Blue* sessions. Kimsey reasoned that with such jewels buried on Stones session reels, he could compile a high-quality facsimile Stones album that would need little work other than the addition of vocal melodies, lyrics and Jagger's voice.

Accordingly, Jagger took control of the project, although saxo-phone overdubs by Sonny Rollins are an example of additional embellishments. With the selected tracks dating as far back as the *Goats Head Soup* sessions, Jagger understandably decided to have them mixed so as to introduce a uniformity of sound. His choice of Bob Clearmountain for this task was perhaps not so judicious. Clearmountain – who had mixed the extended "Miss You" single – executed something sickly rich and drum-heavy that the world did not yet know would unfortunately epitomize music in the eighties.

The album sleeve featured a photograph of Jagger on the front and one of Richards on the back, both men's images overlaid with tattoo designs. Richards wasn't impressed by either that or the last-minute decision by Jagger to change the title from *Tattoo* to that of a well-known brand of skin trans-fers. However, the cover made the album more of an event, with newspapers keen to print pictures of the mildly shocking makeover. One side of the card inner sleeve featured the grotesque paw-in-stiletto design of the "Start Me Up" lead-off single's picture bag, the other side ... absolutely nothing except a dizzying line design. *It's Only Rock 'n Roll* had featured a card inner sleeve on which supporting musicians were not just listed but pictured. When asked in an interview about the lack of the customary list of musicians on *Tattoo You*, Jagger said, "Well, I just got fed up with writing all those credit lists out and everyone wants one above the other one, and then I couldn't remember who is playing, so I thought, Oh, everyone got paid anyway. So it's much easier to leave the whole thing. I mean I didn't get any credits on it except for the songwriting." This waffling disingenuousness was down to the fact that the band were endeavouring not to advertise that the goods they were purveying were not exactly fresh. Richards was hardly any more honest with comments like, "On this album, we took longer. We started to think about this one soon after the last one came out, and we chose the songs a lot more carefully." It was blindingly obvious that the silky guitar on several tracks was not the work of Richards or Wood but the journalists who were prepared to confront the band with their suspicions about the presence of Mick Taylor or Wayne

Perkins, with all the attendant recording-date ramifications, were few and far between.

"Start Me Up" preceded the album it opened, released as a single backed with "No Use in Crying" on 6 August 1981 in the US and 14 August in the UK. Its subject is greasy sex, the narrator positing himself and his partner as machines needing kick-starting and oiling. Vaingloriously, Jagger asserts that once his key is turned, he will never stop. It's not a classic but its staccato riff and anthemic melody were readymade to have people talking of a return to the old Stones sound. That and their subsequent memories of the band's ubiquity in the culture during this period have been enough to lodge it in the public's affections as a landmark record.

"Hang Fire" is a track started at the *Some Girls* sessions. The mildly impressive cooing backing vocals can't much elevate what is a one-dimensional boogie but the lyric is the main problem. With unemployment in Britain hitting record levels, Jagger sensitively handles the issue by stating that in the sweet ol' country where he comes from "Nobody ever works, nothing ever gets done." Depressingly, this is the closest the Stones can now come to social commentary. "Slave" is of *Black and Blue* vintage – which is fine because Billy Preston's organ is wonderful, but then so is the sax from Sonny Rollins by which it is separated by a distance of five years recording-wise. The song feels rather too close chronologically to the similarly themed "Beast of Burden" and smacks suspiciously of a studio jam with overdubs. However, the riff is good stuff and the groove slinky. Curiously, the five-minute track later gained a minute and a half on CD and, in so doing, a feeling of greater worth. "Little T & A" – an *Emotional Rescue* track – is Keith's vocal showcase. It sees him tell model girlfriend Patti Hansen – soon to become his wife – that she is his little rock 'n' roller, his tits 'n' ass with soul. This not-quite-Shakespearian couplet is married to a riff Chuck Berry would have thrown in the dustbin. Richards seems to have made Hansen a happy woman in a domestic sense but she may have felt aggrieved that a dozen years ago Richards was capable of writing the beautiful "You Got the Silver" as a tribute to her predecessor.

"Black Limousine" is credited to Jagger/Richards/Wood.
That it took three men to write this boring, suffocating twelve-
bar blues is something of a surprise to say the least.
Clearmountain's sheen robs it of any grit it might have
possessed, leaving the only thing even slightly impressive
about it Jagger's candid, if hardly sparkling, lyric about the
ravages of age, in which thesis he doesn't spare himself ("Look
at you and look at me"). "Neighbours" is one of two songs
especially recorded for the album. Clearmountain mixes the
echoed drums up to temples-throbbing levels, Jagger virtually
shouts the lyric and Sonny Rollins delivers a dramatic sax part
but all of this sound and fury signifies nothing but another
unimaginative uptempo boogie. The allusion to Richards'
recent eviction from New York apartments for noise-making
makes a tilt for the only sort of rebel credentials the Stones can
still command.

The second side of the album was given over to ballads and
worked far better than side one. "Worried About You" is a
smouldering *Black and Blue*-era track with a virtuoso Wayne
Perkins solo. "Tops" originates from *Goats Head Soup*. A
denunciation (one assumes anyway) of the casting-couch
process, it's the first truly substantial-sounding cut on the
album up to this point if, like the previous track, just slightly
boring. One of the reasons for this tinge of the boring is – also
like on the previous track – Jagger's insistence on falsetto. Mick
Taylor is the author of the classy guitar work. "Heaven" is the
second all-new recording. What should be the slightest thing
on the album is actually arguably its highlight. Richards and
Wood don't even appear on this gossamer, dreamy creation
wherein Jagger delights in the smell and touch of his lover to a
background of phased strummed guitar and tapped drum
ridges. For once, Jagger's falsetto is fitting.

Wood's nagging was clearly having an effect: whereas Taylor
had to sue the Stones for remuneration for his contributions to
Tattoo You, "No Use in Crying" is the second track here for
which Wood receives a compositional credit with Jagger and
Richards. What sounded delicate on the flipside of "Start Me
Up" is almost shockingly rough after "Heaven", and not just
because it's as callous as "Heaven" is gentle. "I ain't never

coming back," the narrator assures his ex-lover in a high-quality, spiritual sequel to "Out of Time". This *Emotional Rescue*
out-take would have substantially improved that album. "Waiting on a Friend" closes the album on an unusual note. This
Goats Head Soup basic track – featuring the long-departed
triumvirate of Nicky Hopkins, Mick Taylor and, on percussion, Jimmy Miller – is augmented by a non-posturing lyric of
which Jagger would probably have been incapable in 1973: a
deliberately ambiguous, mellow statement about not waiting
on a lady but on a friend, gender unspecified. Smoky sax work
completes the agreeable picture.

"Waiting on a Friend" b/w "Little T & A" was the album's
second single, making no. 13 in the US, where it was released on
17 November 1981, and no. 50 in the UK following its 27
November appearance there. 4 March '82 saw "Neighbours"
become the third single stateside. That "Hang Fire" rather than
a new track was the flip might smack of decadence – more than
half of *Tattoo You* was now on single – but this was also commercially fortunate, for it was that side that charted, making no. 20.

The idea that *Tattoo You* received uniformly good reviews is
an American-centric one: whereas sycophancy was the order
of the day stateside, the British music weeklies went in the
opposite direction. Their being offended by the Stones' age
and their lack of hard-left politics was somewhat unreasonable. Their cold-eyed realism about *Tattoo You*'s contents was
less so, with the *NME* accurately adjudging it a good minor
Stones album and then realistically predicting that there would
never be a major one again. However, the popularity of "Start
Me Up" – which reached no. 2 in America and no. 7 in Britain
– and the tsunami of publicity and fond retrospectives accompanying the tour that started three weeks after the album's
release created the sort of mass illusion that dictated that far
from being high-quality only in the sense of being better than
Emotional Rescue, *Tattoo You* was "the best Stones album in
years". Meat Loaf's *Dead Ringer* prevented it from making no.
1 in the UK but *Tattoo You* sat at the top of the *Billboard* album
chart for a scarcely believable nine weeks. The three-month
US tour saw a new, family-friendly Stones playing outdoor
venues in the sunshine and the once demonic Jagger prancing

around in Day-Glo puffa jackets, skateboarder's kneepads and knickerbockers. In the first-ever example of corporate sponsorship in rock, Jovan Musk men's perfume underwrote the tour and – for some – underlined the Stones' status as sellouts. It was the highest-grossing tour in history. A month-long European tour began in May '82.

Although *Tattoo You* was a commercial high-water mark, it also marked a finale for such sales. The band's albums would continue to shift plenty of units but not spectacularly so, while the eighties would be the last decade in which the Stones secured top 10 singles. "Start Me Up" was the Stones' last iconic record, the final one that one could imagine constituting a milestone in people's minds marking a memory, an era or an event. In a world in which a sexagenarian Bob Dylan can secure US no. 1 albums, one hesitates to be certain about *Tattoo You* being the final US no. 1 Stones album, but up to the time of writing that is the case. This would all have been fairly unthinkable in the context of the hoopla of 1981–2. However, the Stones were – gradually but surely – moving on to a different plane, one where they remained titans of music in a manner that rendered their record sales and quality of their current musical output irrelevant. As their albums got less and less interesting, their tours got bigger and bigger, breaking gross and attendance records – their own and those of other acts – each time out.

UNDERCOVER

Sean Egan

UK release: 7 November 1983; US release: 7 November 1983

Produced by: The Glimmer Twins, Chris Kimsey

Charts: UK no. 3; US no. 4

Tracklisting:
Undercover of the Night
She Was Hot
Tie You Up (The Pain of Love)
Wanna Hold You
Feel on Baby
Too Much Blood
Pretty Beat Up
Too Tough
All the Way Down
It Must Be Hell

Bill Wyman had another hit in 1982 when his ultra-melodic "A New Style" reached the UK top 40, while its eponymous parent album was a pleasant affair that included at least one track – "Girls" – that sounded tailor-made for Mick Jagger to wrap his tonsils around but of course was destined never to come to his attention.

A live album from the Stones' American tour called *"Still Life" (American Concert 1981)* was released on 1 June 1982, adorned by the tour's garish backdrop of American iconography. Though the '81 concerts had featured risqué material like "When the Whip Comes Down", "Let It Bleed" and "Star Star", songs of a darker hue like "Gimme Shelter", "Midnight

Rambler" and "Sympathy for the Devil" were missing. Accordingly, the live album is fairly breezy. It is also risible in its between-song patter wherein Jagger can be found extending his American accent from song into spoken announcements as though sticking up two fingers – sorry, one finger – at the Anglocentric punks. Musically, the album is of mild interest as it features the Stones' first-ever foray into rockabilly in the form of Eddie Cochran's "Twenty Flight Rock". Significantly, the most fevered audience reception is not for classics like "Let's Spend the Night Together" or "Satisfaction" but for pseudo-classic "Start Me Up". The LP bequeathed two singles. "Going to a Go-Go" coupled with a standalone live "Beast of Burden" appeared on 1 June 1982 and made no. 26 in the UK and no. 25 in the US. "Time Is on My Side" b/w "Twenty Flight Rock", which failed to chart stateside but made no. 62 in the UK, was released on 24 August (US) and 13 September (UK).

A little more worthy was the documentary film of the tour, *Let's Spend the Night Together*, which premiered on 11 February 1983. The daytime scheduling of the tour's concerts made the title nonsensical and one almost suspects it was chosen by Jagger so as to engineer the spectacle, witnessed at premieres, involving him making young women dissolve into giggling fits by asking, "What's the name of my film?" However, director Hal Ashby provides as interesting a snapshot of the band as *Ladies and Gentlemen The Rolling Stones* had nearly a decade previously, even if like the previous one this film suffers from a lack of backstage footage.

As they moved into 1983, the members of The Rolling Stones were at a stage of their respective lives where taking stock begins to occur. Richards had been reunited with his long-alienated father in the summer of '82, while his own son had entered teenhood. Both Glimmer Twins were due to hit forty that year. Their respective subsequent behaviour has shown that this would not have been a traumatic event for Richards but this, and the lines that had begun to appear on his ultra-fresh face, must have been a big deal for a vain Lothario like Jagger. 1983, of course, also marked the twentieth anniversary of the release of the first Stones record, an event from which at the time it would have been preposterous to extrapolate a two-decade career. Perhaps some or all of these thoughts were running through Jagger's head when he suggested to Richards that for the next Stones album they should work up their compositions before going in the studio. There again, abandoning the age-old spontaneous Stones recording *modus operandi* may have been less a manifestation of his anxiety to prove his enduring artistic worth than of his noted penny-pinching. Certainly the results of these endeavours don't indicate far-reaching creative vision.

The album was heralded on 1 November 1983 by "Undercover of the Night". A return to the subject matter of the fatuous "Indian Girl" might not sound promising, but this time Jagger addresses the issue of Latin American death squads in terms far less like a soap opera. Although his repeated inappropriate use of the word "baby" is the reflex of a man out of time, there is genuine pathos in his litany of the consequences of militia terror ("Once proud fathers act so humble"). Like "Dance (Pt. 1)", it's another song whose non-bluesiness was so despised by Richards that he barely appears on it but its music is galvanizing. Its dance-friendly, uptempo groove is, as with several tracks on the parent album, percussion-heavy. The drama of its stop-starts is heightened by sound effects. The single made no. 11 in the UK and no. 9 in the US, assisted by a lavish story-oriented promotional film – or "video" as the world was now calling them – helmed by noted director Julien Temple.

The B-side was less impressive by the approximate width of a universe. "All the Way Down" is a song about a woman that the narrator met when he was twenty-one. This sets up a lyric that is less a piece of indulgent reflection on the romantic follies of a naïve younger self than a marvelling at the sexual technique (including the physical feat of the title) of the partner in question. Wasting pretty good music – smart, snappy, tuneful – on such juvenile preening would be a feature of the album, as would the single's juxtaposition of songs of thoughtfulness and solipsism.

When the album appeared a week later, any notion aroused by its lead-off that the Stones might be out to acquire *London*

Calling-level relevance was blown asunder by its sleeve, where the "undercover" motif was – in a move of almost unbelievable crassness – turned from a commentary on Third World trag-edy into a peep show theme whereby the consumer could peel away stickers overlaying a naked woman's private parts. Worse was to come. There is nothing wrong in rejoicing in sex, but surely there are better ways to do it than "She Was Hot" (which follows opener "Undercover of the Night"), the boast of a man who engages in a one-night stand and then blames his partner for his transgression ("Honey – where were you?"). The vibrato-inflected energy of its Chuck Berry-isms is quite infectious, but the combination of a complete lack of anything new musically and the grisly lyric – as well as the picture-bag imagery of a naked woman hugging a giant candle when it was released as a single – could almost have been designed to scream "DINOSAURS". And then we immediately have "Tie You Up (The Pain of Love)". It might be unfair that twelve years after "Brown Sugar" the only people who could write a song about S & M without sounding like leering creeps were women and gays – especially considering the ageism implicit in the automatic mental response of "dirty old men" – but there's also no getting away from the excruciating fact that Jagger clearly thinks he's being lovably naughty by addressing the subject. The taut, contracting music once again has some merit.

Keith's chugging vocal showcase, "Wanna Hold You", is remarkable in being barely distinguishable from his previous one, a repetition compounded by the fact that "Little T & A" was not exactly a tour de force. As with a smattering of other Stones cuts of recent years, it alludes to the narrator's poverty, as if the writer is apprehensive that the rarefied stratosphere in which the band members now conducted their lives could not provide a compelling backdrop. "Feel on Baby" is far more sophisticated musically, a sultry five-minute cut with four-man percussion and echo treatment of Jagger's mouth harp. Unfortunately, the lyric is just more narcissism. "You're the hook-up I miss the most," Jagger says before listing surfaces on which he has made love with the woman to whom the song is addressed (which from the sound of it is emphatically not the Texan supermodel with whom he was living and was soon to become pregnant with their first child).

"Too Much Blood" opened side two strongly. This denunciation of the overabundance of violence in both modern culture and modern society (*The Texas Chainsaw Massacre* and a real-life French cannibalism case are discussed in its largely extemporized, mockney, spoken-word lyric) is set within a six-minute-long soundscape that incorporates leisurely horn charts and a fine *noir* bassline. It may be petty and not even particularly pertinent to invoke here blood-spattered Stones material like "Midnight Rambler" or "Let It Bleed" (people's attitudes change). Nonetheless, a listener can't help doing it, and in any event this album has its own moments of playfulness with violent imagery. More rich percussion propels the scuffling "Pretty Beat Up", another song on which Wood secures a co-writing credit with Jagger and Richards. David Sanborn contributes a saxophone solo on a cut that talks of a lover leaving both physical and mental scars but draws the connection unimaginatively. "Too Tough" sees more toying with violence metaphors. The lyric that depicts a man at loggerheads with a former lover scornful of his teenage bride is a largely inchoate affair that seems neither autobiographical nor an imaginative inhabitation of someone else's psyche. The music is mediocre uptempo rock but with some interesting guitar parts. Following "All the Way Down", the album closer, "It Must Be Hell", is propelled by a son-of-"Soul Survivor" riff. The cut explores the fact that whatever problems the West has, they are as nothing compared with the tribulations of those behind the then-extant Iron Curtain. However, we only know this from Mick's interviews: the lyric's imagery is fragmented and unclear. Although not quite boring, the track has outstayed its welcome well before its five-minute playing time is up.

The Glimmer Twins and Chris Kimsey production is an improvement on the overbearing texture given *Tattoo You* by Bob Clearmountain, but even despite the presence of so many percussionists it is tiresomely over-thin, which itself leads to a feeling of aesthetic flimsiness. Revealingly, even though Watts is always inventive and energetic, over the course of the record he becomes irritating, so lacking in "oomph" is his drum work rendered, which one suspects is an attempt to make the rhythm tracks resemble the then modish, weedy synthesized drumming of electropop. The album would have been improved by dropping one of the weaker tracks for "Think I'm Going Mad" – a wistful song of world weariness that appeared as the B-side of "She Was Hot" (released in the US on 23 January 1984 and the UK on 30 January, reaching no. 44 stateside and no. 42 in Britain) – but this would only have been by a marginal amount.

So-so though it is, this would be the last Stones album marked by any significant artistic ambition. From here, they skipped a beat: their increasing ring-rustiness (Jagger said when promoting *Tattoo You* that after the tour he wouldn't even think about the band for six months), the three years between *Undercover* and the next album, the eight years they spent off the road, the dispersion of members to different corners of the globe that made each band reassembly a cumbersome, concentrated effort and special event – all took their toll. Additionally their appetite to prove themselves decreased and was reduced still further by the members having more children (nothing is more guaranteed to make work and even glory seem unimportant than familial bliss).

It was also the last product where any disappointed Stones follower might be able to kid themselves with the mantra of "Let's hope the next one's good" (nobody had been so deluded as to recite the mantra "The greatest rock 'n' roll band in the world" with any conviction for a few years). With their subsequent albums, there was no thread on which to hang loyalty or belief, nothing to remind you why you ever loved this group in the first place. For a band that had made so many contrasting albums in the sixties, this was not a matter of style but simply of quality. The LPs The Rolling Stones would with decreasing frequency issue from hereon were so mediocre-to-plain awful that they would probably never have gained a commercial release had they not been attached to a name of such cachet and history.

DIRTY WORK

Sean Egan

UK release: 24 March 1986; US release: 24 March 1986

Produced by: The Glimmer Twins, Steve Lillywhite

Charts: UK no. 4; US no. 4

Tracklisting:
One Hit (to the Body)
Fight
Harlem Shuffle
Hold Back
Too Rude
Winning Ugly
Back to Zero
Dirty Work
Had It with You
Sleep Tonight

In mid-1984, Jagger appeared on The Jacksons' single "State of Shock". His duet with Michael was an embarrassing catalogue of the laboured, obnoxious mannerisms that had crept into his vocals in recent years. Amazingly, the record reached no. 14 in the UK and no. 3 in the US.

With their distribution deals with the band coming to an end, WEA and EMI took the opportunity for a last Stones payday via the compilation *Rewind*. Released on 29 June 1984 in the UK and 2 July in the US, *Rewind* was the first non-budget-label Stones compilation in a few years to dispense with the apparent policy of selecting tracks by plucking titles from a tombola. It concentrated on the hit singles, although the tracklistings

differed slightly either side of the Pond. Unfortunately, the
damage had been done and the market had been flooded. The
album could only make it as far as no. 23 in the UK and no. 86
in the US. This was despite the fact that it was given promotional assistance via *Video Rewind*, a VCR release containing the
promos for the relevant hits, and in Britain the re-release of
"Brown Sugar"/"Bitch". The latter was now bereft of "Let It
Rock", but the maxi-single had been superseded by the shaped
picture disc: one of the versions took the form of the *Sticky
Fingers* jeans crotch. The single reached no. 58. Consistent with
the spirit of embracing the new, the American version of *Rewind*
was the subject of the release of the first ever Rolling Stones
compact disc. The conclusion of the WEA/EMI deal, incidentally, marked a merciful end to the increasingly embarrassing
and undignified COC and CUN catalogue numbers.

No dissatisfaction with WEA and EMI can be inferred from
the Stones pledging Rolling Stones Records, the band's valuable back catalogue and their next four albums to CBS on
both sides of the Atlantic: loyalty or contentment could not
compete with a guarantee of $28 million. Unbeknown to the
rest of the band, the company's head, Walter Yetnikoff, dangled
a subsidiary carrot before Jagger in the form of a solo deal,
which would come closer than anything else had to wrecking
the Stones. The latter has always been posited as sheer vanity
and selfishness on the part of Jagger, especially by Richards.
While certain aspects of his tilt at going it alone give rise to the
suspicion of a mid-life crisis and an anxiety to define himself
as more than a part of a unit, to some extent Jagger has had a
bum rap on this score. At this point in history, the Stones were
not an appetizing prospect for him for reasons other than ego,
what with his resentment of Richards for demanding a say in
the business in which the guitarist had been completely uninterested during his heroin inertia, Wyman's dalliances with an
underage girl that were to hit the headlines later in the decade,
Wood's continued, interminable drug binges and failed clean-
ups, and the fact that even Charlie Watts – hitherto the most
dependable, upstanding member of the group – had become
an alcoholic and a heroin addict. (One example of Watts'
temporary switch from nicest guy in rock to nutcase was an

incident at a band confab in Amsterdam in November 1984 when he took exception to a drunken Jagger ringing his hotel room and asking "Is that my drummer?" by coming down and flooring him with a punch.) Never the dissolute his public image had (occasionally deliberately) suggested, it is understandable that the cautious, level-headed Jagger would have felt he was drowning in losers. This is not to mention his long-expressed anxiety about the lack of dignity of being an ageing rock star, an anxiety that can't have been lessened by the hostages to fortune he'd left (e.g. "If I'm still singing 'Satisfaction' when I'm 40, I'll kill myself").

The Stones' disunity was there for all the world to see on 13 July 1985. Famine relief concert Live Aid was the perfect summation of the good that popular music can do and nobody had more of a right to be there than titans like the Stones. However, Mick Jagger preferred to perform with Hall & Oates, Eddie Kendricks, David Ruffin, Tina Turner and (on video) David Bowie, leaving Richards and Wood to play atrocious back-up to Bob Dylan in the event's most embarrassing set.

Live Aid occurred literally in the middle of the recording of the new Stones album. With him having just masterminded a massive deal with a new label, it was impossible for Jagger to refuse to participate in these sessions. However, the sessions for his first solo album and the next Stones LP were scheduled so close that they ended up overlapping. When Jagger did attend Stones sessions, his colleagues found him distracted. "Mick didn't seem to be enthused at the beginning," said Wood. "He just wasn't himself." Wyman complained, "We messed around for weeks because Mick was still buggering around with his solo album instead of working with us. He would fly back to London in the middle of it." Richards said of his Glimmer Twin, "in the early stages, we didn't see a lot of him. Ronnie and I had been working for a solid year on riffs, parts and things, you know, we just keep right on going." However, the drug-addled Watts was also posing problems and in any event had to fly home early after cutting his hand. Watts and Wyman don't appear on several tracks. What Richards termed "The Biff Hitler Trio" – himself, Wood plus passing musos like drummer Steve Jordan – stood in for the

Stones much of the time. Accordingly Wood got a high number – four – of co-writing credits. Bobby Womack, band friend ever since they had covered his "It's All Over Now", later told a British newspaper that he had been given $100,000 "under the table" to provide assistance. (He also plays guitar on several tracks.) It does, however, seem strange that Richards couldn't take up the slack: what had happened to the man who could work up stuff like "You Got the Silver" and "Gimme Shelter" largely on his own? When Jagger did give the project his full attention, he seems to have knuckled down to some extent. He claimed in interviews that he wrote all the album's lyrics and vocal melodies, while Richards conceded, "he's done a great job on the lyrics, and a lot of the musical ideas that we had already built up, he changed 'em all around and did a lovely job on them". However, this in some ways is no more a real Rolling Stones album than Jagger's LP.

The album took a cumulative year to complete. After three months, the band felt compelled to turn to an outside producer rather than cleave to their post-1973 policy of bossing around an inventive but subservient engineer like Kimsey. They recruited Steve Lillywhite, famous for helming works by Peter Gabriel, The Psychedelic Furs, U2, Simple Minds and Big Country.

The upshot of all this back and forth and internecine warfare was Mick Jagger's *She's the Boss*, released on 25 February 1985, and The Rolling Stones' *Dirty Work*, which followed a year later. Richards equated Jagger's debut to *Mein Kampf*: "Everybody had a copy, but nobody listened to it." Certainly, it failed to set the world alight sales-wise. Although it reached no. 6 in the UK and no. 13 in the States, those superficially impressive stats were put into context by a subsequent indignity never suffered by Stones product: relegation to the discount racks. However, it's difficult to make a call on whether this was due to its polished but characterless music or other factors. A Jagger solo album of equivalent quality would probably have done well ten years before, but times had moved on, and not just in the sense that the album title is another example of a middle-aged man who doesn't understand that he's not being lovably outrageous in his studied bewilderment at feminism. Jagger was no longer a hero of the young or the counterculture. In fact, he didn't really have much of a public profile, the days by now long gone when he was even remotely a regular turn on chat shows. Technique wise, although he could sometimes turn in a great performance, he did not possess the sort of great voice that could impart a certain thematic unity and gravitas to an album by default. Nor, as touched on earlier, did he have anything particularly to say. His solo albums relied on his being the lead singer of The Rolling Stones rather than being able to boast the proletarian populism of Springsteen, the curmudgeonly thoughtfulness of Neil Young, the divorcée's anguish of Phil Collins, the house-wife-friendly sensitivity of Lionel Richie or the varied but distinctive concerns of Billy Joel. However, Richards' feeling of vindication about Jagger's album is undermined by the fact that he was happy to put his own name to *Dirty Work*, a Stones long-player that is both inferior to *She's the Boss* and a colossal failure on every level.

Dirty Work's problems start with the production. It's no different from many other records of the eighties, plenty of them with multi-platinum sales figures to their credit, but that doesn't mean to say it's not unlistenable. The 1980s was a preposterous decade wherein the musical emperor had no clothes: in the age of the click track, overbearing, echo-drenched rhythm was the in-thing even though it transformed music from a pleasure into a headache-inducing chore. This album enthusiastically adheres to that insane musical fashion. That a band that had been making records when Lillywhite was in short trousers should defer to his decisions and direction simply because they were the accepted standards of the era is both absurd and an indictment of the Stones' loss of belief in themselves. The production would have made the album a disaster even if its songs had not been loudly empty.

For the duration of its opening track, it's possible to believe that *Dirty Work* – despite all the public feuding that had preceded it and given it a pre-release bad rep – could actually be an artistic triumph against the odds. "One Hit (to the Body)" (Jagger/Richards/Wood) features some pleasing sparring of acoustic and electric guitar. Mick's words are, not unusually, obsessed with sex but explore the subject rather more stylishly than usual. The track has a driving urgency and, if the guitar solo provided by Led Zeppelin's Jimmy Page is less special than such a superstar cameo might lead us to expect, only the ringing drumming lets the cut down. However, the second cut is unfortunately far more representative of the record. "Fight" (Jagger/Richards/Wood) is one of a brace of tracks alluding to the seething resentments between Jagger and Richards, although it gets no more analytical than "Going to pulp you to a mass of bruises". The music is featureless, unless the cacophonous drumming counts.

On 26 February 1986 in the US and 3 March in the UK, a cover of the sixties Bob & Earl hit single "Harlem Shuffle" (Bob Relf/Ernest Nelson) was released as the album's first single. Promoting *Dirty Work* with their first lead-off cover job for two decades seemed the ultimate expression by the Stones of a lack of confidence in their own product. It's certainly more tuneful and rich than most other fare here, but courtesy of that metronomic, in-your-face drumming, it's nothing to which you would want to ever return. The single (whose flip was "Had It with You") made no. 5 in the US and no. 13 in the UK.

"Hold Back" is an exhortation to not let circumspection curtail your ambitions. It's tuneless and Jagger's overdramatic vocal and cartoon mannerisms are – as elsewhere – tedious. "Too Rude" (written by Lindon "Half Pint" Roberts) features a Keith vocal on a cover of a track he had heard in Jamaica. The dubwise production mercifully de-monotonizes the drums. On any other album, this would be a sweet and interesting diversion but the fact that the Stones have to pad out this record with a second cover is a depressing sign of desperation.

Side two opens with "Winning Ugly", in which Jagger, in order to denounce a certain eighties mentality, inhabits the consciousness of a man determined to triumph at all costs. The mixing of the drums aside, it's quite good. "Back to Zero" is an above-average, funky track, but the fact that Jagger and Richards needed the assistance of keyboardist Chuck Leavell to compose it is another sign of desperation that slightly spoils our enjoyment and admiration. The lyric

denounces the world powers that, before the fall of the Iron
Curtain, seemed to be endangering the future of the planet.
"Dirty Work" – another co-write between Wood and the Glimmer Twins – has an anti-exploitation lyric that on the surface
sounds noble but, because it is really just a series of lazily written slogans, ends up sounding like dubiously motivated
populism. It's also another track whose tune is not readily
distinguishable from several of the others. The chugging blues
"Had It with You" (Jagger/Richards/Wood) features a deliberately smaller sound – even to the extent of the drums being
mixed lower (or perhaps properly). It began life as Keith's
bitch against Jagger but the latter universalized it by turning it
into a song about a love gone wrong. It's nothing spectacular
– and the average pub band could do as well – but it is a sweet
reminder of the Stones in '64. Neither Watts, Wyman nor
Jagger appears on the (first) album closer, "Sleep Tonight",
which marked the first time Keith had two solo vocals on a
Stones LP. A lullaby love song with dulcet piano from Leavell
and gospel backing vocals, it might well have been as touching
as it strives to be had not that look-at-me drumming destroyed
the mood.

The album really closes with an untitled fragment of piano.
A clue to the provenance is provided by the liner note, "Thanks,
Stu, for 25 years of boogie-woogie." Ian Stewart, who
succumbed to a heart attack in December 1985, had had to
watch in dismay as the Stones tore themselves apart during the
making of the album. At the point at which he died, he probably had every reason to believe that this recording process
would herald the end of the band of which he had been a
founder member.

The sleeve of *Dirty Work* featured the band members
dressed in the sort of primary colours in which their name was
rendered above them, a tableau completely at odds with the
Stones' public image and further evidence of their wanting to
get into step with the gaudy tone of the eighties. The album's
sales were mediocre. Richards' insistence that this was due to
Jagger's refusal to tour may be correct but the record was as
atrocious as the bad smell hanging over it before it was even
released. On 6 May 1986 in the US, and 19 May in the UK,

the Stones released "One Hit (to the Body)" as a single (with "Fight" on the B-side). Had they, as they should have done, released it as the lead-off single, it would have both fared better (it made no. 28 in the US and no. 80 in the UK) and sent out a far more positive (if illusory) message about the album.

Dirty Work was a terrible start to the CBS contract and an unspeakable nadir for the Stones. The latter fact was particularly galling in light of the impression that began to grow that this was not just a substandard LP but a miserable swansong.

STEEL WHEELS

Sean Egan

UK release: 29 September 1989; US release: 29 September 1989

Produced by: The Glimmer Twins, Chris Kimsey

Charts: UK no. 2; US no. 3

Tracklisting:
Sad Sad Sad
Mixed Emotions
Terrifying
Hold on to Your Hat
Hearts for Sale
Blinded by Love
Rock and a Hard Place
Can't Be Seen
Almost Hear You Sigh
Continental Drift
Break the Spell
Slipping Away

In February 1986, the Stones won their first Grammy, the National Academy of Recording Arts and Sciences granting them a Lifetime Achievement award. For some Stones fans saddened by their recent decline and disagreements, this might have seemed a good way of bringing closure to an increasingly unhappy saga. Possibly Mick Jagger subscribed to that point of view.

"If Mick tours without us, I'll slit his throat," Richards told a journalist. Not only did Jagger prepare a tour, he recruited Jeff Beck to play on it, a red rag to a bull for Richards, who detested the moody British guitar virtuoso. Richards' comment was one of the opening salvos in a public war of words that in the early months of 1987 made it apparent that the end of the road that was the Stones' illustrious career had been reached. "It really is all over now", declared *Spin* magazine in their issue dated March 1987. It was the type of groan-inducing headline that British tabloid newspapers had been printing since the late sixties, but what made this one different was the fact that the byline beneath it was that of Nick Kent, who surprisingly after his denunciation of "Angie" became a friend of Keith Richards. He knew plenty of people in the band's circle. Kent quoted Steve Lillywhite as saying of Jagger and Richards, "There's no way I can possibly see them ever working together again . . . It's the end." Those inclined to respond to the producer's musings with a tart "What does *he* know?" were brought up short in the weeks following the publication of that article by an interview with Jagger in the UK's *Daily Mirror*. "I love Keith, I admire him, but I don't feel we can really work together any more," said the singer, bluntly. He also made a pot/kettle/black comment that Richards wanted to run the Stones "single-handedly". Richards was so infuriated that, unusually, he consented to an interview when he had no prod-uct to promote. It was printed in the *Mirror*'s competitor, the *Sun*, the very next day. "He should stop trying to be like Peter Pan and grow up," the guitarist snarled. "We were that close. I didn't change but he did. He became obsessed with age . . . He has told me to my face that he cannot work with me, but he cannot say why. I don't think he knows himself." A couple of weeks later, Wyman was interviewed by MTV's *Music Box*. "It looks that way," he responded to the question of whether the Stones were finished. "It's a pity we didn't go out with a big bang. Instead we went out with a whimper."

It was all sensational stuff, completely lacking the pussy-footing and discretion that usually attends a band conducting a dialogue in the media. Little wonder that Richards later termed this period "World War III". A return to pussyfooting normalcy occurred shortly afterwards, with Wyman talking of "misquotes, off-the-cuff remarks that were taken out of context and blown out of proportion" as regards his MTV

interview, which he requested not be repeated, and a spokesman for Jagger blandly stating, "You know the Stones – they
go through these tribulations. Hopefully things will settle down
to where people can talk again." Richards was past caring,
though, and said, "Mick lost touch with how important the
Stones were for him. He thought that he could just hire another
Rolling Stone and that way he could control the situation
more, rather than battling with me."

Jagger's second solo album was *Primitive Cool*, released in
August 1987. Leaving aside its horribly dated eighties production techniques, it's actually a pretty good record and in the
age-acknowledging honesty and reflectiveness of several tracks
it fulfilled an ambition Richards has been stating for Stones
music since the mid-eighties (sample: "It's a real interesting
position, 'cause we can make this damn thing *grow up*. We're
the only ones around that've kept it together this long"). Had
the album sold well, it's possible that Jagger might have – with
some relief – dispensed with the straitjacket of posturing hard
rock to which the Stones' music had lately been reduced and
gone full tilt into a solo career in which confessionalism was
not going to be scuppered by the ridicule of colleagues worried
that it did not lend itself to anthemic music or chime with the
spirit of rock 'n' roll. Unfortunately sub-*She's the Boss* sales
figures closed off this escape route just as poor critical and
public reception had scuppered his film career. Jagger was
trapped in the gilded cage of The Rolling Stones for the rest of
his life, something confirmed by the devastation of band
investments caused by the recent stock market crash. Jagger
contacted Richards and suggested a new Stones record. Keith
was somewhat taken aback – he was preparing his own solo
album, the contract for which he had only signed because a
resurrection of The Rolling Stones had seemed so uncertain.

"Maybe what we've found out is that Mick really needs The
Rolling Stones more than The Rolling Stones needs Mick,"
Richards told the press. However, for all Richards' caustic
public comments about Jagger and the general perception of
the latter coming back to the Stones with his tail between his
legs, overhanging Richards during this tale had been an aura
akin to that of an abandoned wife. The unspoken question was

why, if he didn't particularly need Mick, was he so desperate
for him to return to the fold? It must have been painful for
Richards to contemplate the fact that when he first worked
with Jagger, the latter was merely a singer very much dependent on him. Moreover, Richards' own solo effort, *Talk Is
Cheap*, released in October 1988, suggested that he needed the
Stones just as much as his colleague, even though its title and
the track "You Don't Move Me" carried on his public putting
down of Jagger. Although the album was talked up by music
journalists who had decided to take sides in the war of the
Glimmer Twins (and with their credibility at stake, they were
hardly going to weigh in on behalf of the supposedly poncified
Jagger rather than the Human Riff, a.k.a. The Living Embodiment of Rock 'n' Roll), it was little more than a respectable
outing. Additionally, whereas Jagger had largely written his
solo efforts on his own, Richards had needed the compositional assistance of drummer Steve Jordan. Nonetheless, the
fact that a combination of the best tracks from *Primitive Cool*
and *Talk Is Cheap* would have constituted the highest-quality
Stones album since *Some Girls* augured well for a Stones reun-
ion the world had got used to thinking it would never see.

On 18 January 1989, Jagger, Richards, Wood and Mick
Taylor participated in a New York ceremony wherein The
Rolling Stones became one of the first inductees into the Rock
'n' Roll Hall of Fame. However, their next album, *Steel Wheels*,
would demonstrate that the artistic powers that had propelled
the Stones into the Hall of Fame were as irrevocably diminished as Mick and Keith's brotherly love (in 2010, Richards
estimated he had not visited Jagger's dressing room for twenty
years).

That The Rolling Stones constituted a cage for Jagger was
proven by the album's lead-off single, "Mixed Emotions",
released on 17 August 1989. It began with the line, "Button
your lip, baby", a return to Stones-by-numbers machismo that
was a complete betrayal of the honesty and lack of posing on
Primitive Cool. Also against the grain of his second solo album
was the feature-free *rock ordinaire* of the instrumentation.
Similarly limply generic was the twelve-bar flipside, "Fancy
Man Blues". The poor quality was probably not the reason for

the fact that its no. 36 UK chart position was the lowest-ever for a lead-off Stones single: although their album sales remained healthy, the UK singles market was collapsing for what the world would soon learn to call "heritage" bands. In the States, where airplay was a factor in chart positions, it made a healthy no. 5.

Steel Wheels featured a dully literal cover design. Although the drums are mercifully not as high as on the Lillywhite-produced abomination, the production that sees the Glimmer Twins reunited with Chris Kimsey still monotonously over-emphasizes Watts' snare. It is also sometimes rather blurred, with individual instruments largely undelineated – with the exception of that wretched snare drum. The tedious opener, "Sad Sad Sad", is like the lead-off single in its *reductio ad absurdum* of the classic Stones sound, as though the band had forgotten how to do it and could now only copy the shapes thrown by their imitators. This applies to several of the uptempo tracks here. The opener's lyric is mildly interesting for the fact that if one reads it as Jagger talking to himself in the second person, the talk of not letting "them" drown you out and – yes – gilded cages seems a cry of despair at being shoved by fate back whence he'd tried to escape. "Mixed Emotions" follows and in this context lines like "Let's bury the hatchet, wipe out the past" become more intriguing.

On "Terrifying", the claustrophobia and pedestrian rock – although not Mick's sex obsession – are dispensed with for a spare and mildly exotic cut featuring trumpet and percussive effects. As with several tracks, Lisa Fischer and Sarah Dash provide dulcet harmony vocals. "Hold on to Your Hat" is more disorderly Stones-by-numbers. The narrator tells a lover to get out of his bed and house and not give him any "lip" or "crap" in the process. The band then lurch straight back to the side of light with "Hearts for Sale" wherein a nimble, loping melody is the setting for a depiction of an attack of melancholia in the midst of merry company, although as with so many Stones lyrics lately it resembles a little too much random phrases lazily thrown together. Jagger executes some extraordinary mouth harp towards the close. "Blinded by Love" is a melodic ballad addressing irrationality caused by infatuation throughout history, whether it be Antony and Cleopatra, Samson and Delilah or the Prince of Wales and "a parvenu second-hand lady". There is much nifty keyboard work, while a fiddle adds colouring without being – as that instrument so often can be – gratingly intrusive. It's a wholly unexpected oasis of sweetness.

The vinyl side two opened with the quite powerful "Rock and a Hard Place", an urgent exploration of the world's ills with agreeably florid words, a cousin-of-"Soul Survivor" riff, some excellent lead guitar and strident brass from The Kick Horns. A respite in which only drums are heard is the sole point that their emphasis works on the album. The track was released as a single on 13 November 1989 with "Cook Cook Blues" (another boring, generic twelve-bar) on the flipside and reached no. 23 in the US and no. 63 in the UK.

"Can't Be Seen" is the first of two Keith vocals. Not the last song by Keith with a you're-too-good-for-me-baby theme, it's an uptempo rock–pop hybrid. It's all right but, like several tracks here, goes on a minute too long. After taking up the compositional slack on the previous album, Wood's reward here is to be cut out of the songwriting altogether. The only non-Jagger/Richards cut is "Almost Hear You Sigh" (Jagger/Richards/Steve Jordan), a leftover from Keith's solo record reshaped by the Stones. A highly melodic song of loneliness in the aftermath of a love affair, it's the best cut on the record. The most impressive sonically is "Continental Drift", which sees the Stones reunited with the Master Musicians of Joujouka by whom Brian Jones had been so entranced that he recorded them for what was arguably the first World Music album. Remarkably, Jagger received a letter from the tribe's current chief at the same time as he was contemplating employing them. Jagger shows restraint in the lyric, cleaving to a surreal impressionistic style appropriate to the elegant, olde worlde Arabic soundscape, even if that feat is slightly undermined by Watts' drumming (or the way it's mixed) being thoroughly Western and eighties. The Joujouka musicians and the massed backing chants build fearsomely. That track would have made a good climactic closer but the record ends on a bit of a damp squib. "Break the Spell" is a mildly mysterious blues that sees Charlie deploying brushes. "Slipping Away", Keith's second vocal, is an exploration of a dying relationship with simpatico brass passages that would be a much more poignant closer without the intrusive drumming.

Steel Wheels got some ridiculously sycophantic reviews, some from critics one suspected knew little about the Stones and some from people who seemed to be caving in to a manufactured groundswell that dictated it was a great comeback – an idea partly created by the media hoopla surrounding the Steel Wheels North American tour, which started on 31 August 1989. "We must be alive to the situation," gushed *Time Out*'s backwards-baseball-capped reviewer to this alleged resurrection. The album is better than *Dirty Work* and the lack of cover versions was a forward step but a sober analysis reveals *Steel Wheels* to be an intermittently good album with absolutely no classics. A handy yardstick for the standards the Stones had set for themselves and everyone else in popular music was provided in America a fortnight before the release of *Steel Wheels* by *The Rolling Stones Singles Collection – The London Years*. A massive three CD/four LP box-set, it rounded up the A- and B-sides of every UK and US Rolling Stones single release to which Allen Klein had rights, and if it took things over-literally ("Sympathy for the Devil" made it on because it was the B-side of a 1976 re-release of "Honky Tonk Women"), nobody was going to complain about the presence of such quality material, nor that rules were bent to allow entry to Jagger's "Memo from Turner". Although in a couple of instances the wrong version of a track was included, it was both a breathtaking collection of music and a highly worthy product that seemed to be seeking to make up for all the shoddy compilations ABKCO had authorized and for their alleged nixing of the original configuration of the worthy *Rolled Gold* project.

Jagger's solo tour had turned out to be a damp squib, with Jeff Beck departing in a huff over payment rates and Mick finding only the bravery to present himself to the less demanding audiences of relative backwaters like Australia and Japan. Richards had toured his album with his band, the X-Pensive Winos but, although that was a happier affair, neither man could hope to match on his own the gargantuan box-office

appeal of the Stones, one massively enhanced both by the fact
that they had been off the road for seven years and by the
understandable conviction of many who had followed their
recent tortuous interrelations that they might never get the
chance to see the band again. Their tour was the biggest and
most high-tech ever seen. The North American leg continued
right the way through to 20 December 1989 and featured a
massive stage set of smoking machinery built around an industrial future theme. The tour moved to Japan in February 1990.
For the May–August European leg, it became the Urban
Jungle Tour, a name change reflecting a downscaling of the set
engendered by the knowledge that lower European ticket
prices would threaten profitability. Before the Japanese leg, at
the insistence of Watts and Wyman, Wood was finally put on
equal financial footing with the other members regarding
concert receipts: despite having been a Stone for fifteen years,
he had hitherto been on a salary.

27 December 1989 saw BBC2 broadcast *25 x 5: The
Continuing Adventures of The Rolling Stones* in their *Arena*
series. An official documentary directed by Nigel Finch, it
ratcheted up the delirious nostalgia for the group even further.
An hour and three-quarters long, it was surprisingly good,
unearthing the type of legendary footage about which Stones
fans were used to reading in biographies but which was rarely
repeated on TV, such as their humiliating treatment at the
hands of Dean Martin on his show in 1964. It was given a
video release in February 1990, gaining twenty-five minutes of
footage in the process. MTV, meanwhile, broadcast their own
Stones documentary on 7 January 1990, apprising the kids of
the video generation, in many cases for the first time, of the
history of a group without which their beloved music-dedi-
cated channel might not even exist. Meanwhile, *Steel Wheels*
was subjected to unprecedented milking. "Almost Hear You
Sigh" b/w "Break the Spell" appeared as a single in the US in
January 1990 and made no. 50. It was issued as a maxi-single
in the UK. One of the additional tracks was a new song, "Wish
I'd Never Met You", which was another written-in-their-sleep
generic blues. The album was mined for an unprecedented
fourth single on 30 July 1990 in – of all places – the UK. But

then maybe "Terrifying" somehow doesn't count, since it was a remixed version released as a CD-only single at a time when the compact-disc player was still considered by many music lovers to be a luxury item. The disc – which reached no. 82 – featured a couple of remixes of others songs among its B-sides, as non-main title songs were still illogically called in this one-sided medium. 25 June 1990 saw the first UK release of *Hot Rocks 1964–1971*, with *More Hot Rocks* following in November. The latter compilation didn't chart but the former climbed as high as no. 3. In the week of its peak placing, *Steel Wheels* was no. 22 in the same chart and *Rewind* at no. 45.

Flashpoint saw the Stones squeezing the tour for yet further money. Released on 2 April 1991 in the US (8 April in the UK), its cover featured an unimaginative, blandly coloured computer-generated drawing of nothing but a burning match and its contents consisted of recent live tracks plus two new studio recordings recorded in a break in the tour in January, "Sex Drive" and "Highwire". The latter addressed the hypocrisy of the West in objecting to Saddam Hussein's warmongering after having originally armed him and was released as a single on 4 March in the US and 11 March in the UK, reaching no. 57 and no. 29 respectively. *Flashpoint* made no. 6 in the US and no. 16 in the UK. There were various singles – regular and "maxi" – spun off the album. The Stones wrung the tour for one last bit of revenue on 25 October 1991 with the release of the live video *Rolling Stones at the Max*.

Perhaps it's unfair to mock such money-maximizing: the Stones were hardly hurting anybody by catering to (or even creating) the market for such products. However, there were a couple of things about the Stones money-making machine that some long-term followers found sad, even pathetic. The Steel Wheels/Urban Jungle tour was sponsored by Budweiser to the tune of £3.7 million. This sponsorship involved the band participating in meet-and-greet sessions with VIPs, a thoroughly un-rock-'n'-roll corporate flesh-pressing exercise that was pretty much the diametric opposite of the spirit of the London Palladium refusenik incident. Meanwhile, the Stones embraced with a vengeance the marketing possibilities afforded by the number of tracks it is possible to squeeze on to CD

singles, with remixes and multiple B-sides of the same A-side
proliferating at a mind-boggling, mercenary pace. For instance,
more than half a dozen recordings from the 1989–90 tour
appeared as B-sides. Such unique but essentially worthless
adjuncts to the main canon will not be addressed by this text,
nor indeed from hereon will any other type of Stones B-sides,
which have gone beyond the point of being worth documenting, let alone listened to.

Flashpoint was probably the first Stones album geared to
the CD age: the vinyl version was missing two of the tracks on
the compact disc, which ran to a massive hour and a quarter,
almost double the optimum length sound quality-wise for a
single vinyl album. Accordingly, the text will from hereon
dispense with references to "sides".

VOODOO LOUNGE

Sean Egan

UK release: 12 July 1994; US release: 12 July 1994

Produced by: Don Was and the Glimmer Twins

Charts: UK no. 1; US no. 2

Tracklisting:
Love Is Strong
You Got Me Rocking
Sparks Will Fly
The Worst
New Faces
Moon Is Up
Out of Tears
I Go Wild
Brand New Car
Sweethearts Together
Suck on the Jugular
Blinded by Rainbows
Baby Break It Down
Thru and Thru
Mean Disposition

Although the Steel Wheels tour had demonstrated that the Stones were more commercially viable than ever before, it by no means marked the end of solo Stones activity.

Keith Richards released the in-concert album *Live at the Hollywood Palladium* in 1991, while his second studio effort, *Main Offender*, followed in '92. Mick Jagger's third album was *Wandering Spirit*, released in 1993. It was a very good record but by now Jagger had probably given up any hope that his solo career could be anything more than an outlet for ideas he felt unsuitable for the Stones, such as this album's bizarre sea-shanty closer, "Handsome Molly".

As for The Rolling Stones, their new distributor was Virgin Records, who secured their back catalogue and a commitment to three new albums for £25 million. The dissolution of Rolling Stones Records that went with the Virgin deal went virtually unnoticed, partly because the lips-and-tongue logo continued to feature on Stones releases.

Bill Wyman did not append his signature to this agreement: he had informed the Stones after the last tour that he was leaving. "I didn't see anything new happening in the future," he later explained. "I realised if we played for another ten years, I'd still be playing 'Jumpin' Jack Flash', 'Honky Tonk Women', 'Street Fighting Man' until we packed up." A newly acquired fear of flying, a desire to start another family and weariness with the endless waiting around for Richards were additional factors. Perhaps surprisingly considering their endless devaluing of his contribution to the band down the years, Jagger and Richards did not take the news with equanimity. Wyman later recalled a charm offensive followed by a nice cop/nasty cop approach to persuade him to change his mind. In the end, the Stones accepted the inevitable. Wyman contented himself among other things with his oldies band, The Rhythm Kings, and his restaurant chain, Sticky Fingers. His departure was at least good news for Wood: without it, it's to be doubted that his colleagues would ever have agreed to extend his equal financial share to equal voting rights.

The UK compilation *Jump Back: The Best of the Rolling Stones 1971–1993* was the first Stones release on Virgin. Despite the plethora of Stones best-ofs in recent years, both pre- and post-1970, and its shoddy cover marking the passage of time via a platform heel and another boot that was supposed to be an equally instant form of visual shorthand for a specific era but was nothing of the sort, it did well on its 22 November 1993 release, making no. 16. The new Stones album, meanwhile, was *Voodoo Lounge*. Its appearance in July 1994 marked almost exactly five years since *Steel Wheels*, the longest gap in

Stones studio albums up to this point despite the fact that there had been no World War IV, or even minor skirmish, among the band members in the interim. The days when the individuals who comprised The Rolling Stones based anything like most of their lives around the group were clearly over.

There were two new arrivals in the band's life with this album, one on bass, the other behind the console. Deciding to go back to a bona fide producer, the Stones employed Don Was, a former member of pop group Was Not Was in his early forties, who had latterly become a fashionable console operator via work for Bonnie Raitt and Bob Dylan among others. Meanwhile, nearly two dozen bassists tried out for the vacant slot in the band's line-up. In the end, the man who would be the rhythm section partner of any newcomer was given the deciding role. Watts plumped for Chicagoan Darryl Jones, a sessioner born in 1961 who had worked for Eric Clapton, Peter Gabriel, Madonna, Sting and (possibly crucially for jazzer Watts) Miles Davis. Jones took on a status below even Wood's former "employee" (Richards' word) role: not only was he merely salaried, he did not appear in band photographs. Although penny-pinching no doubt played a part in that arrangement, it is on one level understandable. With even Wood having now been a Stone for nearly two decades, no new guy – especially one from a younger generation – was ever likely to be properly accepted into this band of brothers. Nonetheless, one will probably never get fully used to photographs of a four-man Rolling Stones. For some, such a jarring sight merely proves that the Stones should not have kept rolling upon Wyman's departure, the logic being that replacing Jones with Taylor and Taylor with Wood on the same instrument was one thing, but once the band starts fragmenting in other ways, how is it The Rolling Stones any more? Of course, life is somewhat more complicated than the purist might wish, and in any case why should the rest of the Stones deprive themselves of a career because one of them has bailed? If only the subsequent product triumphantly justified the determination that the show must go on.

The band made a lot of the fact that they began recording their next album off the back of solo activities by Jagger,

Richards and Wood, but frankly a sense of being well oiled was
not particularly evident on the ensuing disc. Nor did the
strength of the songwriting do justice to Jagger and Richards'
induction into the Songwriters Hall of Fame in June 1993. The
album was styled *Voodoo Lounge* after a sign Keith posted on
the window of the granny flat in Woods' home in which he was
domiciled during preparation. For the third Stones album in a
row (four if you count *Jump Back*), the sleeve was both atrocious and Stones-free, featuring a scratchy illustration of some
sort of dancing imp.

The album was preceded in the UK on 4 July 1994 by
"Love Is Strong". This single did surprisingly well (reaching
no. 14), possibly because of an inventive video wherein a giant-
sized Stones stalked a cityscape. It did shockingly badly in the
US (no. 91), presumably because it was not released there
until 12 September, when the album on which this supposed
lead-off single featured had already been available for two
months. That "Love Is Strong" features "Gimme Shelter"-like
lip-bruising, gargantuan mouth harp and a "Midnight
Rambler"-like menacing, slow-burning ambience is in keeping
with Was' Stones-fanboy approach. However, despite the
grand air, the song turns out to be less than it at first appears,
being just a number of no particular insight about a sexual
infatuation. As with every other track here that attempts to
capture the classic Stones sound, it doesn't even come as close
as the Stones pastiche "Rocks" released by Primal Scream that
year.

The "Hey, Hey!" chants in "You Got Me Rocking" – which
follows album opener "Love Is Strong" – are an attempt to
create an anthemic ambience in a song about a life-battered
man proffered salvation, but this striving is dashed on the
rocks of a lack of a memorable melody or riff. "Sparks Will
Fly" – another rocker, this one apparently kicked off by a row
between Jagger and Jerry Lee Lewis – starts urgently but never
quite takes off. Meanwhile somebody should have told Was
that the high mix of Watts' drums here is sooo eighties. Keith's
vocal "The Worst" is a country number. The track has the
requisites of the genre, including pedal steel guitar, violin and
self-mythologizing self-pity ("I'm the worst kind of guy for

you to be around"). Unfortunately, there's no real pathos, partly because a lifetime of spending up to four consecutive days awake seems finally to have taken its toll on Richards' voice. "New Faces" is decorated with harpsichord played by Chuck Leavell. It's a pretty track, the subject of whose lyric is a man outcharmed by another in the battle for a woman's affections. On "Moon Is Up", the drums are mixed too high and other instrumental passages too low, a recurring problem with Was' production work. Not that rectifying this would have particularly helped an uninteresting, uninflected complaint by a narrator to a woman who has failed him in some unspecified way. "Out of Tears" is a ballad whose narrator is so distraught by the end of a love affair that he can cry no further. It might have worked were the orchestral strings not so faint, although it also drags on a minute or two too long. "I Go Wild" displays the Stones' current penchant for chord-crashing openings, as well as their tendency to not really know quite what to do with the rest of the song after said dramatic entrée. Despite a stirring passage or two, it is more featureless hard rock.

A song that starts with "And" always puts one in mind of somebody trying to keep a conversation going in the absence of something to say. Sure enough "Brand New Car" is a quite pitiful attempt at finding inspiration that comes across as involving no real automobile-related impetus but rather a desire to produce something conforming to a rock song archetype. A horn chart (mixed too low) fails to improve the hackneyed situation. Although the gentle "Sweethearts Together" seeks to recapture the innocence of early-sixties pop, its lyric is incongruously insightful in its analysis of people's desire for a soul mate "to share the pain and laughter in a world beset with fools". That it feels overly self-conscious, as though the Stones are playing with our minds about their place in the musical firmament, is an unfortunate, unavoidable function of the band's longevity. However, only the most curmudgeonly would deny the loveliness of this creation, even if its rhythm drags when it should be perky.

"Suck on the Jugular" encapsulates the faults of Don Was and raises questions about why the Stones – who have worked with him extensively since this album – can't see how massively overrated he is. A funky vibe intensified by call-and-response vocals and wah-wah guitar sets up something potentially very good. However, fascinating-sounding burbles and blasts of instrumentation (including organ, sax, trumpet and harmonica) are infuriatingly barely audible, Was preferring to relentlessly emphasize the drumming. The other newcomer doesn't infuriate but neither is Darryl Jones anything special: unlike with Wyman's work, there are no bass runs that make one's ears prick up at their warmth or dexterity.

"Blinded by Rainbows" is a slow, gentle and thoughtful song about the trade-off between mission and morality in the act of committing terrorism. It features an inappropriately rockin' guitar solo but by then the pounding drumming has already destroyed any prospect of this being more than a slightly above-average cut. The analysis of a deteriorating love affair, "Baby Break It Down" is almost a good song but perhaps needed a non-rock band arrangement to make it sound anything more than everyday. "Thru and Thru" is the second of Keith's two vocals, a tradition that would be continued now that the hour-long albums expected in the CD age – if only to justify their inflated price – allowed their inclusion without forcing Mick to sacrifice a track. Although it is mostly a very spare recording, its six-minute length, thundercracks of drums and massed backing vocals are a tilt at the epic. Disappointingly, however, all this drama is for a lyric based around the mundane theme, "I'm waiting on a call from you".

"Thru and Thru" was clearly intended as the finale, which it was on the vinyl album. However, the new imperative of the record industry was to nudge people into buying CD players, hence "Mean Disposition" being provided to purchasers of the compact-disc version only. This "bonus" transpires to be a nondescript, uptempo piece of bluster on which it's not entirely clear that the main guitar is in tune.

Like *Steel Wheels*, *Voodoo Lounge* is not even as good as any part of the lazy *Goats Head Soup/It's Only Rock 'n Roll/Black and Blue* trilogy. By now, however, the bitter disillusion that would once have greeted such a below-par Stones product was a thing of the distant past. Expecting big things of musicians in their fifties was not a rational notion, not so much because of their age but because more than one pop cycle had turned since their heyday and the passion they had once aroused was accordingly diluted, not least because bands that had succeeded them on the pop timeline had themselves aroused accusations of sell-out, particularly Johnny Rotten/John Lydon (who was more nakedly avaricious in 1983 than the Stones had ever been), The Clash (deemed to have gone all American towards the end of their career) and Paul Weller (who had dismayed many ex-Jam fans by straying further and further from politics in The Style Council). Moreover, if the Stones had an ability to release an album marking an artistic renaissance, it would have happened long before now. Additionally, people had long given up the idea that the Stones were, or even should be, carrying the mantle for the ideals of those who came of age in the sixties. Although Live Aid was an event that brought some of these ideals into focus with a practical, immediate aim, in the eighties popular music as a soundtrack of dissent was otherwise an idea that hit something of a brick wall in light of a zeitgeist that involved so many people embracing an ethos in which financial greed and social authoritarianism were not perceived as unequivocally bad. With odd exceptions, music became merely aural light entertainment. The Stones themselves had been through several different perception wring cycles, from sell-outs to irrelevance to beloved old troopers welcomed back from the wilderness to nostalgia act, with various shades in between. Nostalgia act was the one that was beginning to be set in concrete. *Voodoo Lounge* was a Stones album, and these days that meant no big deal one way or another.

The big deal these days was the Stones tour, which one hesitates to designate "accompanying" because it would suggest that it was less important than the album when it was patently obvious that, in fact, the tour tail was wagging the album dog. It began on 1 August 1994 and lasted an entire year. It worked North America through to December. In January '95, the band embarked on a second leg that by May had taken in South America, Africa, Asia, Australasia and Europe. One of the American dates became the first concert broadcast over the internet. "You Got Me Rocking", "Out of Tears" and

"I Go Wild" were released as further singles from *Voodoo Lounge*. Not only are their variations in B-sides too tedious to list, their chart positions are too irrelevant to document. The transformation of the Stones from rock-'n'-roll band to big business continued apace during the tour when it was announced that the lips-and-tongue logo would soon adorn Rolling Stones Visa and MasterCard credit cards.

Keith Richards has long publicly bemoaned the backarse-wards nature of modern Stones activity: the cumbersome assembling for a new album followed by a tour that engenders razor-sharp, well-oiled musicianship, which is then all wasted as the band resume their separate lives. Wouldn't it be great, he has frequently said, if the Stones made an album right at the end of a tour? They almost did this in 1969 but presumably ended their Muscle Shoals sessions after the superb start of "Wild Horses" and "Brown Sugar" because they realized that Klein would own the results. The idea is now impractical for reasons both personal (the enthusiasm among the band for a long recording process after living out of a suitcase for several months would be low) and financial (no band would want to engage in two world tours in quick succession and in the contemporary market record companies would be reluctant to distribute an album that is not going to be thus promoted). *Stripped* – released by the Stones on 13 November 1995 in the UK and 14 November in the US but recorded during the tour – was a compromise on that ambition. Half a dozen of the four-teen tracks were in-concert performances, the remainder recorded in studios across the globe during the tour, all without overdubs, hence the *MTV Unplugged*-like title. Unfortunately, Richards and his colleagues wasted the small opportunity they had hereby carved for themselves to take advantage of their tour-produced slickness by including no new compositions whatsoever. The songs were from their back catalogue except the Willie Dixon number "Little Baby" and a version of Bob Dylan's "Like a Rolling Stone" that they seemed to have tack-led solely because suggesting it was a song about them was in their eyes amazingly droll. The public were left with just another piece of dispensable Stones product (although that obviously wasn't the opinion of the people who sent it to no. 9 on both sides of the Atlantic). There was a CD-ROM version with special features, while "Like a Rolling Stone" was released as a single. Naturally there was a tie-in video of the *Voodoo Lounge* tour (released on 21 November 1995). There was also a *Stripped* TV programme (December 1995).

Of somewhat greater interest than any current live product was *Rolling Stones Rock and Roll Circus*, released by ABKCO on 14 October 1996. The album featured six tracks by the Stones plus selections from the sets of their invited guests at an event that occurred on 11 and 12 December 1968. At a time when the Stones were off the road but needed to maintain visibility, *Rock and Roll Circus* was filmed for what was projected to be a lucrative TV special. The Stones wrote off estimated costs of £20,000 (big money in 1968) plus the theoretically astronomical worldwide profits because they weren't happy with their own performance. Three decades on, the quality of the performance of the Stones or anyone else was almost irrelevant in the context of what had become a snapshot of a fascinating period in rock history: for example, one of the sets was that of a supergroup featuring Keith Richards, John Lennon, Eric Clapton and Mitch Mitchell. The album reached no. 12 in the UK and no. 92 in the US. A *Rolling Stones Rock and Roll Circus* video was released on the same day. The 2004 DVD added some features, although not the four additional songs Wyman claims the Stones rehearsed.

Robin Eggar's extensive interview with Mick Jagger almost thirty years after Barry Miles' similarly lengthy dialogue with the singer reveals a man who has undergone a surprising transformation – even factoring in that people change considerably between their twenties and their fifties. Many critics claim that the brash, self-aggrandizing persona Jagger projects on stage is actually now merely a cynical conforming to a rock-star archetype. For better or worse, Jagger's cultured, thoughtful comments in this feature suggest this to be true. Additionally, for what it's worth, one exchange seems to give the lie to Keith Richards' latter-day claim that Jagger isn't very well-endowed . . .

SELF SATISFACTION

Robin Eggar

First published in *Esquire*, July/August 1995

In the upstairs room in Henry's Wine Bar overlooking the River Thames a French TV crew are lathering themselves into over excitement. Mick Jagger has arrived, if 40 minutes late.

It is after all a quarter of a mile from his mansion on Richmond Hill. The Stones singer has agreed to do the interview in French. Although rusty, he has a good accent, by the end he is gesticulating freely and cracking the odd Anglo-Gallic pun. He spends a lot of time searching for the correct, the exact, semantic nuance at the expense of the content. Jagger has always been adept at saying nothing, precisely.

Sipping a long cool beer, diamond tooth sparkling in over-size mouth, he promptly admits to finding it all so exhausting. Jagger's attention span is notoriously short, he's all for closing our interview out after 40 minutes as he's taking his parents to the theatre in Richmond that evening. That is the only time he lapses into his faux Cockney come rock star accent, then he reverts to normal. Tying him down is akin to wrestling mist.

Although exceedingly pleasant he has a frustrating habit of starting to answer a question forthrightly, then stepping back before he can commit an indiscretion, before letting it tail away into generalities or nothingness. He hates being nailed to a specific whether it be a date, a friend, a song or the title of the last painting he bought.

Perhaps as a consequence of this the elusive Jagger has become increasingly dismissed as an intellectual lightweight, not so much enigmatic as vacuous. That might be simple jealousy for at 51, grandfather of one and father of five, he has the wiry toned body of a man in his late thirties and the lifestyle of a jet set hedonist. Jagger's fortune is estimated at £100 million, with homes in London, the Loire, New York and Mustique. While his contemporaries grope around the fringes of middle age he continues to do pretty much what he chooses. The years do, at least, plough ever deepening furrows down his cheeks, his face has grown into those caricature lips and his purported inability to remember the past is well documented. For all that he can still recall every song he's ever recorded, and he is acutely aware how The Rolling Stones have become part of popular culture. Mick Jagger, one must conclude, does not want the public to see him as he really is.

Perhaps for Jagger the past is another country, best gone – but not forgotten by other people, for that is how legends grow. More than most of his peers he has always preferred to inhabit the present. It still excites him. As his music still excites millions.

Keith Richards once described you as a nice bunch of blokes. He's said he's never quite sure whether you'll cut him dead the morning after the night before. Who are you today?

I don't know if I can really answer that question, people are different depending on who they are with and what their relationships with them are. I am different with my family than I am at work, same person but you pitch a different side of your personality. I can, for instance be a very patient person, or very calm and friendly until I get angry.

I've been on this bloody tour for almost a year, it feels like I'm on a bus, the same group of people doing the same thing so I become very much into being this rock singer – which is a bit inevitable really. I may not be singing every day but I'm playing that role, being that persona. I do take on this person-ality which is one of the very bad things about it, you get to be very much the centre of attention which cannot be good for you. At the end of the tour I won't be doing it any more so hopefully I'll take up other facets of my personality.

It affects the way I act to people. Right now they come up to me and the awful thing that happens is you instinctively think they are going to ask for your autograph. When I'm not on the road they quite often don't recognise me and ask me the way to the Richmond Odeon, or as happened to me quite recently in a clothes shop "Do you work here? Can you direct me to the men's trousers, is this a 34?"

After this interview you will walk a hundred yards to your home. When you enter those gates is it difficult to stop being Mick Jagger, rock star?

No I just stop when I walk in the door. It's the same trick as being on tour. You have to slough off the onstage personality when you have finished, get rid of it because it is not very attractive in a small room. A lot of people take life as a rock singer too seriously, off stage they are constantly wanting to express themselves in the same way which ends up with you being permanently drunk or out of your mind, or smashing things up. Which is perfectly good behaviour on stage because everyone likes seeing you outrageous but when you get home that isn't how you should behave.

I haven't always been able to do that, there have been long periods when I was playing the rock star 24 hours a day, when I was unable to be anything else and I think they were periods when I was very unattractive. It lasted years and years – probably the whole of the sixties and seventies. Men seem to take an awfully long time to mature for some reason. There wasn't some earth shattering moment when I suddenly realised, but I started to think maybe I shouldn't be behaving like this, that I should have a long look at how I was behaving offstage.

Who brings you down to earth?

Kids can do but I don't think they are a great panacea for everything. A lot of people find kids are so time consuming that they don't have time for any other stuff. I'd already had one lot of kids and they didn't do that for me at all. It's not always children, it is your own sense of what is happening to you with time. Now I'm getting older I want some order, then I can make disorder out of it, I don't want total disorder to start with, I want disorder on the top of order. A bit like the Conservative Party except I don't think they started out with order.

When a band the size of The Rolling Stones is on the road, you are totally protected from the stresses and strains of the real world. Private planes, luxury hotels, bodyguards and it's been that excess all the way – if we are to believe Stanley Booth's The True Adventures of The Rolling Stones *– since the early 1970s. At the centre of this modern day court are the band, the royal family. Unlike the rest of us mortals are you not totally cushioned from reality?*

Well you are when you are on the road but I would question whether you are off it because you have to do the same things as everybody else. People say well you've got a chauffeur . . . well lots of people have chauffeurs, you don't have to be in a rock band to have one, to enjoy other luxuries. I think that part of growing up is to realise that mundane things are sometimes a psychological help to you in getting back into reality. Boring though it is. I hate shopping, even for beautiful, expensive things and I don't like going to the supermarket, but I do find those things make me less buffered from society. Anyway if you want to write it's very good to see how things are going on around you. However you could say I am an artist therefore I don't want to spend my whole time shopping and cooking because then I won't have any time to do what I do well [laughs].

While in the past I might have gone from private plane to hotel to gig, now I don't stay in my room; I go out every single day and see what people are doing in their normal life.

Obviously I don't get to take it all in, you don't get to see much below the surface unless you have a very good eye, when you might see a few details. If you keep your eyes open and your ears open and your nose open you will see and hear a lot going round the world.

Like what?

In Tokyo I got lost which is very easy to do. I've done that a few times and my first reaction is "What am I going to do?", "Where am I?" Then people start to speak to you and you realise it's alright, and you fall into situations where you wouldn't normally be. There's a lot going on in the streets of Tokyo, it's a fascinating place. People say the Japanese have no sense of humour so I'd try to figure out what it is, you have to really work at it if you don't speak Japanese. I'd see groups of drunk office girls out at night, and wonder how do they relax, what do they do. It's very high pressured society, a fantastically crowded environment where they have an incredible amount of rules for behaviour. I saw those rules in operation and wondered do they ever break down. Cyanide gas in the subways shows they do.

Are you no longer the centre of a corrupt court where everything you ever wanted is brought to you?

I think that whole thing is an illusion, people don't really know what it is like to live on the road or to be this rock band thing. In the seventies it was no different from the way it is now. Now there is more money, more things to pamper you with. I am more cosseted so I have to fight more against it, to do interesting things all the time. Sure I fly by private aeroplane but I don't have to be cut off from the world. If I'm in London there might be some wonderful painting exhibition. I try to make sure I meet interesting people.

Who is the most interesting person you have met recently?

I couldn't believe I bumped into Vaclav Havel [President of the Czech Republic and Stones fan] on an airstrip in the middle of Australia. We got a phone call just as we were leaving saying he wants to say hello. I think he is an amazing guy, to have gone from being an underground literary figure to being completely the opposite, an on show politician. It's strange.

Isn't there an increasing connection between rock and roll and politics?

No. The only connection is that politicians like to get pictures with you because it helps their campaign. If it doesn't they avoid doing pictures [laughs].

Should rock stars have a responsibility in politics?

That is a really tough one. In the States there is more of a tradition where people in showbusiness have taken a role in fund raising, showing their support. In England people who own large grocery stores have always given money, unions have given money, but people in showbusiness – at least as far as I know – have not been vociferous in supporting one or the other party. I have always gone along with that.

Did not Tom Driberg [notorious gossip, socialite Labour MP and homosexual] try to recruit you as a Labour MP in 1968?

Tom Driberg was a good laugh, a great old queen of the day, he knew everybody, was fun to be with and outrageous. In those heady days when people thought about me I can't honestly think that the life of being an MP would have suited me. There have been actors who have become MPs but none have been successful as far as I can recall. Look at – whatser-name the MP for Hampstead, Glenda Jackson, maybe I am completely wrong, she will end up ministress for the Arts and will love it.

To be honest, I have never been a party person, I have never thought that one party was so much better than another that I must support it. When I was asked to support the Labour Party they were so unionised and weird. When I was asked to support the Conservative Party I could never agree with many of their policies. I thought Mrs Thatcher had some wonderful things about her but there were so many negatives it all balanced out. It is better to keep my head down than shout out how wonderful it all is.

The current prime minister is the same age as you, the President of the United States is four years your junior while Tony Blair the leader of the Labour Party and widely touted as the next PM is a decade younger and probably used to make out to Stones records.

Yeah he was in a rock band, Tony Blair, did you see the pictures? Obviously it wasn't a very good one or he wouldn't be the leader of the Labour Party now.

How does that make you feel with the leader of the country younger than you, potentially influenced by you?

It doesn't feel strange at all. Everyone gets older and the reins of power pass to a younger generation. What is interesting is that before they were politicians who thought I was a rather odd person who wouldn't have anything to say about anything, now they are the same age or younger and are happy to meet you.

What did you say to Al Gore when you met him last year?

Not an awful lot, we didn't speak very much. I said a few things to Hillary Clinton – I don't want to tell you what they are – I think if you have something on your mind and you have the opportunity to talk to someone in power you must say it. They are politicians, you have elected them, or not, but they are still public servants. If a guy meets John Major or Bill Clinton you can bet your bottom dollar they are going to say, "I hate it that you have just put my tax up you bastard" or "why did you close this hospital?" I will say what is on my mind depending on my pet peeve of the week. You don't get long with such people so I make the most of it.

It's a bit like interviewing a rock star then?

Even shorter usually [laughs].

Your lifestyle is peripatetic, cosmopolitan and international. Your first wife was Nicaraguan, your second American. Do you still consider yourself to be British, European or a citizen of the world?

I don't think it is particularly important. I was born and brought up in England, therefore I am English. Where you belong culturally is what your nationality is rather than what your passport says, the place where you understand all the cultural nuances in society. In England I really understand the culture but there are others I've taken on board. I feel very at home in America because I've spent so much time there and in Australia I only have to be there about three weeks before I understand more or less what's going on in the political and social life. They are both very quick studies because of the language.

France is much more difficult because the language is so different, but after about a week my French gets pretty good, I can understand most of what's going on and even start talking with my hands. Whereas in Japan you might as well be on Mars a lot of the time.

With all the VE Day celebrations just passed do you remember any of it?

I was in my high chair. I was in my mother's house recently and I was demanding "Mum, where's the picture of our street party with me in the high chair?" I don't remember VE Day but I can remember the rationing and austerity of the early fifties. It's one of those things you can never forget.

What do you feel about the European Union and the perceived dominance of the EU by Germany?

It was always going to be like that. The Germans would have been rich anyway because starting from nothing they had the most to gain and nothing to lose from the EU.

I was rather a precocious child politically because my father taught; he always gave me historical references, so I was always pro European. We were all young teenagers who wanted Europe to be closer, to bury all this animosity that had been going on for so long. Ted Heath was our local MP – literally a couple of miles from where I was brought up – he was one of the very first pro Europeans. He spoke very loudly and eruditely for including us in Europe while I remember the Labour Party at that time was fanatically anti Europe, they hated the idea and the trade unions were so protectionist they detested Europe and were real little Englanders, the worst. It is amusing to look at Labour's posturing now.

Now I wonder what this great new economic and political union has really achieved. Not much apart from a disastrous agricultural policy. I can't see anything else. Not much of a financial policy. It hasn't got a foreign policy and I can't see it having a hope of one if it can't prevent a war next door to its borders. There are one or two pluses but when you look around at the most successful emerging economies, great amorphous customs unions have never been big economic successes. The EU's a bit like the Austro-Hungarian Empire. The countries that have been successful have been small and dynamic like Japan – I know it's not small in population but it is in size and resources – Korea, Singapore, England in its day.

Even given my heady days espousing European peace – which still I think is wonderful – is it really going to achieve all these things through a vast faceless bureaucracy? Wouldn't it be wonderful if it did work . . . but I don't see any result from it.

Why do the Stones continue to tour? Surely there is nothing to prove any more.

[laughs] I loved it when you put that in the questions. First of all there is a demand for people to see us, we wouldn't tour if there wasn't. The Rolling Stones really enjoy what they do, go out and do a good show.

It is what I do for a living. Of course I don't have to do it but life would be awfully boring if I just sat on my bum. Just because I've made a few bob I don't sit back and do nothing, that is not how life works, perhaps you don't work as hard or do something different, you don't go on tour 12 months a year.

If you are competitive in any field you prove yourself every time you go out the door. If you are a lawyer you prove your-self every time you make a good deal, an athlete every time you go out and win. Actually I hate all these comparisons with athletes, they are competing directly against someone else, either next to them or kicking their balls in, while in rock and roll there is no such thing.

Every time I go out on stage at the beginning of a new tour, every night I re-prove myself. You might say every time a man has sex he has to prove himself [laughs] . . . there is a certain amount of performance expected in all these endeavours, isn't there. Just because you've done it once doesn't mean to say you can't do it again.

So who is the competition?

There are lots of competitors, like the Pink Floyd, a hugely successful touring stadium band. We tend to talk to each other about how different countries are good some years and not others, we share a lot of personnel on staging and lighting. We're each advancing the other's technology. It was a little like that in the old days with The Beatles but it was much more competitive then.

For instance on the Pink Floyd tour Spain was a complete bust, so we are very cautious of Spain. Let's say there is only one promoter and he loses all his money on the Pink Floyd, he gives them a million dollars, and the market isn't good that year. He loses that money and no longer has a million dollars to give to The Rolling Stones. We have a choice, we can go but it's much more risky because we've got no money in advance and secondly if Pink Floyd didn't do well we might not.

Ah yes, money. There is this public perception that you are The Rolling Stones head while Keith is its heart, which probably makes Charlie the feet. It is often portrayed as if Keith's head is full of musical notes while yours is packed with balance sheets, he reads International Musician, *you prefer the* FT. *So what is the truth?*

I love putting on big shows. Contrary to what people say, I'm not interested in the business side of it – only as an adjunct to getting the show up. To get it up there . . . to me that's an achievement. I'm not that interested in balance sheets. What really interests me in putting on a tour is what it looks like, how does the stage look, how does it appear to the audience when they walk in, how is it lit. Is this enough?

Then an accountant says to me "Well that's great Mick, do you realise it's going to cost $30 million, you are going to have to cut." So I have to listen to a balance sheet person because otherwise The Rolling Stones will make no money and Keith will be the first person to complain [laughs].

I'm not interested in bottom lines per se but like anyone involved in such a big enterprise I have learnt a certain respect for the numbers. I wish I didn't. I wish the gross was so huge I didn't have to worry about the numbers. Then you'd be sitting here asking me why I was charging $300 a ticket.

So you have to learn to make these stages be fantastically beautiful and not spend all your money – most of which goes on putting them up and taking them down. If we were into money we'd just go out on an empty stage with a few spotlights. We are trying to create something. It is commercial art for money.

One other thing that does concern me – if you want balance sheets – is that the ticket price is pitched at the right price so people will turn up. I always ask local promoters how much it is and if it is too much I tell them. It's never not enough, always too high and I always have to reduce it. In Australia and America I'd sit down with Michael [Cohl, tour promoter] and if it's 50 bucks and I reckon it should be 30 then I have to argue about it. It's not the actual amount, it's how many seats at 30, how many at 50, where are they going to be, are there enough cheap seats, are there enough expensive seats. There are people who will pay a lot of money for a seat which always used to be black marketed. Rather than the tout get it we might as well sell 5,000 seats for a lot of money. Once it's done it's done and I never think about it. I don't sit in the dressing room counting the receipts

Do you feel you get misrepresented, Mick's the money man, Keith's the musician?

Obviously yeah. I am more interested in the whole show than just the singing, but the singing is the most important part, but before the singing can happen and before the show goes on a great deal of preparation has to take place. I am not prepared to go out there and not perform to the standards The Rolling Stones have set throughout the years. It is very important to me, it is very important to Charlie too, and we work very hard to make sure that all those things work, that it is a great looking show, the staging is great, the lighting is great, that the seats aren't too expensive, the same goes for all the stuff they sell, the T-shirts.

So you could go out and get a job as a stadium tour manager?

Yeah I probably could because I have been doing it for so long I think I have a lot to offer . . . it would be very frustrating because it is only one aspect of what I do. Performance to me is far more important. Ultimately it's my reputation at stake not the tour manager's or the accountant's. To them it's a bad day but we're exposed to failure.

What is your profession as written in your passport now?

It says Entertainer now and I am quite happy with that . . . actually European passports don't have anything on them now but your height, the colour of your hair or eyes.

How did you and Charlie Watts set about creating the staging for the Voodoo Lounge Tour? Your much quoted wish that "Barbra Streisand couldn't sing on it and Prince Charles wouldn't like it" allows a great deal of latitude.

The trick is to get a set that's not going to take away from the performance but that's going to add to it. We didn't just pick Mark Fisher because he did the last tour. Charlie and I saw three to four stage designers, looked at all their work, then we picked the one we wanted. Then we did lots of sketches, illustrations, looked at architectural books, drawings and argued a lot. Then we started zeroing in on different sketches.

I saw a programme on the TV about an architect called Calatrava. [Santiago Calatrava, born 1951 in Valencia, most famous recent work the Lyons Satolas TGV station.] He did this beautiful [the Almillo] bridge in Seville which you look at and wonder how it stays up. I was very impressed by how clean the lines were, how uncluttered yet how it stood there, so beautiful. I went to an exhibition of his at the Museum of Modern Art in New York full of models and pictures which added to what I'd seen. I became obsessed with these bridges and the idea of things hanging in the air and we decided to go with a modernist approach compared to the Gothic look we had last time. We wanted it very clean and shiny. We came up with these various designs and of course money has to play its part because you can't spend anything. It's like a movie, you are always cutting costs.

The stage has two main themes, the first presents the exterior view of a wired city of the future, a cyberworld of computer networks and limitless communication, the second is an interior look at a modern Voodoo lounge, what Voodoo would be like for a suburban man. To humanise it we added all these inflatable, slightly strange figures that indicate a shrine, a Voodoo shrine – more Mexican than anything else.

The musical tastes of most of your original audience ossified long ago. Some critics suggest the Stones have too.

That's natural; most people liked what they liked when they were teenagers or in their twenties and they don't take anything much new on board. The big problem in the record industry is to get people over the age of 35 to buy records at all; if they do they buy the odd blockbuster hits of The Eagles. To musicians it's very different, we listen more. That is our speciality. There are so many new bands, Oasis, Suede were last year, Blur were in the middle. It's like a shooting star thing. I get these bands who excite me but I don't know whether they are going to come on. Everyone loved Suede and no one bought their second album. I think Oasis are doing some shows with us. I haven't seen them live. The proof of the pudding is in seeing someone play live not just listening to a record. Massive Attack have an interesting sound, but it is so obviously commercial to mix the two. It is a very divided market between rock and dance, it always has been,

Isn't that what The Rolling Stones did?

To some extent yes. Interesting that.

What are your favourite Stones songs?

They are all special to me, each has a different association. I find it really hard to talk about them. I never listen to them at all. Honestly I'm only interested in the new ones, the only reason I play the old ones is if we're trying to work out a stage show and listen to it to see if it is any good, or is it just a memory, how can we rework it to make it part of the show.

Or I don't remember making that one in the first place?

No I remember absolutely all of them. I have this thing that I can remember at least the chorus and a verse of every single Rolling Stones song. I tease Keith and Charlie mercilessly that they can't beat me, however obscure they are. They'll come up with one I can remember part of it and they say "you fucking cheated".

Did Andrew Loog Oldham lock you and Keith in a room and tell you not to come out until you'd written some songs?

[Pauses then says regretfully] I don't think so, though it is a good story. He was rather like a schoolmaster who would say "you have to stay and finish your essay". We came out with a song called "It Should be You", it was really dreadful. Yes I can still remember how the chorus went. It was recorded by George Bean who was one of Andrew's many protégé boys.

Hopefully we've got a bit better since then. While you're writing you can do anything. I would sit around with Charlie playing house music on the keyboards – sort of mad sounds, play Balinese music for a few hours, drive everyone crazy. "Blinded by Rainbows" ["controversial" number from *Voodoo Lounge* which includes the line "when the Semtex bomb goes off"] was all in my head rather than down on paper. I think it's good to have one that shakes you up a bit, otherwise all the songs are about girls and cars and immaturity. The trouble is at the beginning of the tour, when people don't know the record you get: "And now a new song" and they go "Great really great [he claps without any enthusiasm]. Can we hear 'Jumpin' Jack Flash' now?" But eventually they get into it. The time we got to the end of the Steel Wheels Tour they really liked some of it.

Do the Stones simply exist to tour, not to make records? After all you have never sold huge quantities of albums.

No, it's both, they feed on one another. The Stones have never been huge record sellers. The most we've ever sold was *Some Girls* or *Tattoo You* which did about seven million each, but we've never had a *Thriller*. You have to make records, you have to be regenerated every time. I'd quite happily make a record and not tour but I don't like to go on a big tour without new material. The songs are the most important building block of the whole thing, if they don't have it the whole building is weak. You could take out a nostalgic Rolling Stones tour which you didn't bother to write new songs for but I think it's important that the new songs have some quality.

It is 25 years since you starred in Performance, *a film that in many ways set the agenda for how the public have perceived Mick Jagger ever since. Yet according to Marianne Faithfull's autobiography you originally based the character on Brian Jones with a bit of Keith thrown in.*

It was on me too, more on me than anyone else, but that is what acting is. You incorporate other people you have known and studied into your character. That is what happened to Turner.

Do you think he has haunted you? Everyone else who was in Performance *had their lives blighted by it. James Fox got religion, Anita Pallenberg is a recovering heroin addict who was lucky to survive the seventies and Michelle Breton is still alive but in severely reduced circumstances.*

I thought she was dead. I'm glad to hear that, it's big plus. It's odd isn't it, a curse on the characters. Several people did have problems but it never phased [*sic*] me that much. It is an interesting movie and Turner is an intriguing character but he is a character in a movie.

But people have taken the attitude that he is Mick Jagger, the gangster of rock, the man who will do anything for money.

Then I did a good job.

Performance *glorified the drug culture of the time, which had already claimed Brian Jones and Jimi Hendrix. Do you regret the years you spent under the influence?*

I was too smart ever to go that far. But what happened to Brian seems so sad now and it was almost the same with Keith. They must have been very alone. If we'd been a little bit older, a little more mature it could all have been avoided. It was a malaise of the period. Let everyone do what they want to do, don't worry about people killing themselves . . . just don't mention it.

I don't want to give any one liners about the dangers of drugs. People like me have a safety net in life, we have family or we have friends, there is a difference between people who take drugs for kicks and people who take drugs as a substitute for life. But crack is a whole different story.

To change the subject, what are you reading now?

A lot of crap like everybody else, I read biographies and novels mainly, the odd philosophy tract that usually sends me to sleep. I've just finished *Portrait of Power* about John Kennedy's daily diary, about how little he knew coming into office. I've read John Le Carré's newish book, Martin Amis' *The Information*, Simon Schama's book on the French Revolution which was fascinating. I read that James Ellroy book recently, *American Tabloid*, quite dense, a good very long read. On tour I like to have two books going at once. One heavy and one light depending on my mood.

What was the first piece of serious art you bought? Who do you collect and why?

In the sixties I bought Andy Warhol. I was given my first piece of his for a birthday present. I buy paintings from time to time, but I'm not an aficionado of painting of a certain style or period like say Andrew Lloyd Webber loves his Victorian art. The last painting I bought was a watercolour by Ed Burra of a stripper in the Apollo Theatre in the 1930s. [English painter Ed Burra (1905–76) painted *Striptease* in 1934. His best watercolours fetch from £50–75,000.] I am always concerned about the look of things.

So what appeals to you? I gather your house is full of very old English antiques.

It's a real mixture; a bit of continuity and a bit of contemporary, I think that's a good way to be. I have modern pictures, old pictures, antique furniture and contemporary pieces, it works well side by side and that is the way things should be in music. There's no great virtue in just being contemporary.

How do you set about decorating a house?

I just go and shop, much as I hate shopping. Every year Bonham's have a nice exhibition of contemporary British Decorative Art. It's mostly furniture, beautiful new contemporary beds and sofas and pictures and hangings. I went there yesterday and bought a couple of things. I think people don't really appreciate how much talent there is in this country. Some of this contemporary design has a terrific sense of humour and I think if you have things about you that are funny that is good. But most people go out and buy old Victorian things because they know they are safe, they don't make any particular statement and they know no one is going to laugh at them.

You were always a big fan of Nureyev, Tina Turner says you were a painstaking pupil when she taught you the Sideways Pony. Do you enjoy dance as an art form, or is it a stage skill that you have had to master?

I danced yesterday darling. I've been dancing a lot to keep fit. I was planning to see William Forsythe's new untitled ballet at Covent Garden but it's the last night. I don't go to the ballet as much as I should, because I love dance, I always have.

I go to the theatre quite often. I saw Tom Stoppard's *Indian Ink* last week. I liked *Arcadia* too (though some of the physics were a bit beyond me). What I like about Stoppard is he always keeps your interest because you are never stuck in one time period, and he keeps flitting from one to another during the same scene.

A bit like being on tour with the Stones.

Well . . . yes

I hear, like many middle aged folk, you're a keen gardener.

I like looking at gardens. I hate actually gardening; I don't know where people got this idea of my being one.

Back in the sixties the Stones could and frequently did have any women they wanted. How have your attitudes to women changed over the years?

Urgh. I suppose rock bands were exploiting women . . . but maybe they exploited us by their ravenous appetites. I think it is very hard question to come to; first of all I can't really remember what my attitude was then, you can't just lump all women together and say what was your attitude then and now. I find this one hard going . . . I can't do very much on this.

In Richard Neville's Hippie Hippie Shake *he wrote: "Sandy Lieberson, the producer of Mick Jagger's latest soon to be released film,* Performance*, had smuggled the censored offcuts here for a festival premiere. The scene of Jagger in bed with Anita Pallenberg had revealed a salami-sized penis and a scrotum as big as a sugar melon."*

I didn't know that book was out yet. Goodness, isn't that nice, we'll just let that go shall we, I have no comment on that one. [He grins hugely.]

Ian Stewart once said that the one thing he envied you for was having had an affair with Brigitte Bardot. Did you?

No, I never did. What a shame I didn't. I think she was really ready for it but I was too shy, she was too much of a goddess in my eyes for me to take her up on it.

Do the Stones still attract groupies? How old are they?

What a question! On any tour you get people hanging around. I suppose there still are but they're not quite as organised as they used to be. There was this group in the sixties, the Plastercasters, who used to follow the whole tour. Perhaps I shouldn't talk about groupies on tour . . . I don't think they really exist in the same way . . . maybe they just don't fancy me any more . . . we've finished now haven't we?

Not yet. Keith has talked about the Stones like old blues players going on playing into their dotage. Guitarists can always sit down but I can't imagine Mick Jagger not moving on stage. Does the future of the band ultimately depend on your physical fitness and condition?

I don't buy all this old blues stuff. People don't remember Muddy Waters in his prime – fortunately even we are too young to remember that he was this great sex bomb on stage. There is this piece that is going to be on one of the Stones

forthcoming CD-Roms of Muddy doing this really sexy dancing at Newport like a rock and roll star, then of course he got
older, banged himself up in accidents and he had to sit down.
When I went to see John Lee Hooker for the first time when I
was like 17 – I thought, "Wow he's so old. He'll never be able
to carry on much longer." And he must have been about 38
then. And he's still here . . . and so am I.

I'm always a bit worried about becoming obsessed with age.
I mean as long as you can deliver the goods, I think – compose
and sing and make the record and perform – I suppose The
Rolling Stones could just wobble on. Eric Clapton makes this
joke on his *Unplugged* album. "I guess we'll be doing a lot more
of this in the future." There will come a time when I won't be
able to run around on stage. I always say "Yes I will stop" . . . but
you know these promises, they do come back to haunt you. It
was a pretty stupid idea of mine to say that you can only do a
musical idea once . . . I mean Mozart repeated himself. I never
seem to tire of writing and performing.

*How do you cope with being this largely fictitious "icon of popular
culture"? Doesn't it get in the way of making new music?*

Sure I understand the impact the Stones had on a generation,
but I'm not a social historian. I'm very interested in social
history but I detest mythomaniacs in this business who take
themselves so seriously. There're a lot of them about and
they're so boring. In the sixties and early seventies there was a
lot of intellectual posing about popular culture. The first time
there was any serious musical analysis was of The Beatles. It
had never happened before, no one had ever done it to Elvis.
They started analysing popular culture, art and fashion. And
from then on it's never stopped.

Popular music is not only about music. It's about a whole
bunch of other things – where it sits the year it came out, what
else was happening that year; what were the haircuts, the fashion,
the attitudes. Popular music has proved to be a sort of focal point
for popular culture to express itself. I think that is what people
remember – Keith's trousers, the kind of shoes people wore –
Beetle crushers, crepe soled shoes, drainpipe trousers, greasy
hair. And then, of course the music and the way they danced to it.

If you're in it you don't want to be too objective, thinking "this is a cultural moment I'm involved in". And you don't want to be so dumb you don't even notice. But if something has happened, whatever it is, like a march on Washington against the Vietnam war, or a civil rights march, you don't want them just saying I was a nice bloke. You obviously want them to say it was part of a historical moment.

Rock music, and the Stones' output in particular, is thought to capture the spirit of the age. How would you describe the current zeitgeist?

Wavering between consumerism and the millennium.

Are you still reflecting that zeitgeist?

I'll tell you after the next songwriting binge. I hope so. You have to reflect otherwise you are dead. I really vacillate between this thing of whether you are reflecting contemporary culture, while a lot of artists have done well by just being a law unto themselves. If you want to look at painting, Andy Warhol is a good example of someone who really reflected certain periods. I don't see Turner [the English landscape painter] in the same way. The Stones certainly reflected the spirit of the sixties and seventies but we're based on this whole other blues thing which is much longer lasting, much more rooted. We still play 12 bar themes and progressions so you might say that The Rolling Stones are simply representing themselves rather than reflecting contemporary culture. I hope to do both.

Have you succeeded?

We'll see . . . but I don't really care that much.

BRIDGES TO BABYLON

Sean Egan

UK release: 30 September 1997; US release: 30 September 1997

Produced by: Don Was and the Glimmer Twins

Charts: UK no. 6; US no. 3

Tracklisting:
Flip the Switch
Anybody Seen My Baby?
Low Down
Already Over Me
Gunface
You Don't Have to Mean It
Out of Control
Saint of Me
Might as Well Get Juiced
Always Suffering
Too Tight
Thief in the Night
How Can I Stop

The next Stones studio album appeared in lightning-quick time by the Stones' modern standards: three years and two months after its predecessor.

Jagger, in fact, protested that they were making a new album rather too soon and only acquiesced on the condition that they use different producers. "I want to do something that's a bit more groundbreaking," he said in the run-up to the new album. "Producers and engineers always want you to do another *Exile on Main St.* but I want to move on to something that's different and new and a bit more exciting." Laudable though his artistic ambitions were when the blind loyalty of the Stones' fanbase meant he didn't have to care, it was also somehow pathetic that his idea of groundbreaking was to request the services of the likes of the Dust Brothers and Babyface, veritable children whose production techniques were currently fashionable but were destined to become as dated as Steve Lillywhite's already was and which the classic techniques of Jimmy Miller never would. Don Was, Pierre de Beauport, Rob Fraboni and Danny Saber also produced, as well as the Glimmer Twins, in sessions which often amounted to separate Jagger and Richards projects. Such was the studio warfare between Mick and a Keith whose traditionalism made him view the hip, kid producers with contempt that it's not clear whether any of the Dust Brothers' mixes survive. However, it's also unclear that employing the Brothers Dust was any more lacking in wisdom than bringing back, as main producer, the maladroit Was, who once again creates a metallic, cold tone with an overemphasis on the drums. Darryl Jones, who had far more earned a recall than Was even if his work on the previous album was unspectacular, was largely absent, the bass duties handled by more than half a dozen individuals. Although *Stripped* had featured a cover photograph of the Stones, this album went back to the recent tradition of not showing their faces. Instead, a sphinx motif was used. The title *Bridges to Babylon* came from the predictably lavish set for the new tour, Jagger shortening a suggestion provided by, of all people, playwright Tom Stoppard.

The first track, "Flip the Switch", has another of those superficially exciting, drum-oriented openings common to modern Stones fare that then peters out into ordinariness. Lines like "Three black eyes and a busted nose" are in a similar vein of a desperate attempt to capture that old Stones vitality. Symbolically, the track ends pathetically limply, as though everybody lost enthusiasm. "Anybody Seen My Baby?" is a decent song, linear, atmospheric and mysterious. However, the fact that k. d. lang and Ben Mink had to be cut in on the royalties after the similarity was noticed to k. d. lang's "Constant Craving" further demeans a band who have already indicated they feel the need to ask musicians and producers younger than they are how they should operate. An annoying sound effect that apparently confers modernity runs throughout the cut. The track was released on 22 September 1997 as the lead-off single and reached no. 22 in the UK but didn't chart in the States. The mid-tempo "Low Down" is overwrought to no purpose and its guitars are grating.

Quite unexpectedly in the midst of such mediocrity, "Already Over Me" is a great song, not least because this touching ballad has no apparent "side", with Jagger uncommonly coming across as genuine. It's constructed like a classic Stones slowie: sure-footed, highly melodic and boasting a memorable, poignant refrain ("What a fool I've been"). A sweet guitar break completes the sense of faltering old masters rediscovering (if temporarily) their touch.

"Gunface" concerns a man on his way to kill his girlfriend's lover. The contrast between this half-hearted litany of threats against an uninteresting, jerky musical backdrop with that far superior Stones tough-guy anthem, "Crazy Mama", is pitiful. The Richards-sung "You Don't Have to Mean It" is nothing substantial but is enjoyable – especially its lively brass line – and quite possibly the Stones' first successful pure reggae. The slow, ominous "Out of Control" is also moderately successful, with a particularly impressive mouth harp solo. In "Saint of Me" (as in, "You'll never make a . . .") Mick shows off his knowledge of history and the Bible. The mid-paced music is agreeable without being distinctive. The assumption that this is a rebel's anthem undignified for a man of such years is proven wrong: Jagger points out that the requisite self-sacrifice and discipline makes him unfit for canonization. "Might as Well Get Juiced" is a slurred, distorted creation in which Jagger builds a lyric around the title phrase rather unimpressively. As with so many Stones lyrics these days, there's a feeling of settling lazily for slogans. At nearly five and a half minutes, the track is also way too long. Although it strives for modernity, the fashionable production techniques have evidently been toned down, leading to a betwixt-and-between feel. The gentle, acoustic, country-inflected "Always Suffering" is reasonably good but its main point of interest for Stones fans is the fact that though Jagger uses the pronouns expected of a love song, the lyric reads more like a man talking to a comrade-in-arms now estranged. Could this be Mick mourning the loss of his friendship with Keith? The narrator of "Too Tight" warns a lover not to get too attached to him. It's yet another track that is not objectionable musically but during which one waits in vain for something compelling to occur.

Pierre de Beauport is cut in with Mick and Keith on the publishing for "Thief in the Night". How infuriating it must have been for Wyman, Taylor and Wood to see the producer getting a credit based on a riff he'd devised when the same courtesy had not been extended to them in similar circumstances. Wood also might have had an additional issue with it: for the third album in a row, he receives no songwriting credit. Richards sings this number in which the narrator is vexed by a faithless lover. Any hope of enjoyment is crushed by the fact that the guitar picking and ivory tickling are mixed lower than a percussive effect that sounds like rustling paper. In complete contrast, "How Can I Stop" is the only well-produced track on the album. Unfortunately, the slickness and proper delineation of instruments is rather let down by the singing, doubly unfortunate as this was the first time Keith had been granted a third vocal on a Stones album. His halting, wheezing enunciation is a sorry contrast to the velvety backing vocals that attempt to make this a soul number. The Japanese version of the album featured a bonus track in the shape of a live "Angie". Such treats would increasingly be the case with releases in the Land of the Rising Sun, creating another branch of Rolling Stones discography that is both frustrating and expensive for the completist. There were two further singles from the album, "Saint of Me" and "Out of Control".

Bridges to Babylon was released three weeks into the band's latest world tour, which started on 4 September 1997. Had the public who bought advance tickets known that the band were about to release such a relative turkey, it no doubt would not have made a blind bit of difference: the ticket sales were no more dependent on the quality of current product than were sales of the current product itself. It was nostalgia that sent the album into the upper echelons of the charts and the crowds through the turnstiles on a tour that lasted – with two month-long breaks – through to September '98. Naturally, the tour spun off a video/DVD (June 1998) and a live album (*No Security*, November 1998). January 1999 saw the start of a four-month coda to the Bridges of Babylon tour called the No Security tour. Were the Stones really now touring to promote a live album? Well, sort of. Its North America-only itinerary was of arena-sized venues, dispensing with the awe-inspiring bridge with which the group had crossed to a different stage on the previous tour. These days, this was the Stones' version of being men of the people.

That The Rolling Stones were now a touring band first and a recording outfit second was emphasized by the way that the rate of collective Stones activity slowed to a crawl after '98. Richards had apparently had his fill of solo work but Jagger issued a fourth album in 2001 in the shape of *Goddess in the Doorway*. Despite boasting the assistance of the stellar likes of Lenny Kravitz and Bono, it failed to continue the incremental artistic improvement of his solo work. It also sold miserably. He has engaged in subsequent sporadic solo musical activity – even winning with Dave Stewart a Golden Globe for the song "Old Habits Die Hard", a component of their soundtrack to the 2004 remake of *Alfie* – and in 2011 released an album with SuperHeavy, a supergroup that also featured Bob Marley's recording artist son Damian, chanteuse Joss Stone, Eurythmic Dave Stewart and World Music polymath A. R. Rahman. Although *The Very Best of Mick Jagger* (October 2007) featured three previously unreleased tracks, there have to date been no more Jagger albums.

In the June 2002 honours list, it was announced that Mick Jagger had been awarded a knighthood. It was less for charitable works – for which Jagger and the rest of the Stones are in no way renowned – than for the fact that the millions of records and seats the band had sold in their career had been massively beneficial for British commerce and the image of the country. That, though, was not the point for many current and former Stones authorities who viewed the acceptance of the title "Sir Mick Jagger" as both absurd and predictable, the logical, contemptible conclusion of the social climbing and conformism in which the singer had been engaging since the early seventies and which had once been anathema to him. In that camp was Keith Richards, who described his reaction as "cold, cold rage", explaining, "I thought it was ludicrous to take one of those gongs from the Establishment when they did their very best to throw us in jail." After his investiture, Jagger reasoned, "I don't think the Establishment as we knew it exists any more." He elaborated to the *Guardian* in 2011, "I think if you're offered these things, if you refuse it's almost like a parody of being a rebel in a way. If you insist on using your title, then it's really silly. It's almost, in our sort of society, rude to turn things down and silly to take them seriously. As Confucius said: 'All honours are false.'"

It's not known whether Richards was placated by Confucian wisdom but back in 2002 the announcement of Jagger's forthcoming knee-dip had him threatening to pull out of the group's next world tour. In the end, it went ahead, starting in September, lasting a year and taking in venues of varying sizes. It had been five years since their last studio album but the band were not proffering any new material bar four tracks designed to entice the completists into purchasing a compilation album: "Don't Stop", "Keys to Your Love", "Stealing My Heart" and "Losing My Touch". ("Don't Stop" was released as a single in the UK.) The last time the Stones had toured without any new product – 1975 – it was well known that they were in the process of making an album and it therefore seemed nothing more worrying than an unwise commercial move. This time, it seemed a depressing confirmation that the Stones were now nothing more than a glorified version of The Searchers or The Hollies, content to peddle nostalgia to the undiscriminating. It could be argued that they needed to get on the road quickly to commemorate their fortieth anniversary, but the band did not go out of their way to draw attention to that milestone. Ironically, those four tracks were actually rather good, especially the pretty ballad "Keys to Your Love".

The compilation that the new tracks cynically studded was also rather good. Double-CD *Forty Licks*, released on 30 September 2002 in the UK and 1 October in the US, seemed to demonstrate the improving relations between the band and the family Klein as Allen's son Jody increasingly took charge of business affairs. It was the first Rolling Stones best-of unhampered by label or ownership considerations, featuring the prize tracks both pre- and post-1970. It made a US no. 2. Although it was also kept off the top spot in the UK, it is estimated to be the first Stones album to sell a million in their home country. All of this makes it disappointing that for contractual reasons the album is already out of print.

October 2002 also saw the Stones' back catalogue being given a proper remastering job, previous CDs having been very shoddy for such a prestigious act. The British configurations of their first two LPs were unfortunately not part of the programme, although their contents are scattered across various albums that were. In 2003, as a tie-in to the DVD release of Jean-Luc Godard's film, trendy producers the Neptunes, Fatboy Slim and Full Phatt were each permitted to remix "Sympathy for the Devil". The record reached no. 97 in the US but managed the respectable chart place of no. 14 in Britain.

Four Flicks (11 November 2003) was the DVD souvenir of the tour, a massive four-set affair featuring an arena concert, a stadium concert, a theatre concert and a bonus disc of miscellany. The audio souvenir was *Live Licks*, a double-CD no less, released somewhat belatedly on 1 November 2004. The second CD featured songs not often heard from the Stones in concert (including Hoagy Carmichael's "The Nearness of You"), while the first was given over to songs of which there were often already several live versions in the Stones' catalogue. It made no. 38 in the UK and no. 50 in the US.

Although The Rolling Stones were careful not explicitly to draw attention to the fact that 2002 marked their fortieth anniversary, their world tour, autobiography According to The Rolling Stones *and career-spanning compilation CD* Forty Licks *had journalists all over the world noting the landmark and in some cases lengthily musing on the changes to their image and status wrought over that four-decade period by tide and circumstance. Andy Gill was one of them.*

THE STONES AT FORTY

Andy Gill

First published in the *Independent*, July 2002

In a few days' time, The Greatest Rock 'n' Roll Band In The World turns forty. And what better way to celebrate than with another globe-girdling, record-breaking tour?

An iconic presence throughout the second half of the 20th century, The Rolling Stones have managed to successfully fight off the claims of any and all pretenders to their crown, from Led Zeppelin to Bruce Springsteen to REM to U2, with a series of tours that rewrote the record books, upping the ante on every level, from grandiosity of staging to audience size to revenue generated. The sheer scale of a Stones campaign is mind-boggling, and gets more so with each jaunt. In 1989, they played 116 shows around the world, playing to around six million fans, with four shows at the Los Angeles Memorial Coliseum alone generating over $9 million. In 1994, their Voodoo Lounge Tour grossed over $300 million; the following year, a mere seven dates at the Tokyo Dome brought in a whopping $27 million.

The presentation has grown more elaborate accordingly, on the principle that if you're going to charge punters top dollar, you should take pains to make your show the most outlandish and extravagant they'll ever see. The 1997 Bridges To Babylon tour, with its massive circular screen and extending cantilevered bridge out to the middle of the auditorium, is surely the most lavish extravaganza ever staged by a single artist. A week or two after attending the Wembley show, I saw the revitalised, resurgent Aerosmith at the same venue, presenting their grandly-titled Toxic Twin Towers Ball. There was no comparison: for all its gaudiness and energy, the Aerosmith concert was by comparison a piddling little affair, hardly in the same medium, let alone league, as the Stones' flamboyant presentation. The forthcoming tour will doubtless raise the bar even higher, with jet-packs, perhaps, or maybe an airship or two.

It's a far cry indeed from their early days as one of a number of R & B bands scuffling for breaks in the early Sixties. Brought together through the godfatherly interest of Brit-blues pioneer Alexis Korner, the fledgling Stones got their big break when Korner's Blues Incorporated were booked to play a BBC radio *Jazz Club* session, and couldn't fulfil their usual Thursday residency at the Marquee Club; with Long John Baldry stepping up from support to headliner, Korner recommended the Stones as support, and on 12 July 1962, an early line-up (with future Kink Mick Avory on drums, and future Pretty Thing Dick Taylor on bass) made their debut. Band leader Brian Jones wore a trendy corduroy jacket, and guitarist Keith Richards a dark suit, while the singer, a callow LSE student called Mick Jagger, preferred a woolly cardigan, which in those days suggested daringly bohemian inclinations. Harold Pendleton, who booked the club for the National Jazz League, barely tolerated Korner's weekly blues shows, and hated the Stones' less jazz-influenced take on the blues, wasting no opportunity to run them down. His manifest disapproval prompted the new band's leader Brian Jones to pen a letter to *Jazz News* magazine, complaining of the "pseudo-intellectual snobbery" of the jazz scene. "It must be apparent," he wrote, "that Rock 'n' Roll has a far greater affinity for R & B than the latter has for Jazz, insofar that Rock is a direct corruption of Rhythm and Blues whereas Jazz is Negro music on a different plane, intellectually higher but emotionally less intense." Not that the band themselves were that sure of their direction: in an earlier edition of the same magazine announcing their debut, Mick Jagger was quoted as saying "I hope they don't think we're a rock and roll outfit".

Despite the disapproval of sections of the audience, who according to Dick Taylor were openly hostile before they'd even played a note, a contingent of supportive Mods ensured a decent reception, and Pendleton grudgingly used them as a last-minute replacement for bands who failed to show, if he couldn't find anyone else. Eventually, Richards was driven by Pendleton's constant derogation to take more direct action than a sniffy letter to *Jazz News*, responding to one of the booker's put-downs by clobbering him with his guitar. It was the first anyone had seen of Keith's physical side, but not the last. When Australian entrepreneur Robert Stigwood, who helped promote some of their earliest concert tours, refused to pay them £10,000 they were owed, he was accosted at a restaurant by the angry guitarist, who "beat the shit out of him", according to journalist Keith Altham, who was with him at the time. "Keith," said Altham, "why do you keep on hitting him?" "Because the bastard keeps getting up!" replied Keith.

The Stones' career really started taking off during their residency at the Station Hotel, Richmond, where their growing reputation attracted both their future manager Andrew Loog Oldham and Decca A & R man Dick Rowe (a.k.a. "The Man Who Turned Down The Beatles"). Oldham was a lippy 19-year-old PR hustler who, in his own words, had decided to become "a nasty little upstart tycoon shit", in emulation of his hero Phil Spector, whom he had met shortly before. (Indeed, it was advice from Spector that helped Oldham secure the Stones an unprecedented deal: don't use the record company's studio to record the band, he warned, because they'll own the copyright on the recording – pay for your own independent studio session instead, and lease the tapes to the label.) Oldham was instantly drawn to the group. "I knew what I was looking at," he said. "It was Sex. And I was just ahead of the pack."

Oldham's influence was decisive in transforming the raw R & B outfit into a massive attraction, by setting them up as the uncouth antithesis of The Beatles, whose charm and wit had quickly made them beloved of toddlers and grannies alike. Oldham knew that parental condemnation was the surest route to teenage hearts, and set about ensuring that newspaper coverage was critical of the band's sound, their attitude, and

particularly their looks. The *Daily Express* referred to their
"doorstep mouths, pallid cheeks and unkempt hair", and even
the *NME* – not yet the rebellious journal it would become, but
still the voice of youth – described them on their first tour as a
"caveman-like quintet".

Their manager's ideas were often brilliant – he fought long
and hard with Decca to leave the group's name off the cover of
their debut album, thereby bestowing an aloofness on the band
which set them apart from their peers – but he sometimes
went too far. Inspired by Anthony Burgess' *A Clockwork
Orange*, he penned a sleevenote for their second album which
exhorted fans to delinquency. "Cast deep in your pockets for
loot to buy this disc of groovies and fancy words," he wrote.
"If you don't have the bread, see that blind man, knock him on
the head, steal his wallet and lo and behold, you have the loot.
If you put in the boot, good. Another one sold." It was devas-
tatingly effective: questions were raised in the House Of Lords,
and the offending paragraph was eventually deleted from later
pressings of the album.

Oldham established an image and an attitude which continued long after his association with the group was over. In their
prime, The Rolling Stones were a force of nature, able to trans-
mute with ease the raw ore of their own R & B heroes into rock
'n' roll gold, and needing nothing more than an East London
garage wall to relieve themselves against to send tremors of
terror down the spine of the establishment. So potent was their
image that despite the competing claims of such fellow beat-
boom longhairs as The Kinks, The Who, The Animals and The
Pretty Things, the Stones effortlessly assumed the mantle of
number-one folk-devil, a mantle they carried with style and
aplomb from parochial UK origins to the global stage.

Ironically, their very notoriety assured their entry into the
new, supposedly classless society of the Swinging Sixties,
which grasped the ruffians – well, Mick, anyway – to their
bosom. Jagger may have first slipped into the London demi-
monde – that confluence of louche aristos and bohemian
hustlers that pushed back the boundaries of taste and decency
– in pursuit of posh totty, but he soon found its warm and
moneyed embrace irresistible. Mentored by the likes of art

dealer Robert Fraser and antique dealer Christopher Gibbs, he became a staple of the society columns: at a dinner party at the latter's Cheyne Walk flat, he leaned over to fashion designer Michael Fish and whispered, "I'm here to learn how to be a gentleman". He could have been taking the Mick, but somehow one doubts it. It speaks volumes for Gibbs' tutoring that these days, of course, he would be taking the Sir Mick.

All the attitude in the world, however, is useless without the product to back it up, and the Stones soon showed they could compete at the highest level. Listening to a recently-issued four-disc anthology of British blues, it's impossible not to be struck by how quickly the Stones outstripped their fellow enthusiasts of the early Sixties, leaving behind the hand-me-down "authenticity" of nit-picking blues obsessives for a new music which channeled the raw energy of the blues into a more streamlined, potent force. It all happened so fast, as they progressed from basic blues templates like the Buddy Holly/ Bo Diddley knock-off "Not Fade Away" and the Willie Dixon/ Howlin' Wolf knock-off "Little Red Rooster" – the most unlikely number one of 1964 – to the extraordinary sonic invention of "The Last Time", "Satisfaction" and "Get Off Of My Cloud" the following year. And then on from there, pushing the envelope of pop with each successive release, unafraid of using whatever new sounds or strategies their engineers – particularly Ron Malo at Chess Studios, and the gifted Dave Hassinger – could come up with to give their singles that edge over the competition. Reverb, feedback, compression – the Stones employed them all in their search for sonic novelty, only stumbling when all bets were off in the hippy era. Struggling to match The Beatles' rococo invention, the Stones drifted too far from the security of their trusted blues roots and came a kaftan'd cropper with *Their Satanic Majesties Request*, a real rock folly stuffed with space-rock and phasing and hippy hymns, and packaged in a tacky 3D-effect photo, the era's naff precursor to the hologram.

Once bitten, however, they wouldn't make the same mistake again for many a year. The following year's *Beggars Banquet* ushered in an era of unparalleled achievement for the Stones, in which sonic invention was tempered with due regard for

their blues roots. Ironically, for all the charismatic presence of
Brian Jones and Ronnie Wood, few Stones fans would dispute
the supremacy in their catalogue of the albums recorded
between 1969 and 1974 with the more retiring Mick Taylor,
particularly the towering trilogy of *Let It Bleed*, *Sticky Fingers*
and *Exile On Main Street*, with which they negotiated the transition from the Sixties to the Seventies.

It was during this period that the Stones established themselves as the dark lords of rock 'n' roll excess. Extravagant
hedonism had always been a part of showbiz, but the Stones
bestowed upon it a public legitimacy that would become the
template for each successive generation of rockers, from Led
Zeppelin and Aerosmith through to Guns N' Roses and Oasis.
Their American tours of 1969 and 1972 were unparalleled
marathons of sexual and narcotic indulgence. Robert Frank's
1972 tour documentary *Cocksucker Blues* featured scenes of
such casual depravity that Jagger refused to allow it to be shown,
while *Rolling Stone* journalist Robert Greenfield reported vast
quantities of drugs of all kinds, from prescription medications
like Quaaludes and Demerol to pot and acid, and in one instance,
$500 worth of cocaine laid out in a four-foot line on a mirror,
consumed within minutes. Considering their "triumphal
progress", biographer Albert Goldman – never one to mince
words – wrote of a "public image of sado-homosexual-junkie-
diabolic-sarcastic-nigger-evil unprecedented in the annals of
pop culture".

But that was then, and this is now. In recent years, the
Stones have become all about presentation, a parody of their
former scary selves. Mick Jagger, once rock 'n' roll's Pan incit-
ing followers to sybaritic excess, has become the pre-eminent
pantomime dame of rock, whilst their shows have become
bigger, grander, more absurdly conceived than ever before.
Even the announcement, every five years or so, of a new Stones
tour has become a media event in itself, reported with wry
chuckles, just-fancy-that shakes of the head and inevitable
jokes about zimmer frames, as if it were an extraordinary feat
for these sexagenarians to even take to the stage, let alone
travel in the height of luxury across the six inhabited conti-
nents. Their contemporary Bob Dylan, by comparison, keeps

up a ferocious touring schedule with no comparable fuss and
bother, calmly playing hundreds of sold-out shows a year, and
thereby continually rejuvenating his own creative impulses to
produce, in his sixties, work which in its own way equals that
of his youth.

The comparison is instructive on several levels: whilst
Dylan has undergone a creative rebirth by actively confronting
the inevitable ageing process, growing old gracefully with work
of commendable maturity, the Stones seem for several decades
now to have been trying to ignore the fact that they are old
men, using various sleights of presentation to persuade themselves – though few others, surely – that they are still vital
young rockers, still able to punch their weight with younger
pretenders. But the sight of the wrinkled fop Jagger flouncing
his way around the stage, wiggling his bottom "like a duck
shaking water from its tail", to use Philip Norman's memorable phrase, and clapping his hands like a fey flamenco dancer,
has become one of rock's greatest embarrassments. "You
wouldn't want my trousers to fall down, would you?" he once
famously enquired of an audience, the roar of assent recorded
for posterity on a live album. These days, the response would
be more along the lines of Oh God, please no – the very
thought has put me off my dinner!

Worse still, the Stones seem to regard the band as very much
a part-time job, convening every five years or so to crawl back
into the saddle and haul themselves around the world's enormo-
domes. Albums, it seems, are almost an afterthought, cranked
out without passion or wit, then speciously presented as the
raison d'être for the tours – as if they were so inspired by the new
material that they just had to share it with us in the intimate
surroundings of some football stadium or other. So we have the
Steel Wheels Tour, the Voodoo Lounge Tour, the Bridges To
Babylon Tour – the album title always upfront and in our faces,
although it's the last thing any of the audience has come to hear.
Indeed, I cannot recall a single track from the Stones' recorded
output of the past 20 years that would make it onto any reasonable person's home-burnt Best Of The Stones CD.

Instead of focusing their efforts on ensuring that the
company's core business – i.e. records by The Rolling Stones

– are of a standard one might expect from The Greatest Rock
'n' Roll Band In The World, in recent years the various
members seem to take more interest in their individual side-
projects, none of which is worth a light. There are few more
compelling illustrations of rock-group synergy, of the principle of the whole being more than the sum of its parts, than the
Stones. And no wonder: have you heard Mick's last ghastly
solo album, the bargain-bin staple *Goddess in the Doorway*? It's
just utterly, utterly bereft, a pointless exercise which ended up
being little more than a promotional tool for that TV documentary *Being Mick*, when commercial logic dictates it should
have been the other way round. And be honest: who in their
right mind wants to hear Keith sing more than the one token
song, for heaven's sake?

They'll doubtless pull out all the stops again for their upcoming tour, though whether this most barnacled of pop galleons
will ever be as relevant or as inspiring as they were in the Sixties,
when they became, in Can bassist Holger Czukay's apposite
description, "the Volkswagens of rock 'n' roll", is doubtful in the
extreme. As for being The Greatest Rock 'n' Roll Band In The
World, who knows? According to Keith Richards, it's not even
that desirable a status. "On any given night," he once said, "it's
a different band that's the greatest rock 'n' roll band. It's gotta go
up and down. Otherwise, you wouldn't know the difference. It
would be just a bland straight line, like looking at a heart
machine. And when that straight line happens, baby, you're
dead."

Set against the money-spinning triumphalism of the Stones in their fortieth-anniversary year, the reduced circumstances of Mick Taylor captured by Robin Eggar painted a somewhat more forlorn picture, right down to the plugs for his current product and website he clearly insisted be tagged on to the end of the feature . . .

ROLLING STONE IN EXILE

Robin Eggar

First published in the *Sunday Express Magazine*, May 2002

The Rolling Stones turn 40 this year. They will celebrate by embarking on a world tour that will break box office records. Mick Jagger, Keith Richards, Charlie Watts and guitarist Ronnie Wood each stands to earn at least £20 million.

Meanwhile Mick Taylor, the man Wood replaced in 1975, is all but forgotten. Now 54, the most talented guitarist the band ever had finds it hard to get a gig in an English pub. The music he loves to plays does not fit into our hype today gone tomorrow music scene. He makes an ok living overseas but the wealth of Jagger and his band mates has eluded him.

On June 9 1969 The Rolling Stones announced that their new guitarist was to be Mick Taylor, a tall blonde beautiful boy of 21 who looked 17, who could play the guitar like an angel. Within a month his predecessor Brian Jones was found dead in his swimming pool and the band had played their free concert in Hyde Park. It was the start of a five year roller coaster ride of massive tours, Altamont, tax exile in France and ground breaking albums like *Let it Bleed*, *Sticky Fingers* and *Exile On Main Street*. He quit the band in December 1974. For the next 20 years the rock and roll legacy Taylor took with him was not a country mansion but a heroin addiction that almost killed him.

Taylor does not look like he was once a Rolling Stone, nor even a rock star. He is both taller and plumper, his cheekbones do not protrude, his haircut is normal. He wears a pinstripe suit without a tie. He smokes, sips coffee and speaks softly. What bitterness he may have had has been buried alongside his addiction.

During his time with the Stones Taylor dabbled with heroin. "I slowly slipped into it like a lot of other people," he says. "In the band it was thought of as something recreational, something to do at parties. We all did but for some of us like Keith and myself it got more serious. He dealt with it in his way and I dealt with it in mine. I found it more of a struggle when I left because when you are in The Rolling Stones, you get used to people looking after you."

For a decade after leaving the Stones even though his personal life was disintegrating around him Mick held a career together. He cut a solo album and spent two years playing with Bob Dylan (one show was to 450,000 people in Paris). But in 1984 his father died and something snapped. For the next 11 years he was a "total junkie, needles, the works, just as bad as Keith, maybe worse because it went on longer.

"I had never really let my drug problems affect my work up until that point. I always knew I'd be in serious trouble if I ever lost my compulsive need to play. I did lose my way when I didn't pick up the guitar once for two years. If I'd lost the desire to play forever I'd have been in serious trouble. I'm very fortunate to have come out the other side, reasonably intact and in good health, still enjoying what I'm doing and still doing it really well."

Mick does not know exactly how and why he managed to give up heroin. He tried everything, different clinics, cold turkey, his friends were tremendously supportive but nothing seemed to work. "It was always something I fought against," he says, "I never resigned myself into thinking I was going to be a drug addict for the rest of my life. It wasn't until 1995 that I made a full recovery. Maybe I finally grew up. In the end you either get tired of it or it consumes you and you end up on the scrap heap."

The turning point came when Mick moved back to England and settled in Suffolk. "Drugs dig up your roots and burn them. It's taken me a long time to settle down again. Coming back to England was a big part of that. I missed being in England, missed my friends, and missed my family. That was when I started my band for real, went into the studio and started touring on a regular basis."

The Mick Taylor Band is full of consummate musicians like pianist Mike Middleton, guitarist Robert Awhai, bassist Michael "Dreads" Bailey and a choice of drummers. Over the past two years they have played over 170 gigs and are due to tour Sweden in May. Only a handful of those shows have been in Britain.

"I make a living," says Mick. "If you are a good R & B player and you've got a bit of a name there's never a shortage of places you can play in Europe. I've been to the States five times in the past three years. I just don't play in this country. Maybe the stuff I play doesn't have any bearing to the pop scene, which is so transient."

However his most interesting collaboration recently has been with his old friend the Japanese pianist and composer Miyuki. *Mick & I* is a delicate often-beautiful instrumental album, a mixture of new age, jazz and blues, which shows Taylor has lost none of his touch. He and Miyuki, who works regularly with the Ballet Rambert, are planning to do some live shows with other featured musicians tenor saxophone wizard Tim Garland and trumpeter Byron Wallen.

"It is esoteric, shows another side to my playing," says Taylor. "People forget I played on *Tubular Bells*. I've always loved working with keyboard players and I've been fortunate to enough to play with three great piano players, Nicky Hopkins, Max Middleton and Miyuki. I classify myself as an eccentric musician but I suppose my heart and soul is still in R & B."

These days Taylor is very sanguine about his days with the Stones. He is happy, even proud to talk about his time with the band. "I still feel like a Rolling Stone, it's tattooed on my soul," he says. "I'm just not in the band. It has cast a long shadow over my career. It really is a blessing and a curse in equal measure. I wouldn't have missed playing with them for all the world. It was wonderful but it just got a bit crazy in the mid 70s."

Mick's parents (his dad worked for British Aerospace) were early rock and roll fans. They took him to see Bill Haley and the Comets when he was nine and encouraged him to play guitar. He was a natural who at 15 sat in with John Mayall's Bluesbreakers when Eric Clapton failed to show up. Two years later he joined Mayall full time (they are still friends) until the bandleader recommended him to Jagger and Richards. He met them at the recording studio, laid down some guitar on "Honky Tonk Women" and joined the next day.

"The Stones were completely broke. They owed vast sums of money, they had tax problems. I never thought about the money. As I got paid £150 a week it didn't even occur to me. I just wanted to play, Then they signed with Atlantic and it was a new lease of life and a new start for their career."

Legend has it that Taylor was the shy retiring one, content to spend time with his girlfriend Rose, who was then corrupted by the band. Not so he insists. "Lot of Stones fans think I was born at Hyde Park," he grins, "that I suddenly emerged with the butterflies. I wasn't corrupted by them. I had lost my inno-cence a long time before that. I just looked very innocent."

"I always felt part of the group. I wasn't treated like a session musician, I enjoyed the same kind of things everybody else did. I had this image of being the quiet shy and retiring one, not at all, except compared to Mick Jagger I am. I was the youngest and most journalists were only interested in talking to Mick. They didn't want to talk to Charlie or me or Bill and Keith wasn't making any sense most of the time, except when he picked up the guitar."

Throughout his time in the Stones Taylor had to contend with Jagger's dilettante social life following his marriage to Bianca and Keith's heroin addiction. Growing up playing seven nights a week Taylor loved, still loves, playing live. By the end of 1974 the Stones weren't in any state to tour. At times he didn't think Keith would live much longer and the band could not survive without him. Yet even 26 years later Mick is uncomfortable, defensive about explaining his reasons for quitting.

"Well it certainly wasn't the smartest thing to do was it?" he says. "That's all I have to say. I certainly never imagined The Rolling Stones would still be pulling in crowds, doing tours, still be together. There have been various points in their history where they have nearly split up and that was one of them. We were all very worried about Keith. It's well known that they all had their problems with drugs except Bill who is the most strait laced and businesslike. They are all quite extraordinary people, a bunch of eccentrics who deserve each other.

"I didn't leave The Rolling Stones on good terms," he admits. "Lack of song writing credit was certainly a contributory factor. I was burned because there are 5 songs I feel I should have gotten some credit for. I was angry with them for that lack of credit. It doesn't bother me any more now. At the time I thought it was outrageous. Bill Wyman used to get very frustrated as well. He said to me once, 'It's always been like that, you have to get used to it.' Eventually he left too . . . I've never been sure why.

"I got very disillusioned in the early 80s when they basically stopped paying me royalties on the albums I'd played on – which were their most successful ever." Legend has it that he sued them, which Taylor says never happened but he won't expand on the situation, only saying that the problem was "kind of sorted". Others believe he was paid off at a time when he wasn't in a physical or financial position to argue.

The eighties were a bad time for him. He lived between New York and LA and lost touch with his daughter Chloe. "I split up with Rose, my first wife, in 1976. It was very difficult to keep the relationship with Chloe going when I was in America and into the drugs. I have a lot of regrets yes, but I don't spend too much time on them any more." They have mended their relationship. Chloe is now 30 and married with a daughter of her own. Eleanor, three, "is the only one allowed to call me granddad."

Soon after he returned to England Mick had another daughter with an American woman from Boston. That relationship ended on such bad terms that he will not discuss it. Emma, five, lives in Florida with her mother and he has only limited contact with her. "I don't see my little one very often," he says sadly. "These things happen."

Much of Mick's new lease on life and enthusiasm comes from his girlfriend, Marlies Damming. Marlies is 29, younger she admits with a happy grin than Chloe. She is a 6 foot blonde from Drenthe in Northern Holland, blessed with a perpetual smile and a stern work ethic who until last year was studying medicine in Groningen.

Marlies has been a real Stones fan for longer than she can remember. The first time she picked up a guitar she taught herself to play "Love Is Strong" (from *Voodoo Lounge*). Some years ago on holiday at a ski resort she hooked up with a Belgian Stones tribute band called Sticky Fingers and ended up singing lead vocals on "Beast of Burden". In October 2000 she was down in Liege visiting them when she heard that the Mick Taylor band were playing at The Spirit of 66, a nightclub in Verviers.

"My friend knowing how much I liked the Stones suggested I go and see the one that left. He knew one of the security guys and was trying to arrange that I could go back stage," she says, "but this bouncer told me there would be no chance as they had arrived in a terrible mood. After the show when this blond bouncer guy shouted at me 'You! Two minutes! Now!' I just walked into the dressing room. Mick invited me to the next show, which was at Reisen in Holland. That day I had to give two presentations at my University so it was a very tight schedule, but I made it in time."

Since then she's never really left. Both she and Mick commute between Suffolk and Holland but she has taken time out of her degree course and is determined to steer her lover into better times. "Marlies found me a very suitable case for treatment," he laughs. "She says I am the most interesting case she's had, tells her friends she's doing a thesis on me. She's trying to keep me fit. In January she made me go running every day. I've stopped for a bit. My fitness regime hasn't failed. I suffer from Seasonally Adjusted Disorder when it rains every day and I find it harder to get out. There are no indoor tennis courts in Diss. I'm not bad at tennis. I beat her." ("No he didn't," she insists.)

Despite her attempts to wean him off cigarettes he is still a smoker but seldom drinks alcohol as it sends him to sleep. He is teaching her guitar and she can play "Moonlight Mile" (off *Sticky Fingers*) with some aplomb. They work well together. When she is serious it frees him to clown about. She is protective of him but when he picks up his guitar and plays her face softens.

Marlies' philosophy is simple. "Once a Stone always a Stone. You can't really ever leave." Mick Taylor has spent a quarter of a century running from his past. Now he can do what he has always done so well. Play his guitar.

Miyuki's Mick & I *is available on Invoke Records or online from www.sierrabravo.co.uk*

For more information on Mick Taylor's upcoming gigs (and his history) log onto www.micktaylor.com which has had over two million hits.

"Meet-and-greets" are now contractually part of The Rolling Stones' touring process. That music industry bigwigs and lowly employees of the tour's sponsors alike get to shake hands and exchange pleasantries with these larger-than-life characters is not necessarily a bad thing. As Bill German, the editor of a Stones fanzine who became a band friend, noted of one such event, "The whole thing took a minute, but, for those fans, it'd last a lifetime." However, the Stones' history and the unique cachet they once had make the meet-and-greet and its implied corporatism sit oddly with them. Ignacio Julià was one "lucky" fan admitted to the inner sanctum who was left with profoundly ambiguous feelings.

PLEASE ALLOW ME TO INTRODUCE MYSELF

Ignacio Julià

First published in *Pulp-Rock: Artículos y entrevistas 1982–2004* (Milenio, 2005)

In 2002, The Rolling Stones, who as everyone knows have not released an album to live up to their reputation since the mid-Seventies, launch their *Forty Licks* compilation and thus came back to life. The two disc affair includes thirty-six of their most popular songs and, scattered among these, four lively new recordings – what in the Sixties would have amounted to an EP – to encourage sales. Despite the undeniable weight of a selection of bold achievements of 20th-century popular music, the album launch is just the excuse to embark on another long world tour, the main source of income for this financial empire skillfully directed by Sir Mick Jagger. This time the gimmick is the intermixing in the stadia expedition of medium-capacity indoor performances and even a few theatres. The aim is to offer different perspectives on an institution, hoping these different angles lend a new shine to a worn-out icon.

In June 2003, the tour stops in Spain, where in the Sixties the Stones were adored as a scruffy, roguish antidote to the more benign Beatles and have become rock's most popular legend since. I decide to break my cautious refusal to attend their concerts – I did not attend their first visit in 1976 and after that missed opportunity subsequent tours seemed historically too late in their game – and request an invitation. A few days before the event, a call comes from their label inviting me to what is known in the business as a "meet and greet". This ritual consists of record label executives, chain store managers and radio and press people being granted a collective brief encounter with the artist. I am aware that these are usually false and sycophantic ceremonies but how I can spurn the opportunity to shake hands with Keith Richards, the embodiment of all that defines the Golden Age of Rock 'n' Roll? On the afternoon of the day in question, I head to Barcelona's Olympic Stadium where I meet the local representative of their label at the artists' entrance along with the rest of the lucky fifteen permitted to rub shoulders with Their Wrinkled Majesties. Radio and television are the only media allowed in. These are the most powerful media, of course, but an added bonus is the fact that the often malicious verbosity of the rock magazine or newspaper writer is not in their nature.

After a short wait at the gates of the stadium, the inside contact, a gentle PR lady working for the gigantic production team that keeps the tour moving, unquestionably the biggest rock extravaganza in the world, shows up. Walkie talkie in hand and clutching her clipboard, she leads us through the bowels of the stadium, a bustling miniature city full of individuals with both an assigned role and an entitlement to food and accommodation. Production offices, mobile canteens and kitchens, infirmary and dressing rooms go by before we finally arrive at a cubicle consisting of four black canvas walls, about twenty square feet, where the reception will take place. The only decoration is a table of snacks and drinks on one side, and a backdrop of *Forty Licks* promotional material. Here, we will be contained until the group, who we are advised "are late and in a pretty bad mood", show up. If someone feels a physical need, we are told to say so and we will be accompanied, escorted, to the bathroom, just in case we get lost – or sneak into the Sancta Sanctorum, the exclusive Glimmer Twins dressing rooms area, and help ourselves to a bottle of champagne of the type that costs a mere mortal's monthly wage.

That seems not such a bad idea after all: the hostages in here have only insipid Budweiser beer and moistened corn tortillas with bottled, cheap Mexican salsa on which to survive. And to add to the insult of that budget catering, the British matron steadily reads us the protocol: no autographs, no talk if they don't address you – and be sure, they won't – no touching, and so on. We are here for the greetings and the photo opportunity. They ask us to group in front of the promotional canvas for a rehearsal with a warning that we will only be in the picture if we see the camera lens, then dismiss us. We will go back to the same spot when the time comes, the PR lady says. She also jocularly explains that we must watch out for the famous Jagger Trick. The old brat finds it amusing to stand in front of a chosen one in the group so he doesn't make the picture, even shaking his head from side to side to prevent him making himself visible to the camera.

Given the awkwardness of the scene, I choose to get serious and, my second warm beer oozing out of the bottle and wetting the carpet, announce loudly I always preferred The Beatles anyway. Nobody seems to grasp my sarcasm. Just seconds after that, the jolly midwife sticks her head out of the black canvas and happily tells us the band are here. Everyone runs to their spot in time to watch the four Stones enter: here they come, dynamic, just as if they were jumping on stage, hopping, as if fearing somebody is going stop them. First in is Mick Jagger, coming fast towards me and throwing a robotic handshake. The waxy, pale but famous face takes me by surprise, as does the infinite coldness of his stare. Meanwhile, a friendly Ron Wood puts his arm around my shoulder and smiles. The band's court jester, he is the only one with a glimmer of true humanity. At the other end, Charlie Watts poses. I have to reach out to shake Keith Richards' hand – he's wearing a yolk-colored shirt, open to the navel, and dark glasses – and mumble my "delighted to finally meet you" spiel. Flashbulbs explode and, without time for us to really grasp their presence, they disappear as fast as they entered the room. Pathetic, I know, but nobody can now take away our minute with the Stones!

Why do they play out this nonsense? They surely don't need it on a promotional level. The resulting photograph will doubtlessly be placed in prominent spots in corridors, offices and radio studios, but cannot legally be published. The only logical answer, I presume, is an unusual symbiosis between the need for adulation on a small scale – the cries of fifty thousand people they will face in a few minutes is something else, a more abstract and overwhelming adulation – and the nostalgia for an old tradition, a remnant of the showbusiness logistics Jagger closely studied and perfected during the first two decades of the band's existence. It's the only reasonable explanation for this ridiculous scene, reminiscent of the sublime *Mr Bean* sketch in which employees of a London theatre are waiting in line for the Queen and Bean is so nervous his bow turns into a head-butt. On second thoughts, maybe someone should have done something similar to Jagger.

Is this what I deserve after a quarter of a century devoted to these matters? In a way, yes. The experience destroys any vestige of the mythomania which got me started in the business, no doubt reflected in my early (and not-so-early) writing, and reaffirms the idea that, in rock music, financial benefits will always take precedence. Every spectacle contains a fraud, and the rock spectacle may be the most fraudulent of all in its intermingling of rebellion and commerce, art and hyperbole.

When The Rolling Stones finally come on stage that evening, Keith Richards dramatically steps out and promptly messes up the "Brown Sugar" riff – what a guy! – kicking off a set-list that, allied with the spectacular audiovisuals on the screens and the complete commitment of supreme salesman Mick Jagger, will provide an unforgettable night built on nostalgic sentiment that counterpoints the loftiness of musicians never given to mawkishness. I am thinking that this cocktail of finesse and detachment is still irresistible. And then I realize that I am witnessing the last great representation of the validity of rock as we knew it, of a music that had not yet been strayed away from its roots in blues and eagerly sang to that youthful dissatisfaction and curiosity my generation shall never lose.

Who will occupy the Stones' place twenty years from now? What current group will routinely gather fifty thousand people and revive the dormant collective conscience? There seems to be no modern equivalent of the classic rock Olympus. Today everything is mixed, interdisciplinary, virtual, complex, off-centre. We've invented a lot of new dissatisfactions that seem to have no possible satisfaction. Maybe we'll have to keep coming back, poor us, to the source from where this sound emanated, a sound that did not change the world after all, even if it profoundly altered some lives. In rock, like in any artform, only technological progress now seems possible, not an aesthetic or moral one. Who's hitting the notes is still the only thing that matters. In this we have not changed an iota since man first started creating sound to soothe the silence.

A BIGGER BANG

Sean Egan

UK release: 5 September 2005; US release: 6 September 2005

Produced by: Don Was and the Glimmer Twins

Charts: UK no. 2; US no. 3

Tracklisting:
Rough Justice
Let Me Down Slow
It Won't Take Long
Rain Fall Down
Streets of Love
Back of My Hand
She Saw Me Coming
Biggest Mistake
This Place Is Empty
Oh No, Not You Again
Dangerous Beauty
Laugh, I Nearly Died
Sweet Neo Con
Look What the Cat Dragged In
Driving Too Fast
Infamy

August 2005 saw yet another world tour, one that lasted two years, off and on. This time round, the Stones managed to fend off accusations of peddling nostalgia by bringing out a new album, *A Bigger Bang*. It was, of course, a fig-leaf: most of the umpteen millions who saw them on their travels around the globe were long past the point of buying new Stones fare.

However, as they always did when they had a new product, the band sprinkled the set with tracks from it rather than simply churn out exclusively well-known numbers. As was by now routine, they broke box-office records, some set by themselves, during the tour. Particularly noteworthy was their concert on Brazil's Copacabana Beach in February 2006, witnessed in the flesh by approximately one million people. The Stones also secured the prestigious interval spot at Super Bowl. Another of their American gigs was filmed by Martin Scorsese. The celebrated director who has often used Stones music in his films was shooting an in-concert movie that would ultimately be titled *Shine a Light*, thus finally making that *Exile on Main St.* highlight as famous as it should be. *Shine a Light* premiered in April 2008, the same month as a tie-in double-CD appeared.

The front cover of *A Bigger Bang* featured a photograph of the Stones for the first time on a studio album since 1986, although in the day and age of the miniature CD album cover their faces were barely discernible. The Stones' first full-length studio album for exactly eight years – a new record release gap – saw Darryl Jones return on bass, although Richards and – for the very first time – Jagger also took turns on the instrument. The band started from scratch rather than go back to the tapes of the sessions that produced the four new tracks on *Forty Licks*. Wood's recurring drug problems and Watts' treatment for throat cancer meant Jagger and Richards began preparatory work on their own. Watts made a full recovery. It's doubtful that anybody will ever be able to say the same about Wood, who doesn't appear on several tracks. He again receives no songwriting credits on an all Jagger/Richards affair. Nor was there much in the way of auxiliary musicianship. "It's probably the closest that Mick and I have worked together since *Exile on Main St.*," said Richards.

A Bigger Bang's sixty-four minutes meant it was only around three minutes shy of *Exile on Main St.*'s running time. Of course, the fact that the album in no way resembled the sprawling grand statement of that 1972 double vinyl album was not just due to the fact that the vast majority consumed it on its single CD.

"If you go back through Stones albums, I'm sure you'll find

vulnerability along with the swagger. It may not have been as easy to see, though, because it's not my temperament to share that feeling ... This time the songs were written very quickly, and I was in a certain frame of mind. I thought about some of the words afterward to see whether they were too personal, but I decided to just let them stay." Those were Jagger's thoughts on the album. We all think we know to what he refers: Jagger's recent traumatic split with Jerry Hall, the mother of four of his children who had put up with many infidelities until such time as he made a Brazilian model pregnant in 1998. Setting aside the moral plus-point of the old roué finding compositional vulnerability at such an advanced age, it created the bulk of a core of good songs.

The album starts unpromisingly. "Rough Justice" has a couple of good components, including an amusing line wherein the narrator wonders whether he has been transformed from a rooster into "one of your cocks". However, despite the fearsome beat and the dramatic slide work, it's all just a load of bluster, bereft of a good riff or tune, and further proof that the Stones have forgotten how to sound like the Stones.

"Let Me Down Slow", a melodic track wherein the narrator is melancholically aware he is going to be dumped, brings about an immediate improvement. Unfortunately, and not for the last time here, Don Was does his best to ruin a worthwhile cut by mixing the drums too high. "It Won't Take Long" is the third break-up song in a row, this one unconvincingly asserting that the narrator can shrug off the rupture. It's mid-tempo and pretty good. "Rain Fall Down" is more than pretty good, inhabiting the realms of something special. Circular, atmospheric instrumentation accompanies a lyric that is a study in proletarian misery and boredom, although we also get a glimpse into Jagger's more rarefied real-life environs in the shape of a dig at a kiss-and-tell merchant. "Streets of Love" is even higher-class, partly because we infer that this moving, sweet lament of an abandoned lover displays contrition on Jagger's part about his treatment of Hall ("I must admit I was awful bad").

On the twelve-bar "Back of My Hand", Jagger's mouth harp is, as ever, impressive and there are some nicely menacing lines in classic blues tradition ("He says there's trouble, trouble's a-coming") but it's not a particularly distinguished example of a genre into which it's difficult to inject originality. "She Saw Me Coming" is another song that relies for some of its considerable power on what we imagine to be its real-life impetus, in this case a certain young woman with a paternity suit in her hand. "Boy did I get screwed," notes the narrator. Similarly autobiographical elements provide power to "Biggest Mistake", another song seemingly about Jerry Hall, this one even more touching than "Streets of Love". "I took her for granted, I played with her mind," ruefully notes the narrator as he concedes that it may well have been the biggest mistake of his life. In the final couplet he vows that he won't make the same mistake if love comes his way again. Complementing the winning candour is a fine tune and cooing vocal refrain. The Richards-sung "This Place Is Empty" is Keith's own shot at vulnerability as he admits that he hates to be alone in a mellow track addressed to a lover. It's nice enough but as with Richards' vocals lately, his voice is distractingly shaky. Moreover, the line "Come on, honey, bare your breasts" doesn't quite fit into the mood.

"Oh No, Not You Again" – a denunciation of a femme fatale – is more featureless hard rock: no memorable riff, a shouted melody and a flat guitar solo. "Dangerous Beauty" sounds like another song about a femme fatale and in a sense it is, but in this case it concerns the female American soldiers seen posing in horrifying photographs featuring torture victims at Abu Ghraib. It wastes its good intentions with lazy rhymes and a distasteful whiff of Jagger being slightly turned on by the scenario ("If I was your captain, would you salute me?"). Meanwhile, an interesting menacing riff is buried beneath the drums.

In "Laugh, I Nearly Died", Jagger sings rather well, stretching out syllables prettily as he recounts a lonely man's global wanderings. Intricate backing vocals and shimmering guitars add to the lushness. "Sweet Neo Con" is a far superior protest song to "Dangerous Beauty". Mick nails his colours unequivocally to the mast ("I think that you're a crock of shit") in a broadside against the noughties successor to the New Right of the eighties. The instrumentation shadowing his voice on the main vocal refrain makes the melody sound rather stilted but otherwise works up a good staccato groove, helped by Jagger's quality mouth harp. "Look What the Cat Dragged In" possesses a real vitality with its supple-wristed, quick-fire riff, nimble tune, funky groove and dense texture that includes an almost Far Eastern countermelody. Not only that, but the subtle mix means that for once we can enjoy Watts' drumming. The lyric may even be a breakthrough for Jagger, who seems to be admonishing a dirty-stop-out daughter.

"Driving Too Fast" has a powerful riff but falls down in the lyric, which is a metaphor about a manic life or perhaps mentality. "You went straight past the curve and you'll never go back" is about the extent of the insight on offer in lines that feel as if they were devised purely to fill up the space. The album closer, "Infamy", is another Keith vocal. It's a surprisingly toothless and plastic-sounding track, a treated, continuous guitar riff and characterless melody giving it the feel of the looped music proliferating in the charts at this time. The lyric could either be about a love affair gone wrong or Keith's complicated relationship with Jagger but, in any case, is too bare for any pathos. Fans of *Carry On* movies will understand the joke in the title.

That the Stones will now never be hailed as having made an artistic comeback is partly a function of the CD age, which, even though it has passed into history with the advent of the download era's switch to a climate of individual track purchases, has left what used to be called the record-buying public with an expectation of artistic statements lasting an hour or more. A version of *A Bigger Bang* comprising "Let Me Down Slow", "It Won't Take Long", "Rain Fall Down", "Streets of Love", "She Saw Me Coming", "Biggest Mistake", "Laugh, I Nearly Died", "Sweet Neo Con" and "Look What the Cat Dragged In" would have made a solid, impressive album but the day and age when nine strong tracks was preferable to sixteen ones of mixed quality is gone and the album got the appropriate mixed or lukewarm reviews.

The UK singles from the album were "Streets of Love"/"Rough Justice", "Rain Fall Down" and "Biggest Mistake". The special-edition CD/DVD of *A Bigger Bang* featured two album out-takes in the form of "Under the Radar" and "Don't Wanna Go Home", both undistinguished. The four-set tour DVD, *The Biggest Bang*, featured further new tracks. 22 November 2005 saw the release of the Stones compilation, *Rarities 1971–2003*, originally available only in Starbucks branches before gaining a conventional release. Much of it consists of worthless live versions from B-sides, but stuff like "Let It Rock" (a vintage live B-side of uncommon value), "Through the Lonely Nights" and the extended disco mix of "Miss You" (albeit slightly edited here) had long needed mopping up.

Early 2007 brought the revelation that the Stones had managed to remain tax exiles even though Jagger and Watts had relocated to the UK years back. By registering their company in Holland, Jagger, Watts and Richards paid only $7.2 million in taxes on earnings of $450 million channelled through Amsterdam since approximately 1987. The band had perhaps unjustly been accused of meanness when they had postponed UK dates in 1998 because a retroactive tax change introduced by the Labour government had jeopardized the earnings of their large crew, but this latest disclosure stuck in the craws of even those who had always been cognizant that the band had never proclaimed themselves socialists.

The same year saw the release of *Rolled Gold +*. Allen Klein's supposed misgivings about the sales potential of a triple album hardly applied in an age when the release was issued on CD, vinyl, download album with interactive booklet and – in a UK industry first – USB memory card. This expanded version featured twelve additional tracks, including "Brown Sugar" and "Wild Horses".

In July 2008, the Stones signed over their catalogue to Universal in all territories. Most will have stifled a yawn at yet another big money transfer of their post-1970 assets bolted to a new record deal but Universal exploited the back catalogue in a more proactive way than previous labels, with both *Some Girls* and *Exile on Main St.* receiving the bonus-tracks treatment in which the Stones had not hitherto seemed interested. (ABKCO's prior, similar upgrading of *"Get Yer Ya-Ya's Out!"* presumably involved cooperation from the Stones in searching archives and granting relevant release permissions.) Universal have also inaugurated a series of digital "official bootlegs": *The Brussels Affair '73* (17 November 2011), *Hampton Coliseum (Live 1981)* (31 January 2012), *L. A. Friday (Live 1975)* (2 April 2012) and *Live at the Tokyo Dome* (July 2012) are in-concert releases available only as downloads via Google. The release of the deluxe version of *Exile* went hand-in-hand with *Stones in Exile*, an interesting documentary on the making of the album by Stephen Kijak that premiered at the Cannes Film Festival. The deluxe *Some Girls* was accompanied by the release of *Some Girls Live in Texas '78*, a DVD/CD combo. In a bumper year for Stones fans, 2010 saw the release of Keith Richards' autobiography *Life*, a fat tome in which we learnt much we didn't already know even from this frank interviewee, especially about his family, his Dartford background and the Mick–Keith–Anita love triangle of 1968.

A half-century after their first gig, the Stones' story may be coming to an end. The build-up to the January 2013 fiftieth anniversary of the completion of the first classic line-up saw the release of the official and surprisingly good photo-autobiography *50* in July 2012, a band film history *Crossfire Hurricane* in November and the same month another compilation. Though *Grrr!* had an idiotic title and cover picture (a painting of a gorilla's head adorned with the lips-and-tongue logo), it was, like *Forty Licks*, a useful label-spanning best-of, one furthermore that came in multiple editions that included an eighty-track version. However the fact that "Gloom and Doom" and "One Last Shot", the two new songs on the set, marked the first time the group had coalesced in the studio since *A Bigger Bang*'s sessions eight years previously was ominous. More so was the fact that there was no tour announced at the same time. Instead, talk was of a paltry quartet of shows at the year's end, amid rumours that Richards had never truly recovered from brain surgery in 2006 and the difficulty of acquiring insurance for men of the Stones' ages for a long expedition. This of course came as a disappointment to their fanbase. They no longer record material destined to be perceived as classic and the days are long gone when they so clearly constituted a figurehead for a new world order that they scared the Establishment into incarcerating them. Yet the appetite to see and hear The Rolling Stones remains as strong as it was in 1963, 1973, 1983, 1993 or 2003, courtesy of the legend and allure created by some of the best popular music ever recorded. For many millions, they will always be "The greatest rock 'n' roll band in the world".

Surprisingly, Ronnie Wood has been in The Rolling Stones longer than Bill Wyman. Even more surprisingly, he has also been in the band longer than Brian Jones and Mick Taylor combined. He will, though, forever be the New Boy. His mischievous presence is beloved by the fans, especially on stage. His candour is similarly endearing. The release of his autobiography saw him talking to the press. In this interview with Pierre Perrone – originally printed in mid-2007 in several European publications but in different, shorter form – he shirks no questions.

ROLLING ROCK

Pierre Perrone

First published in *L'Espresso*, May 2007

It's the 22nd of March 2007 and the Rolling Stones operation is once again switching to touring mode with the announcement of live dates in Europe throughout the summer. Mick Jagger is in another room, taking part in a webcast, and Ronnie Wood is talking to me, exactly 32 years from the day he met the group for a try-out at Musicland Studios in Munich, Germany. "To the day? Oh that's incredible, a bit of history. Brilliant," muses the thin as a rake guitarist. "That's right! I remember I played the riff that became 'Hey Negrita' and Charlie [Watts, drums] said: 'We hardly know him and he's bossing us around already!' Well, that was all for the *Black And Blue* album." He says of the few weeks he was in contention with Jeff Beck, Eric Clapton, Rory Gallagher, Harvey Mandel and Wayne Perkins to take over from Mick Taylor as guitarist with the greatest rock 'n' roll band in the world, "It was quite a hairy time, quite a mad time, not quite knowing and learning so many different songs and breaking new ones in. Yeah, it was a creative time to say the least. I had always been a fan before I joined and it was a dream come true." He recalls his first concert with the Stones in Baton Rouge in the US on the 1st of June 1975: "It was my 28th birthday. I was thinking not a bad birthday present for a kid who'd always dreamed of being a Rolling Stone."

Even though he now drinks Coca-Cola rather than constantly nursing a glass of wine or a pint of Guinness, Ronnie Wood lives up to most caricatures you've seen of him. Or indeed the paintings the "Renoir of rock", the "Monet of Middlesex" – as Mick Jagger often introduces him – does of himself, his wife Jo, and other musicians. But, since losing both his brothers Ted – "the jazzer" in September 2003 – and Art – "the rocker" in November last year – Ronnie has been taking better care of himself. "I've been checking my own health too, really thoroughly. Everything's all good there. The music just keeps getting better." The guitarist, after another stay in rehab last year – "my fifth or my sixth?" he jokes – seems to have finally won his battle with the bottle. He certainly played better than ever and appeared to be enjoying himself on stage when I saw the band at Twickenham last August. "Definitely! That's one of the reasons why I'm so excited about going out again. I'm playing with this new focus, this new clarity, that is so exciting. Keeping a clear head, it's an on-going struggle but it's getting easier all the time. The rewards from just stopping, from diving in at the deep end, are far greater." He sighs, "Yeah, I was a bit scatterbrained on some of the earlier tours I did. But, since I stopped drinking, I'm playing at my best. We did some filming with Martin Scorsese in New York last year – that will come out later this year – and I maintained a hell of a focus. Mick has had a look at a rough edit and he told me today he was very pleased with what he saw and the live playing. The set list was very unusual." The guitarist often encourages the others to play songs they recorded before his arrival in 1975. "When I joined the Stones, they weren't interested in playing 'Satisfaction', 'Paint It Black' or all the old classics. But that's what I knew the Stones to be, I knew all those songs and that's what I wanted to be up there playing. It's very satisfying for me to get them to play all the songs I used to love as a fan. Now we have a very open mind about the old songs. And we can also do songs that we haven't done too often, old favourites like 'Bitch' and 'All Down The Line'. I get off on playing a bit of slide guitar and seeing Charlie rock. Some nights, he sounds like a fireworks display." Wood sometimes has to remind his guitar partner how various riffs and chord sequences go: "Keith might say: 'Know it? I wrote it!' He may have written it but knowing it? Very often, I have to teach him!"

The last couple of years have been rather eventful for the Stones who have had to cope with the death of Art Wood, Mick Jagger's father and two long-standing friends of the group, Atlantic Records founder Ahmet Ertegun and keyboard player Billy Preston. Watts also had his health worries and won his battle against throat cancer before the Bigger Bang tour started in 2005.

In February 2006, the band played in front of more than a million spectators in Rio de Janeiro. Two months later, after completing dates in Japan, China – another first – Australia and New Zealand, Ronnie and Keith went on holiday together in Fiji. Richards, the inspiration for Jack Sparrow, the character his friend Johnny Depp plays in *Pirates Of The Caribbean*, decided to live up to his buccaneering image and climb up a tree. He promptly fell off and banged his head rather badly.

"I was sitting right behind him when it happened," Wood remembers, "and I heard this massive thud. I spun around, and there he was, on the ground. He'd cut his gums up on impact, he was very bloody, and clutching his head." Richards was instantly flown to New Zealand, where he underwent an operation on his brain. "I think it was a kind of wake-up call for him," says his friend. "His attitude is better now, and you can see it in everything he does. It's like Keith knows he is lucky to be alive, and is well happy about it. I bought him a walking stick with a dried-up skull on the top of it to kind of remind him of what happened. And he loves it. Keith has done his bit with Johnny Depp for the next *Pirates*. He's very excited about that." Wood jokes in reference to the few interviews he and the other two are doing that day, "Keith has got his feet up on an island in the Caribbean. Normally, he's here bossing us around but, this time, he's decided to make us do all the work. We're all coming out of the woodwork. Charlie was on good form today."

Ronnie Wood, the younger brother of Ted – the jazz fan who went on to play drums in Bob Kerr's Whoopee Band

– and Art – who in the mid-sixties formed the Artwoods with Jon Lord, later of Deep Purple, on keyboards – made his stage debut when he joined Ted Wood's Original London Skiffle Group in 1957. "I think it was at the Marlborough cinema in Yiewsley High Street, local boys made good. We went on at the interval between two Tommy Steele films, *The Tommy Steele Story* and *Tommy The Toreador*. I was about nine and I played the washboard. We did a couple of Lonnie Donegan numbers, 'Gambling Man' and 'Putting On The Style'. I even had stage butterflies, Ted had to push me on but then I wouldn't get off. Ted introduced me to the music of Jelly Roll Morton, Bix Beiderbecke, Louis Armstrong and Sidney Bechet. He didn't like a lot of modern music, jazz from the twenties to the fifties was his thing. Art was the blues and rock 'n' roll fan, Chuck Berry, Fats Domino. Ted took me to see Duke Ellington at the Finsbury Park Astoria in 1959 and the Cyril Davies' All Stars with Alexis Korner on guitar and Nicky Hopkins on piano. It was a real rocking band."

The Wood household on the edge of West London in the fifties sounds a real hoot. The boys' father, Arthur, skippered a tugboat when he wasn't leading a 24 piece harmonica big band touring the race tracks of England, everywhere from Good-wood to Royal Ascot, with the motto "Booze, Racetracks and Women". Their mother, Lizzie, gave up her job as a polisher at the HMV plant in nearby Hayes when Art, the couple's first son, was born in 1937. A late addition to the family in 1947, Ronnie Wood soon joined his older brothers in everything they did. "If they were painting, I would paint, and if they played music I would copy them and skip from instrument to instrument," recalls the musician. "We had everything from Chinese woodblocks to old drumkits, tea-chest bass, banjos, guitars, trumpets, saxophone, harmonica, Jew's harps. Ted would let me have a little bash around on his drums. When everyone was out, I would go crazy on the drums and play along with records. I would often split up the fights between my two elder brothers as they'd be roughing and tumbling as the house was clear of parents. I was the peacemaker already."

In 1963, Ronnie followed in the footsteps of both Art and Ted Wood and attended Ealing School of Art, an establishment where the likes of Pete Townshend and David Bowie also studied typography, graphic design and fine art. Towards the mid-fifties, the Ealing School of Art had become a haven for beatniks and a hotbed of musical talent with lovers of bluegrass, trad jazz and blues forming rival bands. Art Wood got his call-up papers and did national service before launching the Artwoods while Ted avoided the army and formed a skiffle group. Having gained valuable experience and musical tips from his brothers, Ronnie Wood launched his own outfit called The Thunderbirds. In 1964, he caught the Rolling Stones at the Richmond Jazz Festival. "They were playing inside a big tent that was bopping up and down. I went in and stood at the back, this awkward little kid totally intrigued by it all. I think I was the last to leave, I even watched them hauling the gear off stage. I went to see them again at the Windsor Tavern. This putrid orange van pulled up, the driver opened the back door and five guys came out with their wrinkled clothes. And yes, I knew I belonged in that band. I've always been a big believer in fate. I just counted on it happening, I thought I'd be patient because it would fall in my lap someday. I just had to wait."

The next couple of years saw Ronnie Wood go from The (British) Birds via mod band The Creation into the volatile Jeff Beck Group in which he played bass and struck up a lasting friendship and songwriting partnership with vocalist Rod Stewart. When Brian Jones left the Stones in 1969, Mick Jagger called Ronnie Wood who was on his wish list ahead of Mick Taylor. "I was round at my mum's one afternoon and there was this phone call, apparently from Mick asking what I was doing," reveals Wood. "I thought it was a wind-up so I said I was busy. Next time, they called me at a rehearsal studio, they got the wrong Ronnie and Ronnie Lane said I was quite happy where I was. I only found out about this years later when Mick Taylor left in 1974!"

Wood and Stewart joined forces with bassist Ronnie Lane, drummer Kenney Jones and Ian McLagan on keyboards as the Small Faces became The Faces, a group more famous for its intake of alcohol than its studio recordings. "True, we were a heavy drinking band," admits the guitarist. "In The Faces' days, it was like we'd know the first number and the last number and, in between, we'd just say: what are we going to do next? And we'd have a crate of white wine and champagne as the support act. Fortunately, the audience would be in the same frame of mind by the time we went on!"

Though Rod Stewart made great solo recordings – *An Old Raincoat Won't Ever Let You Down, Gasoline Alley* – with Ronnie Wood, the Faces only fitfully matched their live potential on the hit singles "Stay With Me" and "Cindy Incidentally" and the *A Nod's As Good As A Wink To A Blind Horse* and *Ooh La La* albums (for an overview of Wood's career, check out *The Essential Crossexion*, the 2-CD anthology released last year). In 1974, with the help of Keith Richards who came and stayed at his Richmond home for four months, Wood recorded his first solo album *I've Got My Own Album To Do* and the pair became inseparable, jamming on what became "It's Only Rock 'n Roll (But I Like It)". "I was on a Stones album before I was even a Stone," stresses Ronnie. The inevitable was about to happen.

The guitarist takes up the story. "Mick Jagger sort of came up to me at a party and said: if Mick Taylor left, do you think you would be interested in helping out? I said I couldn't do anything to break up The Faces but I told him to give me a call if they got stuck, to keep in touch. All the time I was thinking: fucking right, I'd join!"

Even after Wood officially joined the Stones, it was all far from plain sailing as the others put him on a salary rather than make him a full partner. Two years later, Canadian police busted Keith Richards for drugs possession. "That is the hardest memory in all our years of friendship," reflects Ronnie who had himself developed a cocaine habit and was in and out of rehab. "It was just too fucking available. That's not an excuse but, in those days, it was as easy as having a beer or a cup of tea."

Wood made some notable contributions to albums like *Some Girls*, *Emotional Rescue* and *Tattoo You* but, by the mid-Eighties, things had gone from bad to worse. Jagger and Richards were barely on speaking terms and the Rolling Stones hit their lowest creative point with the *Dirty Work* album.

Enter Ronnie Wood the diplomat. "I saw the way things were going and wondered how long I'd be in a job. It was fucking awful, terrible times. You had Mick and Keith who had been childhood mates, who had started the best fucking band, written some of the world's best fucking songs and they were just drifting further and further apart and leaving me in the middle looking for a new job when I'd already landed the best job in the world. But it was obvious neither of them wanted to be the one to split the band."

The guitarist developed a cunning tactic to get his fellow Stones talking: "I'd be over visiting Mick or he would be at my place and I would call up Keith, say a few words then pass the phone to Mick who is not the kind to back off. Then I'd go out of the room and leave them to it. I would do the same if I was with Keith. And eventually everyone was mates again. I was very proud to set them on a good course again."

Veteran of half a dozen different groups, a dozen solo albums and hundreds of jam-sessions with everyone from Bob Dylan to Stereophonics to Prince to The Eagles to The Charlatans, Ronnie was happy to contribute to *Last Man Standing*, the Jerry Lee Lewis album that came out last year. He takes up the story. "Steve Bing, my good friend from Los Angeles, befriended Jerry Lee Lewis and really helped him get his confidence back, made him realise what a great contribution he'd made to rock and roll over the years. He gathered all these people together, Jimmy Page, Springsteen, Ringo [Starr], Keith [Richards], Rod [Stewart] is on it, Mick [Jagger], myself – we did a song called 'Evening Gown' – to make this beautiful duets album. It worked really, really well."

Wood is also ideally placed to assess the Stones' standing and their place in popular culture. "We get four generations in the crowd and, hopefully, we cater to all of them. The Stones are the best, without a doubt! The thing with the Stones is that they are far more professional than all those groups I was in. For a start, even if we rotate the songs, we do have a set list reminding us what to play on stage. I never had any misgivings about joining the Stones. My favourite album is *Beggars Banquet*. It had to be. It's an establishing point. *Beggars Banquet* is a beautiful place to begin. I love *Some Girls*, it's a fantastic album. But you can take a track from almost every album since I've been in the band, two or three tracks from every album. I love what I hear, to be able when we play live to mix new songs but really old ones too, surprises from the past, a good rotation of songs.

"'Look What The Cat Dragged In' is my favourite song on *A Bigger Bang*. I was hoping we might do it for Europe. There are so many good tracks on there that are just asking to be played, you know. Maybe we'll have a look at that when we start rehearsing in May. And I love the photograph on the sleeve, I like the way that photographer worked. He had a lot of things to do really. Our bit was not so long, even though it took up the whole afternoon, it was a hassle, really."

The guitarist also reveals the Stones might yet get round to releasing more outtakes, certainly from his time with the band. "There is plenty of stuff on the back burner, in the archives, tracks that didn't get used. I'm sure one day we'll go through them and find some gems, songs like 'Claudine'. We just released the New Barbarians album from 1979 [*Live in Maryland – Buried Alive*]. I'm amazed how good it sounds."

Life is good for Wood, who can afford to indulge his passion for art in more ways than one. "I've just been to an auction of some of the old master etchings at Sotheby's in London. I was after a tiny little portrait of an old man, a lovely etching by Rembrandt, and some Toulouse Lautrec stuff. I'm really interested in that kind of thing. They can go for amazingly reasonable prices. That was a lovely little artistic adventure."

He is also becoming quite well known for his own paintings. "I've taken on this enormous project with the Royal Ballet at the Royal Opera House – painting all the dancers. It's really fantastic. I'm doing a little bit of a Degas, you know, with pastels, and I've done loads of sketches from rehearsals and I'm getting more oil paintings from *Swan Lake* and various, different ballet shows – *Apollo*. I'm going back to do *Onegin*. It's just great to build up this catalogue of Royal Ballet presentations and get some great images from it. It's going towards a big exhibition." He adds, "I'm so busy all the time. I've got so many different projects going at the moment and, with the tour looming, it's hard to fit everything in but I'm making time.

I'm painting. I have an exhibition of the paintings and drawings I've done of my wife Jo. It's kind of the story of our marriage expressed through art. Jo has been my muse."

Ronnie Wood the artist and art buff makes a refreshing change from the sozzled, drug-addled creature of yore. The guitarist can't wait to get back on the road and play "that whole Scandinavian bit. To me, playing Europe is much more comfortable than being far away in Japan and Australia and all over America. It's a good vibe all over Europe. I'm looking forward to going to The Hermitage in St Petersburg. I can't wait to check out all the paintings there: Matisse, Cézanne, Gauguin, Van Gogh. That's going to be our second time in Russia. We played Moscow before but I kept pushing and pushing for St Petersburg. I can't wait. The happy family is going to be back together. The big gigs, the light show, the big stage. It's going to be really good. The circus is on the road again."

Keith Richards' 2010 autobiography Life *had many admirers, including Mark Ellen, who was so entranced he still wanted to talk to him about it at length the year after its publication. Three decades after the Robert Greenfield* Rolling Stone *interview, Richards' answers (and syntax) – and indeed Ellen's questions – provide a measure of how the guitarist has changed in the interim, particularly the way he has become a byword for a particular type of roguish rock cliché.*

THE RAKE'S PROGRESS

Mark Ellen

First published in the *Word*, June 2011

The doorman holds the lift to admit another passenger. He's delivering "a package for Mr Richards" and headed for the same suite as us, 11 floors above mid-town Manhattan. It's a paper carrier-bag out of which pokes a fake-fur American Indian quiver and a trio of feathered arrows.

This seems on-message for Mr Richards somehow. I have only a few seconds to imagine its purpose – in-office target practice, present for one of his three grandchildren – before we're spilled into his manager's apartment amid such a flurry of greetings, offers of iced water and coffee, and dazzling walls of platinum discs that I completely forget to ask.

Framed pictures cloud your vision – early Stones, the late period line-up in an open car in Cannes, Keith's wife and daughters, his father Bert, the Glimmer Twins in drag, John Lennon, Johnny Depp as Jack Sparrow and a large selection of portraits of Charlie Watts, one in a jazz club holding an alto sax.

Every image of Keith I now relate to his book, the rollicking memoir *Life* published last autumn amid levels of security rarely witnessed outside of the White House. Reviewers were only allowed to look at it for a maximum of six hours and

under close observation at his publishers to ensure they didn't
manage to photocopy the entire brick-like volume and sell
bootleg editions in Camden Market. As a consequence, much
of the panicked press tended to scan it for headline-grabbing
attacks on Mick Jagger and very little else.

But if you've read it, you'll know it's a masterpiece, the most
sustained, colourful and rambunctious rampage through his
67 years imaginable, greatly assisted by the efforts of his author
James Fox who captures his voice impeccably and tracked
down and interviewed some 80 of his fellow travellers – old
girlfriends, classmates, musicians, roadies, managers – to
ensure any lapse of memory was meticulously reactivated.

The unpuncturable optimism and weather-beaten energy of
the leathery party animal of the 21st Century seems directly
hardwired to the cartoonish, short-trousered urchin that emerges
from the coal smoke of Dartford in the 1940s, a character using
expressions like "chiz chiz" and the Bluebottle voice of *The
Goons*, and much given to packing a sheath knife and the pursuit
of "legs-in-the-air laughter". Most of his public profile, you feel,
is self-invented, the rest the result of living up to the folk hero
iconography arranged for him via the joint agencies of the British judicial system and the media. In one touching episode, the
Rolling Stones 2007 tour has reached St Petersburg and Richards settles before his hotel TV and finds himself watching a
ceremony commemorating the 100th anniversary of the Boy
Scouts. "All alone in my room," he remembers, "I stood up,
made the three-fingered salute and said, 'Patrol leader, Beaver
Patrol, Seventh Dartford scouts, sir!' I felt I had to report."

Here he is now, black trilby, candy-striped shirt, a jangle of
skull rings and jewellery, gliding into the room on the thinnest
legs conceivable. Like all the Stones, he has the grizzled
demeanour of a manual worker, someone who's spent four
hours a day for that last 45 years scrubbing wire strings with
his fingers. He speaks, as you know, in that weirdly posh
mangle of vowels, his every utterance funny and thoughtful
and mostly peppered with a self-amused, death-rattling
chuckle. He has the light scent of tobacco about him, and
sparks up the first of five more full-fat Marlboros.

Copies of *Life* line the shelf next to us in 10 languages

including Finnish. I tell him this is what I want to talk about –
any reflections or regrets, some high and low points revisited,
some missing bits installed. "Fine," he beams with apparent
relish, swirling the ice in his cardboard water cup. "Whatever
you got, just fire away."

*The 10 year-old Keith Richards seems like one part Molesworth,
one part* The Goons *and one part* Just William. *Is that about right?*

Roughly right. Yes, that's a good proportion. But it's so long
ago, it's like talking about somebody else, but at the same time
the continuity holds, so realised that was me. It was another
world, the Fifties. The things you can remember, the essence,
it was so totally different then. Telephones were a rarity, TVs
maybe one in five houses. Is this the same world?

Did you recognise yourself in it?

Oh yeah but I'm still recovering from the book quite honestly.

In what way?

Well in the way that somebody says "time to put the story
down". I'm not going to be working for a year or two and it
seems like a good time to reflect but then, in doing it, you're
actually living your life twice. As if living it *once* isn't enough.

Is that enjoyable or painful?

It's (*laughs*) . . . it's interesting. At the same time you come out
the other end feeling you've been through the mangle.

*Your grandfather was gassed in the First World War and your
father wounded in the Second, and you present a lot of your life
like a military campaign – getting "burnt by a pyro" onstage, the
Stones "liberating Prague". Is that how you see yourself, in some
sort of line of noble warriors?*

There's always been that strain in me, and maybe in the family,
not that they were military-minded. They all got sucked into
being a warrior through no desire of their own, they just kind
of got caught up in it. But in a way I suppose it rubbed off.
There was no real war on, at least for Englishmen, when I was
growing up so I invented one.

Why did you feel the need to?

I think the English society at the time was still living in the
Thirties, that was the mindset of everybody. Yeah, but it's the
Fifties! "Before the war" prefaced just about every statement
that anybody made. "It wasn't like this before the war!" Well *I*
don't remember *before the war*. I imagined the Thirties – until
I found out – to be some kind of idyllic situation where every
Englishman was perfectly happy but I soon got disabused of
that. But at the same time you grew up thinking "I wish *I'd*
been born before the war" as they were apparently having
such a great time, as that's all they ever talked about. I felt I'd
missed the boat or something. I mean we had rationing! So my
war was against that generation. We were all rebels at that age
anyway but I guess I took it a little further.

*There's a theatrical flair to the early part of the book as if you're
constantly waiting for an audience – there's a great line about an
escapade in a letter to your aunt Patty: "exits amid deafening
applause". How old were you when you started seeing your whole
life as a performance?*

It was a very theatrical family. Everyone was in amateur
dramatics, everything was "who could pull off the best line?"
So in a way it sort of fell into place. Once I *had* a place I felt
comfortable there [in the Stones]. Instead of being overawed
by being famous I thought, "About bloody time, you know!"

*Your relatives have bits knocked off them, marriages don't seem to
work, you're an only child so you have to fight for any friendships.
You seemed to accept that life's a struggle. Was that useful when
the Stones started?*

Yes, but as I was growing up I just sort of put the struggle on
even terms. And of course the Rolling Stones was the perfect
vehicle for my mentality.

In what way?

Well at least I was on level footing with everybody. (*American
accent*) You gotta listen to what I'm doin'! In a way, I was no
longer a bystander. I was the youngest one in the group and I

was just trying to grow up really and find a niche. Also I wanted
some money! But it wasn't a shot in the dark, you know.
Something inside, from being in this impoverished flamboyant
family, said, Well *one* of us has got to make a move. But I only
realised later that you've got to take every opportunity you
can. To me, the Stones in the beginning, I was like a missionary, you know? Everybody should hear the blues! If they don't
hear it, they are *bereft*. All five of us were like that. If we could
turn a few more people onto this incredible music that turned
us on so much. We were looking for the fountain of the blues.
And suddenly the missionary bit goes out of the window 'cos
success has taken you over.

*You needed such self-belief. Brian even invents a whole new char-
acter for himself and becomes blues evangelist Elmo James.*

Oh we all thought we were black. We were ashamed of being
white. But if you wanted to be a star in England, the worst
bucket you could put yourself in was the blues bucket. Now you
realise the real strength of popular music – since recorded music
actually – stemmed from the blues, black people in America that
were living in some duress. And probably still are.

*Extraordinary to think Muddy Waters was in overalls painting
the offices at Chess Records and then these white educated English
blues students like the Stones reactivated these old guys' careers.*

In other words our missionary work paid off. In spades!

In spades! Are we still allowed to say that?

I think we are (*chuckles*). Especially with a chuckle thrown in.
(*America accent*) "It takes you guys from England to turn
America on" – to a *white* audience! So in a way it was a successful mission, from the idealistic point of view that we turned
white America back onto their roots, onto black music, that
was all around them and they weren't listening to. And it took
a couple of – I wouldn't say *pretty* – white boys from England
to re-steer their minds.

*There wasn't much "pretty white boys" from Dean Martin when
he introduced you on the Hollywood Palace TV show in '64*

*– "The Rolling Stones are backstage now, picking the fleas off
each other." Why were you so forgiving about it?*

You kind of felt a bit sorry for Dean, for slipping up, that he was
no longer up with the times. We were kind of leading him along,
letting him make a joke or two. But that kind of thing would have
been tough if The Beatles hadn't knocked the door down first.
They didn't knock it down, they kicked it in. Without The Beatles,
the Stones would never have made it. We weren't the door-kick-
ers. We need the latch open to get in! We were too raw. They were
streets ahead of us and writing their own songs. We were just
playing the blues – "here's a great song by Muddy Waters". It
was interesting how easily Mick and I fell into song writing. We
had songs inside of us without us realising it, but without
Andrew's prodding and gouging it might never have happened.

*There's a lovely old-world sepia tint to the book – London in the
'40s is "horse shit and coal smoke", police officers are "turnkeys",
judges are "wigs", Anita's family are a "a blur of syphilis and
madness". Do you think you've over-romanticised any of it?*

I don't think you can really. I mean in a way it's a fairy story,
certainly looking at it from this end. When you're 14 or 15 all
you want to do it be a guitar player in a great rock and roll
band, and it actually happens – of *course* it's a fairy story. "You
got three wishes." I only want one! (*Holds up badly gnarled left
index finger.*)

*My God, what happened to your finger? Is that the one you
dropped the paving stone on when you were 10?*

No, that's this one (*right hand*). That one's arthritis. Of the
benign variety. I don't feel it but it just gets in the way a bit.

Does it affect your playing?

If I was a classical player, yeah, but you can put deformities to
work in my game! Hence I have a very weird style of playing.
They all work (*displays 10 knobbly and misshapen digits*) – it's
just that they've got lumps on them.

*There's a moment around '67 when the lower middle-class rock
bands on the rise meet the daughters of the aristocracy on the razz*

– the Marianne Faithfulls, Anita Pallenbergs, the Lady D'Arbanvilles – and both sides discover whole new worlds. "I don't know whether we were snobbing or they were slumming" as you put it so perfectly. It seems such a big part of pop culture. Why is that?

What *I* realised was the daughters of the upper crust were just as pissed off with the situation as the rest of the rabble, and they wanted to reconnect as well. You got invited to a debs dance so to us it was like "Wahey! – this should be interesting!" But at the same time once you got in there – a lot of my friends were semi-aristocratic for a while, some of them still are and are still pretending to be gypsies – once you met that upper crust who were the same age as us, they felt the same way. Something's got to give.

What were they rebelling against?

I suppose that things weren't moving fast enough. It's like Harold Macmillan – "You've never had it so good." Well it could be better! Maybe it was a matter of the post-War generation, something inside of the whole nation. The whole country has been through this tremendous blood-letting, and it's got to *mean* something. You can't say "Before the war" again as that means you're going to have another one. So without knowing what direction to go in, we felt whatever direction it is, it's got to be different. And we were all part of that. You couldn't do it in a vacuum. Obviously the audience felt the same way too.

At one point you say the "feral body-snatching girls could do everything they'd been brought up not to do at a Rolling Stones concert". What did you mean by that?

That it's OK to let go. There was energy looking to be channelled, that was on the loose – with no particular place to go. And I suppose The Beatles and ourselves crystallised that energy and that force that was bubbling around. Under very disapproving eyes.

You wake up in bed with Ronnie Spector in 1964 and register this as a high point, the same when you see people hanging off the rafters at the early shows. Was it hard over the next four decades to feel life was still improving?

Well the trouble with peaks is you're always looking for a higher one. Some of the peaks at the time I thought were peaks but they were drug-induced euphorias, but then drugs were just something to do, it wasn't "drug time". There were no decisions made about it. Living that kind of life on the road with other musicians you were going to be confronted with it. We'd be in the States, two shows a day sometimes, five hundred miles apart, and 80 per cent of them would be supporting very experienced black musicians – to us very old, some of these cats might be in their mid-30s. And we'd sort of manage to drag our ass to get there and so eventually we asked, man, how do you do this? We're barely 23 and we can't keep up with you. How are you ready for showtime? And they'd say, (*delves into inside pocket*) "Well you take one of these, and you take one of those . . ."

I've never been much good at drugs, in fact I haven't taken any since a night out with Julian Cope in 1981, but they always seemed . . .

Doing what?

Horrible cheap speed.

(*Professional disdain*) I've never been much of a speed freak myself.

But drugs always seemed to have this magnetic hold on you right from the start. What possessed you to start taking your mother's period pain pills?

I took anything to see what would happen. When I found out how many drugs were actually available I sort of turned myself into a laboratory for a while. It was an experiment but a *controlled* experiment. Some people don't know when to stop. Jimi Hendrix would still be with us.

What gave you that sort of appetite in the first place?

That's between me and God – if there is one. I have no idea. I go for medical check-ups and they say, "You're 45 years old and you don't smoke." And I say, this is where your charts are screwed up. All their statistics go by the board. I had Hepatitis C and cured myself. I didn't even know I had it.

If you went for an all-over body scan tomorrow then . . .

. . . the news would be good. I wouldn't recommend my life for anybody else but I never felt I was ever physically endangering myself particularly. I mean I made one or two slips-up but it didn't stop the experiment from going on.

What's your definition of a slip-up?

Taking bad shit, occasionally. I always had to be careful with the quality, the purity etcetera. But once in a while you're stuck in a place where there's no choice. I think I took something with strychnine in it once. I'm lying on the bed. (*Points at lifeless body*) "He's dead!" (*Mimes trying to move paralysed face*) I'm trying to say I'm OK! "He's not breathing!" There you don't want to go. It was only when people pointed out I was a junkie that I realised I was. I thought I was just "experimenting with heroin".

There's a moment of preposterous decadence on the '72 American tour which Stanley Booth remembers very colourfully – "Once you've seen sufficient fettuccine on flocked velvet, hot urine pooling on deep carpets and tidal waves of spewing sex organs, they seem to run together. Seen one, you seen 'em all. The variations are trivial." Was he underselling it, do you think?

(*Laughs*) Well, that was obviously what caught *his* eye! Hot urine I'm a little perplexed about. I never took the temperature of that stuff. But it would give a rough idea of what it was like. It was crazy. It *was* crazy. And nobody saw the reason why it shouldn't carry on being crazy. And see how *crazier* it could get. There was always people far crazier than us – fans, other musicians, guys deliberately going over the top. This is why I decided to control the experiment. I like getting high but not *that* high. I can't stand the atmosphere up there.

I have to ask you this, I've wanted to know for 35 years. In 1976, the Stones played Knebworth Park . . .

Everything that could go wrong at an outdoor gig did go wrong.

Too true – and you crashed your Bentley on the way back to London. A hundred thousand people were there, quite a few of them probably reading this magazine now. There was a 90-minute delay before the second last act, 10cc, which meant the Stones didn't come on 'til just before midnight. Three years later I interviewed Eric Stewart for the NME *who told me Keith Richards was so out of it he had to be taken up to Knebworth House and put to bed and that, to buy some time, the Stones roadies had cut through the multicore cables leading to the PA system, which took 10cc's road crew 90 minutes to repair. Hence the delay. Stewart was still comically furious about it. Is this true?*

Is this the guy in The Hollies?

That's the other guy, Graham Gouldman, wrote songs for The Hollies. Is this true?

(*Uproarious evasive laughter.*) Well from *our* point of view it's "the show's delayed for a couple of hours, great 'cos I could use a kip".

So this was a deliberate piece of vandalism by the Stones roadies?

I don't know if they did it deliberately. That's another thing that will be lost on the mists of time. Maybe it was accidental.

How can you "accidentally" cut through a multicore cable?

I don't know, run over them with a flat tyre (*smiling*). You've got to realise that backstage guys and crews have their own rules and law. They shouldn't go on for a couple of hours! "*I'll* fix it." I was just told there was a delay.

We were near the stage – a giant inflatable tongue – and I remember someone strapping a guitar onto you and seeing you tottering down the slope and hitting this tremendous wrong chord.

(*Shakes head, laughing.*) They were probably overworking me.

There's a kind of Stones' Law that applies to the group and nothing outside. Things happen that aren't allowed to happen in real life. Mick sleeps with Brian's girlfriend Pat (the mother of his third child) and yet the group carries on. How does that work?

Who's sleeping with who is not really that important. I mean I've no doubt there were a few scars down the road about that one, and Mick was rather famous for having to have everybody else's woman – so I paid him back in *spades* on that. Sex was just . . . no big deal. Sex, drugs and rock and roll. In what order (*shrugs*) . . . not bothered.

Mick sleeps with Anita, you sleep with Marianne. About a week later the four of you spend 10 days together on a yacht on the Med. Again, real life dictates that this does not work.

We had a very aristocratic way of looking at it. Was Queen Victoria really William the Fourth's daughter? Apparently not, so . . . It didn't seem to be that important. Usually these things were just one-off. Who had who? "Sorry, can't remember who I had. It was very nice but I didn't know who it was. The room was dark. I walked into the wrong room. Nobody complained." It was kind of like that in those days. There were other things more important.

Like the collective value of the group overcoming these sort of obstacles?

We thought it would overcome *us* at one point. We've suddenly got this enormous monster and you realise you created it, you're no longer in control of it. But they were great times and it's a lot better than chopping wood.

There's a moment in the late '90s in Jamaica when you feel the need to get out of the house and hire a room at the local brothel . . .

Bum Bum and Cindy? Remember them well. Bum Bum is now respectably married and lives in Coventry. I'm not in touch personally but I know. I'm sure she's read the book.

Again, this is Stones' Law. If I went to a brothel for a bit of breather, I don't think my wife would be that thrilled to be honest. How come yours doesn't mind?

(*Amused and slightly pitying look.*) 'Cos our relationship goes deeper than that. Patti used to come down to that joint too, great dancing. I mean we never had *relations*. All I did was give a couple of girls a night off. They went to sleep on the bed in their bikinis and I wrote a song ["You Don't Have To Mean It"]. It had this red, gold and green couch and zebra-skin ceiling and I asked them to imagine we lived there and how they'd redecorate it. And about what they said to the men who came there – they said you can say anything, say you love them, you don't have to mean it. When I got in trouble with the odd line I'd give them a nudge and try it out on them and change it and they'd go back to sleep. I knew the guy who ran the joint, used to be a bouncer when we used to work the Tottenham Court Road. Here he is running the biggest whorehouse in Jamaica. "Keith!" What are you doing here? "I'm running this show!"

Can I defend Mick Jagger for a second? He gets a monumental kicking in your book. He's presented as tight and mean-spirited and mistrustful, and a cold, rather controlling crumpeteer, yet you're inseparable friends at the beginning, so connected you can second-guess each other's thoughts. Did you mean to be that harsh?

No, I understand that but what else can I say? And who else would say it? I'm there to tell the truth the way it was. Without saying what I said about Mick I would just be skirting the issue and just be flim-flamming, and people would be able to understand more the kind of tensions that go on if you're trying to run a band for 50 years.

I approve of your honesty, I admire it in fact, it's just that it's . . .

Is it a little brutal?

Yes, it's brutal! You're emotional about all these other people – Gram Parsons, Bobby Keys – but so unemotional about Mick.

I'm *very* emotional about Mick. Otherwise I wouldn't say it. It's just on the other end of the scale. Without presenting the Rolling Stones as they actually were, bare bones and all, the story would just have drifted. I would have just skated over the tensions between Mick and myself. I wouldn't have been telling the story.

By emotional I suppose I meant warm and affectionate. So you're vicious towards him because you care so much?

Exactly. I'm just as emotional that way as I am in a soft way. I've known Mick longer than anybody else in the world. We've known each other since we were four. Many gaps, different

schools and stuff, but if I don't try and put some understanding into the relationships of the Rolling Stones then it *would*
just be a fairy story. He can take it. He's got a skin like a rhinoc-
eros. Sometimes it's very hard to get anything real out of Mick.
Sometimes you have to be a little over the top to get a
reaction.

What was his reaction in the end?

I saw him two weeks ago and, yeah, he's a little hurt. But I said
to him, "There is nothing in there, Mick, that didn't happen
and ain't true. And if you saw a different take on it you're on a
different planet, 'cos everybody else . . ." I mean he was quite
willing to dump us [*the Stones didn't tour from '82 to '89*], and
that hurt.

If he was to write his version tomorrow, what . . .

He tried once and had to give the money back. I knew he was
trying to write a book. This was in late '80s and I'm getting
phone calls from Mick saying "What did we do in August of
1966, man?" You're writing a book aren't you? Otherwise you
would never have called me with such mundane questions.

What would he say about you?

Probably some very venomous things but at the same time I
said, "Mick, we can just look at it as all water under the bridge
– all right water under *two* bridges", and we both laughed and
kind of left it at that.

*When Mick puts the Stones on hold, you form the X-pensive
Winos and play a 40,000-seater venue in Argentina clearly
because you're desperately missing the sound of the crowd. Describe
that feeling.*

It's amazing. And what's even more amazing is you can get
used to it. You walk into a stadium somewhere and someone
says there's 85,000 and you say, no, 87,000. You can tell just by
looking – and you like a full house. And after a million, who's
counting? [*They played to 1.3 million on Copacabana Beach in
2006.*] But if you want to blame anybody, blame the
audience.

How do you mean?

'Cos I wouldn't *be* there otherwise, bless their hearts (*laughs*). You realise that you started this thing off but how can you get off this bus? I can't let down all these people. You can't not hack it. You can't not feel like it tonight. The number of times you hear, "Ladies and gentlemen, the Rolling Stones!" and you haven't slept and whatever and you think, I wonder if I can deliver what these people have paid to see. And you get up there and Woooooow, suddenly . . . the energy, the *exchange* of energy with the audience. It doesn't matter really how big it is – you might be playing a small theatre, it's more concentrated in a small place – but the transference of energy back and forth is unbelievable. It's more difficult to give up than heroin. The one thing I will never give up, if I can avoid it, is the Rolling Stones. You can't go to rehab for that.

Elton John said it was completely addictive. You play to 60,000, you've got to play to 70,000 the next night. And so on.

"Why aren't there more people?" Reg, there's no more room. There's not any more seats! He *still* wouldn't be able to grasp it, bless his old heart. But we prefer playing theatres as it's a controlled environment. God is not going to join in – with thunder and lighting and wind. When you're playing outdoors all the time, there's one member of the band you can't count on (*points crooked finger skywards again*) – Him!

I don't personally care whether members of the Rolling Stones make good parents – as a consumer I'd rather you were writing "Ruby Tuesday" than doing the school run – but your daughter Angela was born when you and Anita were addicts and you handed her over to be raised by your mother. Have you ever felt regretful about that?

There's no sentence living with my mum. She's a barrel of fun, and Angela and I can connect because of it – she grew up in Dartford, she was at school there, she did her bit. And she's expecting a baby! We're all preparing to go over for the delivery. What *I'm* thankful for is that none of my kids have got big heads. They don't think they're something special because I'm their dad, and that is kind of the proof of the pudding. I've got some great kids who've grown up very stable and do their own thing without being bothered who dad is. My kids never run riot and never bothered anybody. I mean my daughter [Theodora] *did* get popped a month ago for like a *minuscule* amount of marijuana so I told her to give up being arrested and she agreed with me but, apart from that, my kids are the straightest guys in the world.

I'd love to hear the conversation where Keith Richards tells his daughter not to get arrested.

I just said, Stop that, it's no fun, and she said you're right. And she didn't let on who her parents were, she spent a night in the tank and kept schtum, and I said, That's the way to handle it. Stupid thing – bored, waiting for her sister and some cop with nothing better to do – in *this* city! – brought her in. But apart from that, none of my kids have been in trouble. I took the heat for the whole family for several generations.

When you first heard Chuck Berry you assumed he was white, and that Jerry Lee Lewis was black, but since the arrival of the internet, and MTV for that matter, it's rare to hear new music without already having some sort of mental image of the people who made it. Do you think that kind of preconditioning makes people less adventurous?

Yeah, and you have a generation growing up with this image of this song being thrown at you, so a lot of bad records sold many millions of copies 'cos their image was great. This is like the book and movie. You read a great book and you see the movie and it's not the way you pictured it 'cos everybody's got their own individual picture. *This* is what it looks like – it's not Warren Beatty.

So it constricts the imagination?

Exactly. The imagination is being channelled more and more by technology – and technology can do no wrong (*hollow laugh*).

You had dogs called Syphilis and Ratbag and a yacht named Mandrax. Are you "on" all the time?

I just never wanted a dog called Rover. Why would you? You're in the park and someone says, "Come here, Rover"! He's not Rover, he's *Syphilis*! I suppose I wanted to make a mark, even taking a dog for a walk. But I have the freedom to be "on" if I want, to be goaded into outrageousness, know what I mean? To liven up your lives a bit. Come on, you know, what's the worst that's going to happen? Give someone with theatrical inclinations a chance and they'll be trying to take over the whole stage. At least I haven't done that. Which you could never say of Mick Jagger.

Do you think songs are in a permanent state of evolution?

Yes, you write these songs – especially in the early days and you're straight into the studio a day later and it's set in concrete. That's the moment it got captured but it's out before you've even got to know it. So for the rest of your life – I play "Satisfaction" thinking, Shit I could have played that or I could have twisted it or overdubbed that. So onstage you start throwing in a few variations on the theme.

Are there songs you've improved on?

It's very hard. I should think "Beast Of Burden" we've done onstage a lot better than on record, and it's a very good record. And "Jumpin' Jack Flash", some of the variations are at least as good as the record. But there's no way you could play "Jumpin' Jack Flash" the way it's recorded 'cos it's just me with eight guitars. Some songs on record might be just Charlie and me and Mick with a bit of tambourine. Or it might be mostly Mick and Charlie and I'm barely there. You make a record then you've got to play it live. It took us a long time to play "Satisfaction" right.

When did you last hear a song on the radio so good you wanted to slap the dashboard?

Only to knock it off. "Turn that off!" (*laughs*) I mean . . . technology. There's a whole lot of things going on that are bruising my ears – as well as a whole of other people's. Digital sound is a poor, poor substitute for analogue sound. It doesn't pop, it doesn't bounce, it's homogenised and stuffed together between one and zero. I like to go to 11 or 12! Analogue can do that. The sound off disc is so much better. But you're not going to fight technology, you're going to learn to live with it. After all you're only providing a service. Hey, what is music? It's a luxury. First the food and the water! Though I could live off music and not eat. Don't try that at home.

Any song you wish you'd written?

Songs from the '30s and '40s, those beautifully crafted songs. Hats off to Irving Berlin, Cole Porter, Hoagy Carmichael, Jimmy Van Heusen, Sammy Cahn, Duke Ellington, Billie Holiday. The bar's up there. The bar's up there, as a songwriter you think . . . actually *forget* about it! I won't do the high jump, just the limbo. It's pop music, it's not supposed to last. I mean nobody has ever dared – or bothered or tried – to make another hit out of "Peggy Sue", one of the most brilliant rock and roll songs of them all, as the essence is embodied in the record not just the song. Or "Summertime Blues" or "C'mon Everybody" – again a record not just a song. It's a sound.

Anyone you envy?

Lots of them but they're mostly painters. Picasso for starters – just for his ability to express himself. But at the same time I understand that Picasso was also very lucky being there at the right moment. In that sense alone we're just about on the same level.

Keith Richards now occupies the place in Stones fans' affections in regards to Mick Jagger that John Lennon has long occupied in those of Beatles devotees in regards to Paul McCartney, i.e. the acknowledged keeper of the group's flame who acts as antimatter to the supposed sell-out to orthodoxy. The publication of Life *saw the sycophants out in full force, with the guitarist's autobiography not only receiving (reasonably deserved) plaudits but Richards himself being reflexively placed atop a pedestal of unimpeachable rock-'n'-roll integrity. Bill Wyman was one critic who viewed Richards, his book and his code with somewhat more scepticism. Furthermore, for the first time in his journalistic career he was able to exploit the coincidence of the fact that his name is the same as the one assumed by the band's long-time bassist as he set up in his review a brilliant conceit (by which some readers were actually taken in) whereby Jagger had passed on his written feelings on the book to him under the misapprehension that he was his erstwhile colleague.*

PLEASE ALLOW ME TO CORRECT A FEW THINGS

Bill Wyman

First published on slate.com, November 2010

Editor's note: On a recent morning, the journalist Bill Wyman received a UPS package containing a typed manuscript. On reading it, he saw that it seemed to be the thoughts, at some length, of singer Mick Jagger on the recently published autobiography of his longtime songwriting partner in the Rolling Stones, Keith Richards. A handwritten note on an old piece of Munro Sounds stationery read: "Bill: For the vault. M."

From this, Wyman surmised that the package was intended for Jagger and Richards' former bandmate, the bassist Bill Wyman, who has assiduously overseen the band's archives over the past five decades and with whom Wyman the journalist coincidentally shares the same name. Wyman the journalist, a longtime rock critic, was once threatened with a cease-and-desist letter from the bassist's Park Avenue attorneys and felt no compunction about perusing the contents of the package. The manuscript he received is reprinted below.

I am, I see here, marginally endowed, if I read Keith's sniggering aright. I do not sing well, either. I am not polite to employees; indeed, I have even been known to say, "Oh, shut up, Keith," in band meetings. I do not appreciate the authenticity of the music or the importance of what we do. I want to "lord it over" the band, like James Brown. I am "insufferable." I slept with Anita.

Most of that is in just the first quarter of this overlong book, but a tattoo of my failings sounds all through it and culminates in almost 20 full pages of rambling invective near the end.

I don't mind this, really, for reasons I hope are understandable and will get into later. This is all from a guy pushing 70 for whom gays are still "poofters" and women "bitches." I think so many things about Keith. We were close, the two of us, for many years. We had known each other in grade school, if you can believe it, in the same undistinguished eastern suburb. Then we bumped into each other in a train station at 18 or so and started talking about the blues. We were different; I'd already been on TV with my father, who was a fairly notable expert on physical education at the time. Keith was . . . rougher, let's say. For the next nearly 10 years, we were rarely apart. Even after we were famous, we lived at each others' flats or houses. We were still very young, and, like puppies, we'd cluster together.

We were barely a band before our lives changed, but I think still of the time we spent, squalidly, before we were a group, in a very cold and small flat, more filthy than you can imagine. Our flatmate Jimmy Phelge was a veritable comic virtuoso with a pair of soiled underwear. Certainly we – I – wanted to be famous, but can I point out our road to it was not absurd, exactly, but unthinkable, in the sense that we couldn't even imagine a way to do it? The London music scene was entirely insignificant, and we didn't even play the trad jazz (Charlie's métier), which dominated.

Still, we practiced day and night out of some unspoken impetus, innocent suburban boys abruptly living quite near the edge of a dark milieu. This brings me to Brian, who played guitar very well and was a brittle devil. We knew that because of many things, not least that he spent an inappropriate amount of time beating up his girls in the next room. I'm not proud of that. Keith gives himself (too much, I think) credit for rescuing Anita, eventually, from Brian; but that of course was years later. Earlier, we both listened to or watched his cruelty, in the bedroom and elsewhere; we paid no attention to the half-dozen kids he'd fathered and ignored the savagery he accomplished on tour. We didn't know better; we were priapic jackals ourselves, fucking even one another's girlfriends if they got left, as it were, unattended. But it was wrong to have let Brian do that, and Keith should have owned up to this in the book.

I supposed it is a karmic justice for Brian that we continued to watch as he descended from there to hell, harried by the police and increasingly incapacitated artistically, which further estranged him from us. Oh, that's not true; we didn't just watch. We ushered him along, ridiculing him, you might say, to death as he began to lose his ability to contribute. Again, we were young. What were you doing at 25? We didn't know about depression, insanity, addiction, or what acid might have done to him. It's unclear to me whether the drugs diminished his ability to contribute or whether the drugs were in effect a way to cover up something that wasn't there. The first song Keith and I wrote was a hit single; Brian couldn't write a song to save his life, literally. And let's remember that he was a total asshole.

I'm digressing but I'm trying to explain where we came from. We didn't have a template. Nothing against Steven Tyler, but there's a difference. We felt around in the dark; we were famous within weeks; and, in the end, we left a body or two behind us. We did these things, good and bad, together; we were friends.

The second important thing is Keith's talent. We took it for granted, in a way, as he says. We felt it was our duty to get together and write a song, one good song each day we worked. He is kind to say I could take what he gave me and run with it. But he is the one who gave me the actual song to write the lyrics to. He wrote a dozen Top 10 hits in five years, and, after the band added Mick Taylor and essentially grew up, he wrote most of *Beggars Banquet* and *Let It Bleed*. Again: What were you doing at 25? It's interesting to me how no previous song we'd recorded would have a respectable place on those albums; and any song on them would have seemed out of place even on *Aftermath* or *Between the Buttons*. Keith's lurch forwards was amazing. As a pure rock (not folk or pop) songwriter, I think he is not just without peer. I think he is unrivaled in depth and growth, from "As Tears Go By" to "Satisfaction" to "Jumpin' Jack Flash" to, I don't know, "Gimme Shelter". "Monkey Man". "Street Fighting Man". The primal feel of the chording. The musicality of the intros and breaks. The innovation of the recording – cruder, no doubt, but I will argue far more emotionally powerful than The Beatles'. The winding, inter-mixed guitars he almost desperately loved. Without him, what would I have been? Peter Noone? It is hard to use a word like integrity about a band as compromised, as self-bloodied, as we were. But for some years, unlike any other group, The Beatles included, we declared war on that silly, hypocritical, repressive, and arbitrary society in which we lived. The only ammunition we had were Keith's songs. The lyrics, I confess now, may have been in their defiance just épater la bourgeoisie and in their poesy derivatively Zimmerman-esque. Even when they weren't, no one would have paid attention if the chords weren't arresting, irrefutable. The songs spoke primarily through their music, not their words. Keith's doting fans nattering on about the ultimate avatar of rock 'n' roll authenticity irritate me, it's true; but he may to this day be underappreciated.

So those two things I think, are important. Our bond; his talent. We blink at that point, and go 40 years forwards, and he has written a book that says, essentially, that I have a small dick. That I am a bad friend. That I am unknowable.

The reviewers, who idolize Keith, don't ask why this is all in here. We have rarely spoken of such things publicly, and tangentially even then. We don't talk about it in private, either, and, no, he hasn't been in my dressing room in 20 years. I thought we both learned that there is no point in sharing anything at all with the press, save a few tidbits for the upbeat

The Stones are back in top rocking form! article that accompanies each of our tours. I think Keith never appreciated the tedious hours I had to spend with Jann Wenner to accomplish that.

But I know why it is all here.

In the book we get the stories.

Oh, the stories. The rock, the girls. The car wrecks, the arrests. You read them on the printed page, delivered in what, I must admit, is a pretty fair written representation of Keith's slightly tangential, drawling, effeminate delivery, resting charmingly just this side of the incomprehensible.

I was generally made familiar with the stories in a different context. They were generally related by an assistant or a lawyer, tour manager or a publicist, poking their head into a room. Keith's disappeared. Keith's asleep backstage and can't be roused for the show. No one will wake him because he keeps a loaded gun under his pillow and grabs it and points when riled. Keith fell asleep in the studio again. No, Keith isn't mixing the album. He flew off to Jamaica, and, no, we don't know when he will be back. Keith's asleep. Keith's asleep. Keith's asleep.

The scamp. Those are but one tier, and a fairly innocuous one, of the many times I was vouchsafed news of my partner. The next tier is more colorful. Keith (or his favorite sax player/ drug runner/drug buddy/hanger-on) has slugged a photographer/destroyed a hotel room/gotten into a fistfight with the locals/fallen into a coma. Oh, yes, and the police are here. (Because police are whom you want backstage at a rock concert or at a recording studio.)

Or: The bandmate Keith personally vouched for is freebasing again. This last was of some interest to me, because it meant that I got to sing at a stadium backed by not one but two guitarists falling over onstage. Keith likes to talk a lot about his getting clean from heroin. It is not correspondingly apprehended that he replaced the heroin comprehensively with liquor. Given a choice I select the slurring alcoholic over the comatose junkie as a lifelong professional partner, and I say this with some knowledge of the two alternatives. But neither is strictly desirable.

And, yes, they do fall over onstage. (Or asleep on a chair in the studio.) I laugh at it now and blame no one but myself. Why, Keith gave me his "personal guarantee" Woody would not be freebasing on tour.

And yet I was surprised when it happened. I take the point that professionalism, one's word, rock 'n' roll merriment . . . these are fungible things in our world. It is a fair charge that I have become less tolerant in these matters over the decades. In our organization, inside this rather unusual floating circus we call home, I am forced into the role of martinet, the one who gets blamed for silly arbitrary rules. (Like, for a show in front of 60,000 people for which we are being paid some $6 or $7 million for a few hours' work, I like to suggest to everyone that we start on time, and that we each have in place a personal plan, in whatever way suits us best, to stay conscious for the duration of the show.)

So I will take that point. All of the forgoing was just . . . a little outré behavior on tour. Let's go to the next tier – again, of matters one is informed of with some regularity, this not over months, not years, but entire decades. Keith's been arrested with a mason jar full of heroin and a shopping bag full of other drugs and drug paraphernalia and is charged with drug trafficking. That was his baggage for a weekend in Toronto. It is hard to play a show with a catatonic guitarist, harder still when he is in jail for 10 years. I won't even get into the fact that this came right when I had every record label in the world fighting to sign us, and in an instant my negotiating power was vaporized. Here's a baroque bulletin from the archives: Anita's 17-year-old boyfriend has accidentally shot himself, in Keith's house – Keith's bedroom – with a gun Keith left lying around. Young Marlon, then perhaps 10, saw Anita, covered in blood, coming down the stairs distraught, and God knows it could have been Marlon playing with the gun. Or: Keith's driven his car off the road (again) with Marlon inside (again). In his book Keith stands back, amazed at the things that just . . . happen to him. He is frequently the victim of faulty wiring in the hotels in which we bivouac; a surprising number of times this phenomenon has caused fires. Ritz-Carltons are not built the way they used to be, I guess. Redlands burned down a couple of times as well, as did a house he was renting in Laurel Canyon. It's a wonder Marlon survived his childhood. A third child Keith disposed of by sending her off to his mum back in Dartford to raise. The second? That was another son, who was left with his paranoid, unstable, heroin-addict mother and didn't make it past infancy. Keith says he blames himself, and on that at least I think we can agree.

It is said of me that I act above the rest of the band and prefer the company of society swells. Would you rather have had a conversation with Warren Beatty, Andy Warhol, and Ahmet Ertegun . . . or Keith, his drug mule Tony, and the other surly nonverbal members of his merry junkie entourage? Keith actually seems not to understand why I would want my dressing room as far away as possible from that of someone who travels with a loaded gun. And for heaven's sake. No sooner did Keith kick heroin than Charlie took it up. In the book Keith blames me for not touring during the 1980s. I was quoted, unfortunately, saying words to the effect of "the Rolling Stones are a millstone around my neck." This hurt Keith's feelings. He thinks it was a canard flung from a fleeting position of advantage in my solo career, the failing of which he delights in. He's not appreciating the cause and effect. Can you imagine going on tour with an alcoholic, a junkie, and a crackhead? Millstone wasn't even the word. I spent much of the 1980s looking for a new career, and it didn't work. If I had it to do over again I would only try harder.

When I came back I resolved to do at least something well. Which brings us to money. We did not entirely mismanage our career in the 1960s, save for the calamity of signing with Allen Klein, who, with fatal strokes of our pens, obtained the rights and total control of our work throughout the 1960s. It was my responsibility. Keith downplays this, but the fact is we signed the thief's papers. It was all done legally. Klein was a Moriarty, truly; he didn't wait to sign us to steal. The signing was the theft, a product of a scheme so encompassing that in the end, he paid us a pittance and walked off with our songs. This is by far the single most important nonmusical event in our history, and yet it is rarely remarked on. I was not 30 and had lost us a historic treasure.

In the 1970s, we worked very hard, and with *Some Girls* we eventually sold a lot of records, but in reality you couldn't make much money back then, even touring. In the early 1970s we might play for a period of, say, two months, 10,000- and 20,000-seat halls at $6 or $10 a ticket. Back then, we were lucky to take half the gross home. You do the math. Then take out expenses and manager and lawyer fees . . . and split the remainder five ways. Nor did we live frugally. It got better over the decade, and Keith and I had the songwriting, of course, but compare us with Paul or Elton during the 1970s (who outsold us by many times, for starters, and among other things did not split their income with anyone) and our fame was entirely inconsistent with our bank accounts.

In 1981, I put us in stadiums and charged a more reasonable tariff and might have made us more money that summer than we'd earned in our entire career up to that point. And I've done it several times since – each time, I mean, to be precise, literally earning close to as much as we had the previous 30 or 40 years in total, including those previous tours. The Bigger Bang outing grossed more than $558 million – more than a million dollars a day for 18 months – and we pocketed the lion's share of it. If the promoters didn't like it they could raise the price of the nachos, or the parking. And I'm not even mentioning the sponsorships, the ticket fees, the merchandise . . .

I sound, now, like the accountant who earns my bandmates' jeers. But I don't remember Keith complaining about these sums, or, incidentally, that it took me 20 years to remember to give Ronnie a full share, just as we both pretended not to hear when Mick Taylor, or Ronnie, asked for credit for songs they'd written.

Does Keith really sigh for the good old days on tour? Shabby theaters, shitty sound? Wound-up kids standing for hours in the hot summer sun in dreadful mid-American cities waiting for a chance to race recklessly for general-admission seats? Us enduring a day of hassle and travel to take home perhaps $3,500 each? I remember Keith asleep or not showing up until hours after the scheduled start time. Our feral fans running, fighting, throwing rocks at police. Today, the shows start promptly, there are video screens for the folks in the back, and we offer $1,000-a-seat ducats for the fat cats.

Here's the thing: I'm a rock star. What is the measure of my success if not the biggest rock and roll tour of all time?

I know what you're thinking. It's what Keith thinks, too.

What about the music? Isn't it all, in the end, about the music?

I must note that the Stones rarely get a bad review, no matter how poor our albums. (Jann again, and so many wannabe Janns; how is it that we somehow manage, again and again, to record our "best album since *Some Girls*"?)

But let me ask you to imagine yourself, as I was, unimaginably, partnered with the writer of "Satisfaction", "Paint It Black", "19th Nervous Breakdown", "Honky Tonk Women", etc. And then imagine that your partner, seemingly overnight, lost some essential part of his talents. Not, as is commonly supposed, sometime perhaps in the 1980s, when The Rolling Stones' decline in creativity was on obvious display, but earlier. A lot earlier. Like, say, 1972 at the latest.

Those who like *Exile on Main St.* like its denseness, its mystery, its swampy commitment. Accidentally and amid no little chaos, we conjured up something dirty, impenetrable, and, in parts, compelling. But I think its murk promises depths that aren't there. There are decent but no major songs on *Exile*. Let's go back an album, to *Sticky Fingers*. I wrote "Brown Sugar". Mick Taylor wrote "Sway" and most of "Moonlight Mile", and made "Can't You Hear Me Knocking" his own. Keith and I together did most of the rest, like "Wild Horses", but, in the end, he didn't write most of the thing's best songs.

From there, there's *Exile*. Some nice tracks – "Rocks Off", "Happy" – but there is no "Gimme Shelter" or "Let It Bleed". Chords that once threatened society in some significant way now rarely radiated outward.

The next few years were difficult. I don't want to say Keith wrote no songs. He did. But successively, in each album, the process became more difficult, as both his capacity for the job declined along with the quality of what he did write. He mocks the disco songs – "Hot Stuff", "Miss You", "Emotional Rescue". But what would the commercial impact of those albums have been without those immediate hits? We were being outsold by everyone from Supertramp to the Doobie Brothers as it was. At the same time I had to come up with tracks and weasel promising material out of our cohort and not give up songwriting credit, which I accomplished in all but one or two cases.

The resulting albums are, with perhaps the exception of *Some Girls*, flaccid and unconvincing. The aforementioned disco hits. A little lyrical naughtiness ("Starfucker", "Some Girls"). The earnest ballad in which the incorrigible Stones display some unexpected touches of maturity ("Memory Motel", "Waiting on a Friend"). Lots and lots of undistinguished filler, clavinet playing by Billy Preston, Motown covers . . . And for some of the good stuff Keith wasn't even there. For *It's Only Rock 'N Roll* I did the title single with Woody and Bowie. Taylor and I constructed the splendid "Time Waits for No One", a fantasia, alluring to this day, for percussion, piano, and guitar. (I don't think Keith has ever let us play it live.) ("Sway", either.)

I will testify that Keith was intermittently sentient during some part of the recording of *Some Girls*. Yes we were fully Manhattanized at this point, because I live here and that's what I found interesting. The geographic location of Keith's talent, being nowhere, wasn't available for evocation.

By the time of *Tattoo You* I was exhausted. Entirely drained of ideas. I told Chris Kimsey to ransack the archives. "Start Me Up" was a very old song, with some 20, 30, 40 takes as a reggae . . . and one with a real rock guitar. It turned out to be our last real hit, and the arc of our career would look a lot different if we hadn't found it. With it, we could plausibly at least claim to be hitmakers in the 1980s. "Waiting on a Friend", that symbol of our new-found maturity, was, if memory serves, from a centuries-old session with me and Mick Taylor. About our work from the rest of the 1980s and 1990s, the less said the better. Can you sing a single chorus from *Dirty Work*? Name a single track? We certainly don't play songs from those records in concert if we can help it.

I go into such detail to describe the arc of our decline accurately but also note this sad corollary: Keith brought something

out of me, way back when. Through *Exile*, I felt I had to rise to
his songs. When he checked out creatively, I lost something
important. While there is some spark, I guess, in "Some Girls"
or "Shattered" or whatever, however contrived, I know most
of the other songs sucked. In the 1980s and '90s it got worse.
I could conjure up only the most banal cliché or the most
pretentious polysyllabic nonsense. Compare "Sympathy for
the Devil" with "Heartbreaker". One Godard made a film
about. The other is a TV movie. I literally wrote a song called
"She's So Cold" and then, a few years later, one called "She
Was Hot".

Now, Keith went through the same thing. I think this is why
Keith lost himself with heroin and now drinks: to stave off the
pressure to match himself and dull the knowledge that he can't
any more (and, back then, couldn't). It's trite, maybe, but
there's a reason a guy spends a decade in a haze, and the three
decades since in a stupor. Keith's rancor is almost entirely
based on the fact that it was not, in the end, easy to keep the
appearances of what in the public mind is the Rolling Stones,
and the process wasn't always pretty. But I did it, and, among
other things, to this day it is hardly in the public mind that
Keith Richards hasn't written a significant rock 'n' roll song in
nearly 35 years.

For that I get Keith's book.

Why did he write it? Or, rather, having decided to write it all
down, why did he devote so much of it to carping about me?

Well, he's not talking about me, really. He's just trying to get
my attention, I think, in the end. The remaining part of the
rancor comes from the fact that he knows he lost me, many
years ago. It's funny – Keith doesn't write good rock songs
much any more, but what he does do, every four or five years,
is craft a beautiful little ballad. Since *Tattoo You* Keith's written
and sung a couple of tracks per album. (We had a huge fight
about his putting three on *Bridges to Babylon*; I didn't like it,
but didn't have anything else to offer, even with three years
since the previous album. Why one of the songs I did write is
now co-credited to k. d. lang is a matter to be discussed on
some other day.) Generally, one of these is a throwaway, and
the other . . . is something gorgeous. Put them all together

along with songs he wrote solo and sang from the early years – "You Got the Silver", "Happy", and so forth, all the way up to "Thru & Thru" and "All About You" – and you have a CD of no little power and emotion. (I've done it.)

These songs are more honest than his book. In "The Worst", he says something about "I'm the worst kind of guy for you to be around." That's a song that might ring true for many people. It makes me think about how Keith lost me only after I lost him. In an older song, he explains a worldview I find a bit disturbing, and I would like to point out that since from most peoples' perspective I have flirted the edge of total decadence my entire life I can make that observation with some authority:

> *Slipped my tongue in someone else's pie*
> *Tasted better every time*
> *She turned green and tried to make me cry*
> *Being hungry*
> *Ain't no crime*

Again, the honesty is bracing. I think Keith puts just about any of his manifold urges on a par with hunger, and I think we can agree the world would be a dangerous place if that was the norm. It explains many, many of his actions over the years. In the book he tells the story of going to meet Patti Hansen's parents for the first time – drunk, holding an open bottle of Jack, and with one of his fucktard friends in tow. You can imagine how the evening ended. I'm sure Keith thinks it's OK. ("Being nervous ain't no crime.") ("Oh, shut up, Keith," I think.) With that perspective – and the added benefit of being rich and famous and having most of his deplorable actions do nothing but burnish his image – Keith's way in the world has been, in a certain way and ignoring, for the moment, the people who died, a blessed one.

I certainly bless it. I stood by him and propped him up and didn't fire his ass for many, many years. It would have ended the Stones, of course, so maybe I was being selfish. In a way, even comatose he had a marquee name; as my meal ticket, you might say, it suited me to let him doze. I took the reins until, when he finally woke up, he found that he had no place in the

management. He's angry about that, too. Yes, let's let Keith
Richards have a hand in overseeing an operation that gener-
ates $1 million a day in revenue. I don't know what else I could
have done. Later, one grows older and becomes more informed
about such things, and I saw I was supposed to have held an
elaborate ceremony called an "intervention." Society could
have effectively halted the upheavals of the 1960s simply by
requiring all of us to "intervene" with one another. In any
event, considering half our circle was on heroin and the rest
were coke fiends, I think it wouldn't have been efficacious in
our circumstances.

He talks about me, too, in his solo songs, less subtly: "I'm so
sick and tired of hanging around jerks like you." People ask me
why I let him put these on the album. I think: Oh, why not? It's
a great song, and he can sing it, and he can write the book, too.
He's trying to get my attention. To connect. To have it be how
it once was. At our age, I think there's no basis for it. Keith
celebrates his own unchanging character, and I have had quite
enough of that.

But, still, when I think of Keith, I think sometimes of how
someone different from the book comes out through these
songs. Once in a great while he detaches and looks down at his
corporeal self. "I think I lost my touch," he sings on one of
them; "It's just another song and it's slippin' away." Rock and
roll is strange. When a song is beautiful – those spare guitars
rumbling and chiming, by turns – the words mean so much
more, and there, for a moment, I believe him, and feel for him.

Or I think about "How Can I Stop", which may end up
being Keith's last great song.

"How can I stop . . . once I start?" he murmurs, over and
over again. "How can I stop once I start?"

It's about rock 'n' roll, of course, and playing guitar, and his
tenure, and mine, in our unusual coalition. It's also about
heroin and everything else he can't stop ingesting. But again
it's about Keith himself, who once started never did stop –
through the fame, the songs, the concerts and the women and
the drugs; and the violence and senselessness, the addictions
and the deaths, the ruined lives, the petty and large-scale cruel-
ties. At the end Keith got Wayne Shorter to do a sax solo that

is itself almost an out-of-body experience, perhaps the loveliest moment on one of our records. It goes on and on over the last two minutes of a very long track, and the end is almost a . . . an exaltation, perhaps? I am lost there. It's something I'm not sure I ever saw evidenced in real life, and something that isn't in his book. It's the sound – or at least the closest thing Keith Richards will ever admit to it – of a conscience.

*A previously unpublished snapshot reflection from an ex-*NME *journalist who, not content with holding the unofficial world record for interviewing the Stones more times than anyone else in the sixties, went on to become their publicist.*

ROLLED OVER

Keith Altham

The first time I glimpsed The Rolling Stones was on a rainy Sunday afternoon in September 1963 at the Royal Albert Hall. "The Great Pop Prom" was sponsored by the teen magazines *Valentine, Roxy* and *Marilyn*, published by Fleetwood Publications for whom I then worked as a cub journalist. I was just nineteen.

This scruffy-looking bunch of long haired, London-based toe-rags opened the show with their first ever chart single "Come On", written by Chuck Berry. The Beatles closed it with a string of their recent hits. On the only occasion the two groups ever appeared on the same bill, the Stones won hands-down. The Stones always were a better live band than The Beatles. Perhaps the latter just did not try because they could not be heard above the screaming, but the Stones were different, dangerous and more musically adept. Their unique blend of rock and blues was underscored by the androgynous sexual appeal of Mick Jagger and Brian Jones.

Backstage at the Hall, I interviewed the latter. He was the Stones' self-styled leader (the band were angry later to discover Brian had sneakily successfully insisted on an extra five pounds a week from their agent on the basis that he was "in charge") in the Sir Henry Cole Room where there was a luxury VIP suite overlooking the Albert Memorial. In those early days Brian drew most attention from "the scream-agers" with his charismatic blond good looks. His upper middle-class charm made his adoption of the role of spokesman with the Media almost reasonable. "Basically we just play bad Chuck Berry," said *sotto voce* Jones when I spoke to him for *Marilyn*. "It's just a sound we use as the basis of the rhythm and blues style we play. My nickname in the band is 'Elmo' because I love the work of blues slide guitarist Elmore James."

Though it was Brian who named the band in response to *Jazz News'* advertising manager's enquiry, later Mick claimed to have made up the name. Despite being an attention-grabber with his sulky good looks, young Jagger was yet to dominate the group with his writing partner Keith Richard – as he was then "s"-lessly known – and broodingly watched Brian holding court with media and fans.

That day, Keith compensated for the boredom of the hospitality room by picking his nose and flicking the results at the flock wallpaper. Seeing me cringe, Brian just laughed and said, "You were lucky. It must have been a black one. He eats the green ones." Brian finished our chat and then distinguished himself by passing out over the buffet table. He was carried back to the dressing room. I was intrigued to see if he could recover in time for their evening gig at the Richmond Station Hotel where I had an invitation to see "what we really can do".

Mick meanwhile kept walking past an upstairs window to gauge the reaction of the girls outside. He was screamed at, and wasn't visibly bothered that the hysterics down below were because they thought he was a Beatle. He tried another walk by, which produced the same result. He preened and shook his hair to more screams. The late Ian Stewart, their founder member and keyboard player who was renowned for his pithy but often profound remarks, told me once, "Mick is trying to find out who and what he is, and when he does it will probably be the end of The Rolling Stones."

The Stones had jumped on the R & B bandwagon that Alexis Korner and Blues Incorporated started in late 1962. I had seen Mick, Brian and Keith guesting on numbers like "Got My Mojo Working" with Alexis and Cyril Davies and mingling with the crowd which occasionally included Long John Baldry, Rod Stewart and Paul Jones, known then as P. P. Pond. At one point, the band that became the Stones tried to enlist Pond as their vocalist. It would have been interesting to see how pop history would have played out had Jagger landed the job Pond ultimately did, fronting Manfred Mann. "We knew Paul Jones had the better voice," Brian Jones admitted once to me. "But Mick was something else. There was just something different about him. No one ever looked, sung or sounded like him before or since. He is an original."

After the Albert Hall matinee, I drove with fellow journalists Penny Valentine (from *Boyfriend*) and Maureen O'Grady (*Rave*) to Richmond. Our names were not on the guest list as had been promised and it cost seven shillings and sixpence to get beyond the front door, which bore a mis-spelt handwritten note announcing "The Roling Stones Bloose Party" written by their original manager Giorgio Gomelsky and scored underneath "No free tickets." We put it down to expenses – er, experience.

We passed what we thought were a couple of girls in the doorway involved in a hair-pulling spat. It proved to be the hirsute Mick and his new girlfriend Chrissie Shrimpton, the younger sister of the famous model Jean Shrimpton. Chrissie later tried to sell Jagger's love letters to the *News of The World* but in a landmark legal battle Jagger proved that she might own his letters but he held the copyright.

By the time the Stones took the stage, the low-ceilinged, small, sweaty and eye-stingingly smoky room was packed with teenagers, some standing on tables and chairs. On the tiny stage up front, I could just see Mick doing a cramped skip and singing in a strange, cockney-inflected but nonetheless effective manner while the band tore the guts out of rhythm and blues classics like "Got My Mojo Working", "You Better Move On" and "Poison Ivy" plus a few old rhythm and roll chestnuts. The white boy had stolen the blues and added the wonder ingredient of sex appeal. It was exciting and reeked of dangerous liaisons.

Brian might have been the star but there was something hypnotically grotesque about the way Mick carried himself. He was slightly camp but not effeminate, a little loutish but not brutish and projected just the right amount of strutting insouciance to be sensual rather than objectionable. Even so, while there were a few cries of "Mick" and "Brian" from the girls, there was not yet a lot of screaming.

Ian Stewart on piano, tambourine and maracas stuck out like a sore thumb among his beautiful long-haired colleagues with his short-back-and-sides and a chin that jutted like the edge of the South East of England. Like him, Brian and Mick wore ties and sports jackets but their fringed bouffants just made the neatness seem ironic. "Stu", as he was known to all, had paid for that advertisement in *Jazz News*. (Drummer Charlie Watts joined last and to this day bears the bewildered look of an old jazzer wondering why he is sitting behind a poncy rock vocalist.)

Though he still did a turn with them on stage, Ian in fact had been ruthlessly fired a few months ago on the orders of their new manager Andrew Loog Oldham, ostensibly because "the great British public cannot count up to six for a beat group". Stu's big chin, un-bohemian hair and Scottish stolidity did not fit their image and he wasn't about to change. He became a lifelong friend to both me and the Stones. As we both lived in Ewell and he drove their Bedford van in the early days, he was often my lift home from Stones gigs, conditional on me helping load the van.

I recall one occasion travelling with the Stones from London to Aylesbury Odeon where they were due to appear on a bill with Dave Berry, Marty Wilde, The Swinging Blue Jeans and the raunchy American girl group The Ronettes. Stu was cautiously driving through a thick green pea-souper in the old white Bedford van. Keith was asleep in a sleeping bag in the rear. Bill was as usual up front ("Can't travel in the back, it makes me car sick," he lied for years so that he got more leg room), with Charlie and I crammed in alongside. Suddenly, Stu spotted Brian on the other side of the dual carriageway in his unmistakable white Ford Galaxy headed in the opposite direction, the guitarist clearly completely lost. "We are now officially a quartet," said Stu resignedly as Brian hurtled blindly past us back towards the Smoke . . . We motored on up the A1. Just outside Aylesbury we hit the curb of a roundabout. Keith shot in his sleeping bag up in the air and off the van roof. His theatrical moan was less funny when we arrived five minutes later at The Aylesbury Odeon and opened the back doors: Keith rolled out unconscious with a bump on his

forehead the size of pigeon's egg. "Right," said a phlegmatic
Stu. Turning to me, he stated, "I'll unload the gear and you go
and explain to the promoter The Rolling Stones are now a
trio." Fortunately Keith came round and they acquitted themselves well as a quartet.

Mick spent a considerable amount of time in The Ronettes'
dressing room on that tour, much to the consternation of Phil
Spector – lead singer Ronnie's husband – at home in the US.
Spector eventually felt compelled to issue instructions to have
their dressing room declared off-limits to all Rolling Stones.
Not only did you have to lock up your daughters in those days,
but it was wise to secure your wife. "He is like a sexy black
hole from which nothing escaped," Stu once informed me of
Jagger.

"I was offered the job of personal manager or road
manager," said Stu in a quote that typified his adorable bluff-
ness. "I chose the latter because equipment does not answer
back." He affectionately referred to his charges as, "My little
three chord wonders – my little buckets of shit" (or a variation
thereof) when urging them on stage. He was the only one they
allowed such familiarities and as such was probably the only
totally honest voice the Stones heard from the moment they
became stars until his untimely death in 1985. When Stu
succumbed to a heart attack, Keith Richards commented,
"Who's gonna tell us off now when we misbehave?" At Stu's
memorial concert at the Marquee Club, Pete Townshend, Jeff
Beck, Eric Clapton and the Stones turned up to play in tribute.

In the early Seventies, I left journalism behind to become an
independent press agent and worked with some of the biggest
acts in the business. Perhaps it was inevitable that in 1980 I
secured The Rolling Stones as a client. By this time, Brian was
long dead, his replacement Mick Taylor long gone and my
adoration of the band a thing of history. I always loved the
early Stones far more that the later models when drugs took
over and they became kings of stadium rock. They were always
exciting live performers but in a context in which contact
between them and the audience is fractured, they are almost a
tourist attraction. There is something slightly pathetic about a
68-year-old man singing "(I Can't Get No) Satisfaction" and

wagging his bum about. This was little less the case when I became their PR when Mick was a stripling of 37. However, he and the Stones had already reached an iconic status that made them indestructible. As for me, I had once given the awful *Their Satanic Majesties Request* a rave because I thought they deserved a break after that terrible year of '67, so loyalty to them was hardly going to be a problem now.

I saw Stu in our local pub in Ewell just after I got the job and he delivered one of his famous straight-from-the-shoulder jabs. "Congratulations on getting the job as Mick's butler," he said. I was slightly miffed but it soon became apparent that Mick did indeed see me more in that role than the PR I was supposed to be. Stu was spot-on again.

Mick was determined to rule the roost. "Keith is never available anyway 'cos he's always off the hook," Mick disingenuously informed me at the start of my tenure. "Bill is boring, [also not true] Charlie doesn't want to do interviews and Ronnie does what I tell him – so you report to me." "Nice," I thought, remembering more egalitarian times and the close-as-brothers bond between him and Keith that had now been severed to leave only a business relationship. However, I kept my mouth shut and just did as I was told. In retrospect it might have been an error but – also in retrospect – it would have been suicidal to get between Mick and the band. I chose the coward's way out and dealt exclusively with Jagger. That is, exclusively apart from his insufferable secretarial protection squad. Mick had seized the role of unofficial band manager but, to be fair to him, without his diligence and intelligence the band would probably have disintegrated years ago. "Someone had to take charge," sniffed Mick. "I don't want to be the one but it seems like if I don't do it no one else would – decisions had to be made and Keith was out of it."

He once listed his worst fault as "treating my friends badly". I can understand why he would say such a thing but in the early Sixties when I travelled with the Stones in England and Europe, he was as likeable and funny as the rest of the band. In that decade, the music press hugged him to their bosom in a way unimaginable today. He was an underdog, struggling against an establishment clamour for his head on a pike, especially when there seemed to be a police penchant for busting a Rolling Stone a month (that *annus horribilis* of 1967). As time went by, though, this charming, artistic young man on the side of light changed. At least to my eyes. Stu had apparently seen through him from the beginning. "When I first met him, I thought he was something special but I also thought he cared more about the fame and the money than the music and I never changed my mind," Stu once said to me when we were working on a book together. Stu had the good grace not to say "Told you so" when Jagger peremptorily sacked me after three years' service despite the fact that via my efforts his face was just about to be plastered over the colour supplements. However, there was no mistaking the knowing look in Stu's eye.

Jagger was always a social climber and he never started anything unless he thought he could finish it. Inevitable then that he achieved his lifelong aspiration to join the upper classes with his knighthood. By then, rock 'n' roll was all just an act to him. Mick had a set routine before meeting the press which he would go through with me: "Let's check, got me long hair, got me sardonic smile and me couldn't-care-less attitudes – let's go." Mick could change like a chameleon to suit his background and once the band hit the road morphed into what was expected of a Rolling Stone: the accent became a Cockney whine and the attitude guttersnipe. That he acts out this "rock god" role is one reason he can never really convince playing anybody else. You take one look at the character he is attempting to play on film and it is impossible to believe he is anyone other than his greatest invention – Mick Jagger.

Mick lets no one into his private world and works the press better than any other major artiste I ever represented as a publicist. "You wanna find out the truth about us then go read my lyrics – they are like a diary," he scolded one reporter who asked an intrusive question in my presence and then grinned like a split coconut before informing him, "But unfortunately you are going to need the key to the code and only I know it." And so the music journalists do what journalists always do – when the legend becomes fact we print the legend. It has helped make The Rolling Stones' extraordinary rep, one that ensures that should they so wish they can play their greatest hits for the rest of their lives. Whether they do so wish may hinge on the sniping that goes on in books and papers.

"When is the bitching going to stop between you and Mick?" one reporter asked Keith.

"Better ask the Bitch," the reply shot back.

On it goes.

And finally, Gary Pig Gold settles matters . . .

TEN REASONS WHY THE ROLLING STONES *WERE* THE WORLD'S GREATEST ROCK AND ROLL BAND

Gary Pig Gold

Originally published on www.cosmik.com, December 2002

1. BRIAN JONES' HAIR
Not only the longest, and the blondest, but the most *distinctive* coif to come out of the (first) British Invasion . . . hence his invariably being positioned as the focal point of the band's publicity photos, not to mention album covers. "Personally, I always make a point of cleansing my hair after every meal," a young Brian would defiantly inform the press when asked if the band, as their promo boasted, bathed only during months with an "R" in them.

2. ANDREW LOOG OLDHAM
Take equal parts Col. Parker and Phil Spector, mix with a liberal helping of Laurence Harvey (cf: *Expresso Bongo*), garnish with a dash of Anthony Burgess, and you have the wonderlad who transformed himself from failed pop crooner Sandy Beach to frustrated Brian Epstein gofer to chart-topping svengali of the world-famous anti-Beatles all in a mere eighteen months. Needless to say The Rolling Stones, not to mention Malcolm McLaren, would not – in fact, *could* not – have ever risen to successfully battle the rock wars without the skilled example of Andrew Loog.

3. THEIR STAGEWEAR
As a young impressionable tyke of nine, I remember how totally dumbstruck I was when chancing upon the Stones on a Red Skelton special in '64. After months spent innocently

bopping to squeaky-clean moptops on *The Ed Sullivan Show*, imagine my stupefaction when Mick Jagger, striped sweatshirt hanging, first suggestively shook his maracas in my parents' living room. Keith hunched menacingly black and pirate-like over his guitar. The rhythm section, shaggy and sullen. And, ever the individual, Brian Jones nattily attired in a modish three-piece, every golden lock in place. It must've worked: My grades, to say nothing of my standards, started tumbling the very next day.

4. THE "PRODUCTION" ON THEIR RECORDS

The scene is Olympic Sound Studios, London, May 10, 1963 as recording of "Come On", The Rolling Stones' first release, has just been completed:

Roger Savage (engineer): "What about the mixing?"

Andrew Loog Oldham (producer): "What's *mixing?*"

And thus the stage was shakily set for decades of recordings which in many ways gave birth to, and in retrospect certainly define, the very essence of garage (a.k.a. grunge, roots, and/or punk) rock. From their initial cacophonous Oldham-by-the-seat-of-his-Levis sessions straight on up to their current multi-million-dollar-yet-*still*-somehow-Portastudioesque-sounding productions, Rolling Stones records are best-selling examples of the fine art of Feeling over Finesse; of Emotion over Edification. And the *ultimate* irony? "Come On" is now available on SACD.

5 CHARLIE WATTS' DRUMMING

Especially on "Paint It, Black"!

6. THEIR ALBUM COVERS

From *December's Children* to (the untruncated original issue of) *Some Girls*, without forgetting *Through The Past Darkly*, *Sticky Fingers* (particularly the *Spanish* edition!) and the until-recently-banned *Beggars Banquet*, Stones songs have always come both lovingly and luridly packaged inside the most quintessential photos, graphics and liner notes this side of *The Who Sell Out*. Grand Prize Winner? Without a doubt the bloody-morning-after portrait adorning the superb *Between the Buttons, again* starring Brian "Miss Amanda" Jones. (Runner-up: the infamous she-male sleeve on the "Have You Seen Your Mother, Baby, Standing In The Shadow" single).

7. "CHARLIE IS MY DARLING"
Forget *A Hard Day's Night, Lonely Boy* and even *Gimme Shelter* for a *true* docu-style glimpse of those once-swinging Sixties, *Charlie Is My Darling*, produced, of course, by Andrew Oldham, boldly treads where no Arriflex had been before (e.g.: into an Irish hotel ballroom circa 3 a.m., where them shit-faced Glimmer Twits butcher "Return To Sender" whilst sliding tumblers full of champagne back and forth across a grand piano top). Also watch the band being savagely attacked *on* stage, and hear Brian describe what "surrealism" means to him. I wonder why this has *still* never been screened in America?

8. THEIR INSPIRED CHOICE OF SONG MATERIAL
Nary a Stones album or concert has existed solely on the works of Jagger/Richard(s) ... some dusty old (rhythm 'n') blues tune has been given the nod, and been performed in testament to, the moss upon which the band has always rolled (excepting during that *Satanic Majesties* detour). Hands-down Number One fave cover-tune Of All Time, however, has to be their little-heard manic mangling of "I Wanna Be Your Man" which, with all due respects to Ringo, absolutely *shreds* the Fabs' version. And howzabout that Dylan cover on *Stripped,* huh?! Anyways ...

9. THEIR IMPECCABLE FLAIR FOR SELF-PROMOTION
From the early daze of urinating on gas stations ("we piss anywhere, maaann ...") in 1965 to their jet-setting, trend-setting string of designer drug busts in the Seventies, the Stones have always been their own best press agents. Not surprisingly either, having graduated with dayglo colours from the Andrew Oldham "As Long As They Spell The Name Right" school of PR. And long after most of his bass-playing contemporaries had retired to Britain's loftier cricket estates

and dry-out clinics, the oldest Stone was still taunting ires by marrying every schoolgirl-slash-model within reach. I *miss* Bill Wyman.

10. LEWIS BRIAN HOPKIN JONES, 1942–1969
R.I.P.

SELECTED BIBLIOGRAPHY

BOOKS

Appleford, Steve, *Stories Behind the Rolling Stones' Songs: It's Only Rock 'n' Roll* (Carlton, 1997).

Bockris, Victor, *Keith Richards* (Omnibus Press, 2002).

Bonanno, Massimo, *Rolling Stones' Chronicle: The First Thirty Years* (Plexus Publishing, 1990).

Booth, Stanley, *The True Adventures of the Rolling Stones* (Chicago Review Press, 2000).

Carr, Roy, *The Rolling Stones: An Illustrated Record* (New English Library, 1977).

Clayson, Alan, *Brian Jones* (Sanctuary Publishing, 2004).

——, *Charlie Watts* (Sanctuary Publishing, 2004).

——, *Keith Richards* (Sanctuary Publishing, 2004).

——, *Mick Jagger: The Unauthorised Biography* (Sanctuary Publishing, 2005).

Cowan, Nick, *Fifty Teabags and a Bottle of Rum* (Quartet, 2008).

Dalton, David, *The Rolling Stones* (Star Books, 1975).

——, *Rolling Stones in Their Own Words* (Music Sales Corp, 1980).

——, *The Rolling Stones: The First Twenty Years* (Thames and Hudson, 1981).

Davis, Steven, *Old Gods Almost Dead* (Aurum Press, 2003).

Egan, Sean, *The Rough Guide to The Rolling Stones* (Rough Guides, 2006).

——, *Rolling Stones and the Making of Let It Bleed (Vinyl Frontier)* (Unanimous, 2007).

Egan, Sean and Gered Mankowitz, *Rolling Stones (One on One)* (Insight Editions, 2012).

Elliott, Martin, *The Rolling Stones: Complete Recording Sessions (1962–2002)* (Cherry Red Books, 2003).

Faithfull, Marianne, and David Dalton, *Faithfull* (Penguin Books Ltd, 1995).

Gambaccini, Paul, Tim Rice and Jonathan Rice, *British Hit Albums* (Guinness, 1990).

——, *British Hit Singles* (Guinness, 1995).

German, Bill, *Under Their Thumb* (Villard Books, 2009).

Goodman, Pete, *Our Own Story by the Rolling Stones as We Told it to Pete Goodman* (Bantam, 1965).

Greenfield, Robert, *A Journey Through America With The Rolling Stones* (Panther, 1975).

——, *Exile on Main Street* (Perseus Publishing, 2008).

Hector, James, *The Complete Guide to the Music of the Rolling Stones* (Omnibus Press, 1995).

Hoffmann, Lee Ann, and Frank W. Hoffmann, *Cash Box Singles Charts (1950–1981)* (Scarecrow, 1983).

Jagger Mick, Keith Richards, Charlie Watts and Ronnie Wood, *According to the Rolling Stones* (Phoenix Press, 2004).

Kent, Nick, *The Dark Stuff: Selected Writings on Rock Music* (Da Capo Press, 2002).

Lysaght, Alan, *The Rolling Stones: An Oral History* (McArthur, 2004).

Needs, Kris, *Keith Richards: Before They Make Me Run* (Plexus Publishing, 2004).

Norman, Philip, *The Stones* (Pan, 2002).

Oldham, Andrew Loog, *Stoned* (Vintage, 2004).

——, *2stoned* (Vintage, 2003).

Paytress, Mark, *Rolling Stones: Off the Record* (Omnibus Press, 2003).

Rawlings, Terry, *Brian Jones – Who Killed Christopher Robin?* (Helter Skelter, 2004).

Richards, Keith, *Life* (Orion, 2010).

Salewicz, Chris, *Mick and Keith* (Orion, 2003).

Sanchez, Tony, *Up and Down with The Rolling Stones* (New American Library, 1980).

Sandford, Christopher, *Mick Jagger: Rebel Knight* (Omnibus Press, 2004).

Savage, Jon, *England's Dreaming: The Sex Pistols and Punk Rock* (Faber and Faber, 1991).

Scaduto, Anthony, *Mick Jagger* (W. H. Allen, 1974).

Wells, Simon, *Butterfly on a Wheel – Rolling Stones: The Great Drug Bust* (Omnibus Press, 2012).

Whitburn, Joel, *The Billboard Book of Top 40 Albums* (Watson-Guptill, 1995).

——, *The Billboard Book of Top 40 Hits* (Billboard, 1996).

Wohlin, Anna, and Christine Lindsjoo, *The Murder of Brian Jones* (John Blake, 2001).

Wood, Ronnie, *Ronnie: The Autobiography of Ronnie Wood* (Macmillan, 2007).

Wyman, Bill, *Stone Alone* (Viking, 1990).

——, *Rolling With the Stones* (Dorling Kindersley, 2002).

Various, *The Rolling Stones* (Rolling Stone Magazine, 1975).

——, *Rolling Stone Illustrated History of Rock and Roll* (Picador, 1981)

CD-ROM

Aeppli, Felix, *The Rolling Stones 1962–2002 The Ultimate Guide To The First Forty Years* (Mathis, 2003).

WEBSITES

aeppli.ch/tug.htm

www.beatzenith.com

www.chartstats.com

www.edsullivan.com

www.everyhit.com

www.frayed.org

www.iorr.org

newspaperarchive.com

rockpopgallery.typepad.com

www.rollingstones.com

www.timeisonourside.com

ACKNOWLEDGEMENTS

CYRIL DAVIES AND THE STONES IN JANUARY 1963 © John Pidgeon, 2009; THE BACK LINE © John Pidgeon, 1978. Reprinted by permission of the author.

THE ROLLIN' STONES – GENUINE R & B! © Norman Jopling, 1963. Reprinted by permission of the author.

THIS HORRIBLE LOT – NOT QUITE WHAT THEY SEEM by Maureen Cleave © 1964, *Evening Standard*. Reprinted by permission of *Evening Standard*/Solo Syndication.

THE ROLLING STONES: OUR FANS HAVE MOVED ON WITH US © Keith Altham, 1967; ROLLED OVER © Keith Altham, 2012. Reprinted by permission of the author.

MICK JAGGER *INTERNATIONAL TIMES* INTERVIEW © Barry Miles, 1968. Reprinted by permission of the author.

THE BITTERSWEET SYMPHONY © Rob Chapman, 1999. Reprinted by permission of the author.

THE ROLLING STONE INTERVIEW: KEITH RICHARD © Robert Greenfield, 1971. Reprinted by permission of the author.

IT ISN'T ONLY ROCK AND ROLL © Robert Christgau, 1975; SOME GUYS © Robert Christgau, 1978. Reprinted by permission of the author.

AND SITTETH AT THE RIGHT HAND . . . © Jonh Ingham, 2007. Reprinted by permission of the author.

SELF SATISFACTION © Robin Eggar, 1995; ROLLING STONE IN EXILE © Robin Eggar, 2002. Reprinted by permission of the author.